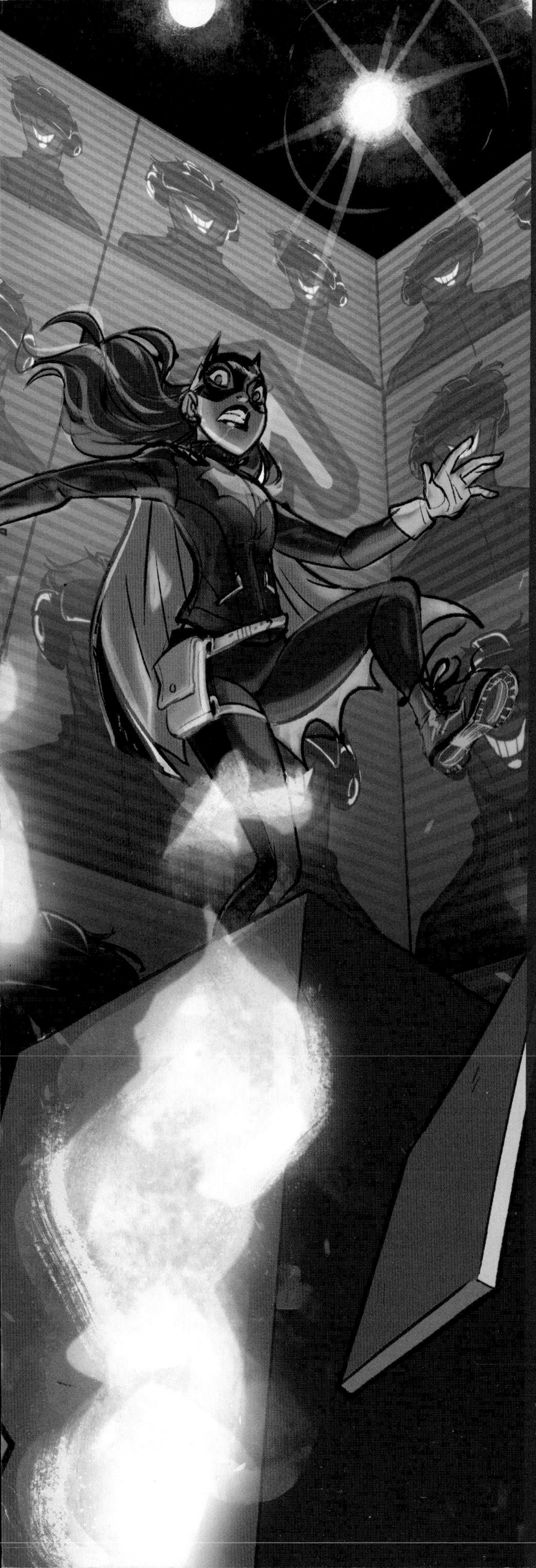

BATGIRL

VOLUME 2
FAMILY BUSINESS

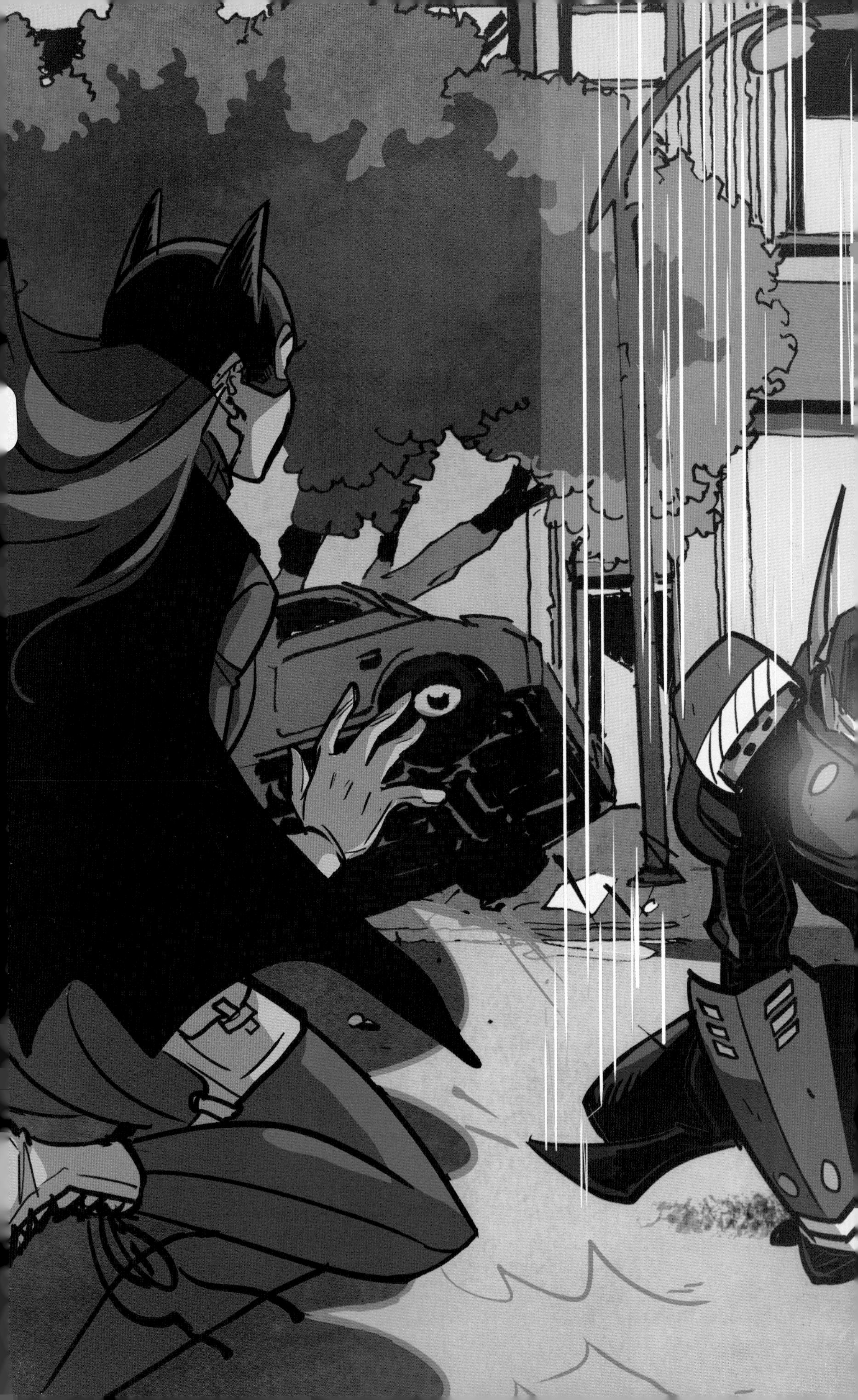

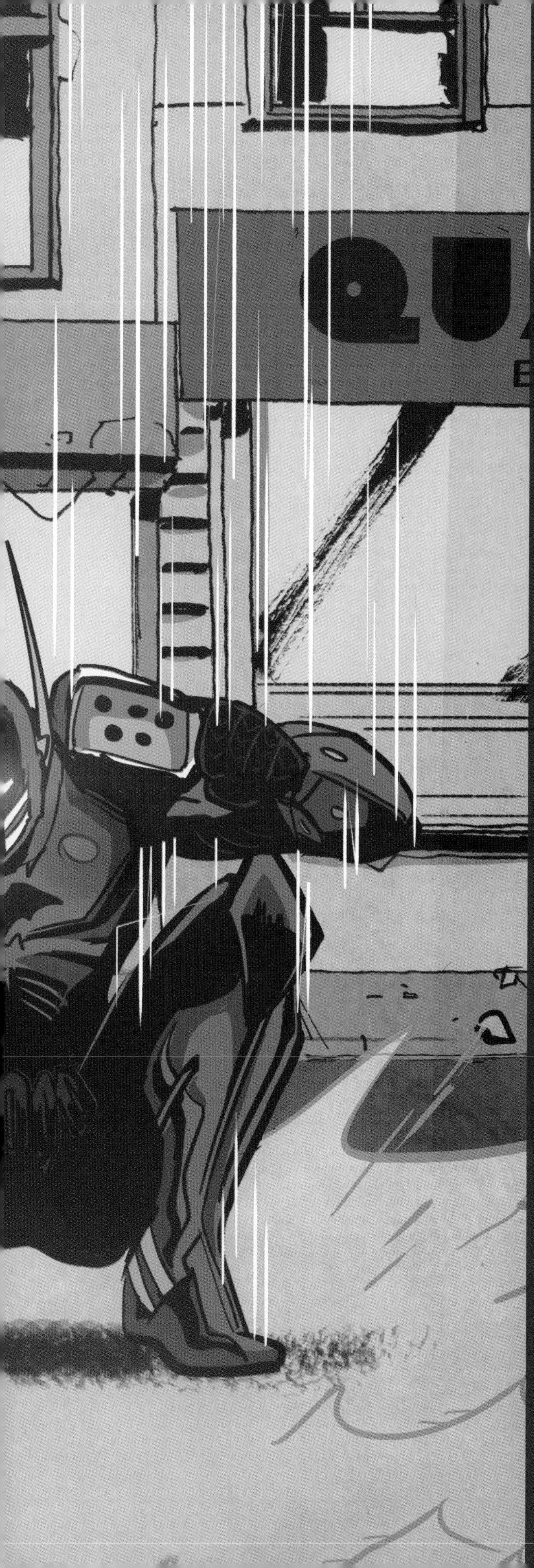

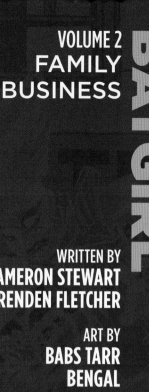

BATGIRL

VOLUME 2
FAMILY BUSINESS

WRITTEN BY
CAMERON STEWART
BRENDEN FLETCHER

ART BY
BABS TARR
BENGAL

ADDITIONAL ART BY
JOEL GOMEZ
JAKE WYATT
MICHEL LACOMBE
DAVID LAFUENTE
MING DOYLE
MINGJUE HELEN CHEN
JUAN CASTRO

COLORS BY
SERGE LAPOINTE
BABS TARR
BENGAL
GABE ELTAEB
IVAN PLASCENCIA
MINGJUE HELEN CHEN

LETTERS BY
STEVE WANDS

COLLECTION COVER ART BY
CAMERON STEWART

BATMAN CREATED BY
BOB KANE
WITH **BILL FINGER**

CHRIS CONROY Editor – Original Series
DAVE WIELGOSZ Assistant Editor – Original Series
JEB WOODARD Group Editor – Collected Editions
ROBIN WILDMAN Editor – Collected Edition
STEVE COOK Design Director – Books
DAMIAN RYLAND Publication Design

BOB HARRAS Senior VP – Editor-in-Chief, DC Comics

DIANE NELSON President
DAN DiDIO and JIM LEE Co-Publishers
GEOFF JOHNS Chief Creative Officer
AMIT DESAI Senior VP – Marketing & Global Franchise Management
NAIRI GARDINER Senior VP – Finance
SAM ADES VP – Digital Marketing
BOBBIE CHASE VP – Talent Development
MARK CHIARELLO Senior VP – Art, Design & Collected Editions
JOHN CUNNINGHAM VP – Content Strategy
ANNE DePIES VP – Strategy Planning & Reporting
DON FALLETTI VP – Manufacturing Operations
LAWRENCE GANEM VP – Editorial Administration & Talent Relations
ALISON GILL Senior VP – Manufacturing & Operations
HANK KANALZ Senior VP – Editorial Strategy & Administration
JAY KOGAN VP – Legal Affairs
DEREK MADDALENA Senior VP – Sales & Business Development
JACK MAHAN VP – Business Affairs
DAN MIRON VP – Sales Planning & Trade Development
NICK NAPOLITANO VP – Manufacturing Administration
CAROL ROEDER VP – Marketing
EDDIE SCANNELL VP – Mass Account & Digital Sales
COURTNEY SIMMONS Senior VP – Publicity & Communications
JIM (SKI) SOKOLOWSKI VP – Comic Book Specialty & Newsstand Sales
SANDY YI Senior VP – Global Franchise Management

BATGIRL VOLUME 2: FAMILY BUSINESS

Published by DC Comics. Compilation and all new material Copyright © 2016 DC Comics. All Rights Reserved.
Originally published in single magazine form in BATGIRL 41-45, BATGIRL ANNUAL 3 and online as DC SNEAK PEEK: BATGIRL 1
Copyright © 2015 DC Comics. All Rights Reserved. All characters, their distinctive likenesses and related elements
featured in this publication are trademarks of DC Comics. The stories, characters and incidents featured in this publication
are entirely fictional. DC Comics does not read or accept unsolicited submissions of ideas, stories or artwork.

DC Comics, 2900 West Alameda Avenue, Burbank, CA 91505
Printed by RR Donnelley, Salem, VA, USA. 1/15/16.
First Printing. ISBN: 978-1-4012-5966-2.

Library of Congress Cataloging-in-Publication Data

Names: Stewart, Cameron, 1976?- author, illustrator | Fletcher, Brenden,
author. | Tarr, Babs, illustrator.
Title: Batgirl. Volume 2 / Cameron Stewart, Brenden Fletcher, Babs Tarr.
Description: Burbank, CA : DC Comics, [2016]
Identifiers: LCCN 2015037665 | ISBN 9781401259662 (paperback)
Subjects: LCSH: Graphic novels. | BISAC: COMICS & GRAPHIC NOVELS /
Superheroes. | GSAFD: Comic books, strips, etc.
Classification: LCC PN6728.B358 S75 2016 | DDC 741.5/973—dc23
LC record available at http://lccn.loc.gov/2015037665

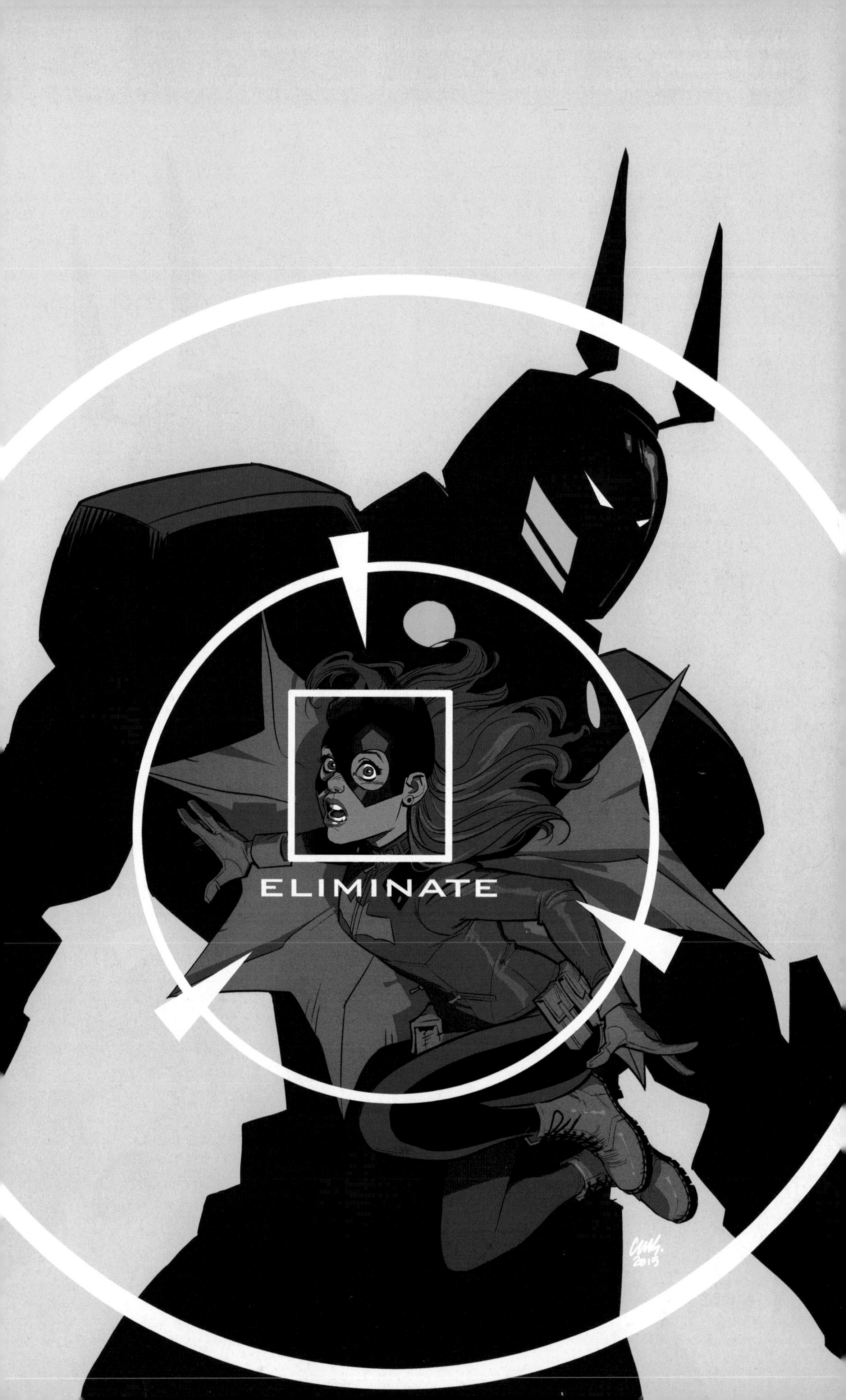
ELIMINATE

SNEAK PEEK CAMERON STEWART & BRENDEN FLETCHER writers BABS TARR artist & colorist STEVE WANDS letterer

INTERFERENCE

CAMERON STEWART & BRENDEN FLETCHER writers BABS TARR artist JOEL GOMEZ background artist SERGE LAPOINTE colorist STEVE WANDS letterer cover by CAMERON STEWART

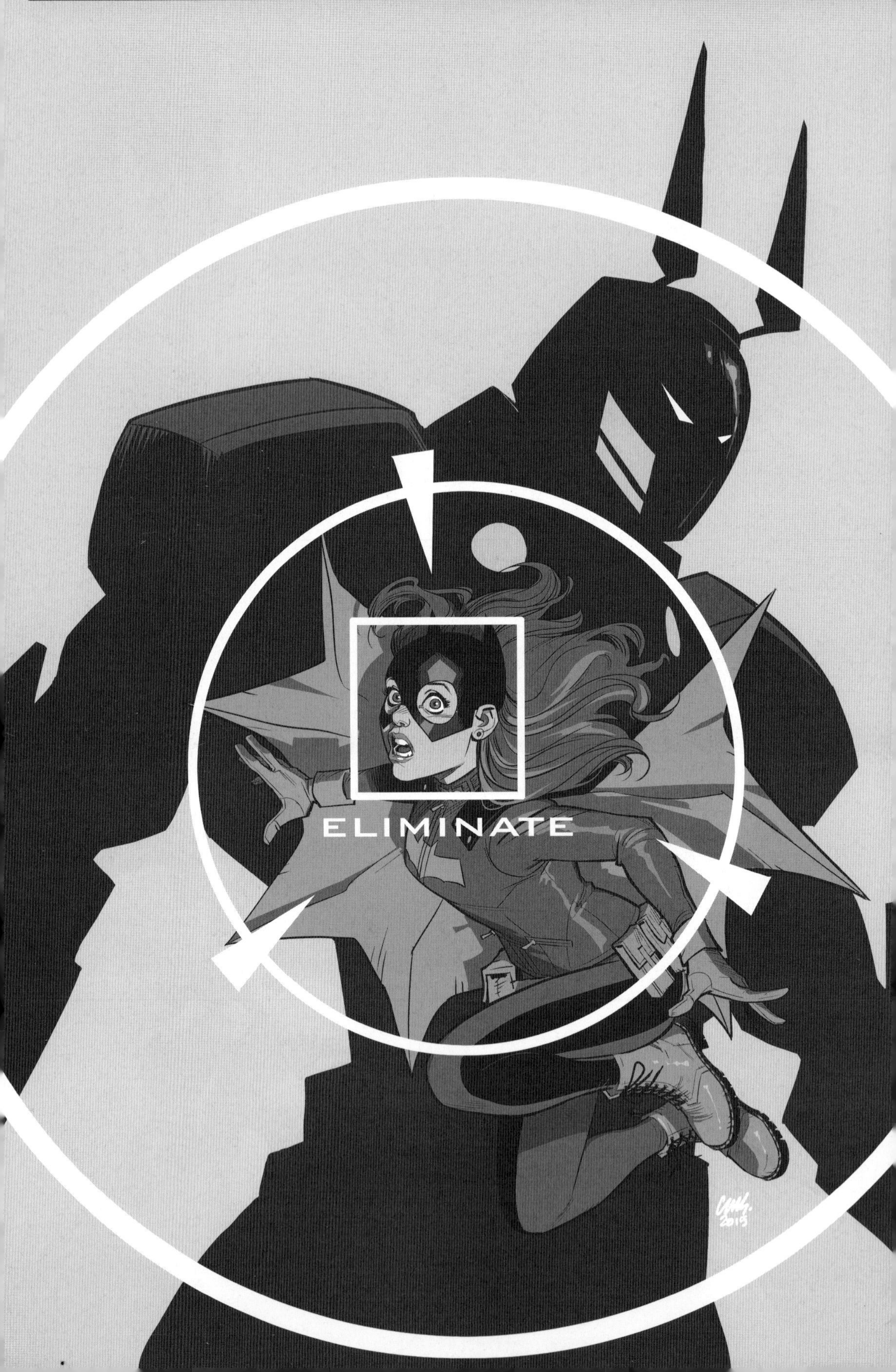
ELIMINATE

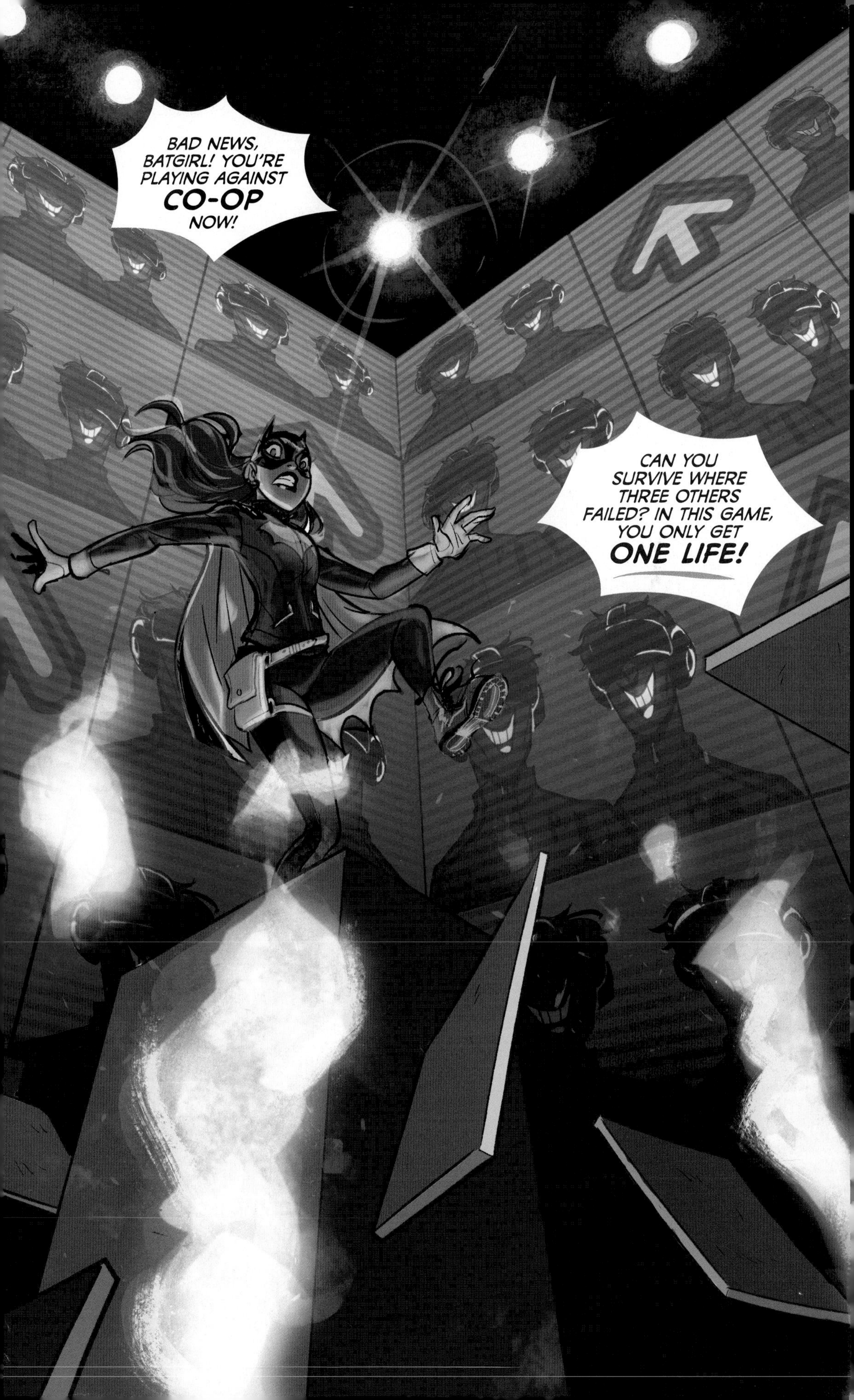
BAD NEWS, BATGIRL! YOU'RE PLAYING AGAINST CO-OP NOW!
CAN YOU SURVIVE WHERE THREE OTHERS FAILED? IN THIS GAME, YOU ONLY GET ONE LIFE!

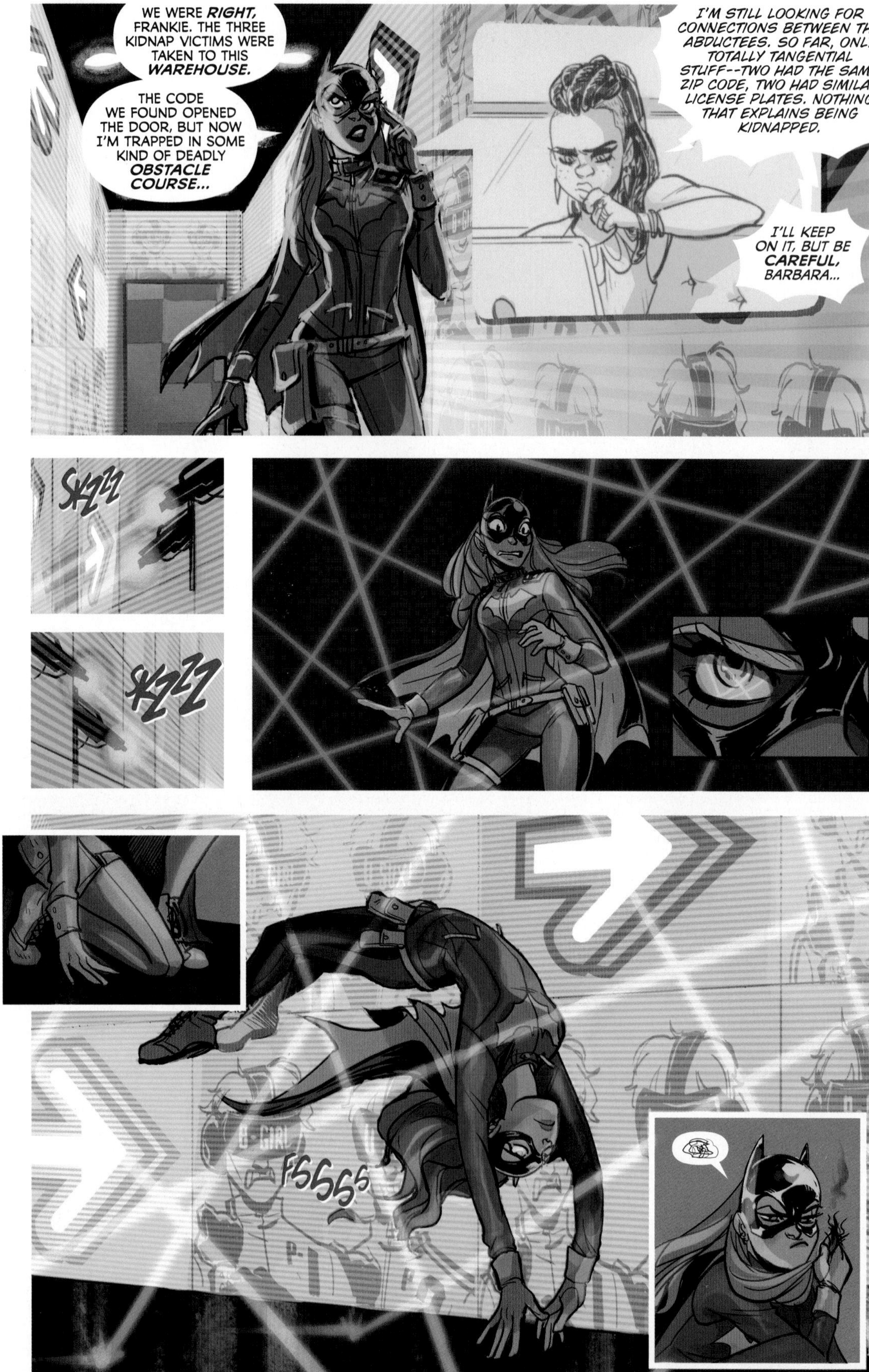
WE WERE **RIGHT,** FRANKIE. THE THREE KIDNAP VICTIMS WERE TAKEN TO THIS **WAREHOUSE.**
THE CODE WE FOUND OPENED THE DOOR, BUT NOW I'M TRAPPED IN SOME KIND OF DEADLY **OBSTACLE COURSE...**
I'M STILL LOOKING FOR CONNECTIONS BETWEEN THE ABDUCTEES. SO FAR, ONLY TOTALLY TANGENTIAL STUFF--TWO HAD THE SAME ZIP CODE, TWO HAD SIMILAR LICENSE PLATES. NOTHING THAT EXPLAINS BEING KIDNAPPED.
I'LL KEEP ON IT, BUT BE **CAREFUL,** BARBARA...
SKZZZ
SKZZZ
FSSSS

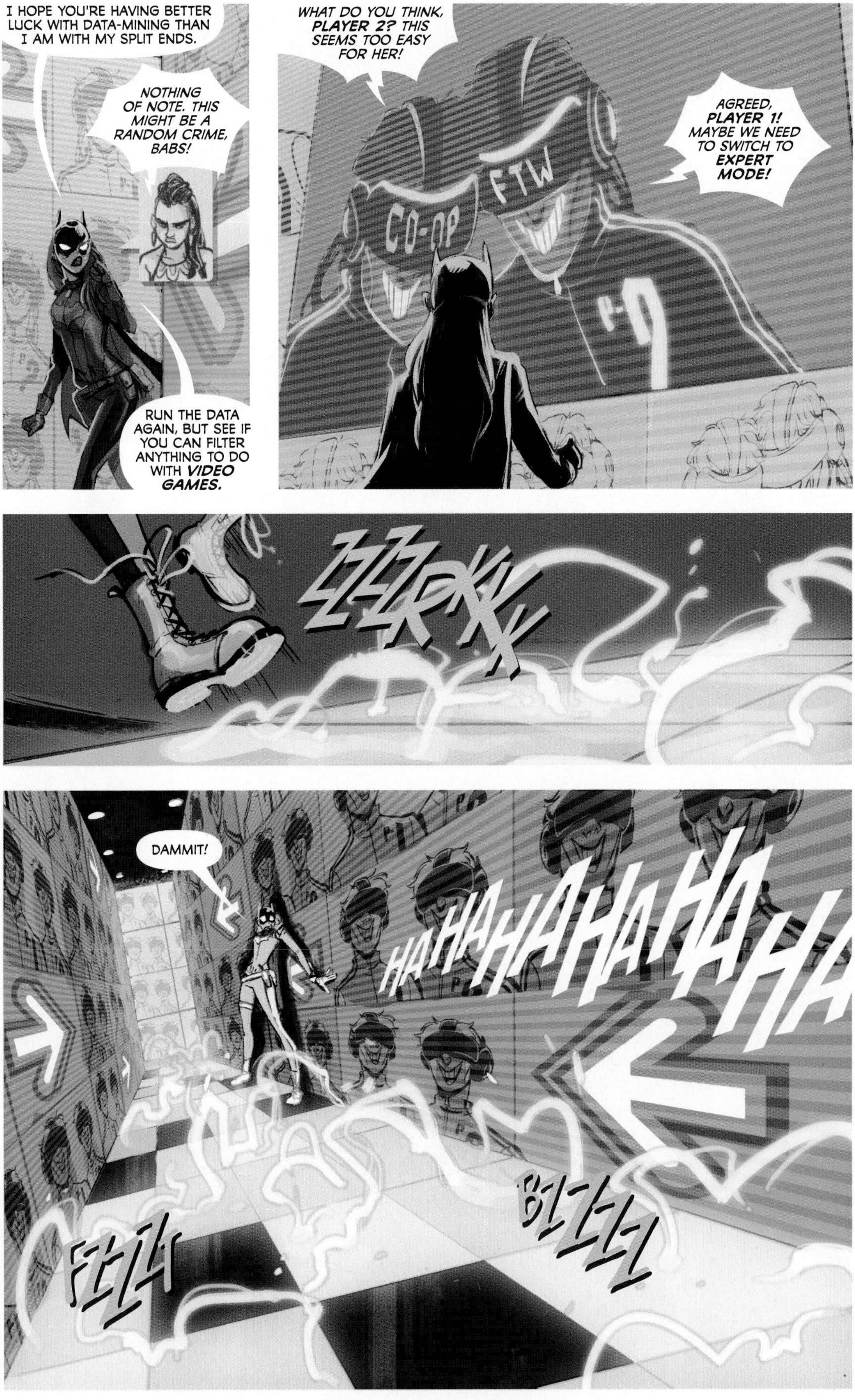
I HOPE YOU'RE HAVING BETTER LUCK WITH DATA-MINING THAN I AM WITH MY SPLIT ENDS.
NOTHING OF NOTE. THIS MIGHT BE A RANDOM CRIME, BABS!
RUN THE DATA AGAIN, BUT SEE IF YOU CAN FILTER ANYTHING TO DO WITH *VIDEO GAMES.*
WHAT DO YOU THINK, **PLAYER 2?** THIS SEEMS TOO EASY FOR HER!
CO-OP
FTW
AGREED, **PLAYER 1!** MAYBE WE NEED TO SWITCH TO **EXPERT MODE!**
ZZZRKK
DAMMIT!
HAHAHAHAHAHAHAHA
FZZZT
BZZZZ

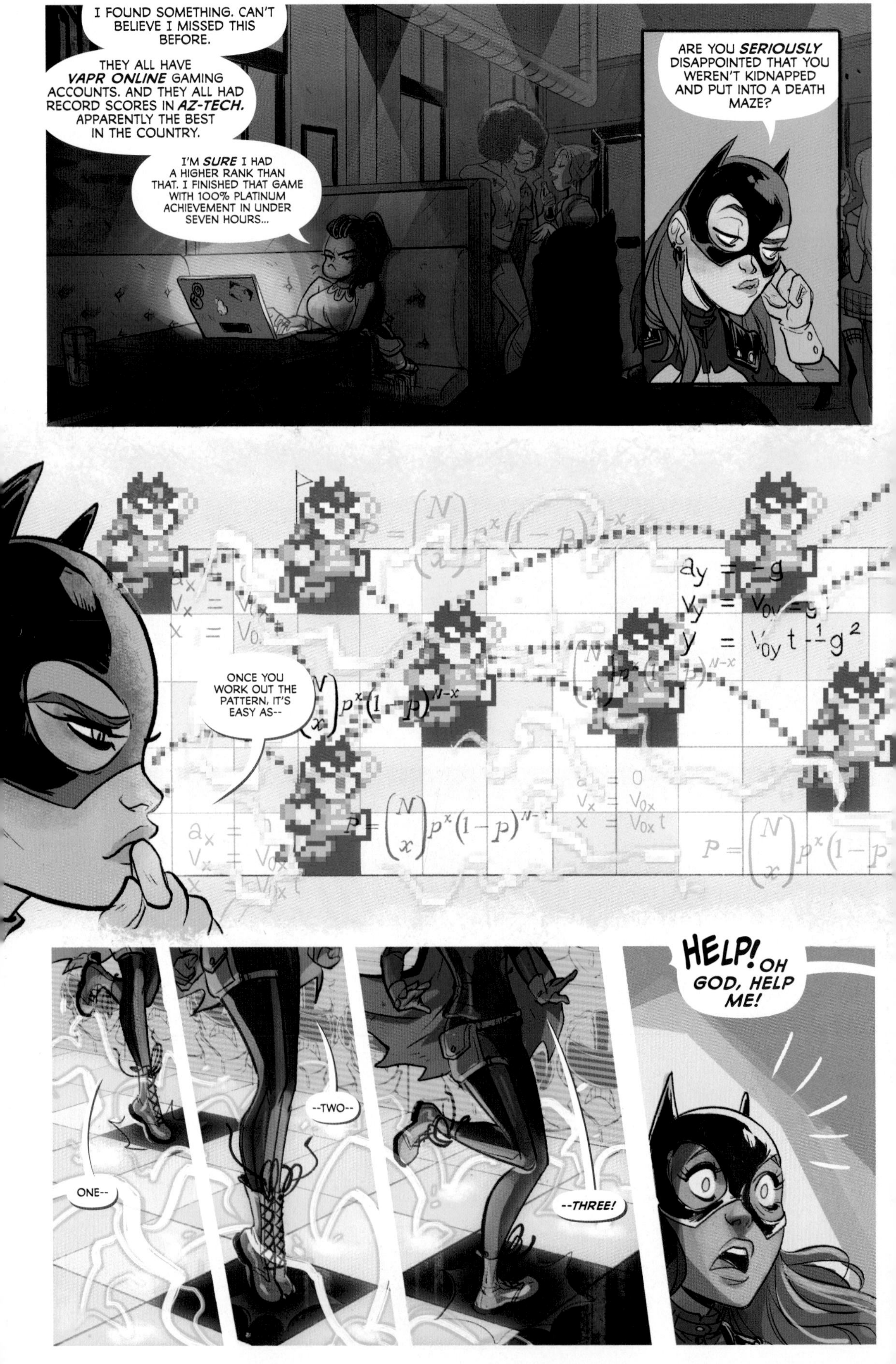
I FOUND SOMETHING. CAN'T BELIEVE I MISSED THIS BEFORE.
THEY ALL HAVE VAPR ONLINE GAMING ACCOUNTS. AND THEY ALL HAD RECORD SCORES IN AZ-TECH. APPARENTLY THE BEST IN THE COUNTRY.
I'M SURE I HAD A HIGHER RANK THAN THAT. I FINISHED THAT GAME WITH 100% PLATINUM ACHIEVEMENT IN UNDER SEVEN HOURS...
ARE YOU SERIOUSLY DISAPPOINTED THAT YOU WEREN'T KIDNAPPED AND PUT INTO A DEATH MAZE?
ONCE YOU WORK OUT THE PATTERN, IT'S EASY AS--
ONE--
--TWO--
--THREE!
HELP! OH GOD, HELP ME!

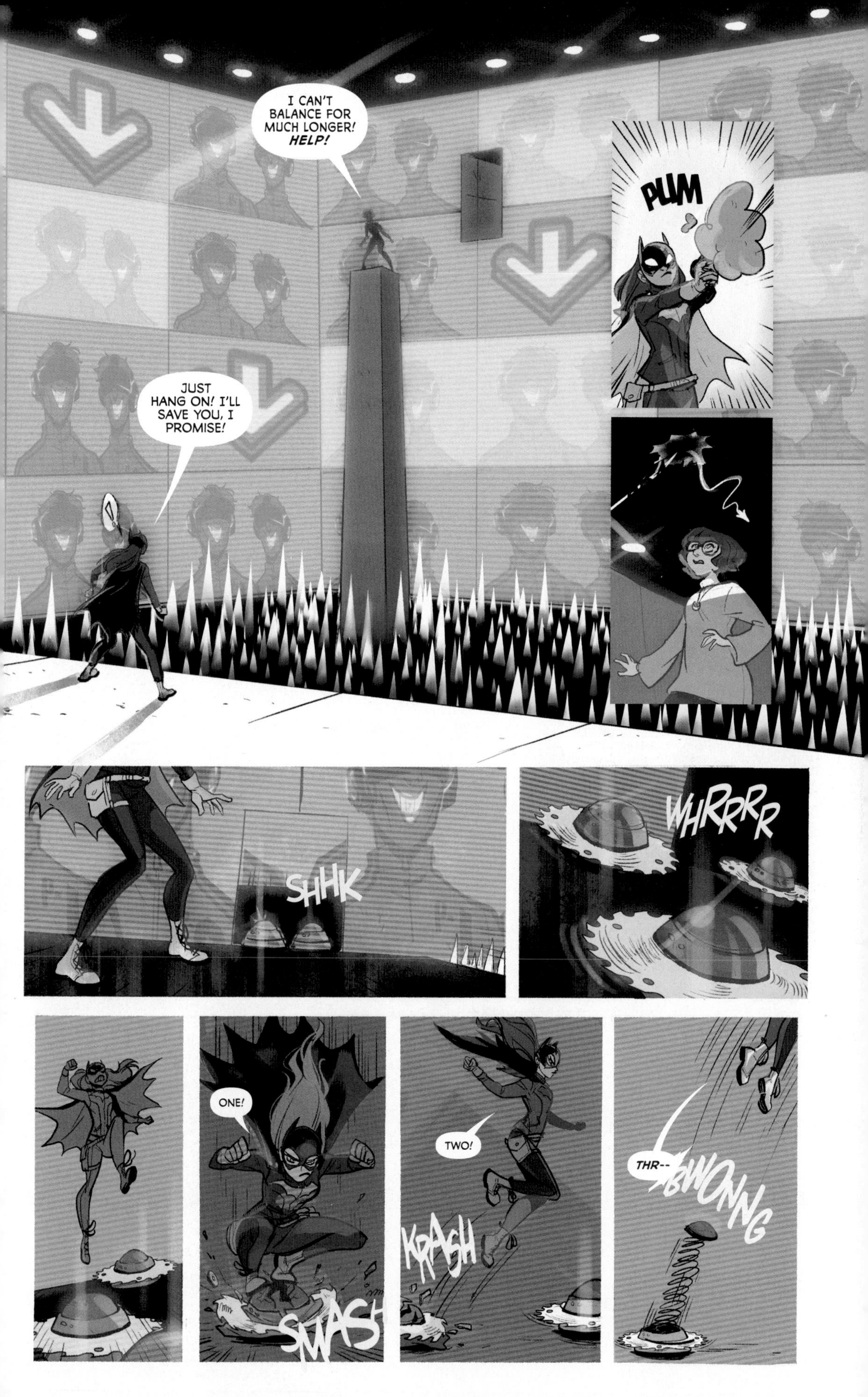
I CAN'T BALANCE FOR MUCH LONGER! *HELP!*
JUST HANG ON! I'LL SAVE YOU, I PROMISE!
PUM
SHHK
WHRRRR
ONE!
SMASH
KRASH
TWO!
THR--
BWONNG

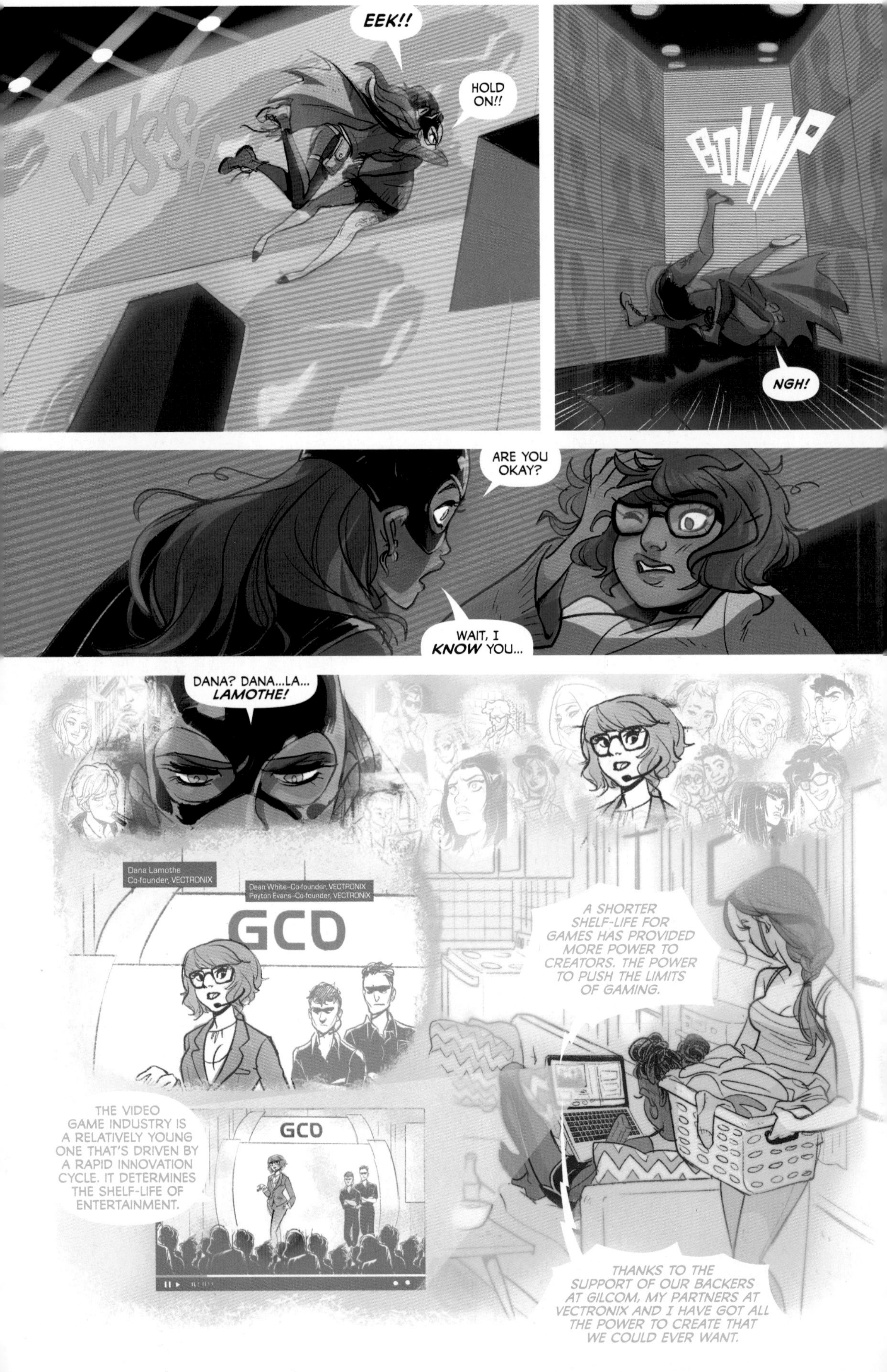
EEK!!
HOLD ON!!
WHSSH
BOUMP
NGH!
ARE YOU OKAY?
WAIT, I KNOW YOU...
DANA? DANA...LA... LAMOTHE!
Dana Lamothe
Co-founder, VECTRONIX
Dean White–Co-founder, VECTRONIX
Peyton Evans–Co-founder, VECTRONIX
GCD
A SHORTER SHELF-LIFE FOR GAMES HAS PROVIDED MORE POWER TO CREATORS. THE POWER TO PUSH THE LIMITS OF GAMING.
THE VIDEO GAME INDUSTRY IS A RELATIVELY YOUNG ONE THAT'S DRIVEN BY A RAPID INNOVATION CYCLE. IT DETERMINES THE SHELF-LIFE OF ENTERTAINMENT.
GCD
THANKS TO THE SUPPORT OF OUR BACKERS AT GILCOM, MY PARTNERS AT VECTRONIX AND I HAVE GOT ALL THE POWER TO CREATE THAT WE COULD EVER WANT.

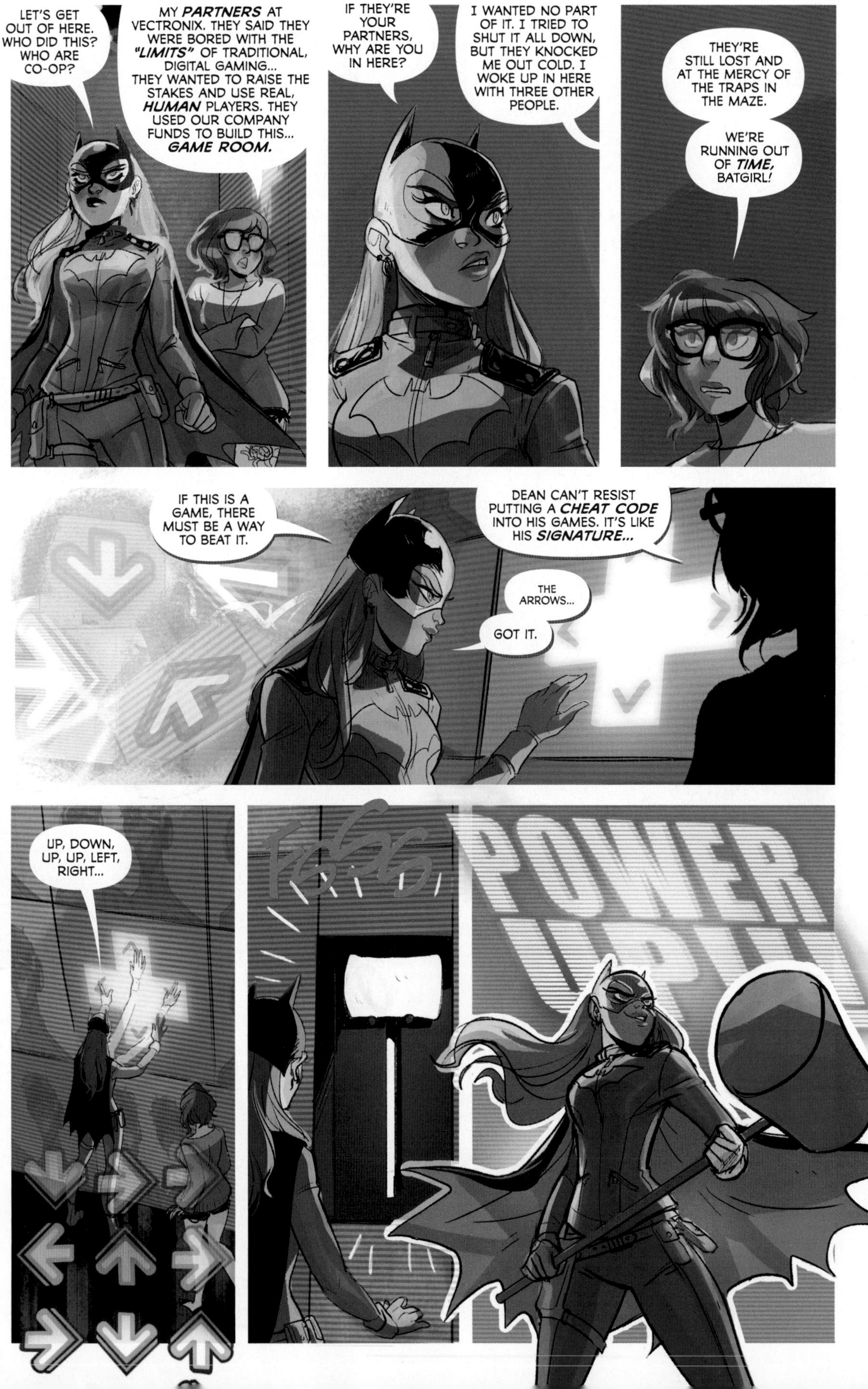
LET'S GET OUT OF HERE. WHO DID THIS? WHO ARE CO-OP?
MY PARTNERS AT VECTRONIX. THEY SAID THEY WERE BORED WITH THE "LIMITS" OF TRADITIONAL, DIGITAL GAMING... THEY WANTED TO RAISE THE STAKES AND USE REAL, HUMAN PLAYERS. THEY USED OUR COMPANY FUNDS TO BUILD THIS... GAME ROOM.
IF THEY'RE YOUR PARTNERS, WHY ARE YOU IN HERE?
I WANTED NO PART OF IT. I TRIED TO SHUT IT ALL DOWN, BUT THEY KNOCKED ME OUT COLD. I WOKE UP IN HERE WITH THREE OTHER PEOPLE.
THEY'RE STILL LOST AND AT THE MERCY OF THE TRAPS IN THE MAZE.
WE'RE RUNNING OUT OF TIME, BATGIRL!
IF THIS IS A GAME, THERE MUST BE A WAY TO BEAT IT.
DEAN CAN'T RESIST PUTTING A CHEAT CODE INTO HIS GAMES. IT'S LIKE HIS SIGNATURE...
THE ARROWS...
GOT IT.
UP, DOWN, UP, UP, LEFT, RIGHT...
POWER

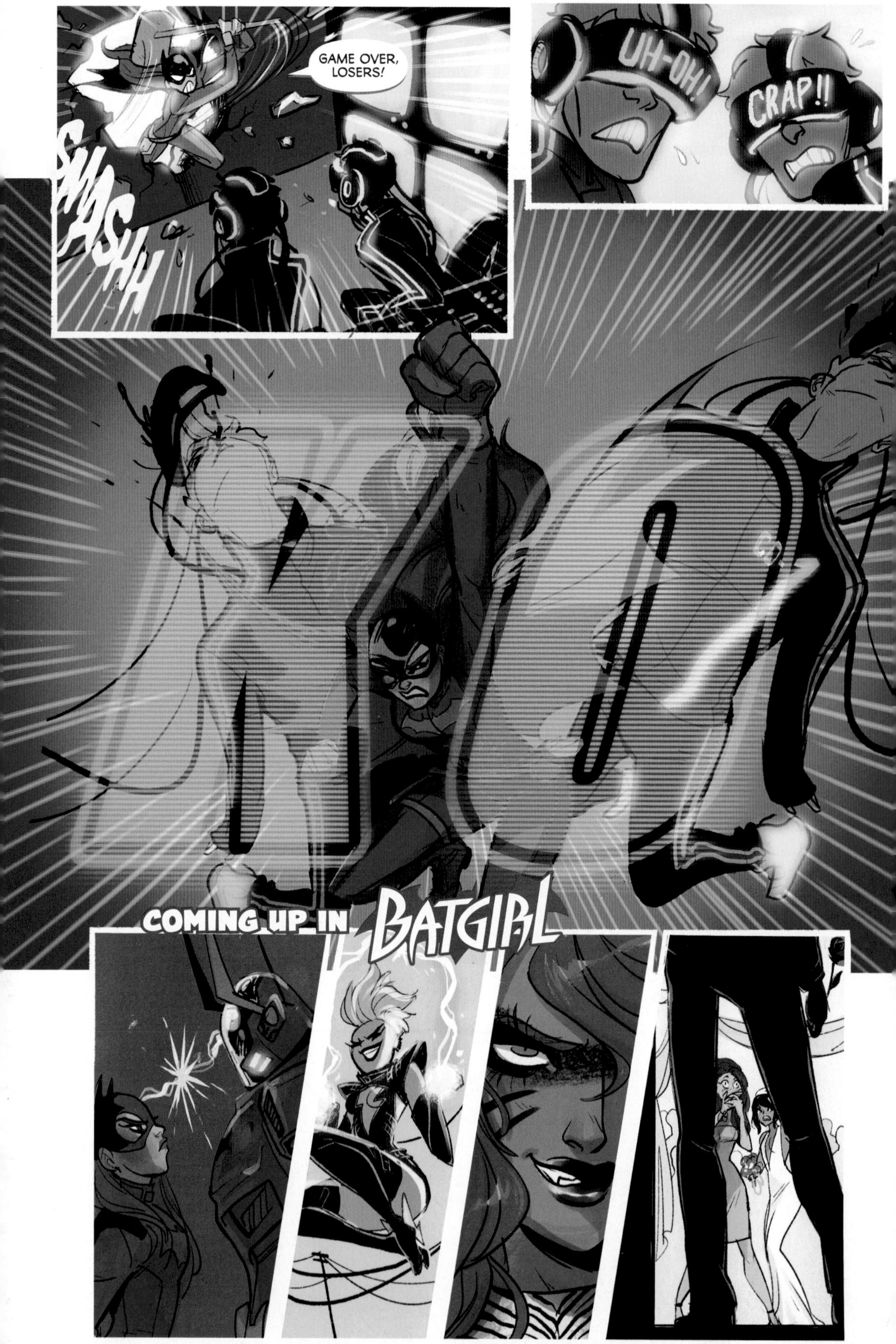
GAME OVER, LOSERS!
SMASHH
UH-OH!
CRAP!!
COMING UP IN BATGIRL

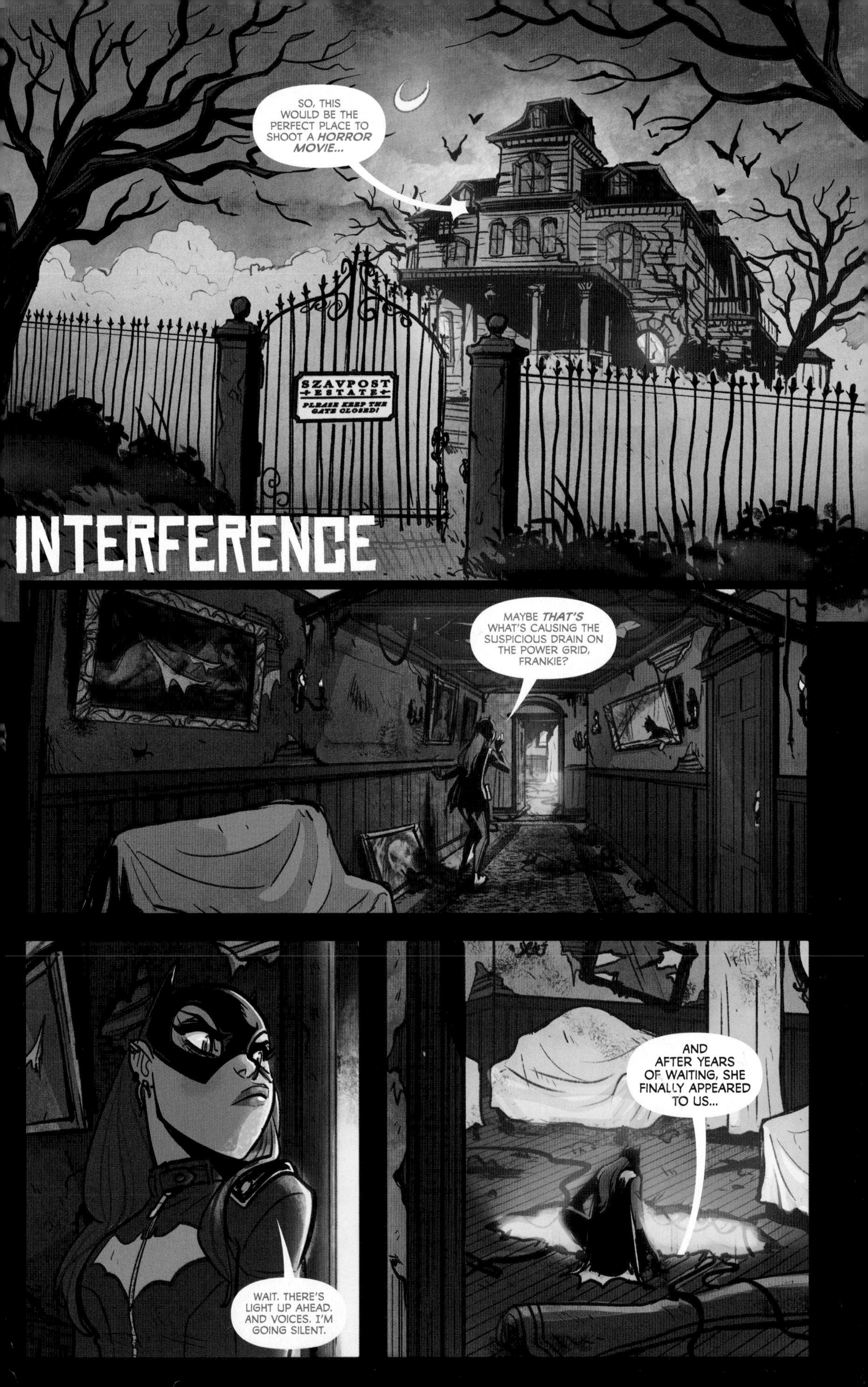
SO, THIS WOULD BE THE PERFECT PLACE TO SHOOT A *HORROR MOVIE...*
SZAVPOST ESTATE
PLEASE KEEP THE GATE CLOSED!
INTERFERENCE
MAYBE *THAT'S* WHAT'S CAUSING THE SUSPICIOUS DRAIN ON THE POWER GRID, FRANKIE?
WAIT. THERE'S LIGHT UP AHEAD. AND VOICES. I'M GOING SILENT.
AND AFTER YEARS OF WAITING, SHE FINALLY APPEARED TO US...

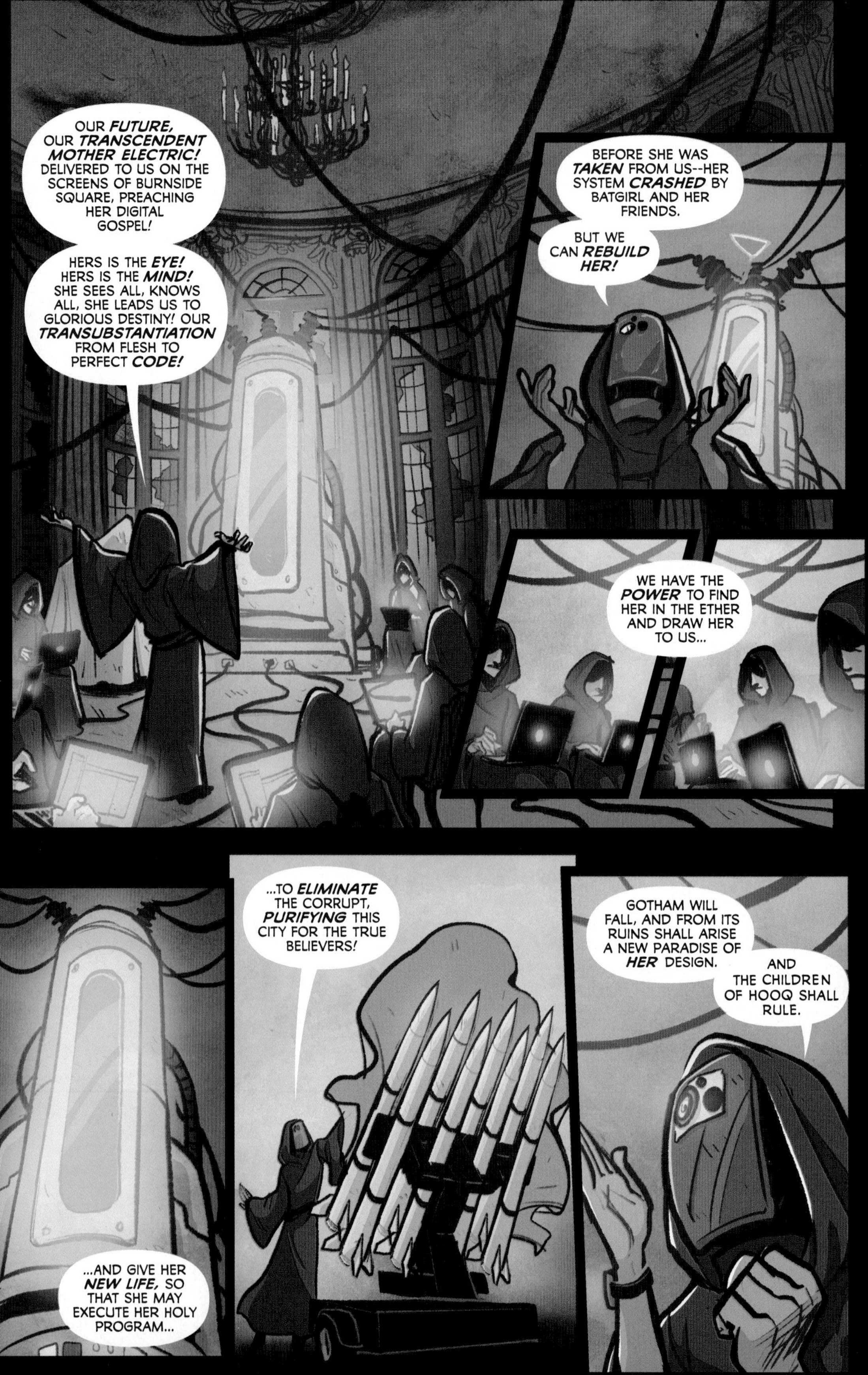
OUR FUTURE, OUR TRANSCENDENT MOTHER ELECTRIC! DELIVERED TO US ON THE SCREENS OF BURNSIDE SQUARE, PREACHING HER DIGITAL GOSPEL!
HERS IS THE EYE! HERS IS THE MIND! SHE SEES ALL, KNOWS ALL, SHE LEADS US TO GLORIOUS DESTINY! OUR TRANSUBSTANTIATION FROM FLESH TO PERFECT CODE!
BEFORE SHE WAS TAKEN FROM US--HER SYSTEM CRASHED BY BATGIRL AND HER FRIENDS.
BUT WE CAN REBUILD HER!
WE HAVE THE POWER TO FIND HER IN THE ETHER AND DRAW HER TO US...
...AND GIVE HER NEW LIFE, SO THAT SHE MAY EXECUTE HER HOLY PROGRAM...
...TO ELIMINATE THE CORRUPT, PURIFYING THIS CITY FOR THE TRUE BELIEVERS!
GOTHAM WILL FALL, AND FROM ITS RUINS SHALL ARISE A NEW PARADISE OF HER DESIGN.
AND THE CHILDREN OF HOOQ SHALL RULE.

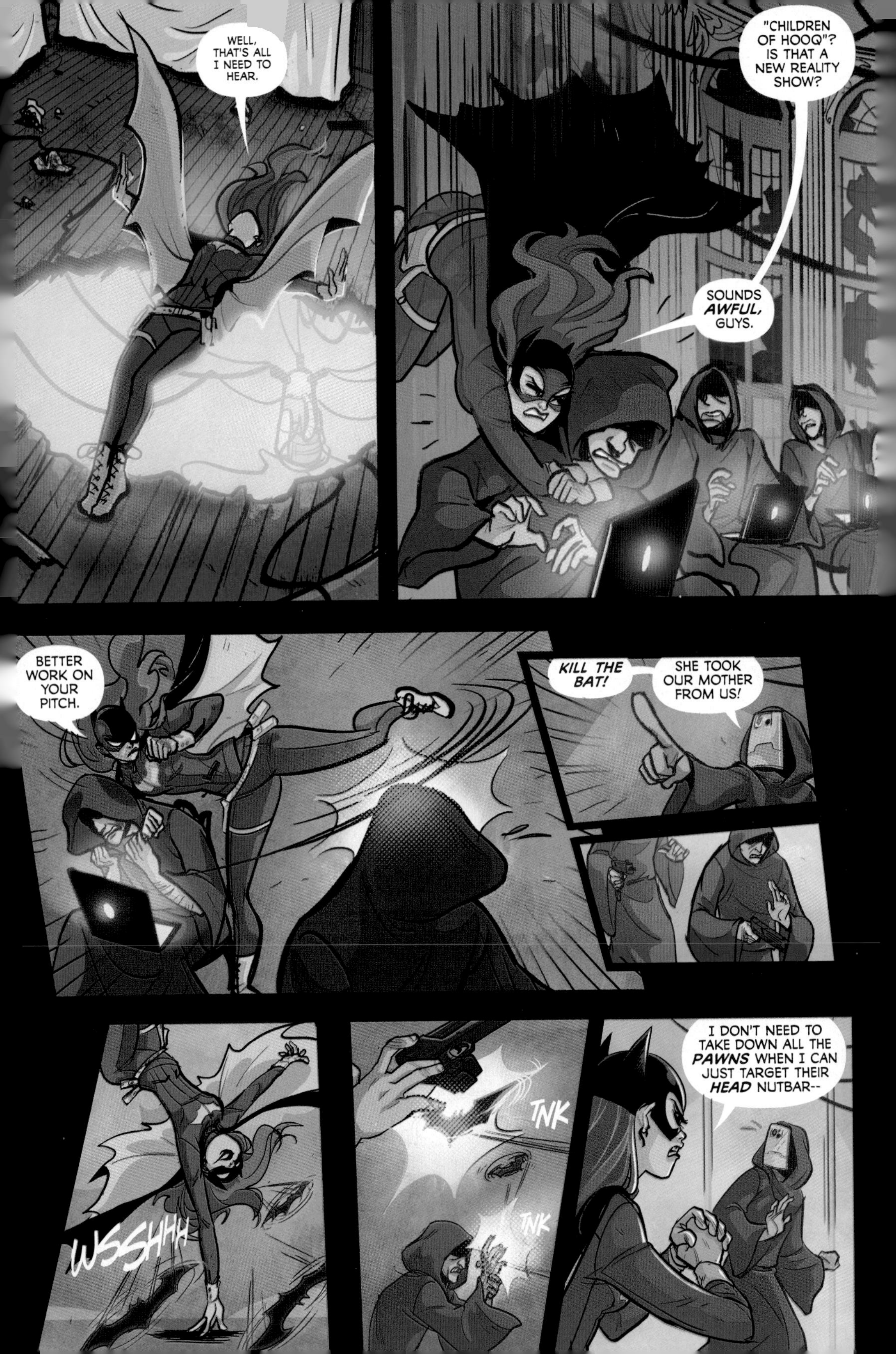
WELL, THAT'S ALL I NEED TO HEAR.
"CHILDREN OF HOOQ"? IS THAT A NEW REALITY SHOW?
SOUNDS *AWFUL,* GUYS.
BETTER WORK ON YOUR PITCH.
KILL THE BAT!
SHE TOOK OUR MOTHER FROM US!
WSSHHH
TNK
TNK
I DON'T NEED TO TAKE DOWN ALL THE *PAWNS* WHEN I CAN JUST TARGET THEIR *HEAD* NUTBAR--

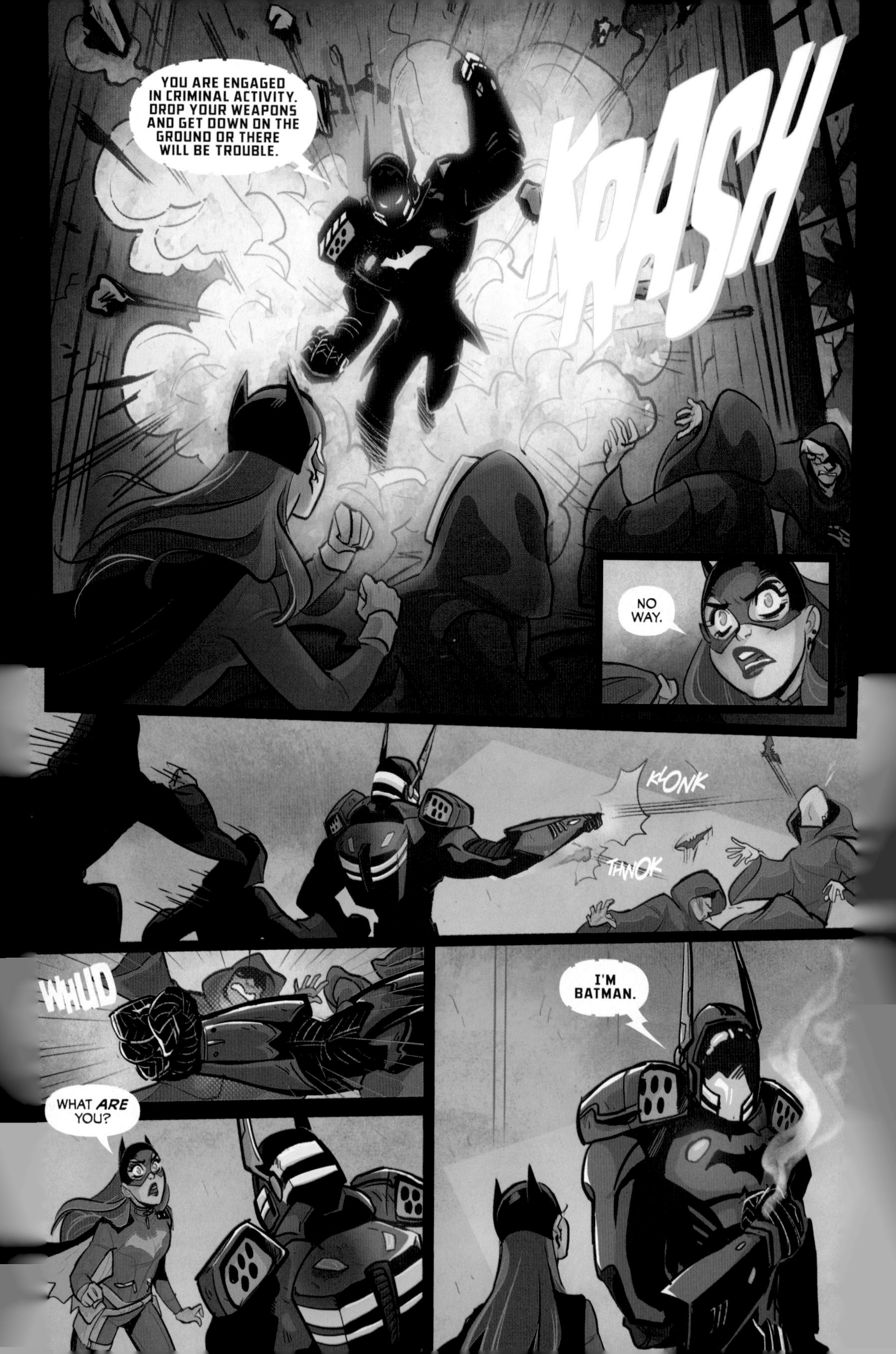

YOU ARE ENGAGED IN CRIMINAL ACTIVITY. DROP YOUR WEAPONS AND GET DOWN ON THE GROUND OR THERE WILL BE TROUBLE.
KRASH
NO WAY.
KLONK
THWOK
WHUD
WHAT ARE YOU?
I'M BATMAN.

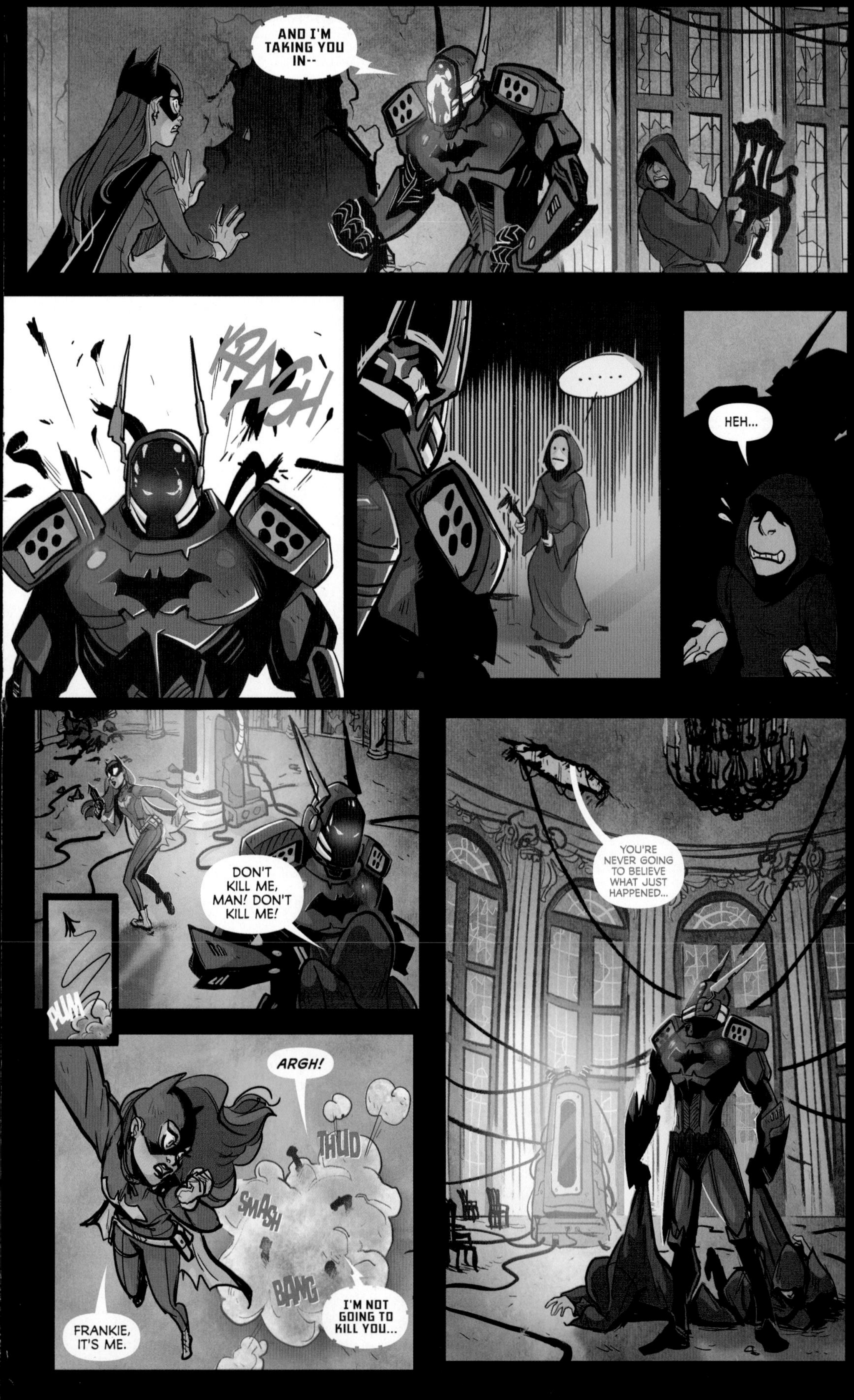
AND I'M TAKING YOU IN--
KRASH
.....
HEH...
DON'T KILL ME, MAN! DON'T KILL ME!
PUM
ARGH!
THUD
SMASH
BANG
FRANKIE, IT'S ME.
I'M NOT GOING TO KILL YOU...
YOU'RE NEVER GOING TO BELIEVE WHAT JUST HAPPENED...

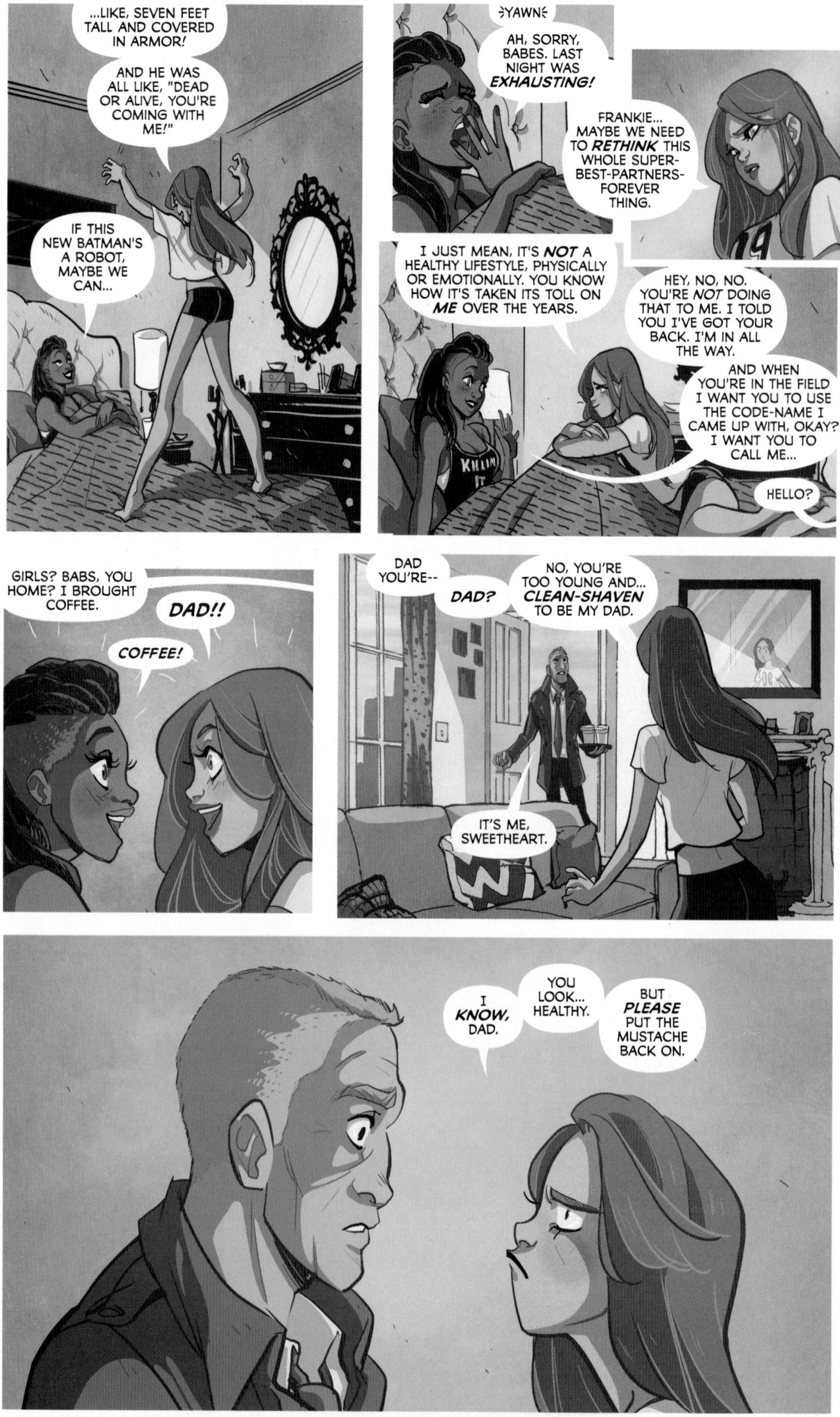
...LIKE, SEVEN FEET TALL AND COVERED IN ARMOR!
AND HE WAS ALL LIKE, "DEAD OR ALIVE, YOU'RE COMING WITH ME!"
IF THIS NEW BATMAN'S A ROBOT, MAYBE WE CAN...
YAWN
AH, SORRY, BABES. LAST NIGHT WAS EXHAUSTING!
FRANKIE... MAYBE WE NEED TO RETHINK THIS WHOLE SUPER-BEST-PARTNERS-FOREVER THING.
19
I JUST MEAN, IT'S NOT A HEALTHY LIFESTYLE, PHYSICALLY OR EMOTIONALLY. YOU KNOW HOW IT'S TAKEN ITS TOLL ON ME OVER THE YEARS.
HEY, NO, NO. YOU'RE NOT DOING THAT TO ME. I TOLD YOU I'VE GOT YOUR BACK. I'M IN ALL THE WAY.
AND WHEN YOU'RE IN THE FIELD I WANT YOU TO USE THE CODE-NAME I CAME UP WITH, OKAY? I WANT YOU TO CALL ME...
KILLIN' IT
HELLO?
GIRLS? BABS, YOU HOME? I BROUGHT COFFEE.
DAD!!
COFFEE!
DAD YOU'RE--
DAD?
NO, YOU'RE TOO YOUNG AND... CLEAN-SHAVEN TO BE MY DAD.
IT'S ME, SWEETHEART.
I KNOW, DAD.
YOU LOOK... HEALTHY.
BUT PLEASE PUT THE MUSTACHE BACK ON.

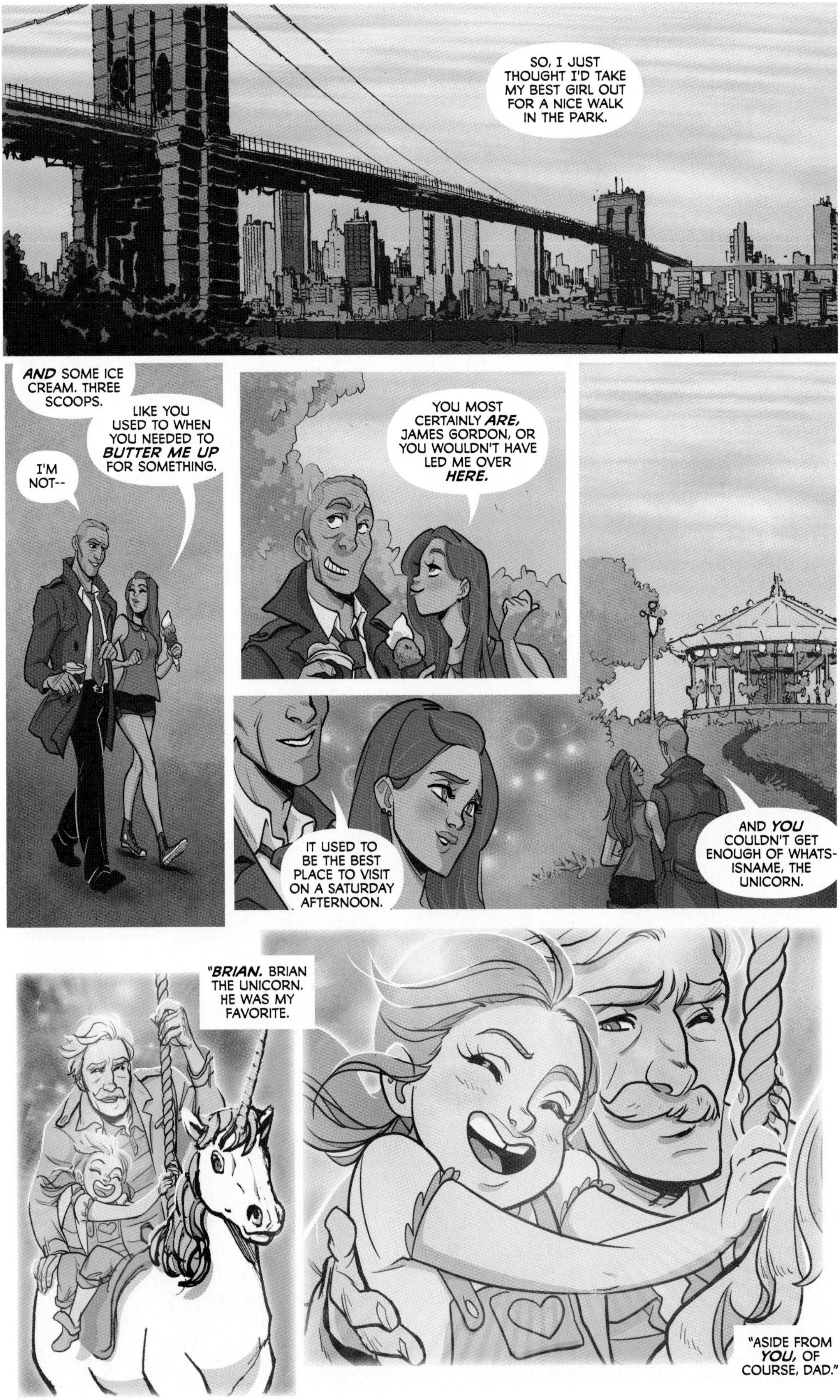
SO, I JUST THOUGHT I'D TAKE MY BEST GIRL OUT FOR A NICE WALK IN THE PARK.
AND SOME ICE CREAM. THREE SCOOPS.
I'M NOT--
LIKE YOU USED TO WHEN YOU NEEDED TO BUTTER ME UP FOR SOMETHING.
YOU MOST CERTAINLY ARE, JAMES GORDON, OR YOU WOULDN'T HAVE LED ME OVER HERE.
IT USED TO BE THE BEST PLACE TO VISIT ON A SATURDAY AFTERNOON.
AND YOU COULDN'T GET ENOUGH OF WHATS-ISNAME, THE UNICORN.
"BRIAN. BRIAN THE UNICORN. HE WAS MY FAVORITE.
"ASIDE FROM YOU, OF COURSE, DAD."

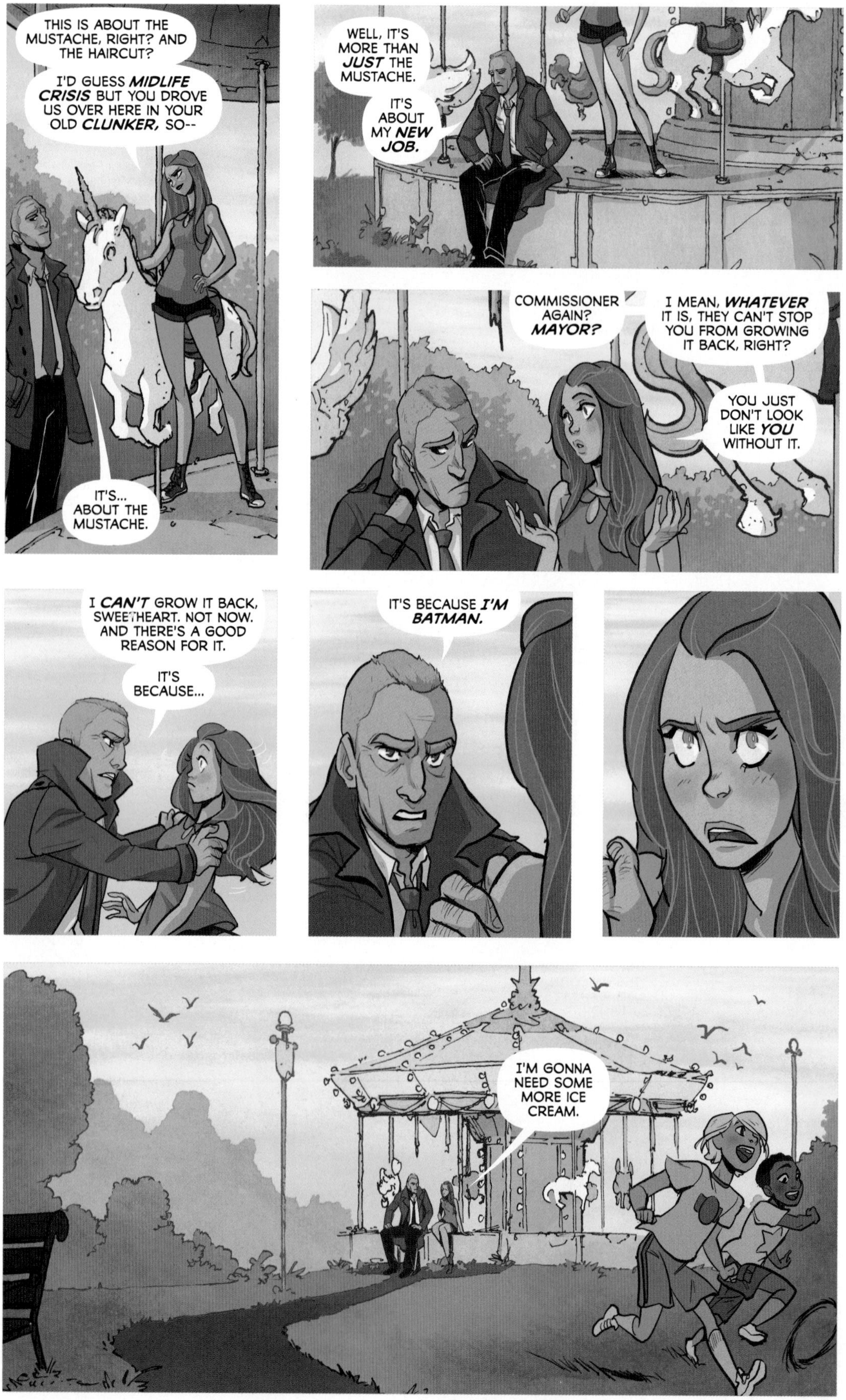
THIS IS ABOUT THE MUSTACHE, RIGHT? AND THE HAIRCUT?
I'D GUESS MIDLIFE CRISIS BUT YOU DROVE US OVER HERE IN YOUR OLD CLUNKER, SO--
IT'S... ABOUT THE MUSTACHE.
WELL, IT'S MORE THAN JUST THE MUSTACHE.
IT'S ABOUT MY NEW JOB.
COMMISSIONER AGAIN? MAYOR?
I MEAN, WHATEVER IT IS, THEY CAN'T STOP YOU FROM GROWING IT BACK, RIGHT?
YOU JUST DON'T LOOK LIKE YOU WITHOUT IT.
I CAN'T GROW IT BACK, SWEETHEART. NOT NOW. AND THERE'S A GOOD REASON FOR IT.
IT'S BECAUSE...
IT'S BECAUSE I'M BATMAN.
I'M GONNA NEED SOME MORE ICE CREAM.

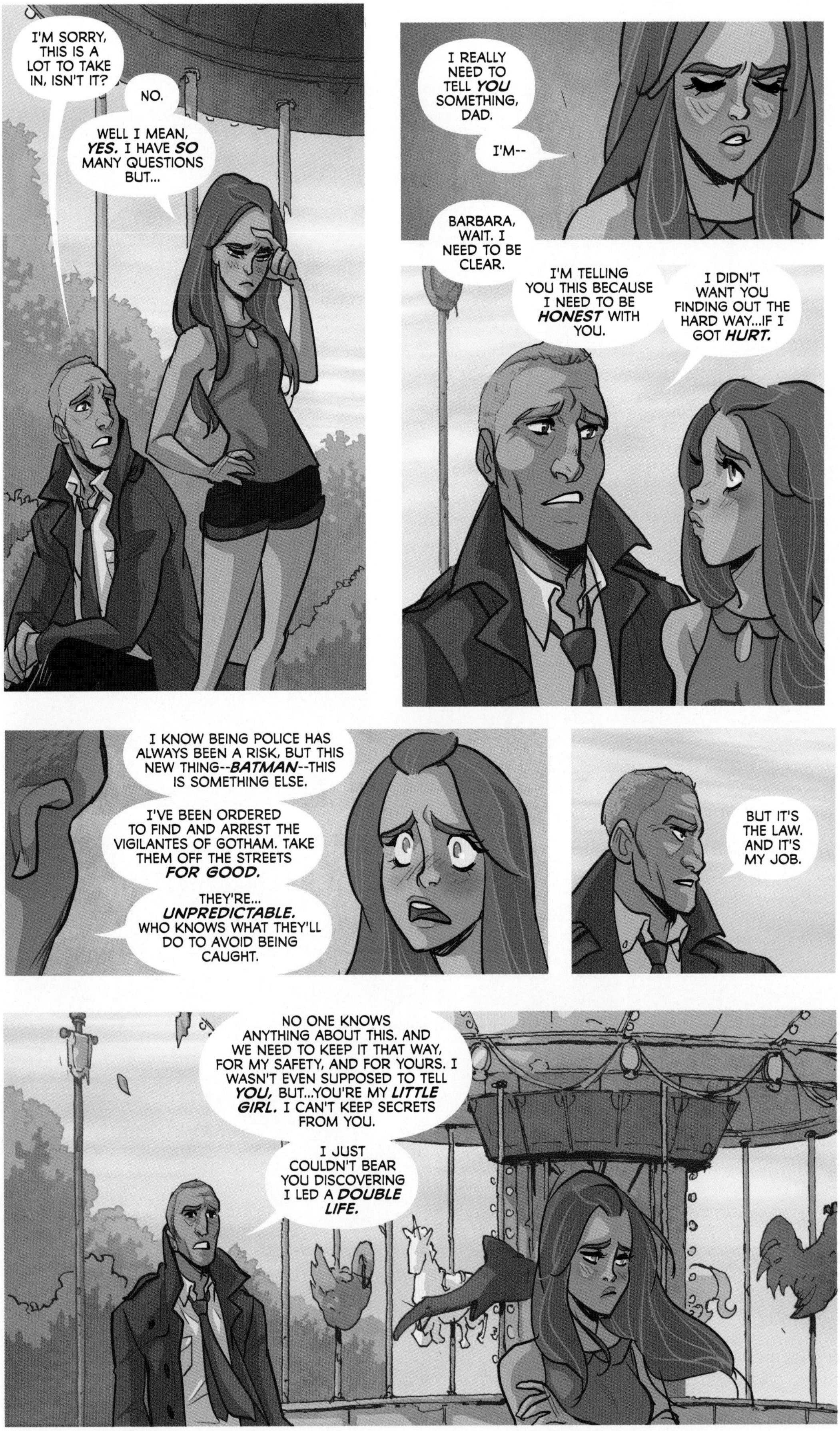

I'M SORRY, THIS IS A LOT TO TAKE IN, ISN'T IT?
NO.
WELL I MEAN, YES. I HAVE SO MANY QUESTIONS BUT...
I REALLY NEED TO TELL YOU SOMETHING, DAD.
I'M--
BARBARA, WAIT. I NEED TO BE CLEAR.
I'M TELLING YOU THIS BECAUSE I NEED TO BE HONEST WITH YOU.
I DIDN'T WANT YOU FINDING OUT THE HARD WAY...IF I GOT HURT.
I KNOW BEING POLICE HAS ALWAYS BEEN A RISK, BUT THIS NEW THING--BATMAN--THIS IS SOMETHING ELSE.
I'VE BEEN ORDERED TO FIND AND ARREST THE VIGILANTES OF GOTHAM. TAKE THEM OFF THE STREETS FOR GOOD.
THEY'RE... UNPREDICTABLE. WHO KNOWS WHAT THEY'LL DO TO AVOID BEING CAUGHT.
BUT IT'S THE LAW. AND IT'S MY JOB.
NO ONE KNOWS ANYTHING ABOUT THIS. AND WE NEED TO KEEP IT THAT WAY, FOR MY SAFETY, AND FOR YOURS. I WASN'T EVEN SUPPOSED TO TELL YOU, BUT...YOU'RE MY LITTLE GIRL. I CAN'T KEEP SECRETS FROM YOU.
I JUST COULDN'T BEAR YOU DISCOVERING I LED A DOUBLE LIFE.

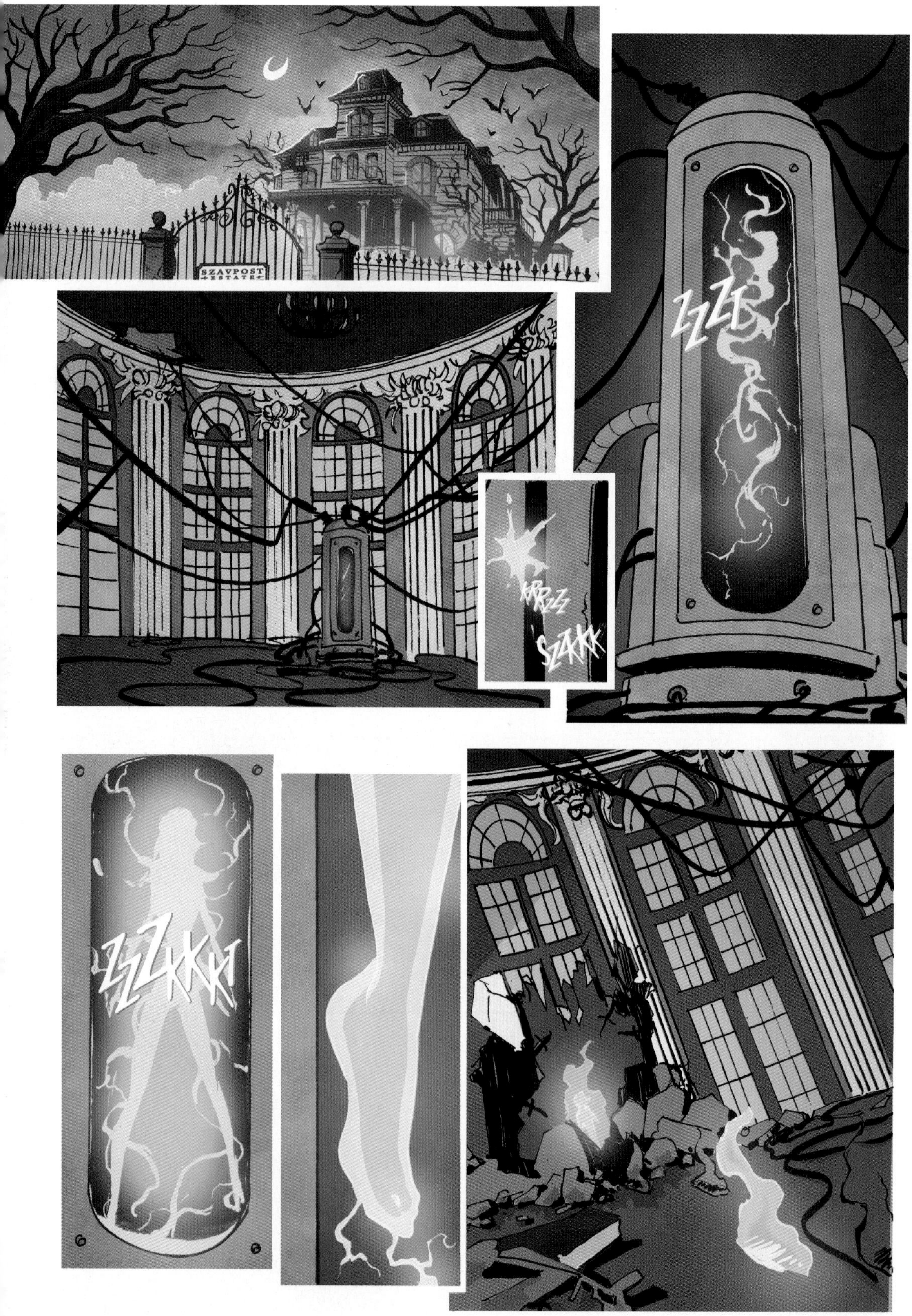
SZAVPOST ESTATE
ZZZT
KRRZZZ
SZZKKK
ZZZKKKT

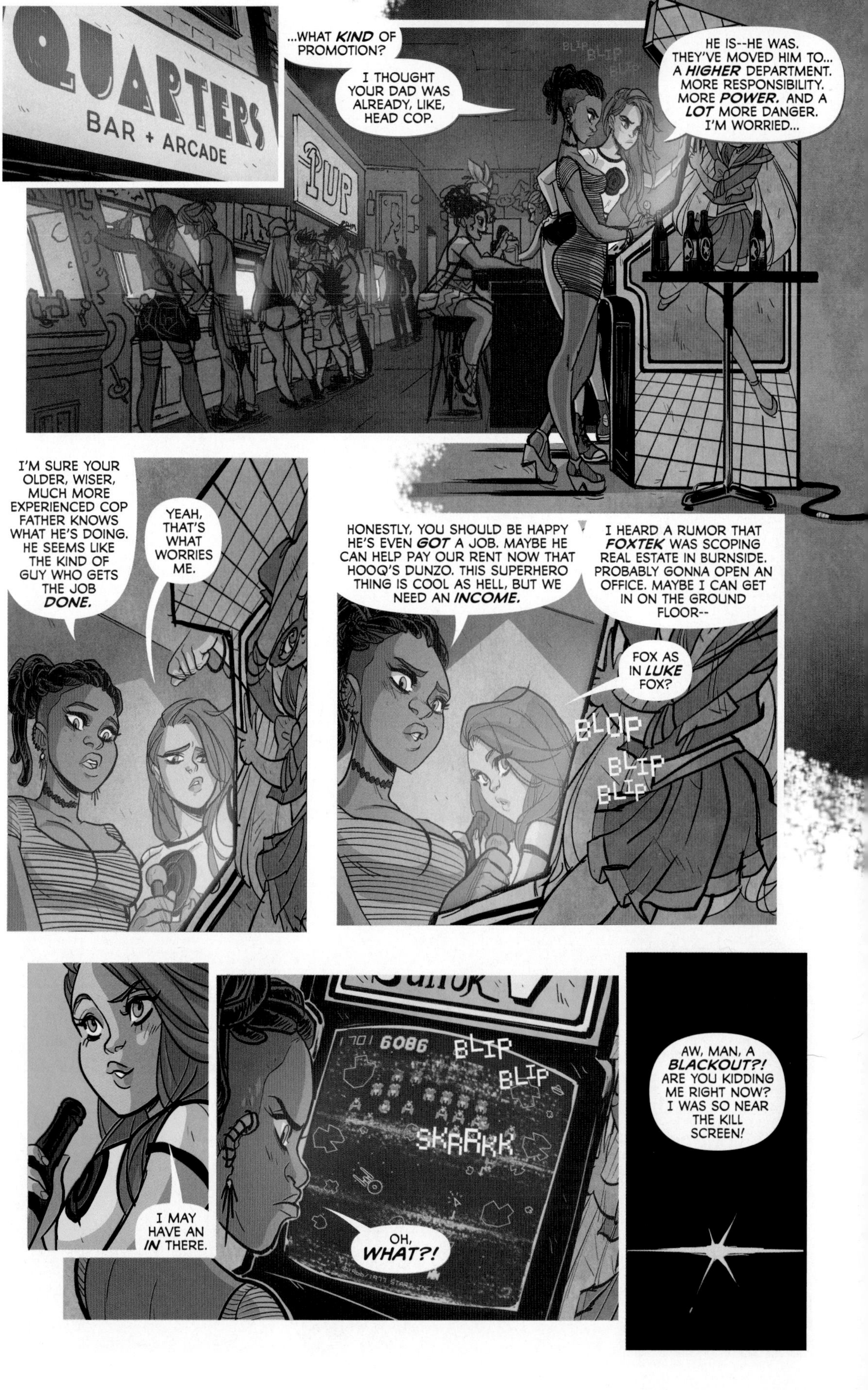
QUARTERS
BAR + ARCADE
...WHAT *KIND* OF PROMOTION?
I THOUGHT YOUR DAD WAS ALREADY, LIKE, HEAD COP.
1UP
BLIP BLIP BLIP
HE IS--HE WAS. THEY'VE MOVED HIM TO... A *HIGHER* DEPARTMENT. MORE RESPONSIBILITY. MORE *POWER.* AND A *LOT* MORE DANGER. I'M WORRIED...
I'M SURE YOUR OLDER, WISER, MUCH MORE EXPERIENCED COP FATHER KNOWS WHAT HE'S DOING. HE SEEMS LIKE THE KIND OF GUY WHO GETS THE JOB *DONE.*
YEAH, THAT'S WHAT WORRIES ME.
HONESTLY, YOU SHOULD BE HAPPY HE'S EVEN *GOT* A JOB. MAYBE HE CAN HELP PAY OUR RENT NOW THAT HOOQ'S DUNZO. THIS SUPERHERO THING IS COOL AS HELL, BUT WE NEED AN *INCOME.*
I HEARD A RUMOR THAT *FOXTEK* WAS SCOPING REAL ESTATE IN BURNSIDE. PROBABLY GONNA OPEN AN OFFICE. MAYBE I CAN GET IN ON THE GROUND FLOOR--
FOX AS IN *LUKE* FOX?
BLOP
BLIP
BLIP
I MAY HAVE AN *IN* THERE.
6086
BLIP
BLIP
SKRAKK
OH, *WHAT?!*
AW, MAN, A *BLACKOUT?!* ARE YOU KIDDING ME RIGHT NOW? I WAS SO NEAR THE KILL SCREEN!

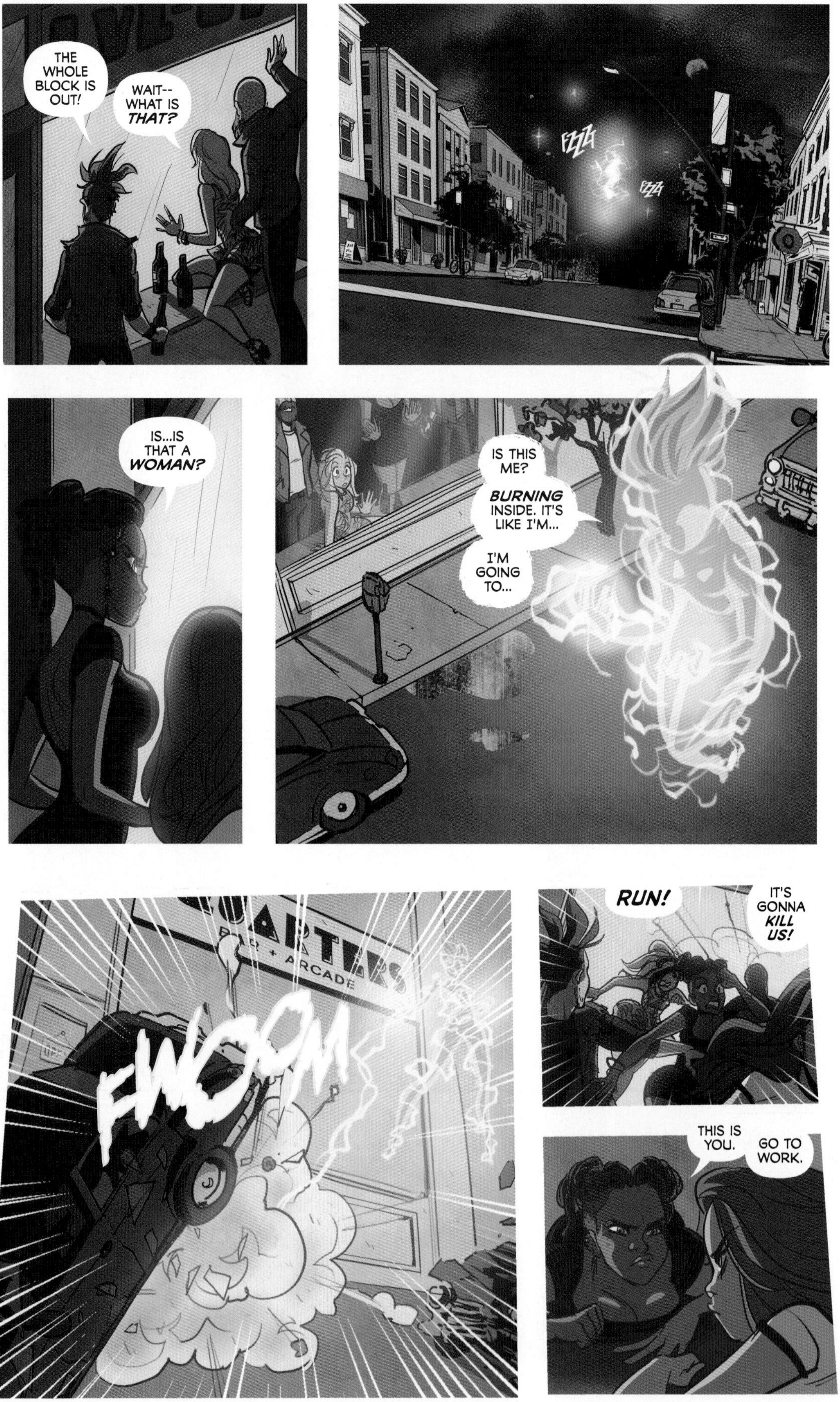

THE WHOLE BLOCK IS OUT!
WAIT-- WHAT IS *THAT?*
FZZZ
FZZZ
IS...IS THAT A *WOMAN?*
IS THIS ME?
BURNING INSIDE. IT'S LIKE I'M...
I'M GOING TO...
QUARTERS BAR + ARCADE
FWOOM
RUN!
IT'S GONNA *KILL* US!
THIS IS YOU.
GO TO WORK.

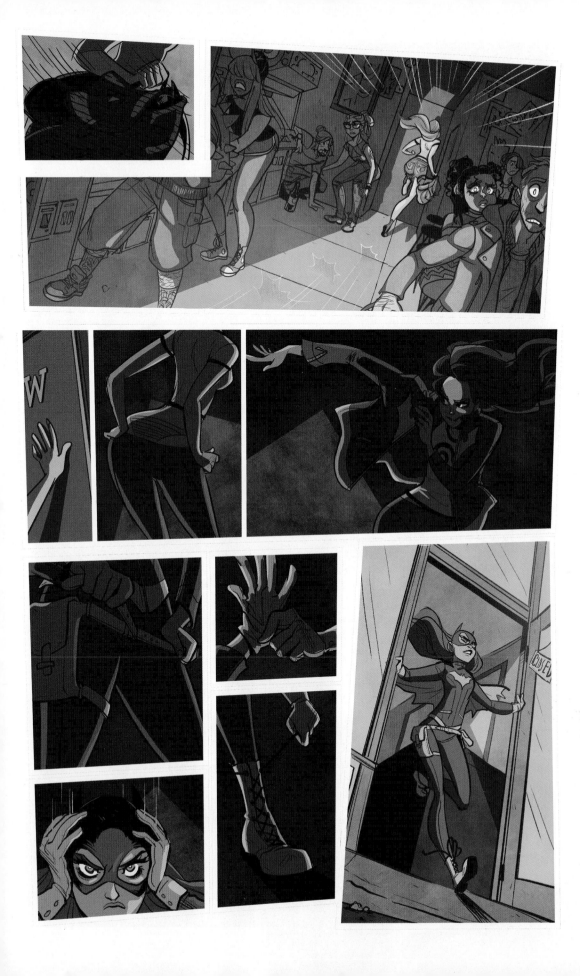

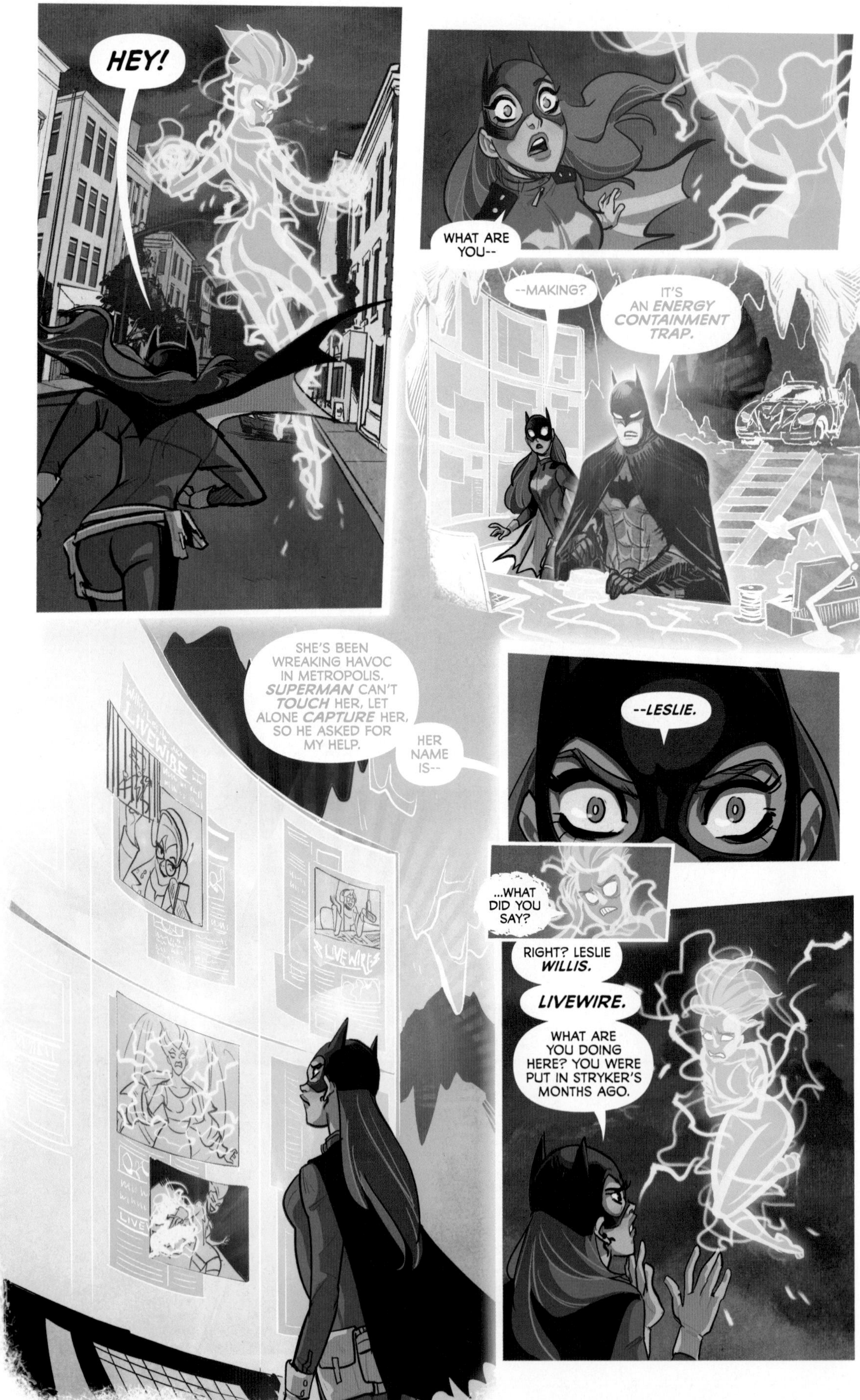

HEY!
WHAT ARE YOU--
--MAKING?
IT'S AN ENERGY CONTAINMENT TRAP.
SHE'S BEEN WREAKING HAVOC IN METROPOLIS. SUPERMAN CAN'T TOUCH HER, LET ALONE CAPTURE HER, SO HE ASKED FOR MY HELP.
HER NAME IS--
--LESLIE.
...WHAT DID YOU SAY?
RIGHT? LESLIE WILLIS.
LIVEWIRE.
WHAT ARE YOU DOING HERE? YOU WERE PUT IN STRYKER'S MONTHS AGO.

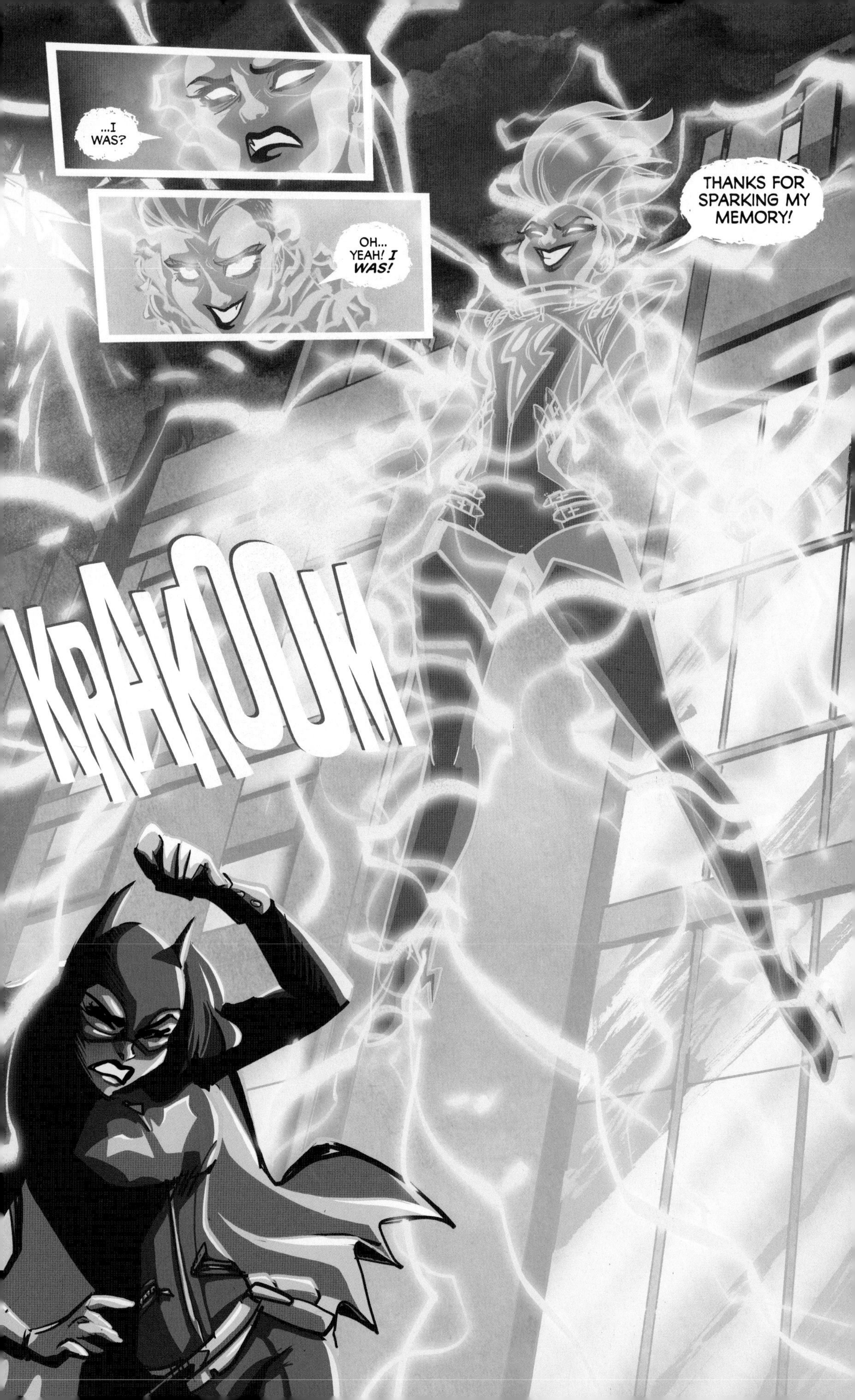
...I WAS?
OH... YEAH! I WAS!
THANKS FOR SPARKING MY MEMORY!
KRAKOOOM

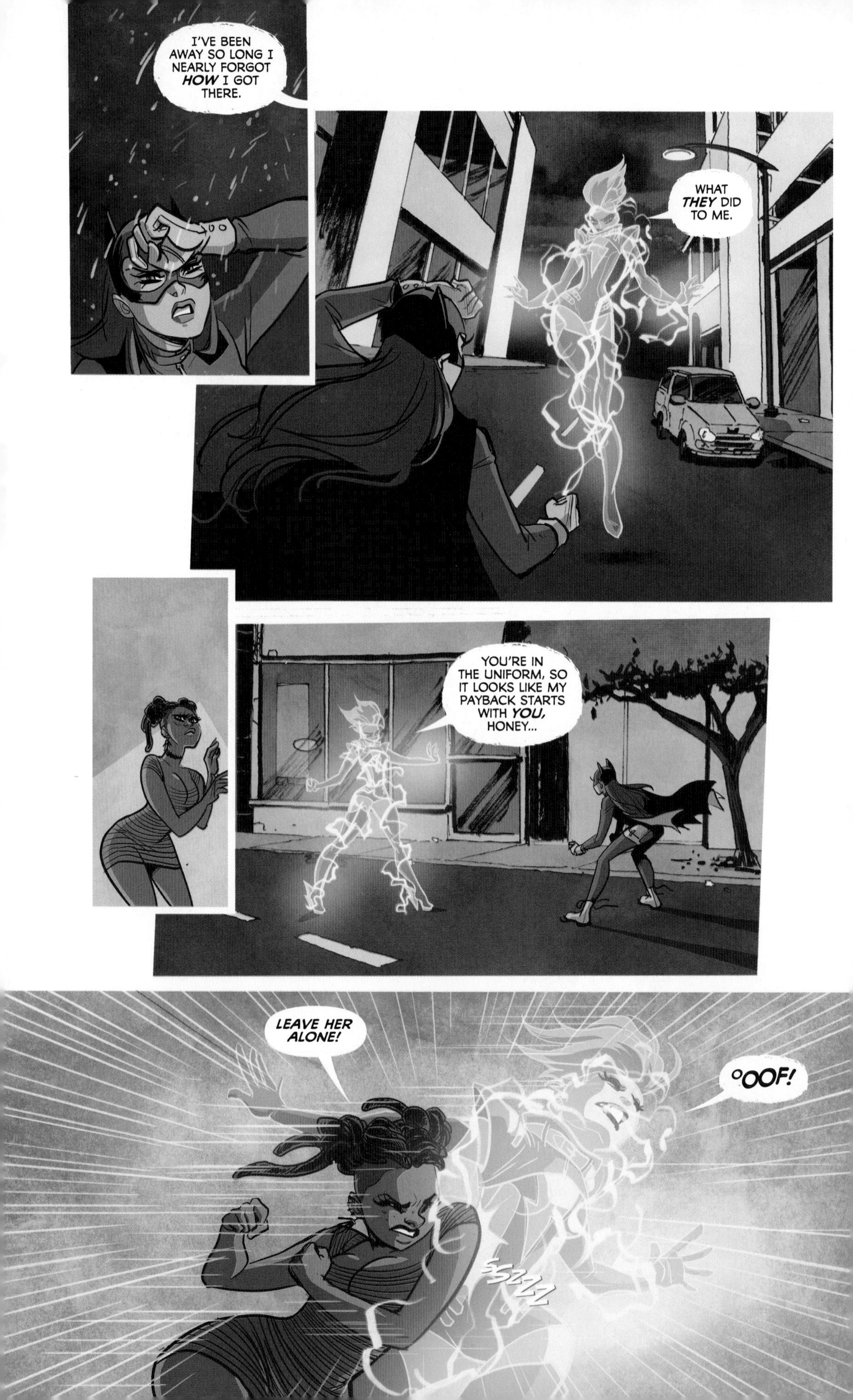
I'VE BEEN AWAY SO LONG I NEARLY FORGOT HOW I GOT THERE.
WHAT THEY DID TO ME.
YOU'RE IN THE UNIFORM, SO IT LOOKS LIKE MY PAYBACK STARTS WITH YOU, HONEY...
LEAVE HER ALONE!
OOOF!
SSZZZ

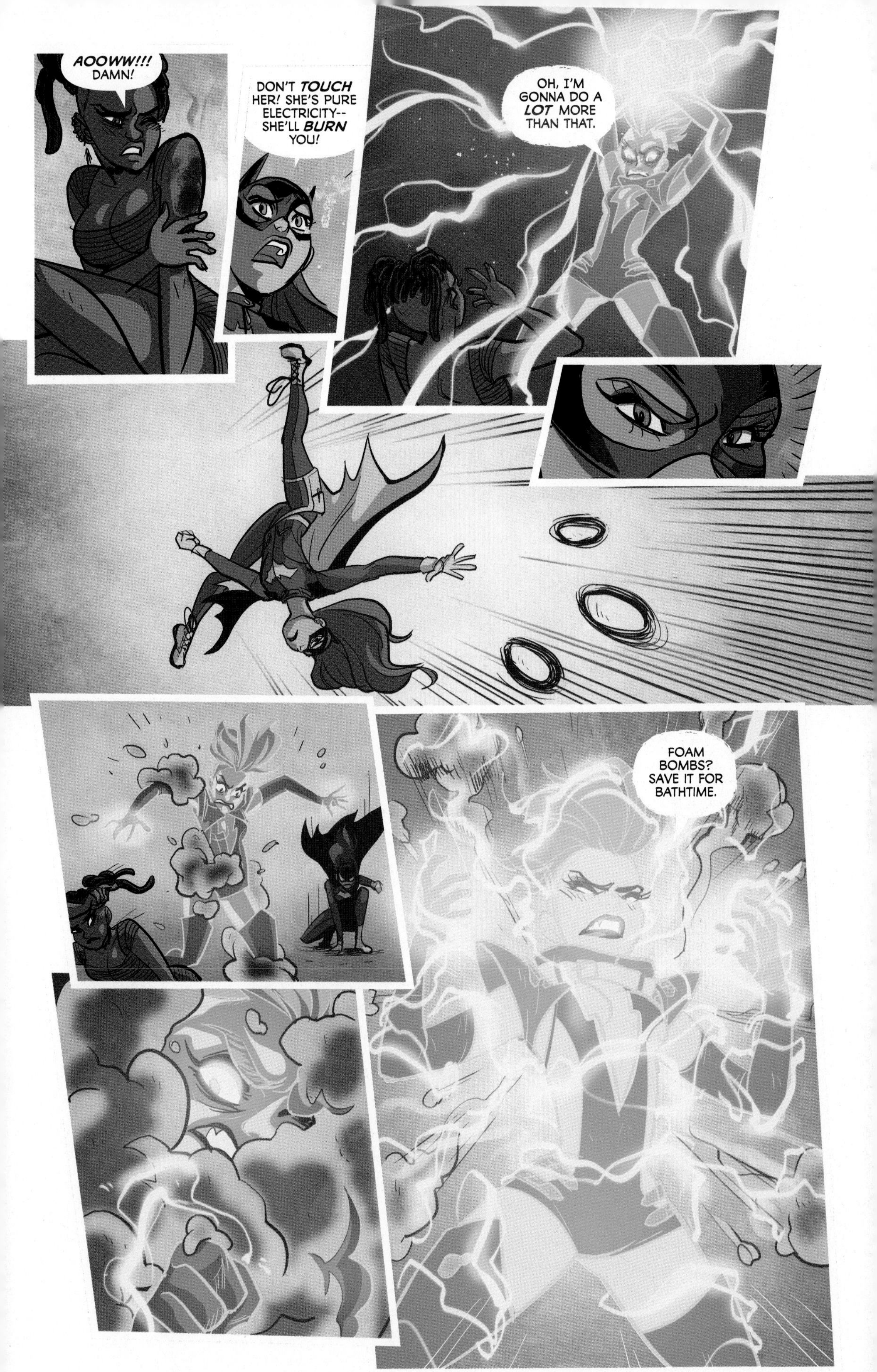
AOOWW!!! DAMN!
DON'T TOUCH HER! SHE'S PURE ELECTRICITY-- SHE'LL BURN YOU!
OH, I'M GONNA DO A LOT MORE THAN THAT.
FOAM BOMBS? SAVE IT FOR BATHTIME.

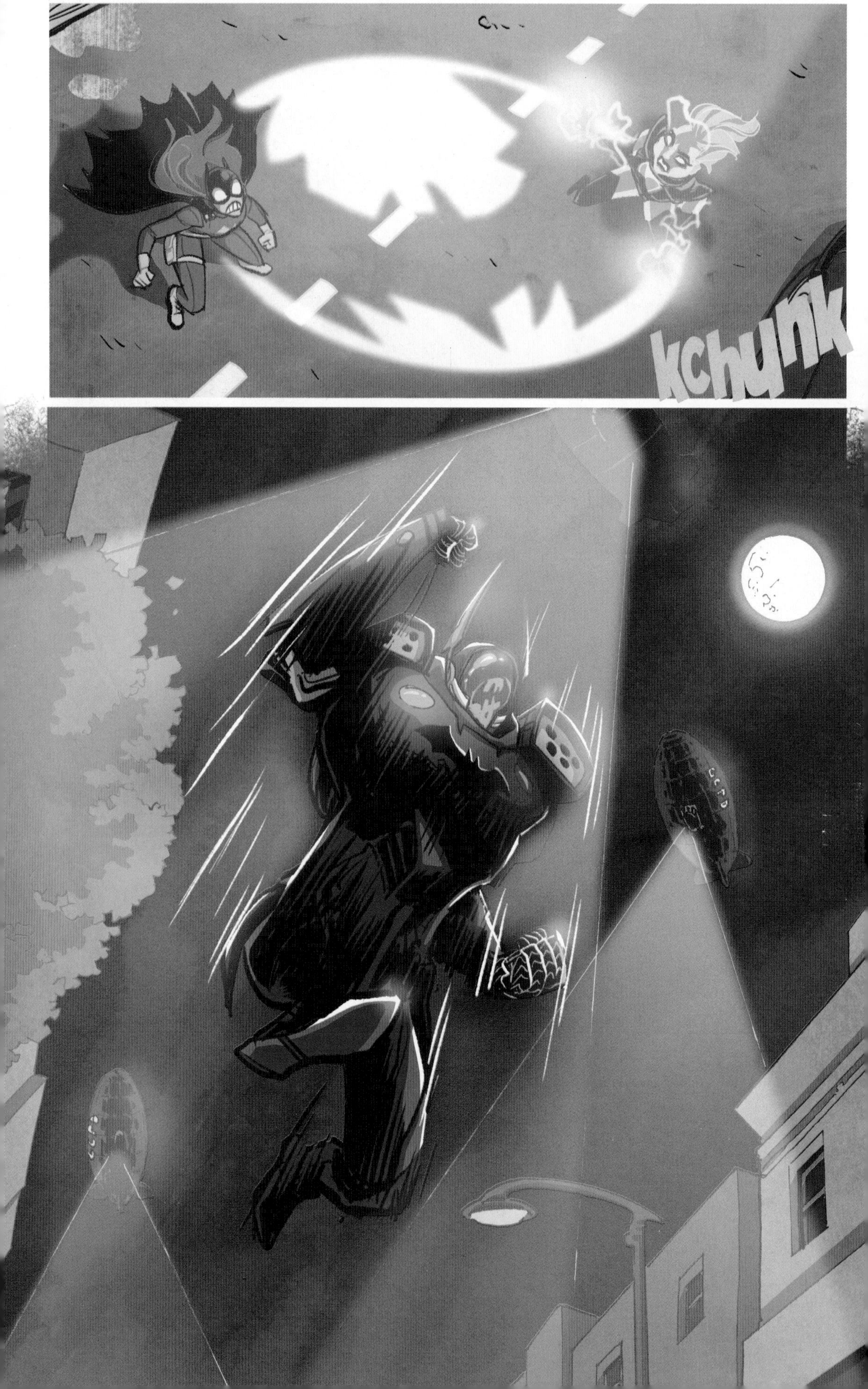
kchunk

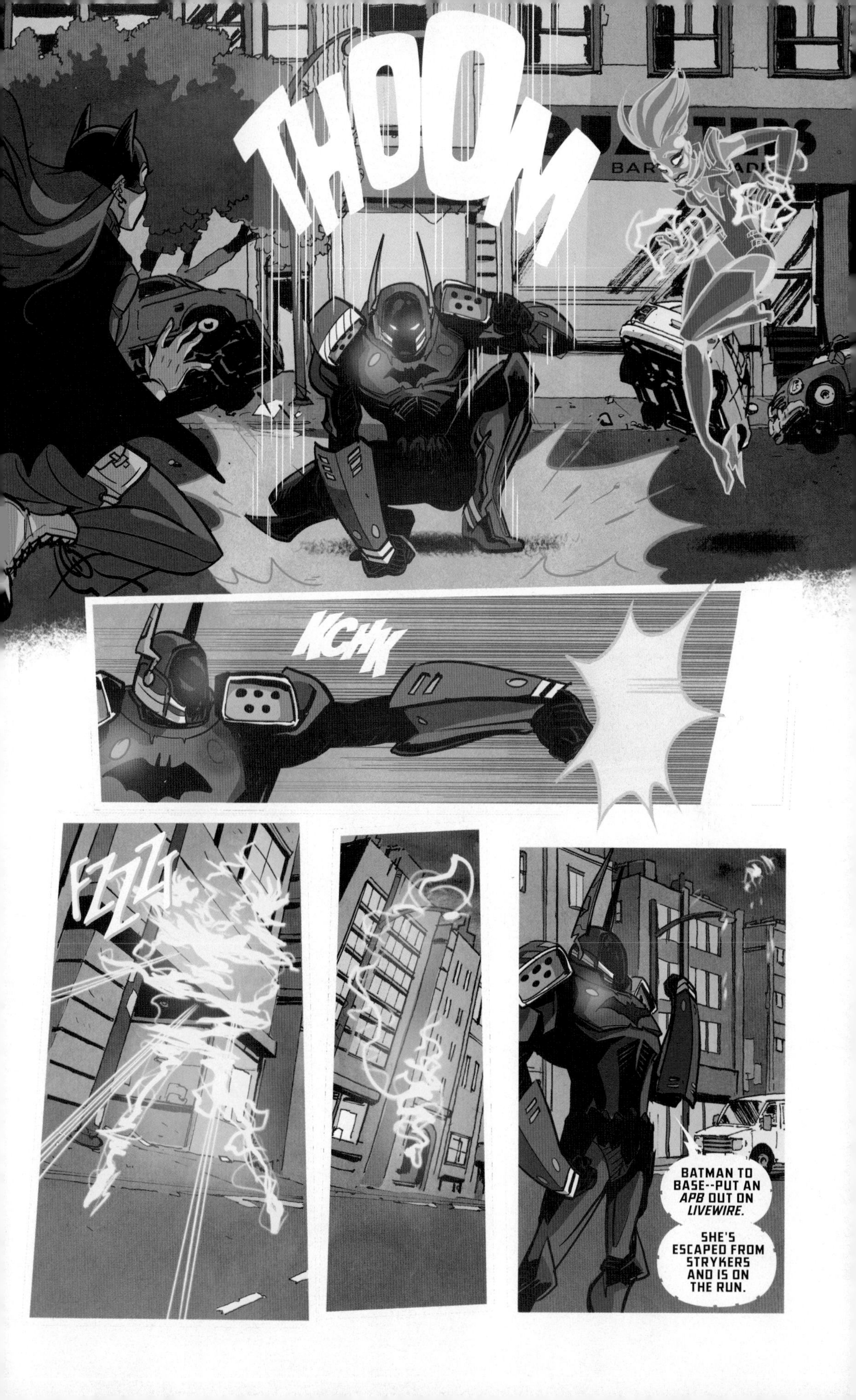
THOOM
KCHK
FZZZT
BATMAN TO BASE--PUT AN *APB* OUT ON *LIVEWIRE*.
SHE'S ESCAPED FROM STRYKERS AND IS ON THE RUN.

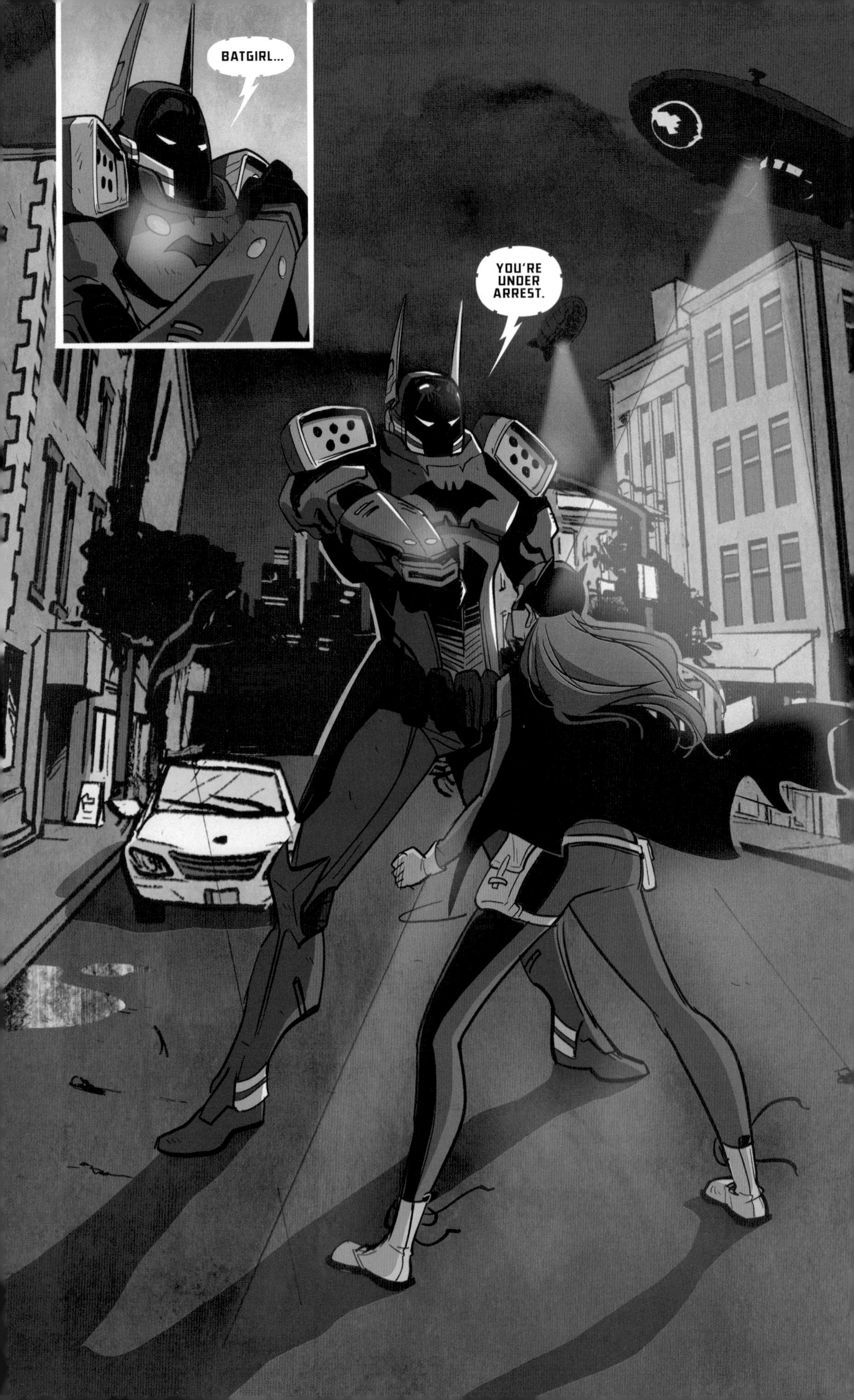
BATGIRL...
YOU'RE UNDER ARREST.

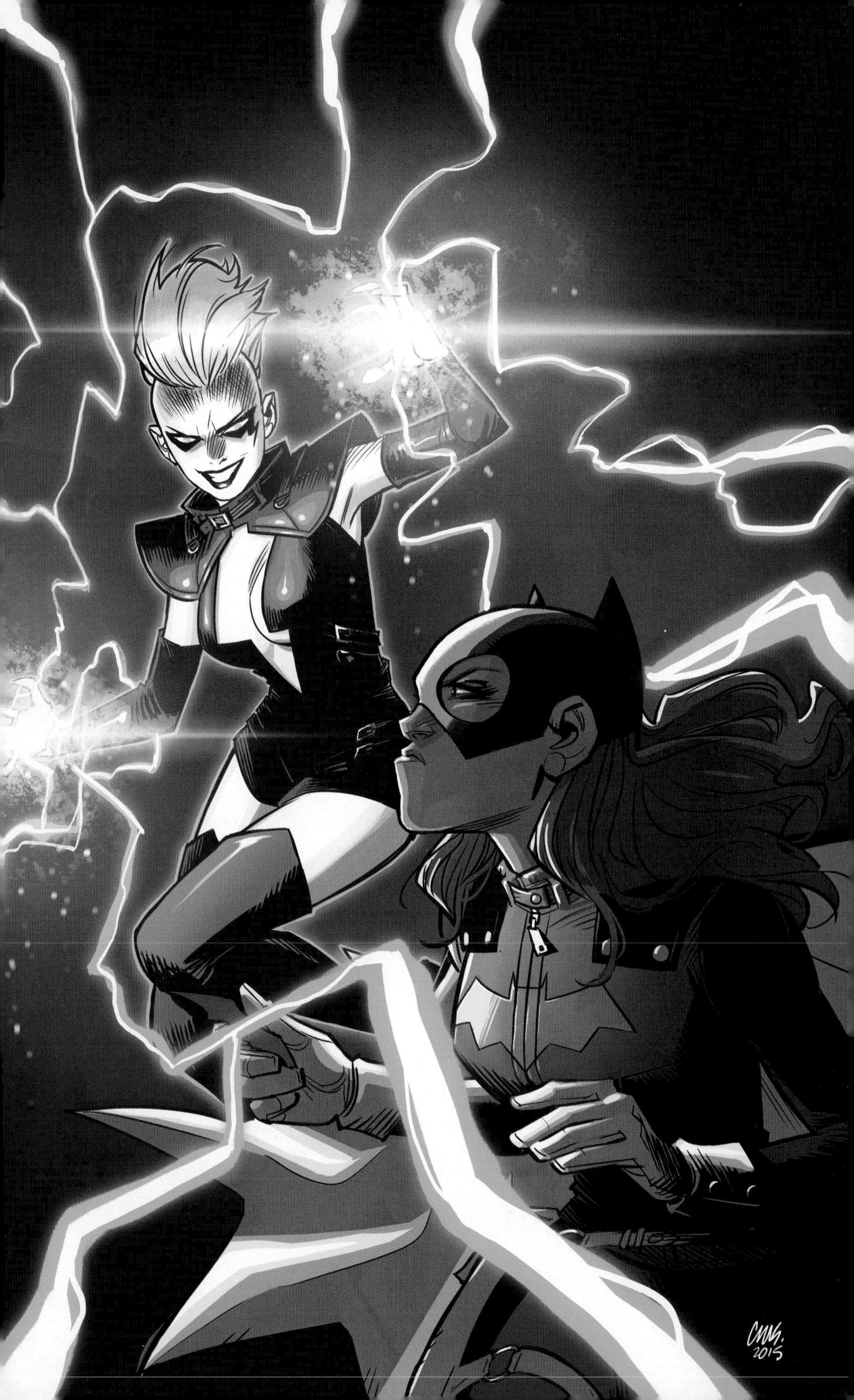

CAMERON STEWART & BRENDEN FLETCHER writers BABS TARR artist JAKE WYATT MICHEL LACOMBE breakdown artists
SERGE LAPOINTE colorist STEVE WANDS letterer cover by CAMERON STEWART

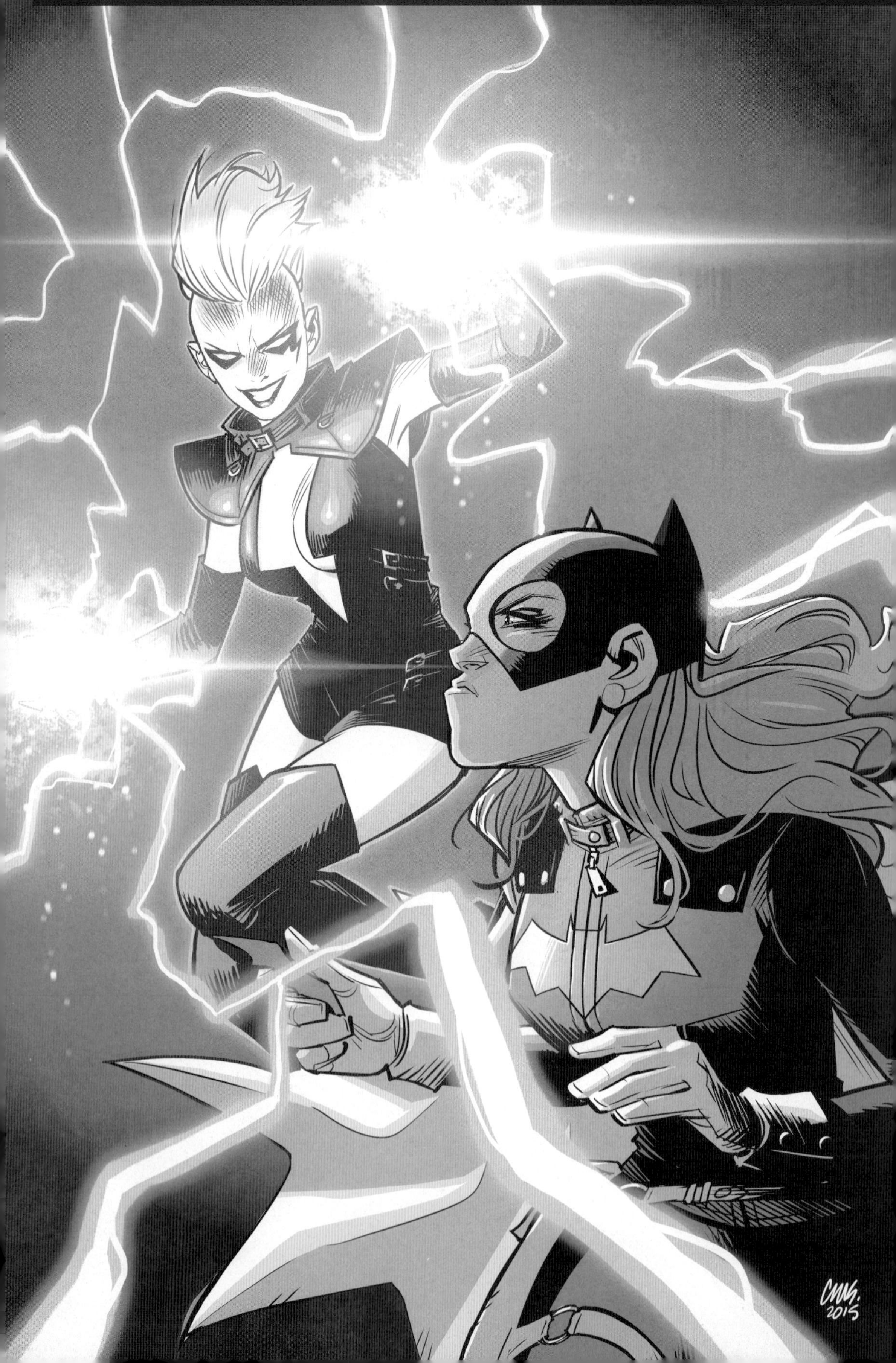

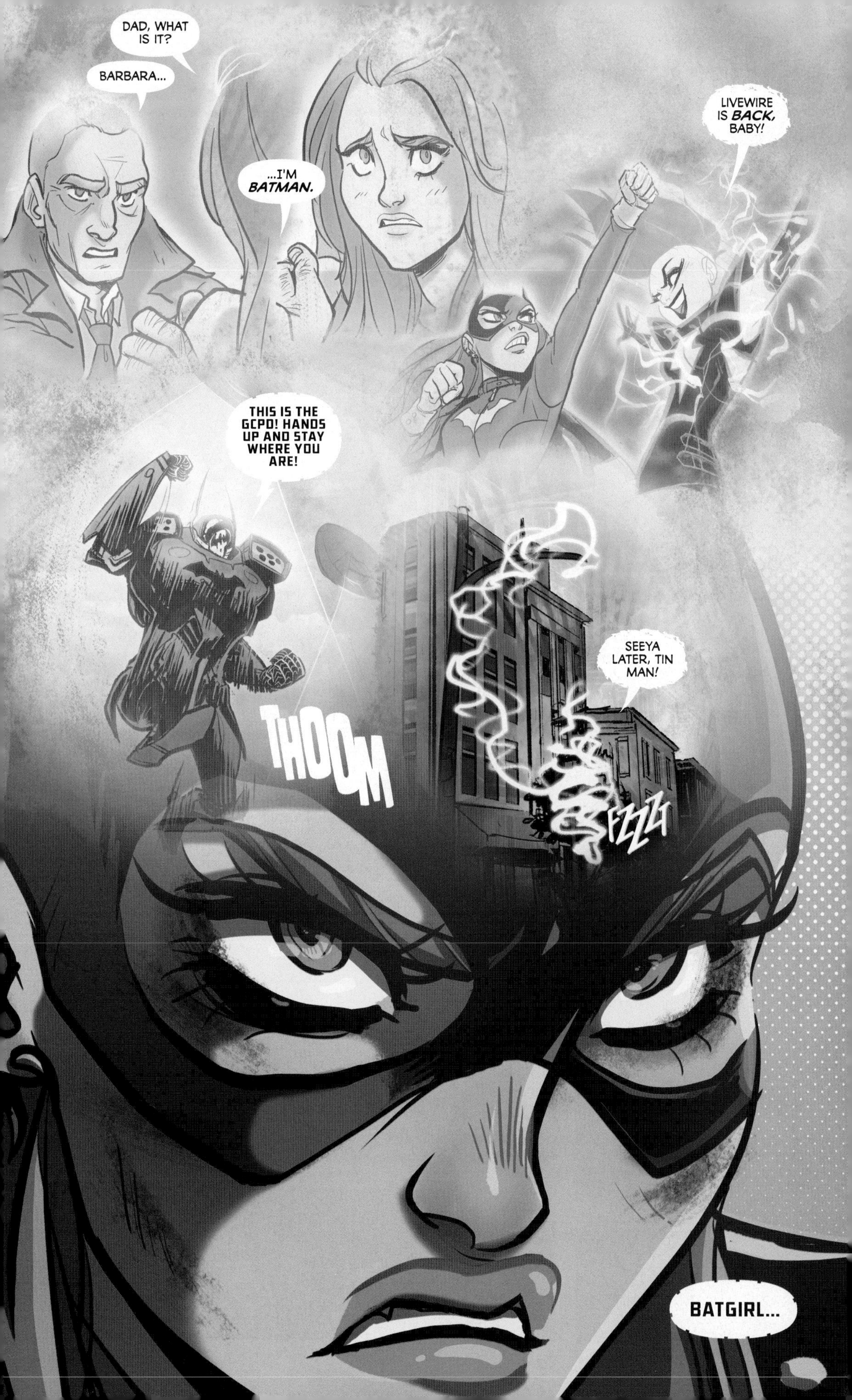

DAD, WHAT IS IT?
BARBARA...
...I'M BATMAN.
LIVEWIRE IS BACK, BABY!
THIS IS THE GCPD! HANDS UP AND STAY WHERE YOU ARE!
THOOM
SEEYA LATER, TIN MAN!
FZZZ
BATGIRL...

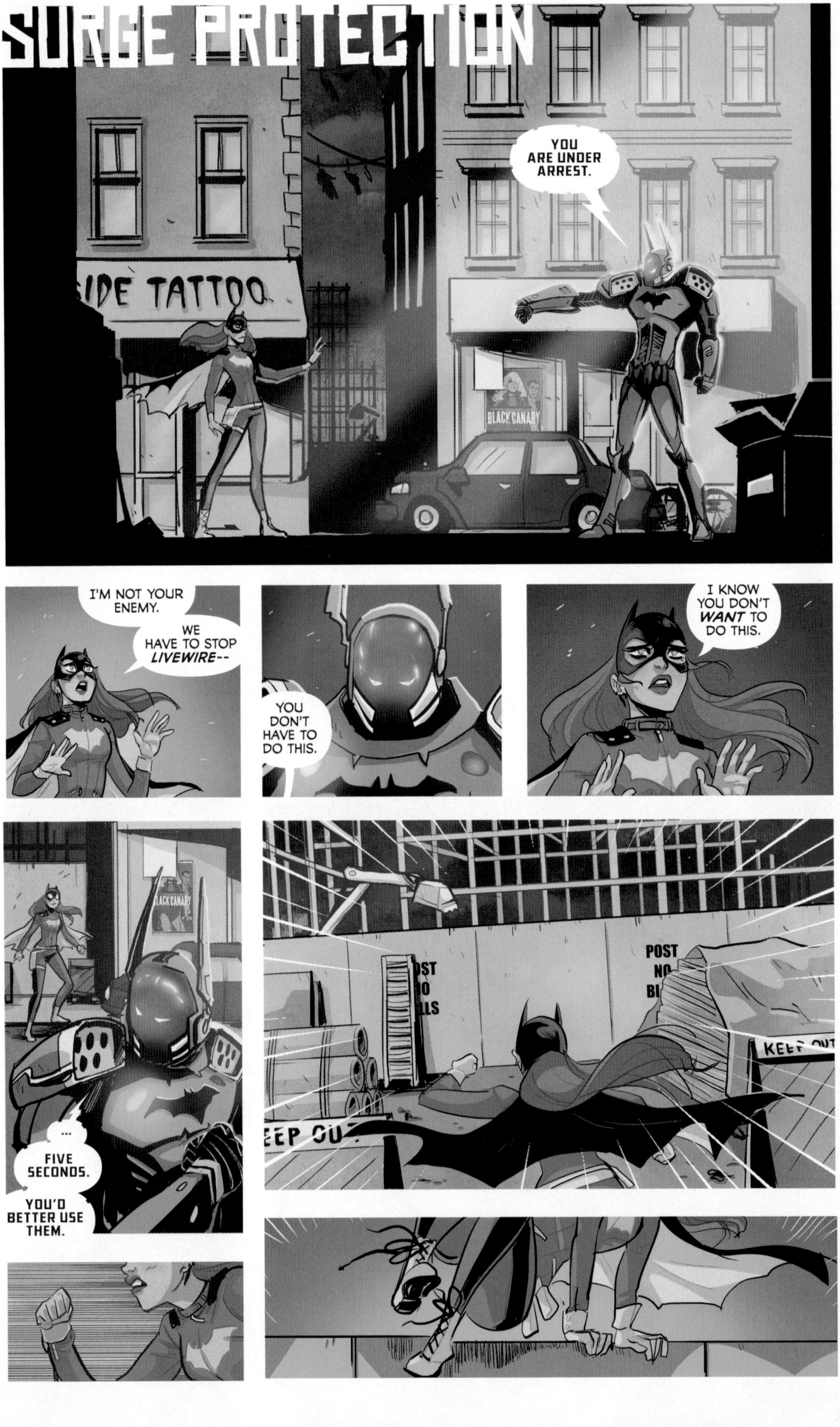
SURGE PROTECTION
YOU ARE UNDER ARREST.
BLACK CANARY
I'M NOT YOUR ENEMY.
WE HAVE TO STOP *LIVEWIRE*--
YOU DON'T HAVE TO DO THIS.
I KNOW YOU DON'T *WANT* TO DO THIS.
BLACK CANARY
...
FIVE SECONDS.
YOU'D BETTER USE THEM.
POST NO

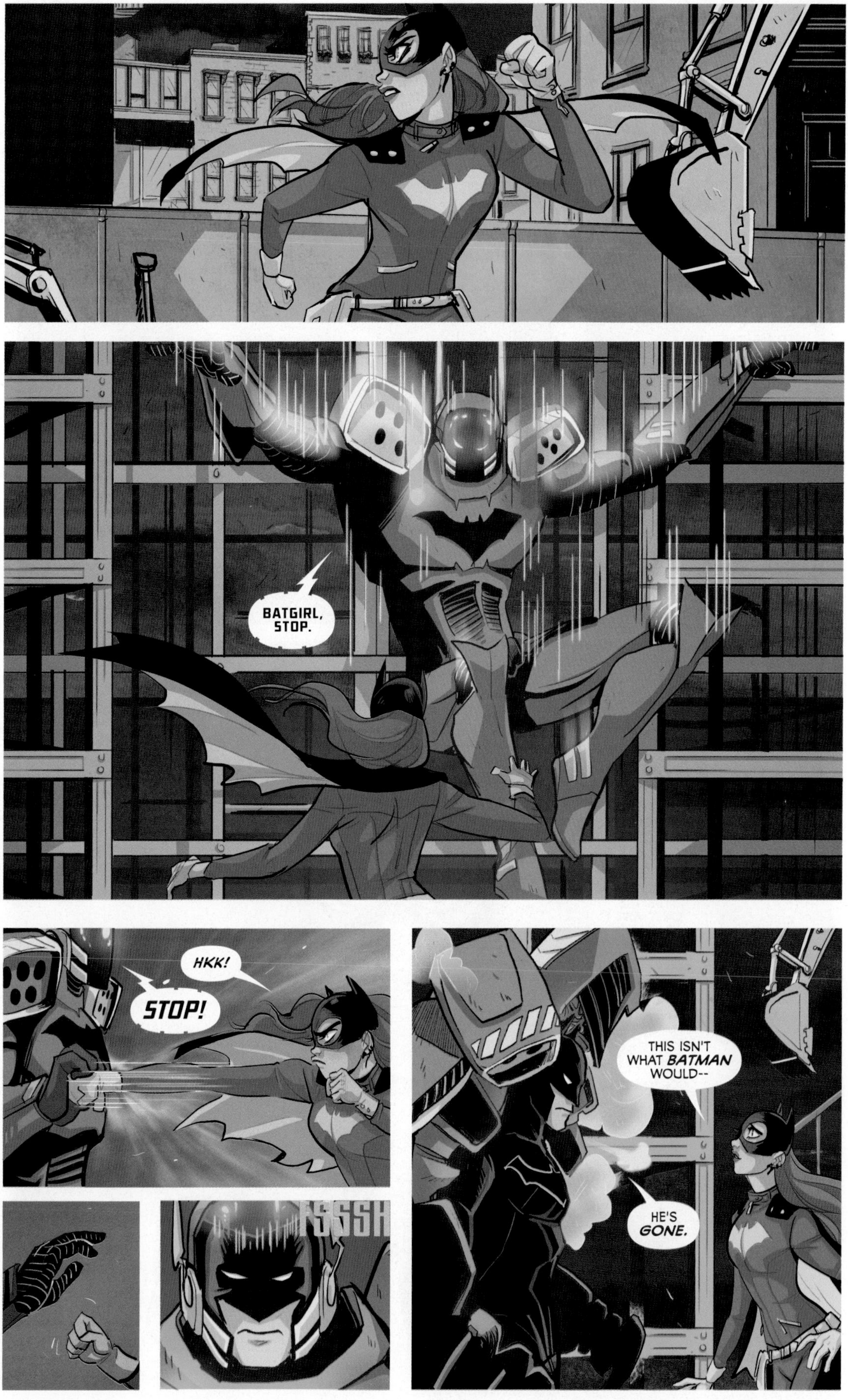
BATGIRL, STOP.
HKK!
STOP!
FSSSH
THIS ISN'T WHAT BATMAN WOULD--
HE'S GONE.

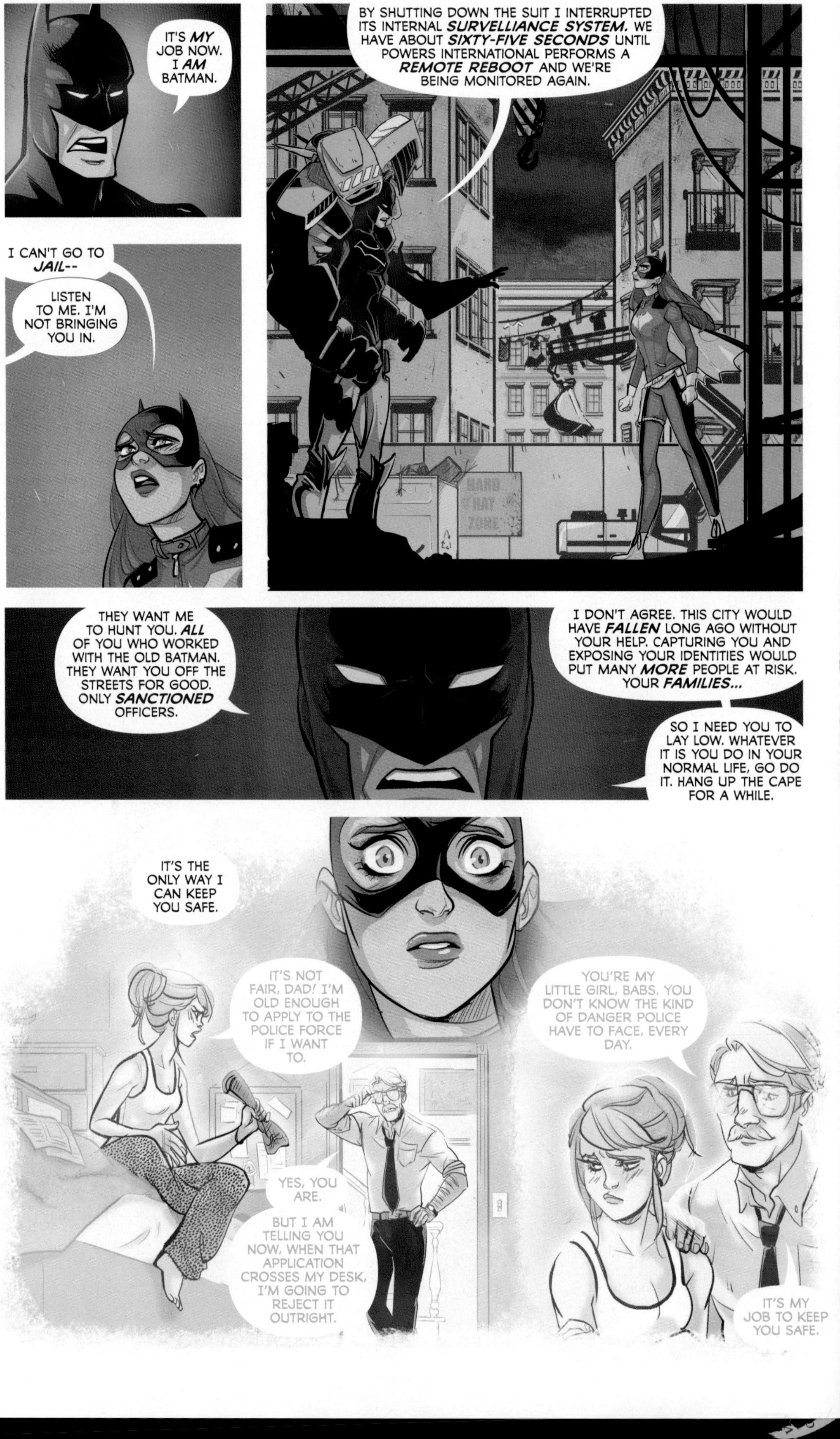
IT'S MY JOB NOW. I AM BATMAN.
BY SHUTTING DOWN THE SUIT I INTERRUPTED ITS INTERNAL SURVELLIANCE SYSTEM. WE HAVE ABOUT SIXTY-FIVE SECONDS UNTIL POWERS INTERNATIONAL PERFORMS A REMOTE REBOOT AND WE'RE BEING MONITORED AGAIN.
I CAN'T GO TO JAIL--
LISTEN TO ME. I'M NOT BRINGING YOU IN.
HARD HAT ZONE
THEY WANT ME TO HUNT YOU. ALL OF YOU WHO WORKED WITH THE OLD BATMAN. THEY WANT YOU OFF THE STREETS FOR GOOD. ONLY SANCTIONED OFFICERS.
I DON'T AGREE. THIS CITY WOULD HAVE FALLEN LONG AGO WITHOUT YOUR HELP. CAPTURING YOU AND EXPOSING YOUR IDENTITIES WOULD PUT MANY MORE PEOPLE AT RISK. YOUR FAMILIES...
SO I NEED YOU TO LAY LOW. WHATEVER IT IS YOU DO IN YOUR NORMAL LIFE, GO DO IT. HANG UP THE CAPE FOR A WHILE.
IT'S THE ONLY WAY I CAN KEEP YOU SAFE.
IT'S NOT FAIR, DAD! I'M OLD ENOUGH TO APPLY TO THE POLICE FORCE IF I WANT TO.
YES, YOU ARE.
BUT I AM TELLING YOU NOW, WHEN THAT APPLICATION CROSSES MY DESK, I'M GOING TO REJECT IT OUTRIGHT.
YOU'RE MY LITTLE GIRL, BABS. YOU DON'T KNOW THE KIND OF DANGER POLICE HAVE TO FACE, EVERY DAY.
IT'S MY JOB TO KEEP YOU SAFE.

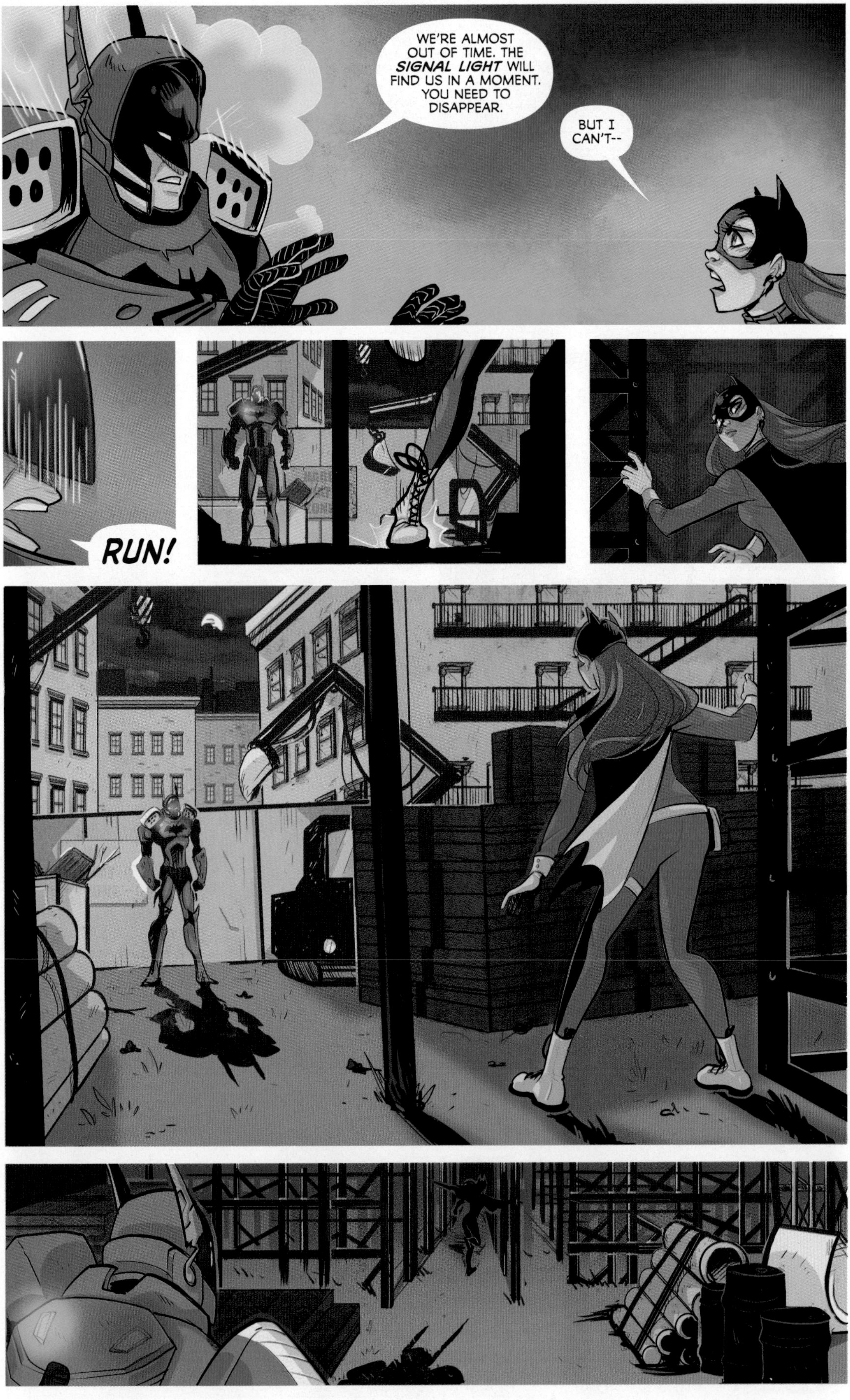
WE'RE ALMOST OUT OF TIME. THE SIGNAL LIGHT WILL FIND US IN A MOMENT. YOU NEED TO DISAPPEAR.
BUT I CAN'T--
RUN!

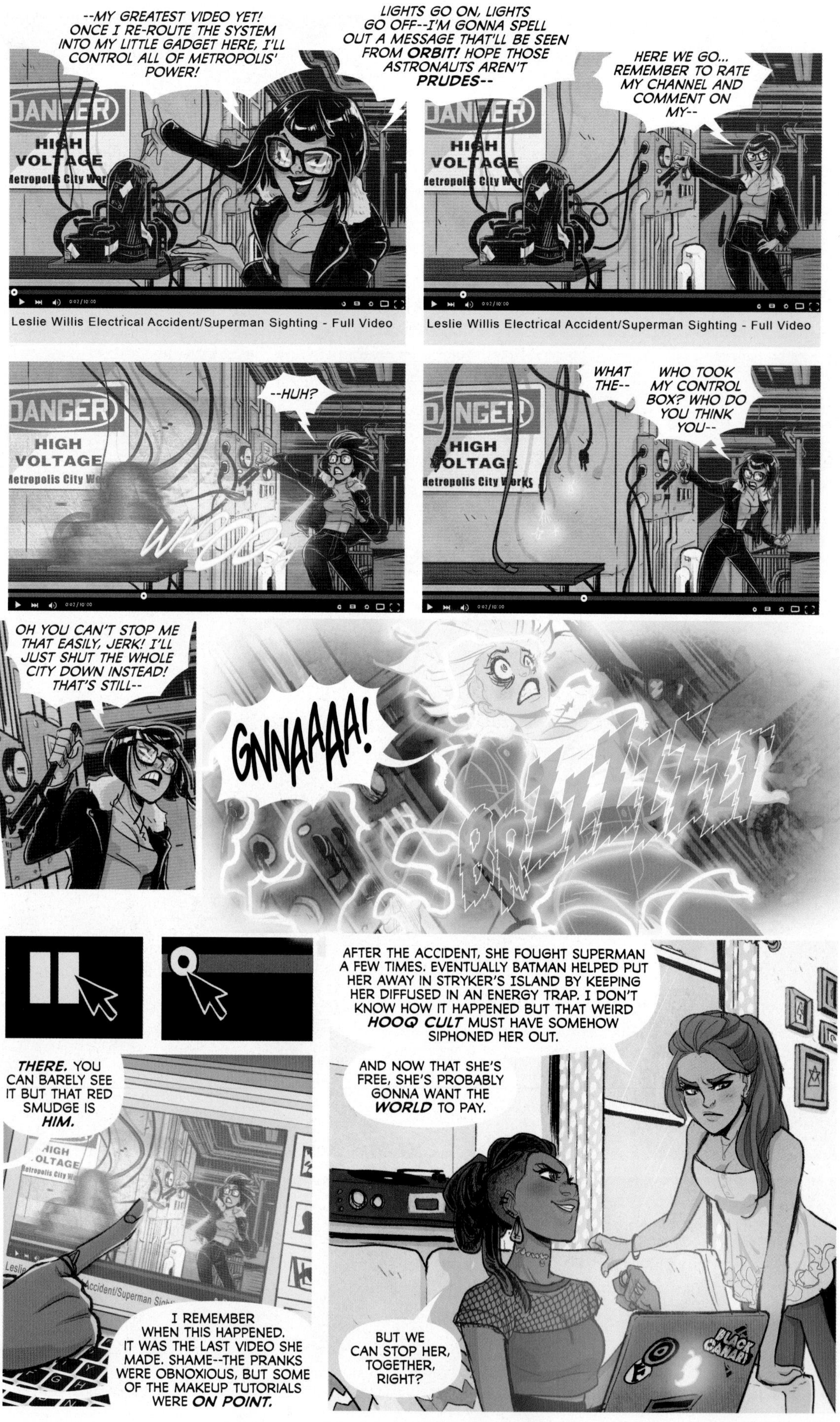
--MY GREATEST VIDEO YET! ONCE I RE-ROUTE THE SYSTEM INTO MY LITTLE GADGET HERE, I'LL CONTROL ALL OF METROPOLIS' POWER!
LIGHTS GO ON, LIGHTS GO OFF--I'M GONNA SPELL OUT A MESSAGE THAT'LL BE SEEN FROM ORBIT! HOPE THOSE ASTRONAUTS AREN'T PRUDES--
HERE WE GO... REMEMBER TO RATE MY CHANNEL AND COMMENT ON MY--
DANGER
HIGH VOLTAGE
Metropolis City Works
Leslie Willis Electrical Accident/Superman Sighting - Full Video
Leslie Willis Electrical Accident/Superman Sighting - Full Video
--HUH?
WHOOOSH
WHAT THE--
WHO TOOK MY CONTROL BOX? WHO DO YOU THINK YOU--
OH YOU CAN'T STOP ME THAT EASILY, JERK! I'LL JUST SHUT THE WHOLE CITY DOWN INSTEAD! THAT'S STILL--
GNAAAA!
BRZZZZZT
THERE. YOU CAN BARELY SEE IT BUT THAT RED SMUDGE IS HIM.
I REMEMBER WHEN THIS HAPPENED. IT WAS THE LAST VIDEO SHE MADE. SHAME--THE PRANKS WERE OBNOXIOUS, BUT SOME OF THE MAKEUP TUTORIALS WERE ON POINT.
AFTER THE ACCIDENT, SHE FOUGHT SUPERMAN A FEW TIMES. EVENTUALLY BATMAN HELPED PUT HER AWAY IN STRYKER'S ISLAND BY KEEPING HER DIFFUSED IN AN ENERGY TRAP. I DON'T KNOW HOW IT HAPPENED BUT THAT WEIRD HOOQ CULT MUST HAVE SOMEHOW SIPHONED HER OUT.
AND NOW THAT SHE'S FREE, SHE'S PROBABLY GONNA WANT THE WORLD TO PAY.
BUT WE CAN STOP HER, TOGETHER, RIGHT?
BLACK CANARY

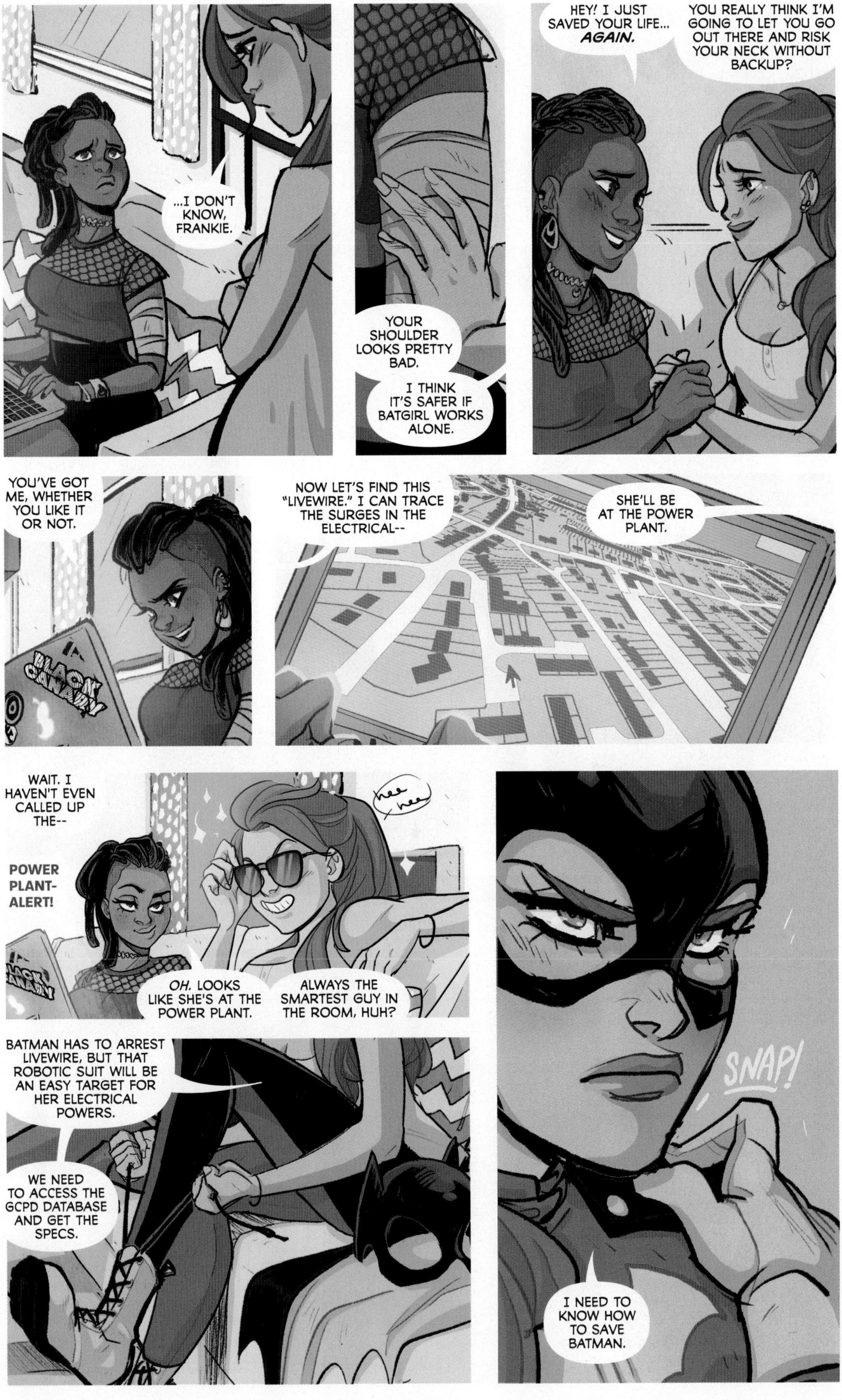
...I DON'T KNOW, FRANKIE.
YOUR SHOULDER LOOKS PRETTY BAD.
I THINK IT'S SAFER IF BATGIRL WORKS ALONE.
HEY! I JUST SAVED YOUR LIFE... *AGAIN.*
YOU REALLY THINK I'M GOING TO LET YOU GO OUT THERE AND RISK YOUR NECK WITHOUT BACKUP?
YOU'VE GOT ME, WHETHER YOU LIKE IT OR NOT.
BLACK CANARY
NOW LET'S FIND THIS "LIVEWIRE." I CAN TRACE THE SURGES IN THE ELECTRICAL--
SHE'LL BE AT THE POWER PLANT.
WAIT. I HAVEN'T EVEN CALLED UP THE--
POWER PLANT-ALERT!
hee hee
OH. LOOKS LIKE SHE'S AT THE POWER PLANT.
ALWAYS THE SMARTEST GUY IN THE ROOM, HUH?
BATMAN HAS TO ARREST LIVEWIRE, BUT THAT ROBOTIC SUIT WILL BE AN EASY TARGET FOR HER ELECTRICAL POWERS.
WE NEED TO ACCESS THE GCPD DATABASE AND GET THE SPECS.
SNAP!
I NEED TO KNOW HOW TO SAVE BATMAN.

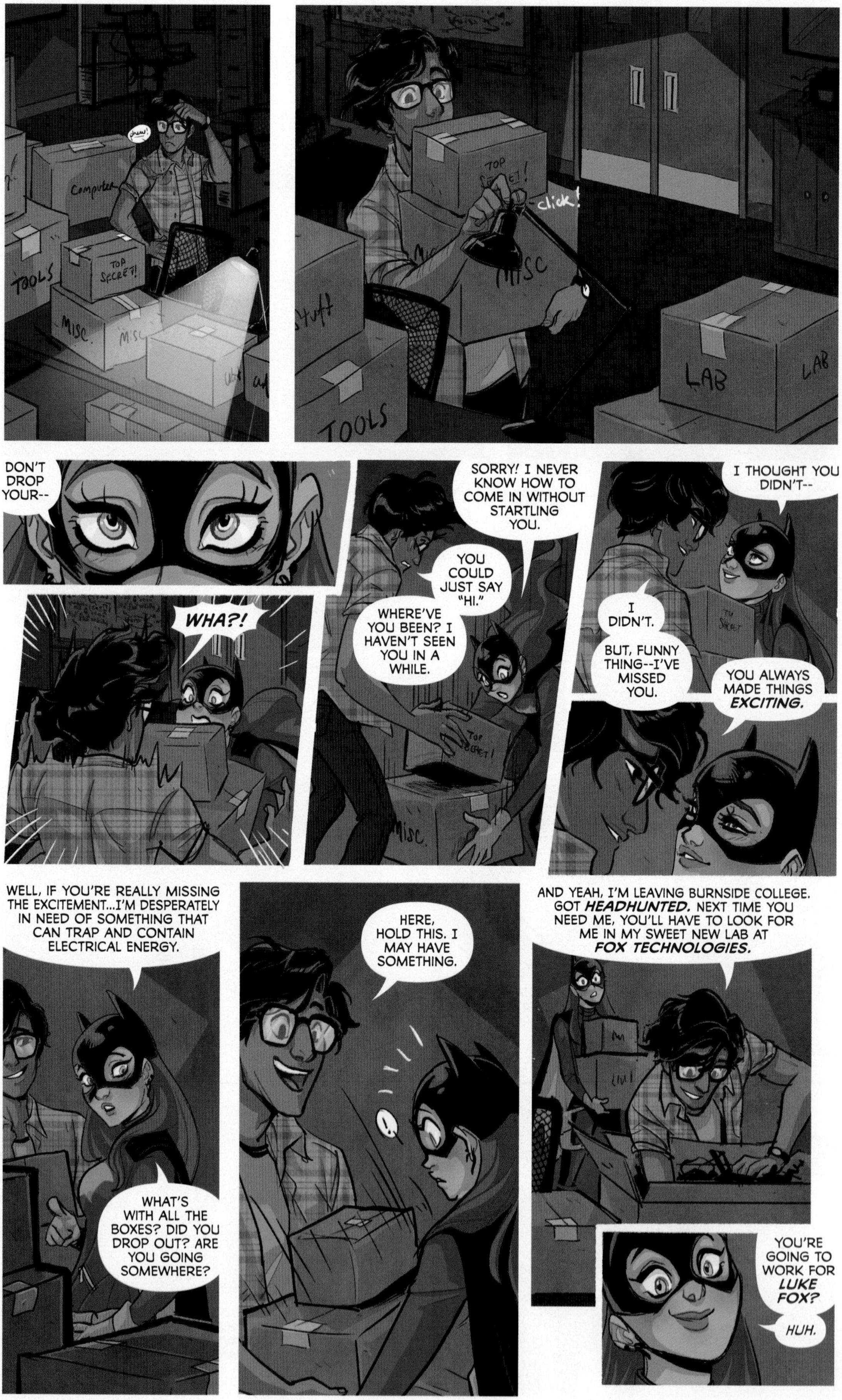
phew!
Computer
TOP SECRET!
TOOLS
MISC.
TOP SECRET!
click!
MISC
LAB
TOOLS
DON'T DROP YOUR--
WHA?!
SORRY! I NEVER KNOW HOW TO COME IN WITHOUT STARTLING YOU.
YOU COULD JUST SAY "HI."
WHERE'VE YOU BEEN? I HAVEN'T SEEN YOU IN A WHILE.
I THOUGHT YOU DIDN'T--
I DIDN'T.
BUT, FUNNY THING--I'VE MISSED YOU.
YOU ALWAYS MADE THINGS *EXCITING.*
WELL, IF YOU'RE REALLY MISSING THE EXCITEMENT...I'M DESPERATELY IN NEED OF SOMETHING THAT CAN TRAP AND CONTAIN ELECTRICAL ENERGY.
WHAT'S WITH ALL THE BOXES? DID YOU DROP OUT? ARE YOU GOING SOMEWHERE?
HERE, HOLD THIS. I MAY HAVE SOMETHING.
!
AND YEAH, I'M LEAVING BURNSIDE COLLEGE. GOT *HEADHUNTED.* NEXT TIME YOU NEED ME, YOU'LL HAVE TO LOOK FOR ME IN MY SWEET NEW LAB AT *FOX TECHNOLOGIES.*
YOU'RE GOING TO WORK FOR *LUKE FOX?*
HUH.

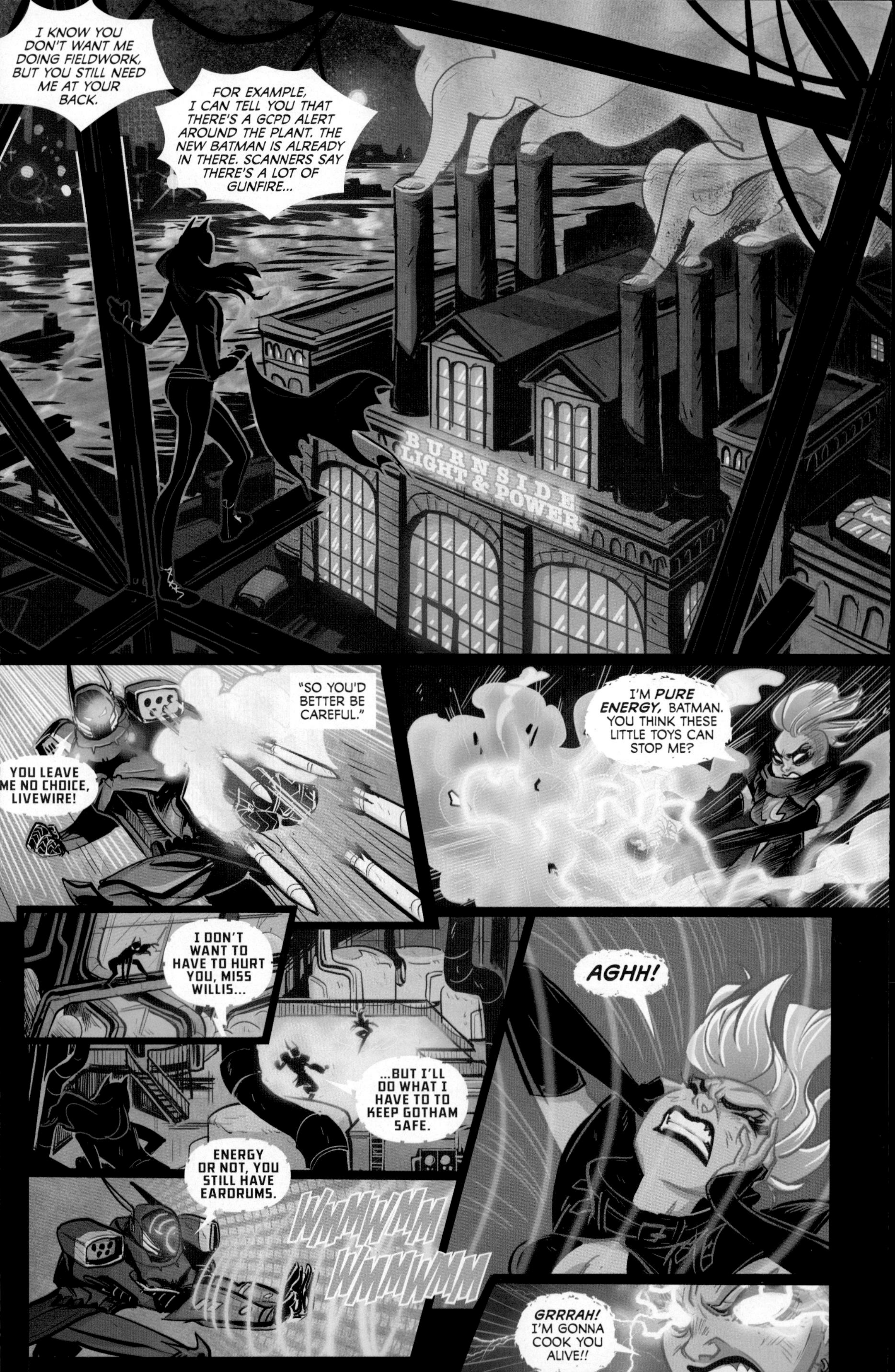
I KNOW YOU DON'T WANT ME DOING FIELDWORK, BUT YOU STILL NEED ME AT YOUR BACK.
FOR EXAMPLE, I CAN TELL YOU THAT THERE'S A GCPD ALERT AROUND THE PLANT. THE NEW BATMAN IS ALREADY IN THERE. SCANNERS SAY THERE'S A LOT OF GUNFIRE...
BURNSIDE LIGHT & POWER
"SO YOU'D BETTER BE CAREFUL."
YOU LEAVE ME NO CHOICE, LIVEWIRE!
I'M *PURE ENERGY,* BATMAN. YOU THINK THESE LITTLE TOYS CAN STOP ME?
I DON'T WANT TO HAVE TO HURT YOU, MISS WILLIS...
...BUT I'LL DO WHAT I HAVE TO TO KEEP GOTHAM SAFE.
AGHH!
ENERGY OR NOT, YOU STILL HAVE EARDRUMS.
WMMWMM
WMMWMM
GRRRAH! I'M GONNA COOK YOU ALIVE!!

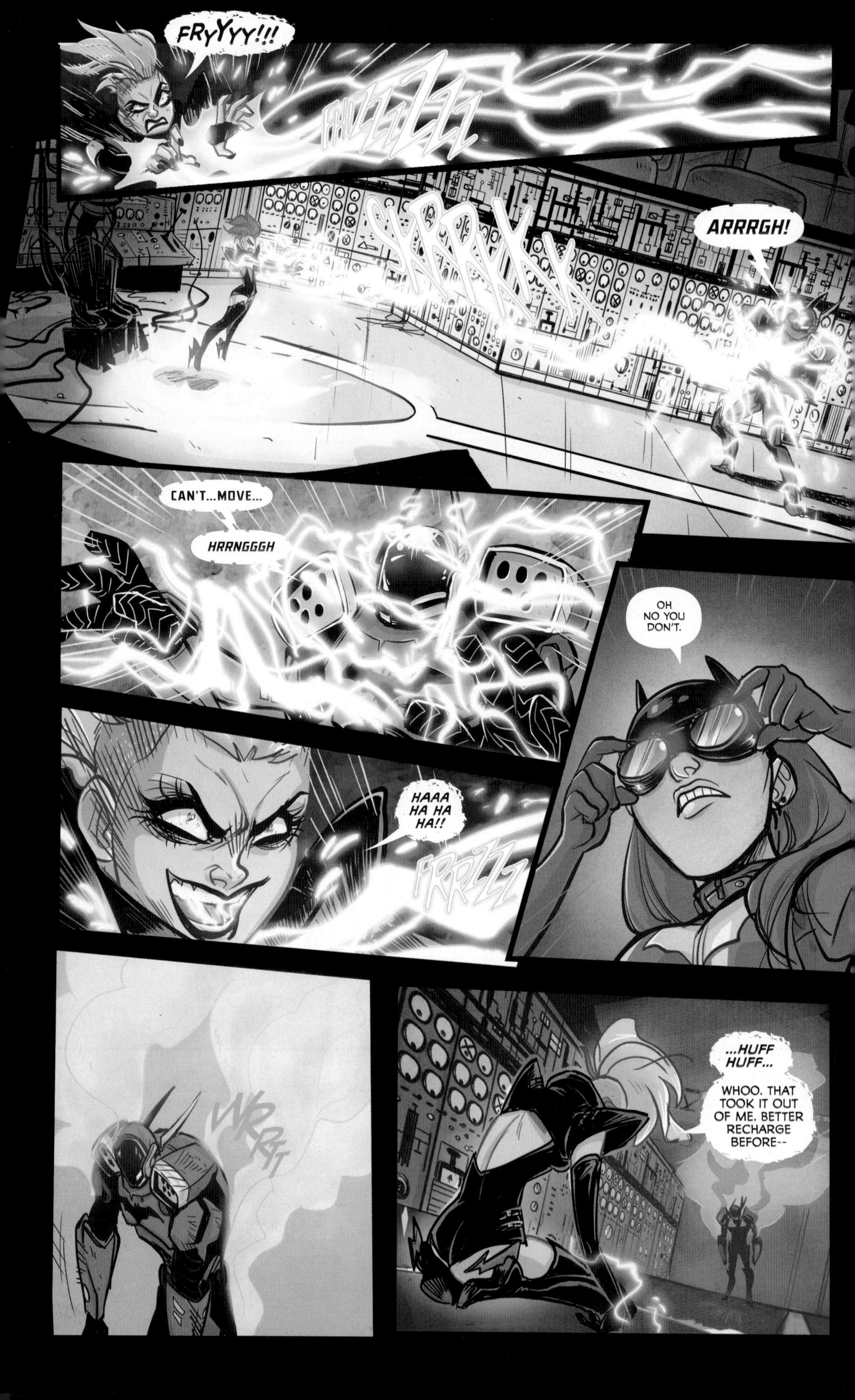
FRyYYY!!!
FHZZZZZZZZ
SKRRKKK
ARRRGH!
CAN'T...MOVE...
HRRNGGGH
OH NO YOU DON'T.
HAAA HA HA HA!!
FRRZZZ
...HUFF HUFF...
WHOO. THAT TOOK IT OUT OF ME. BETTER RECHARGE BEFORE--

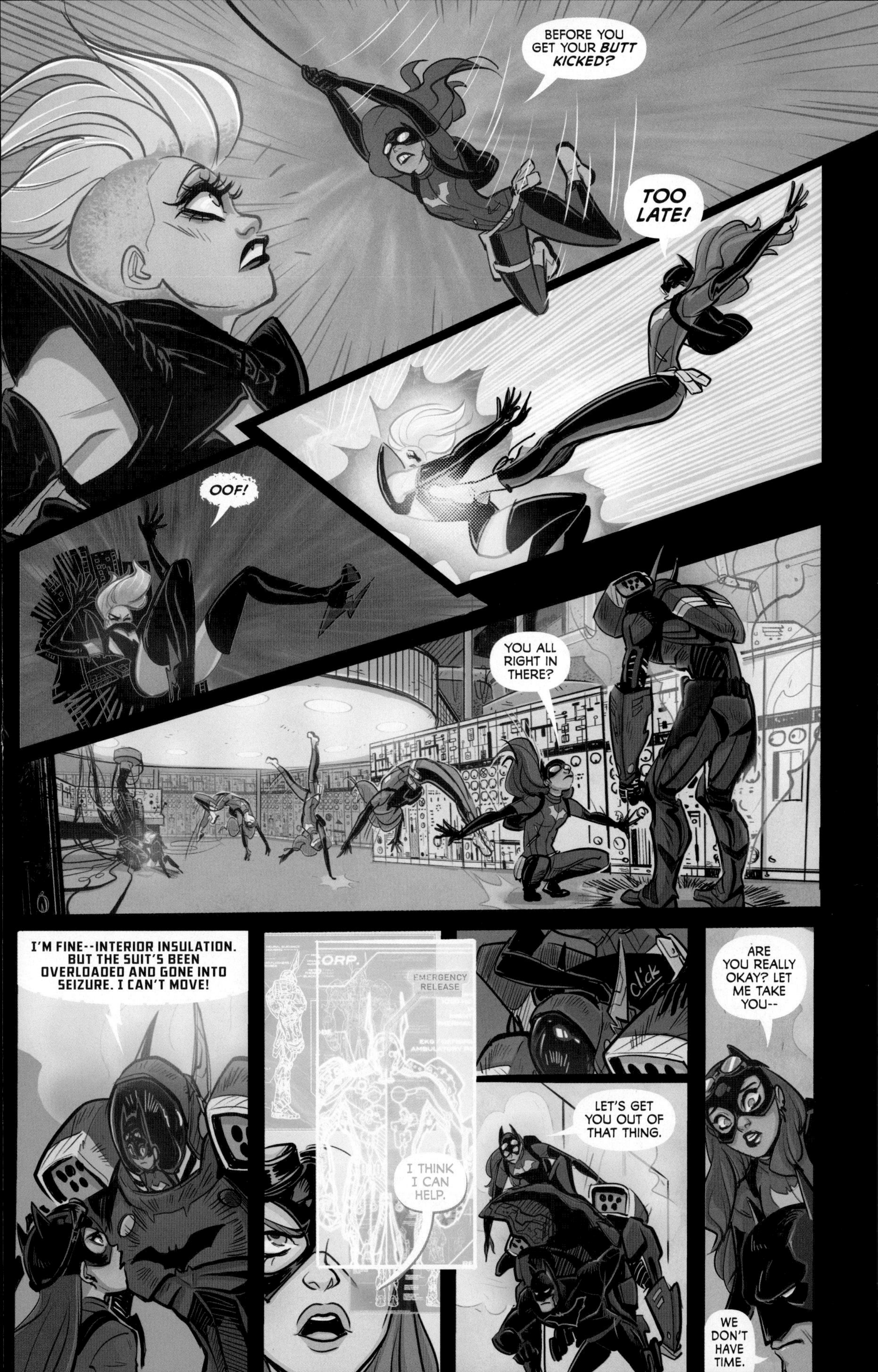
BEFORE YOU GET YOUR BUTT KICKED?
TOO LATE!
OOF!
YOU ALL RIGHT IN THERE?
I'M FINE--INTERIOR INSULATION. BUT THE SUIT'S BEEN OVERLOADED AND GONE INTO SEIZURE. I CAN'T MOVE!
EMERGENCY RELEASE
I THINK I CAN HELP.
click
LET'S GET YOU OUT OF THAT THING.
ARE YOU REALLY OKAY? LET ME TAKE YOU--
WE DON'T HAVE TIME.

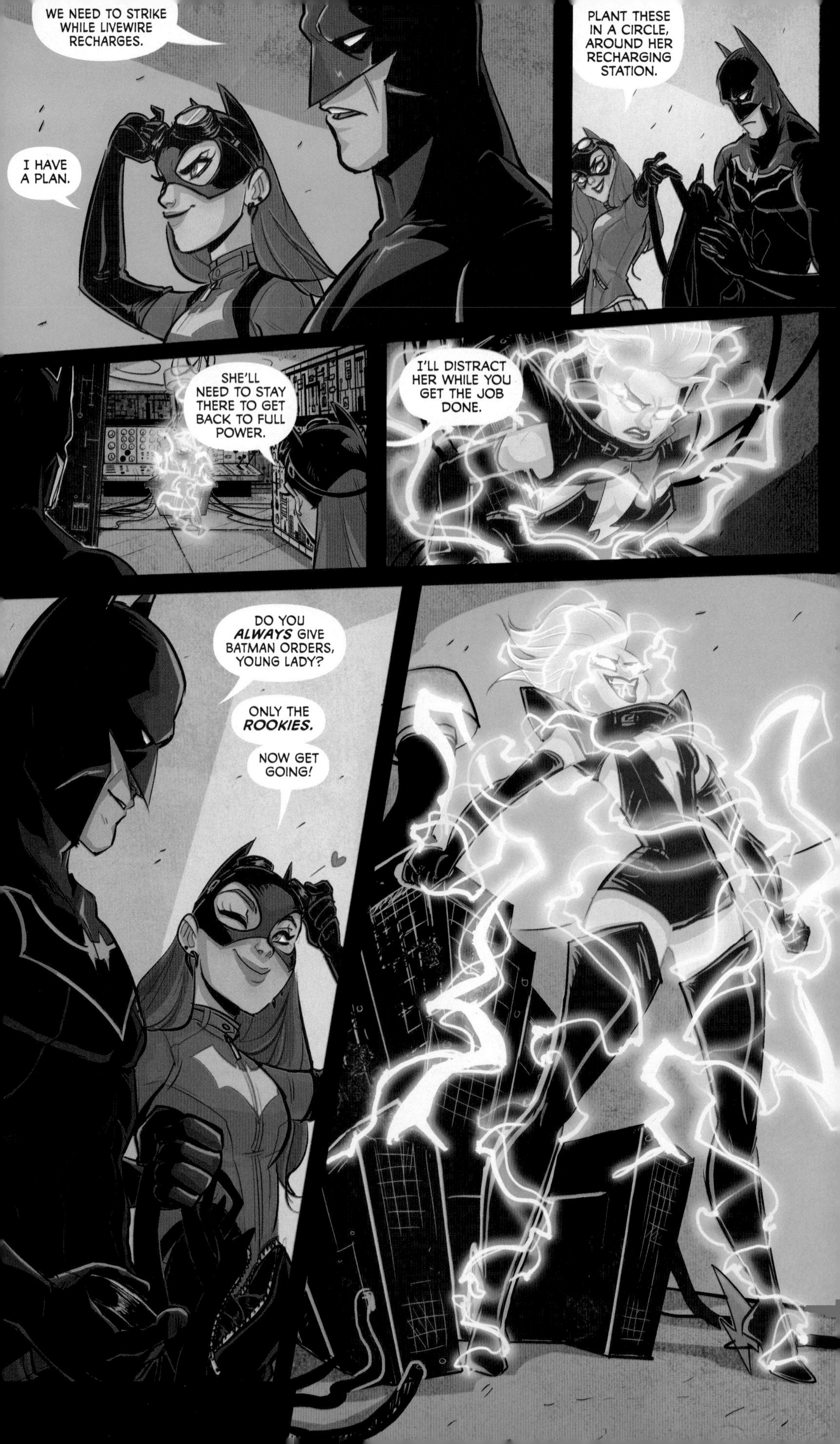
WE NEED TO STRIKE WHILE LIVEWIRE RECHARGES.
I HAVE A PLAN.
PLANT THESE IN A CIRCLE, AROUND HER RECHARGING STATION.
SHE'LL NEED TO STAY THERE TO GET BACK TO FULL POWER.
I'LL DISTRACT HER WHILE YOU GET THE JOB DONE.
DO YOU ***ALWAYS*** GIVE BATMAN ORDERS, YOUNG LADY?
ONLY THE ***ROOKIES.***
NOW GET GOING!

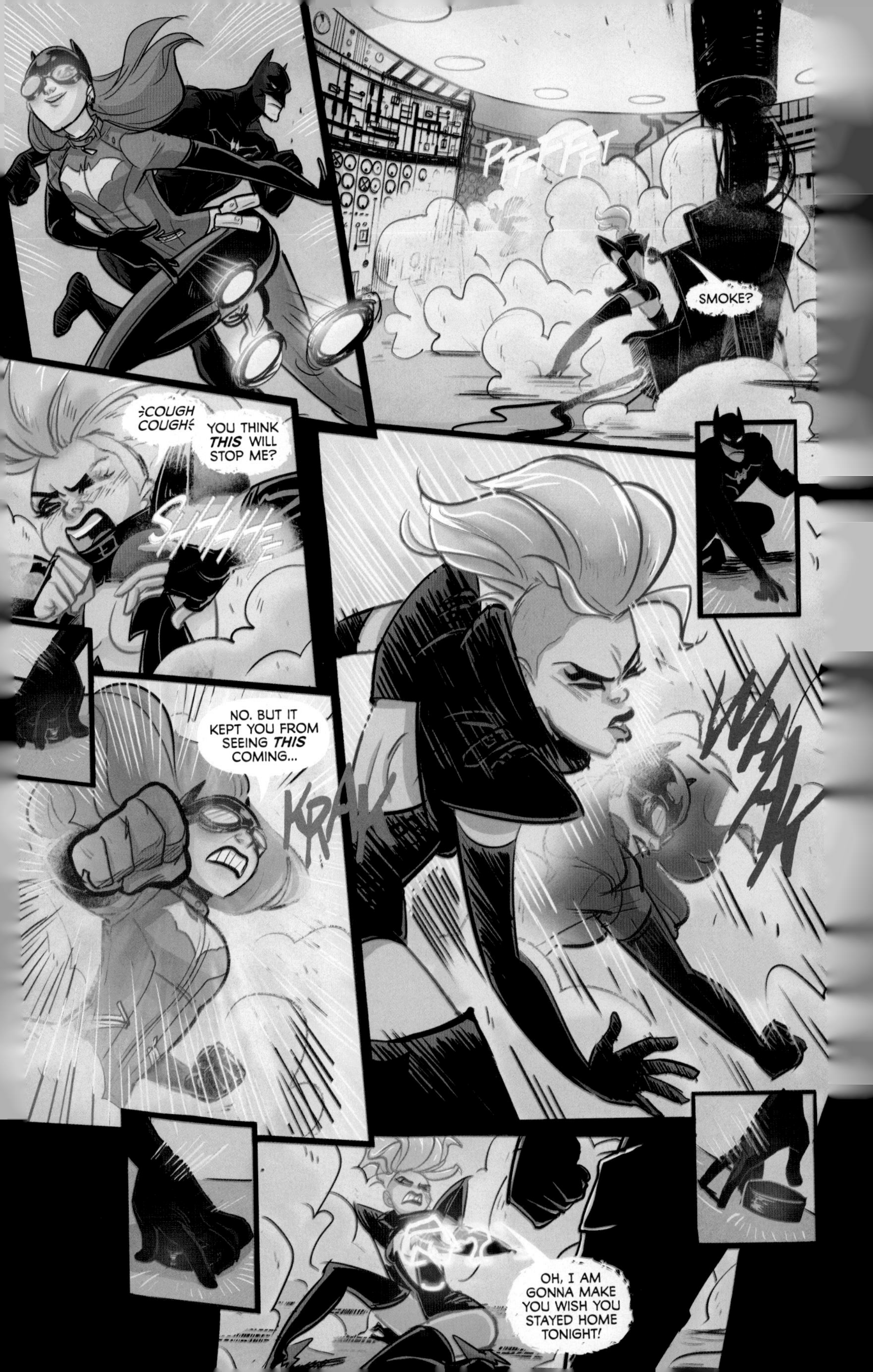
PFFFFT
SMOKE?
;COUGH COUGH;
YOU THINK THIS WILL STOP ME?
SHHHE
NO. BUT IT KEPT YOU FROM SEEING THIS COMING...
KRAK
OH, I AM GONNA MAKE YOU WISH YOU STAYED HOME TONIGHT!

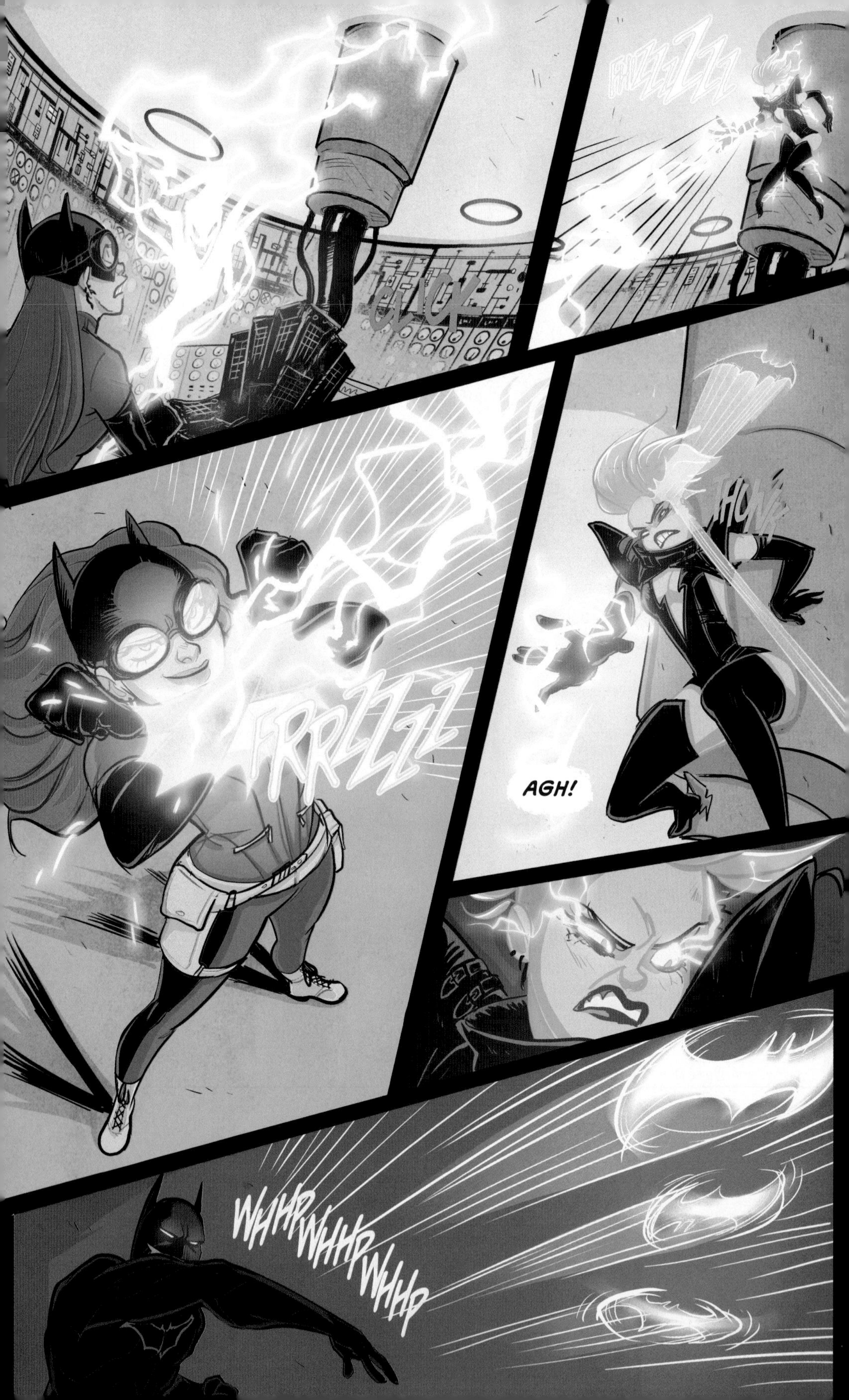
CLICK
FRRZZZZ
AGH!
WHHP WHHP WHHP

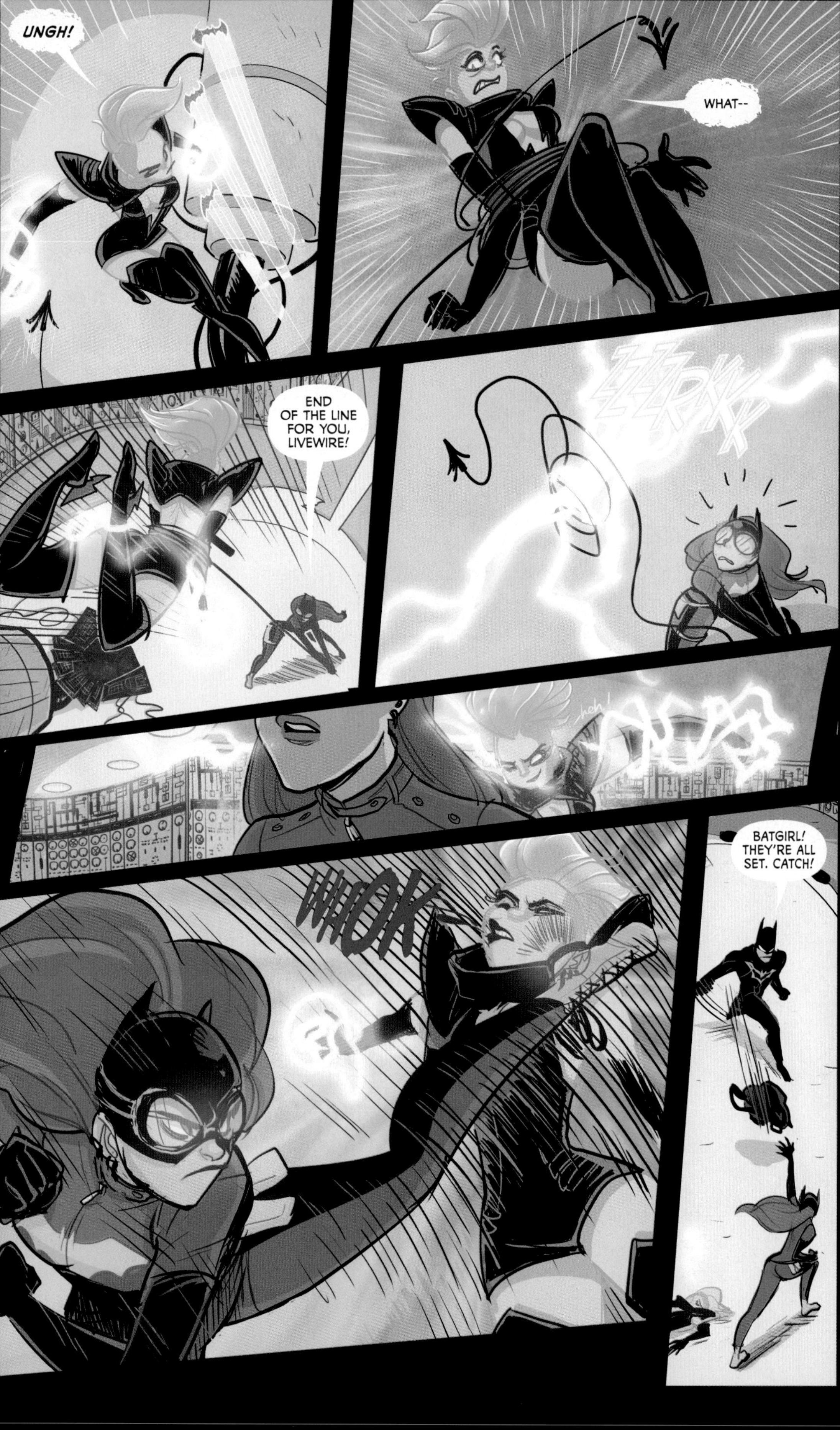
UNGH!
WHAT--
END OF THE LINE FOR YOU, LIVEWIRE!
heh!
BATGIRL! THEY'RE ALL SET. CATCH!
WHOK

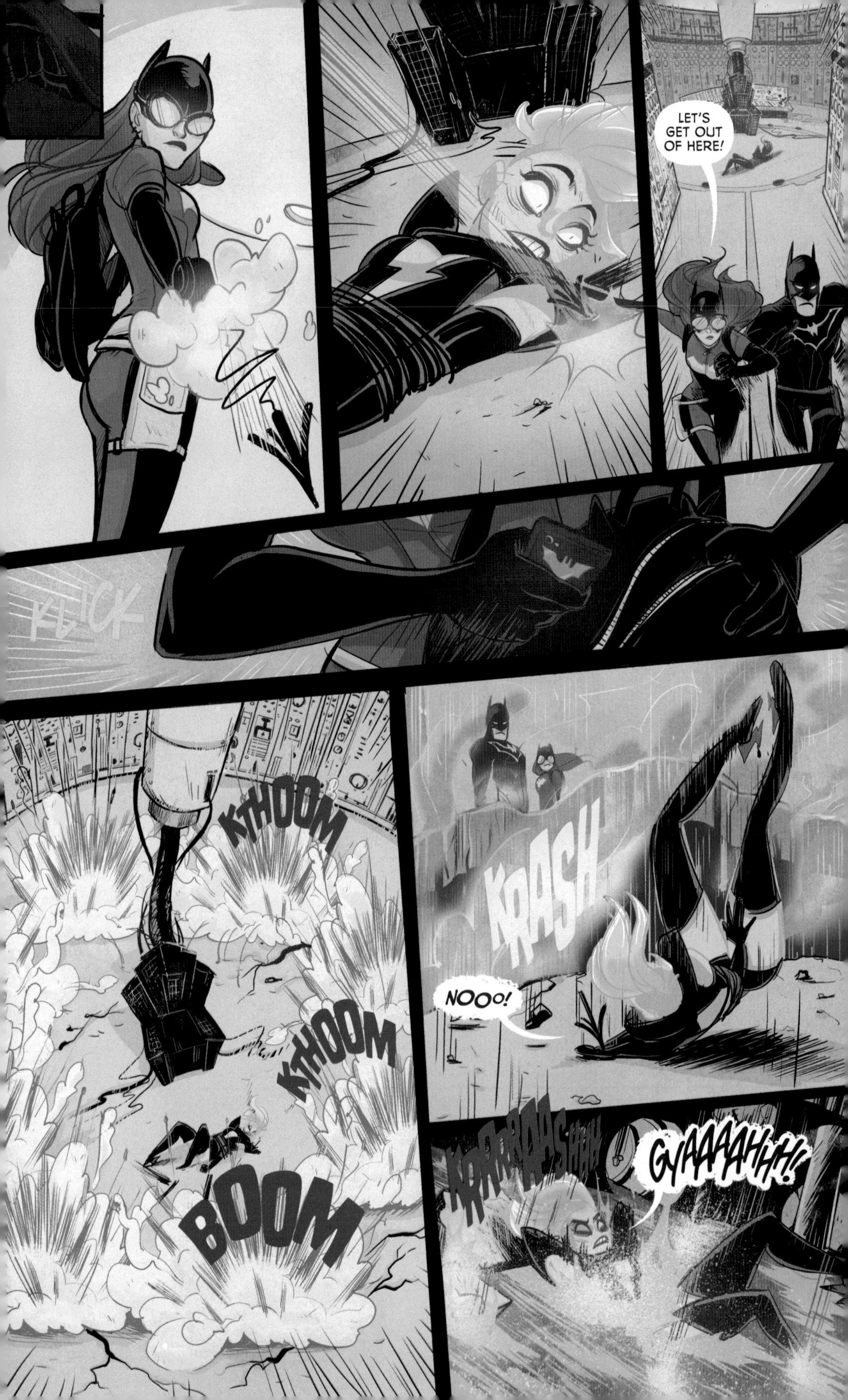
LET'S GET OUT OF HERE!
KLICK
KTHOOM
KTHOOM
BOOM
KRASH
NOOO!
KRRRRAASHHH
GYAAAAHHH!!

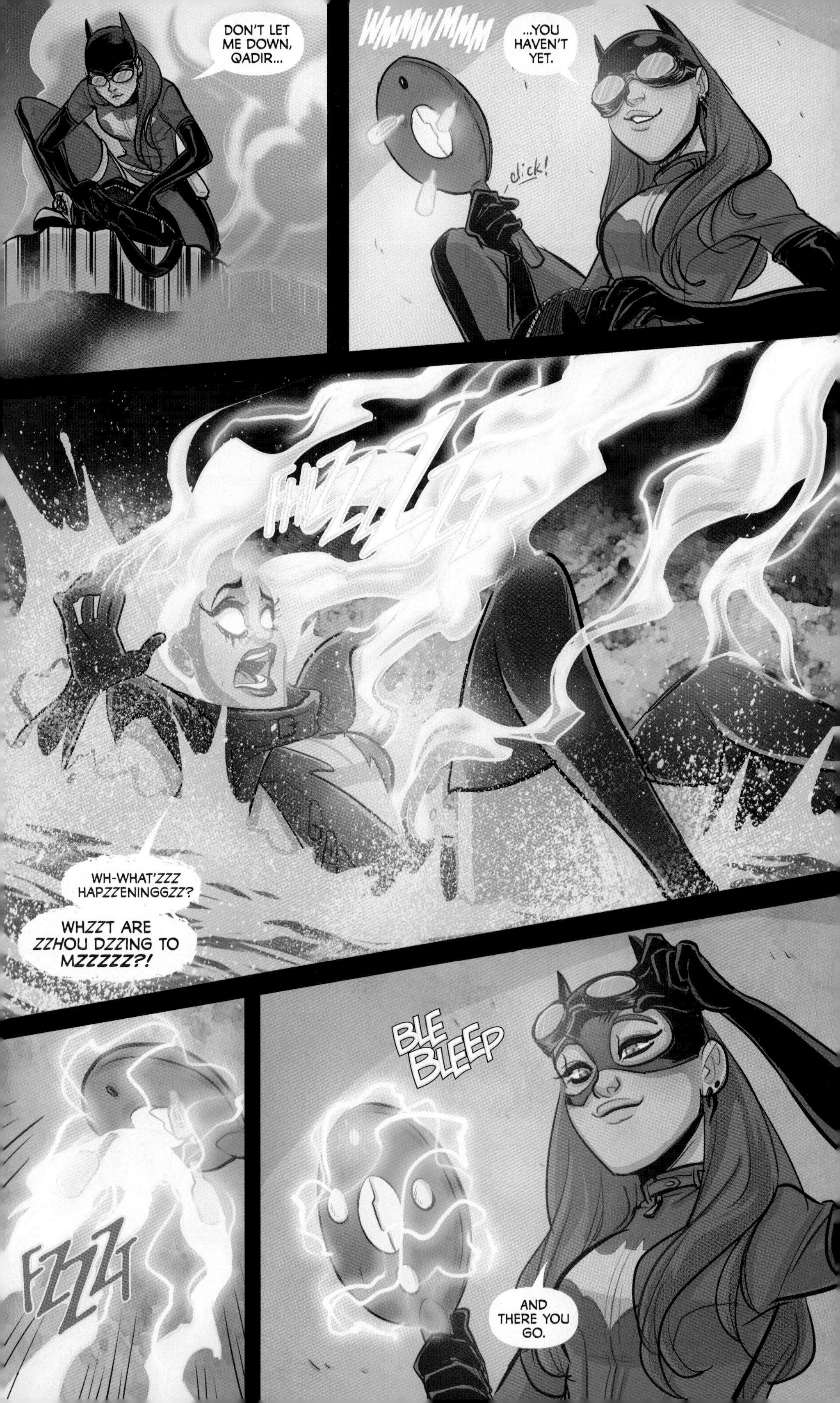
DON'T LET ME DOWN, QADIR...
WMMWMMM
...YOU HAVEN'T YET.
click!
FHHZZZZZZ
WH-WHAT'ZZZ HAPZZENINGGZZ?
WHZZT ARE ZZHOU DZZING TO MZZZZZ?!
FZZZT
BLE BLEEP
AND THERE YOU GO.

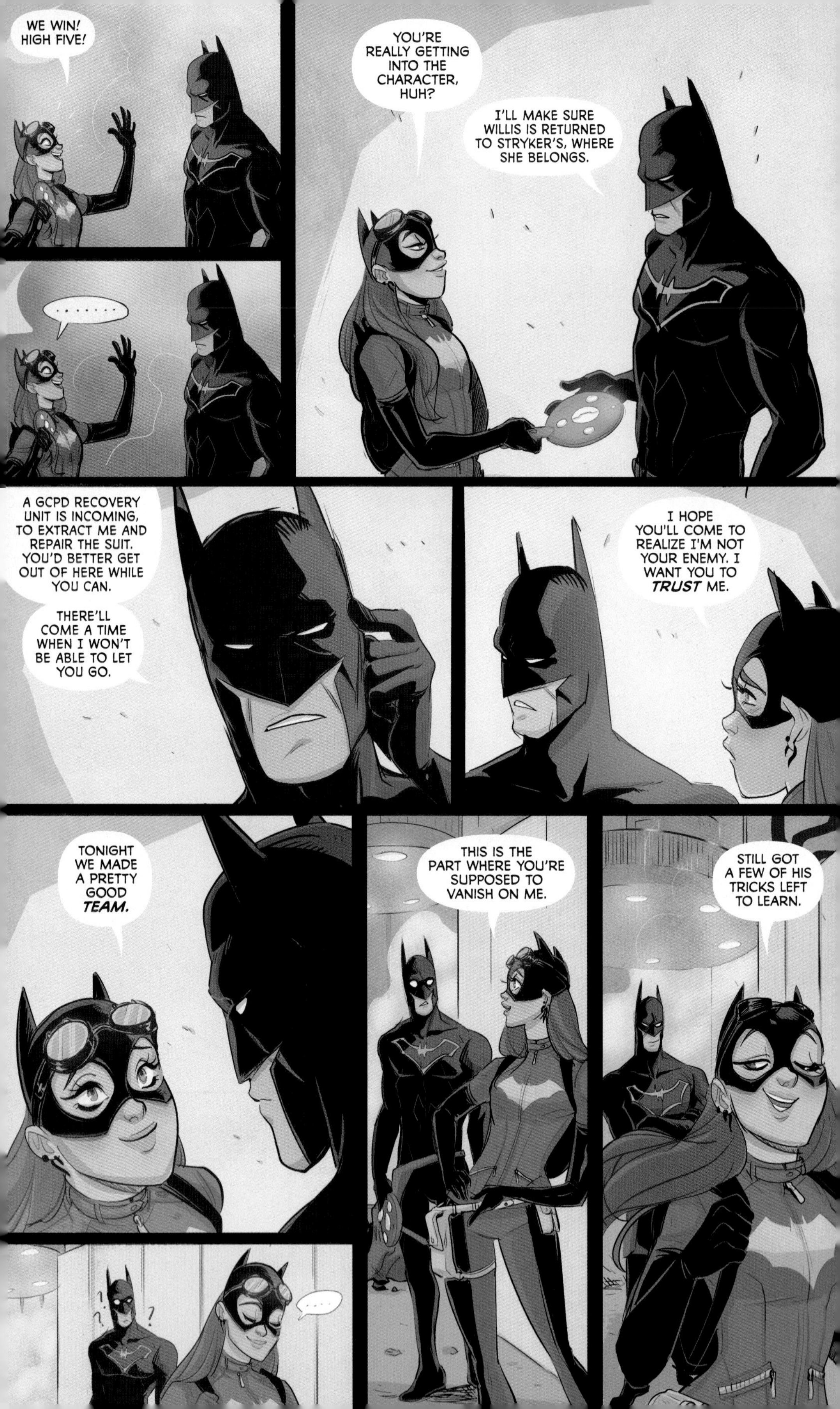
WE WIN! HIGH FIVE!
. . . .
YOU'RE REALLY GETTING INTO THE CHARACTER, HUH?
I'LL MAKE SURE WILLIS IS RETURNED TO STRYKER'S, WHERE SHE BELONGS.
A GCPD RECOVERY UNIT IS INCOMING, TO EXTRACT ME AND REPAIR THE SUIT. YOU'D BETTER GET OUT OF HERE WHILE YOU CAN.
THERE'LL COME A TIME WHEN I WON'T BE ABLE TO LET YOU GO.
I HOPE YOU'LL COME TO REALIZE I'M NOT YOUR ENEMY. I WANT YOU TO TRUST ME.
TONIGHT WE MADE A PRETTY GOOD TEAM.
. . . .
THIS IS THE PART WHERE YOU'RE SUPPOSED TO VANISH ON ME.
STILL GOT A FEW OF HIS TRICKS LEFT TO LEARN.

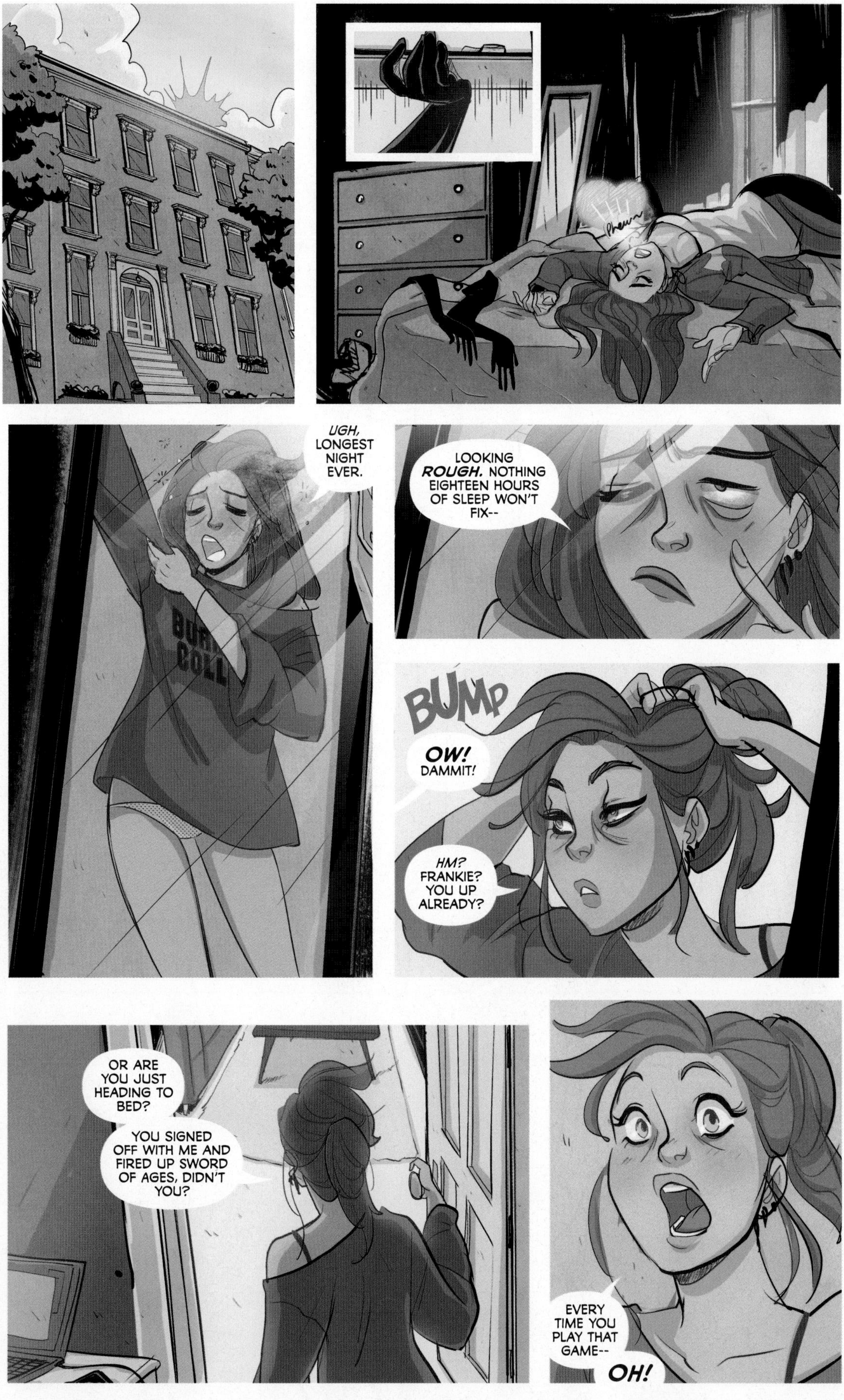
Phew
UGH, LONGEST NIGHT EVER.
LOOKING ROUGH. NOTHING EIGHTEEN HOURS OF SLEEP WON'T FIX--
BUMP
OW! DAMMIT!
HM? FRANKIE? YOU UP ALREADY?
OR ARE YOU JUST HEADING TO BED?
YOU SIGNED OFF WITH ME AND FIRED UP SWORD OF AGES, DIDN'T YOU?
EVERY TIME YOU PLAY THAT GAME--
OH!

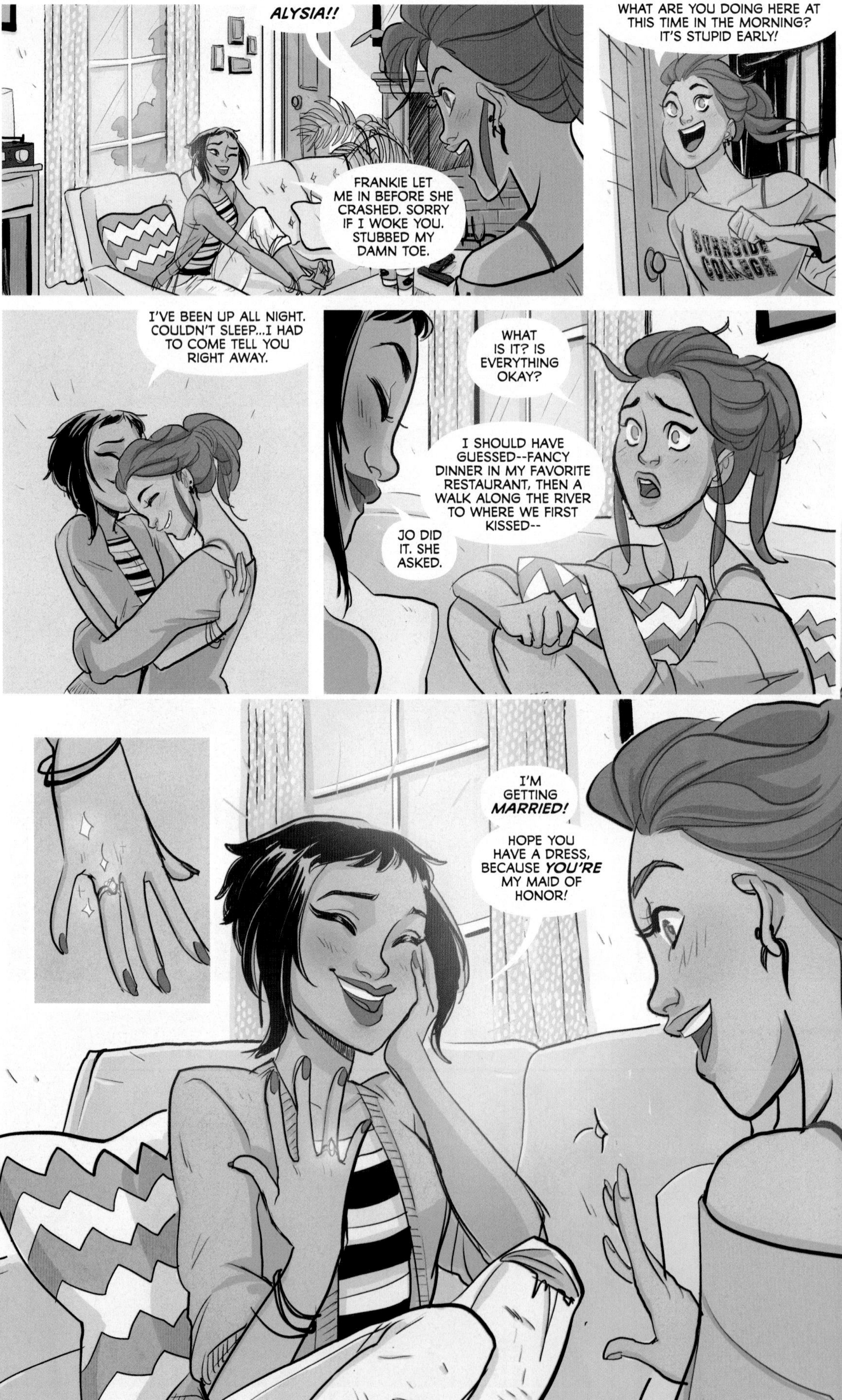
ALYSIA!!
FRANKIE LET ME IN BEFORE SHE CRASHED. SORRY IF I WOKE YOU. STUBBED MY DAMN TOE.
WHAT ARE YOU DOING HERE AT THIS TIME IN THE MORNING? IT'S STUPID EARLY!
BURNSIDE COLLEGE
I'VE BEEN UP ALL NIGHT. COULDN'T SLEEP...I HAD TO COME TELL YOU RIGHT AWAY.
WHAT IS IT? IS EVERYTHING OKAY?
I SHOULD HAVE GUESSED--FANCY DINNER IN MY FAVORITE RESTAURANT, THEN A WALK ALONG THE RIVER TO WHERE WE FIRST KISSED--
JO DID IT. SHE ASKED.
I'M GETTING *MARRIED!*
HOPE YOU HAVE A DRESS, BECAUSE *YOU'RE* MY MAID OF HONOR!

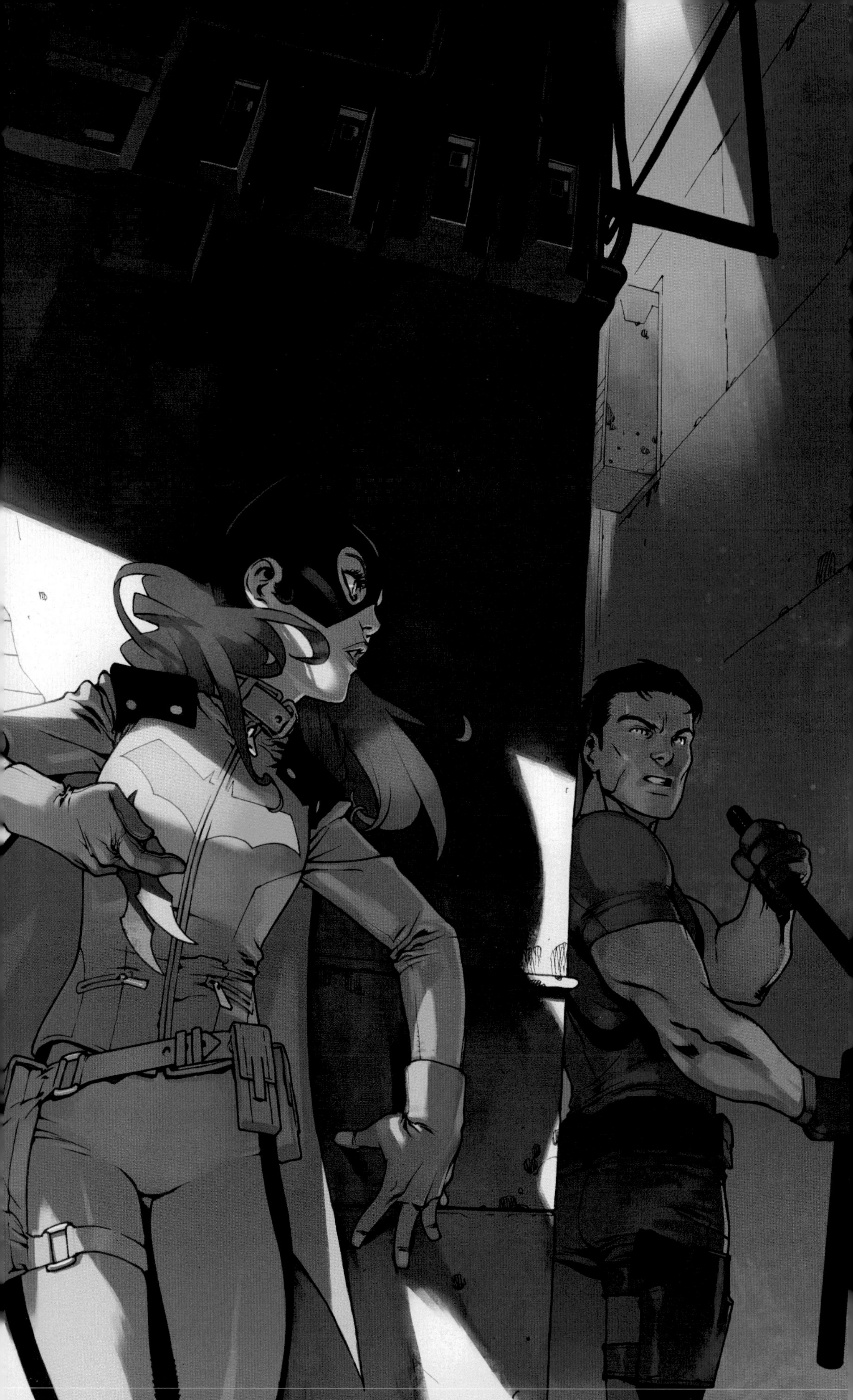

CAMERON STEWART & BRENDEN FLETCHER writers BENGAL DAVID LAFUENTE MING DOYLE MINGJUE HELEN CHEN artists
BENGAL GABE ELTAEB IVAN PLASCENCIA MINGJUE HELEN CHEN colorists STEVE WANDS letterer cover by BENGAL

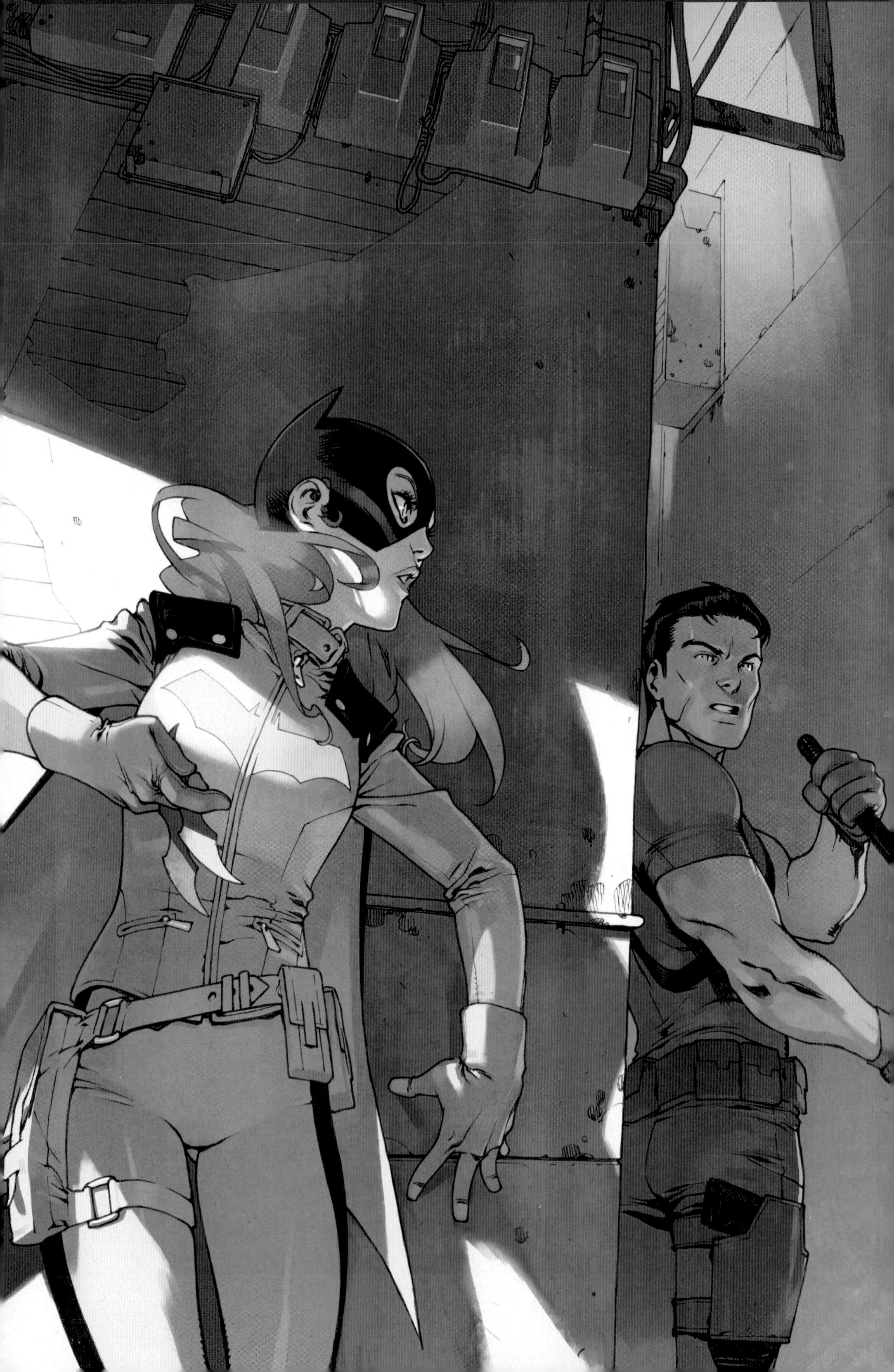

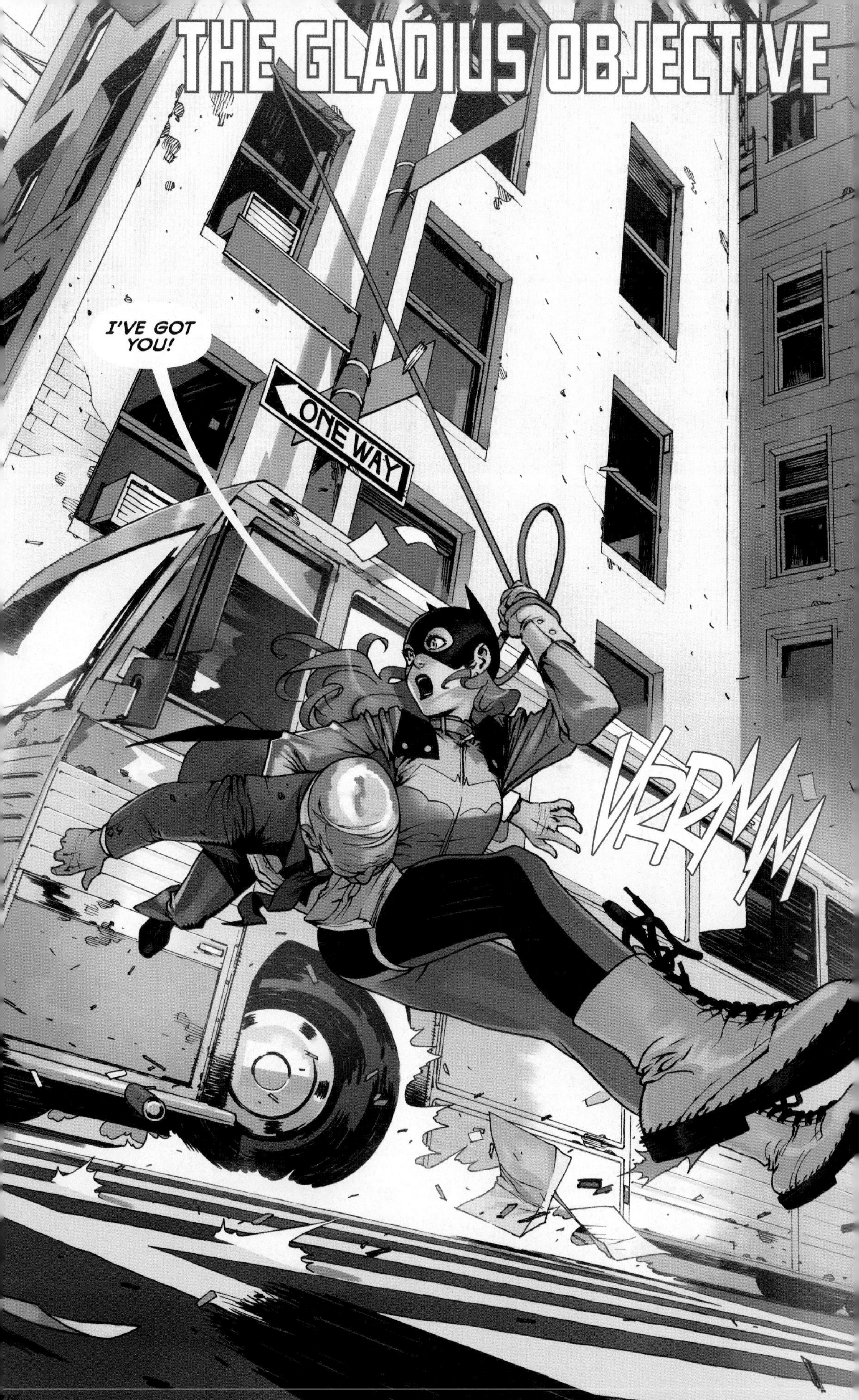
THE GLADIUS OBJECTIVE
I'VE GOT YOU!
ONE WAY
VRRMMM

GOTTA BE *CAREFUL,* WALKING OUT IN THE ROAD LIKE THAT--HEY, ARE YOU *OKAY?* LOOK AT ME... WHAT'S YOUR NAME?

I--I DON'T...MY HEAD...CAN'T FIT THE *PIECES...*

MY NAME...W-WHAT YEAR IS IT?

WHAT IS THE NEGAHEDRON?

FIRST THINGS FIRST...

LET'S SEE IF WE CAN FIGURE OUT WHO YOU ARE.

CLIK

SEND TO: FRANK CHARLE

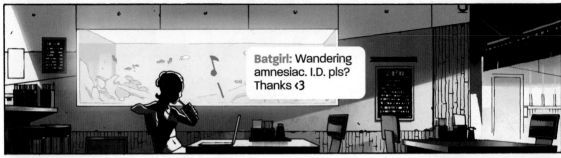

Batgirl: Wandering amnesiac. I.D. pls? Thanks ‹3

NEVER A DAY OFF...

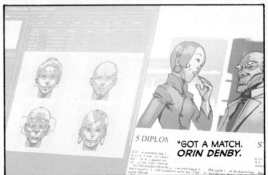

5 DIPLOM

"GOT A MATCH. *ORIN DENBY.*

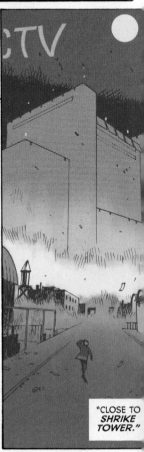

CTV

"CLOSE TO *SHRIKE TOWER.*"

"PRESIDENT OF THE UNITED NATIONS ECONOMIC AND SOCIAL COUNCIL.

"WENT MISSING NINE DAYS AGO...

"...ALONG WITH FOUR U.N. DIPLOMATS.

"GOT HIM ON CCTV FROM EARLY THIS MORNING. OVER THE RIVER, GOTHAM DOCKLANDS.

Frankie: He should have just blown it up :-D

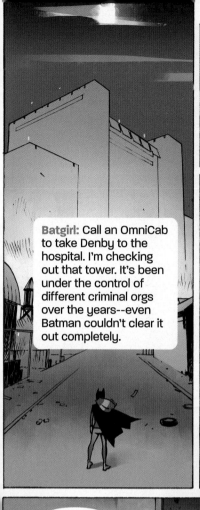

Batgirl: Call an OmniCab to take Denby to the hospital. I'm checking out that tower. It's been under the control of different criminal orgs over the years--even Batman couldn't clear it out completely.

AH!

WH-THUNK

ANOTHER STEP AND I AIM SIX INCHES TO THE *LEFT.*

WHY ARE YOU *THIS* SIDE OF THE RIVER, BATGIRL? THOUGHT YOU WERE THE QUEEN OF *HIPSTERVILLE.*

I LOOK OUT FOR *ALL* OF GOTHAM, NOT JUST BURNSIDE.

I'M FOLLOWING A *LEAD.* FOUR DIPLOMATS ARE MISSING AND I'M NOT GIVING UP UNTIL I'VE FOUND THEM.

WHO ARE *YOU?*

CALL ME *DIRECTOR.* I'M TRACKING A *DEVICE* STOLEN FROM OUR AGENCY BY TERRORISTS. IT REQUIRES MULTIPLE PEOPLE TO OPERATE...MAYBE OUR CASES ARE *RELATED.*

WE CAN GO IN TOGETHER. SHARE THE *WORKLOAD*...

"AGENCY." SO YOU'RE *GOVERNMENT?*

...SURE.

WELL, IF YOU PROMISE NOT TO *SHOOT* AT ME AGAIN.

DEAL.

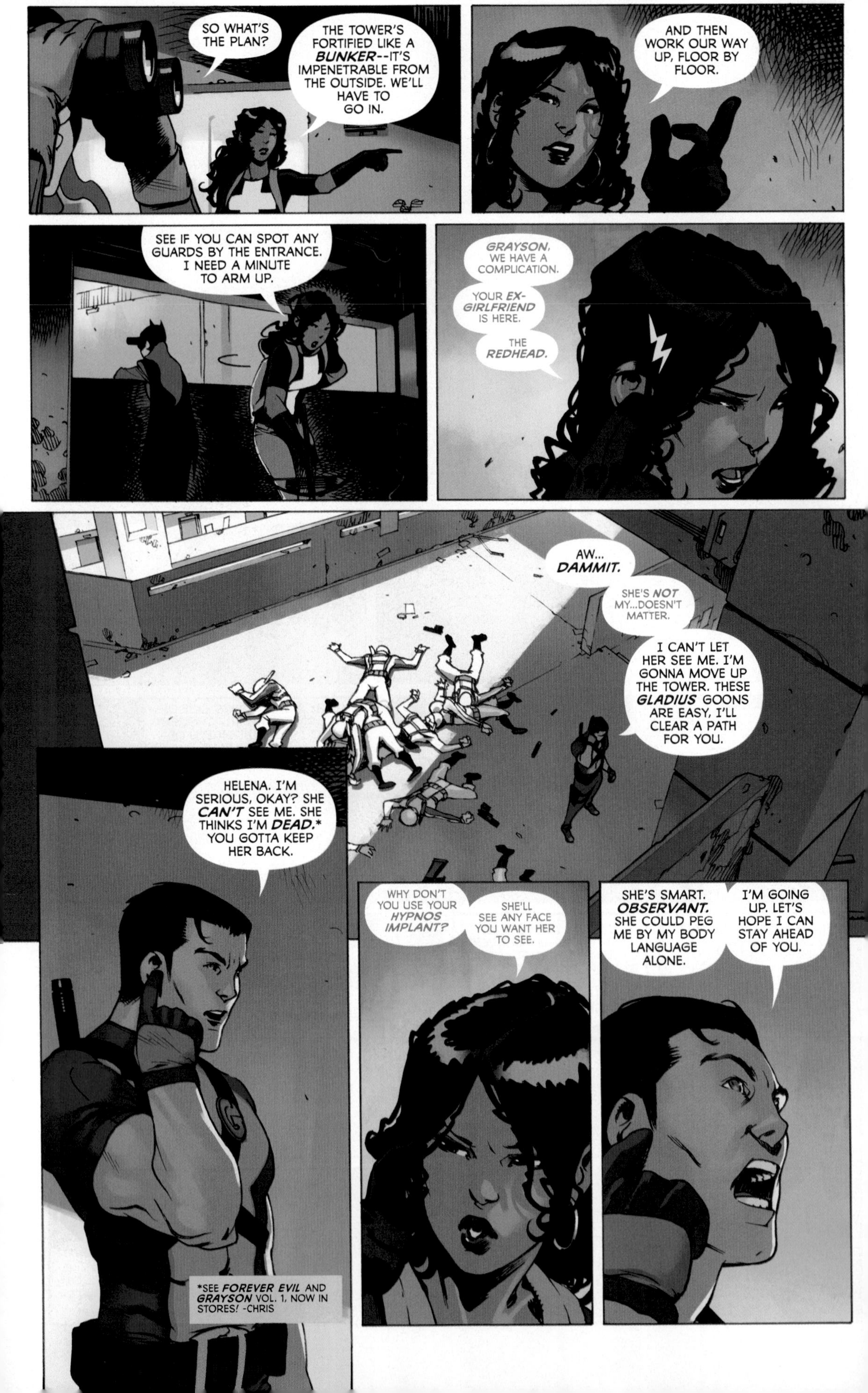
SO WHAT'S THE PLAN?
THE TOWER'S FORTIFIED LIKE A BUNKER--IT'S IMPENETRABLE FROM THE OUTSIDE. WE'LL HAVE TO GO IN.
AND THEN WORK OUR WAY UP, FLOOR BY FLOOR.
SEE IF YOU CAN SPOT ANY GUARDS BY THE ENTRANCE. I NEED A MINUTE TO ARM UP.
GRAYSON, WE HAVE A COMPLICATION.
YOUR EX-GIRLFRIEND IS HERE.
THE REDHEAD.
AW... DAMMIT.
SHE'S NOT MY...DOESN'T MATTER.
I CAN'T LET HER SEE ME. I'M GONNA MOVE UP THE TOWER. THESE GLADIUS GOONS ARE EASY, I'LL CLEAR A PATH FOR YOU.
HELENA. I'M SERIOUS, OKAY? SHE CAN'T SEE ME. SHE THINKS I'M DEAD.* YOU GOTTA KEEP HER BACK.
*SEE FOREVER EVIL AND GRAYSON VOL. 1, NOW IN STORES! -CHRIS
WHY DON'T YOU USE YOUR HYPNOS IMPLANT?
SHE'LL SEE ANY FACE YOU WANT HER TO SEE.
SHE'S SMART. OBSERVANT. SHE COULD PEG ME BY MY BODY LANGUAGE ALONE.
I'M GOING UP. LET'S HOPE I CAN STAY AHEAD OF YOU.

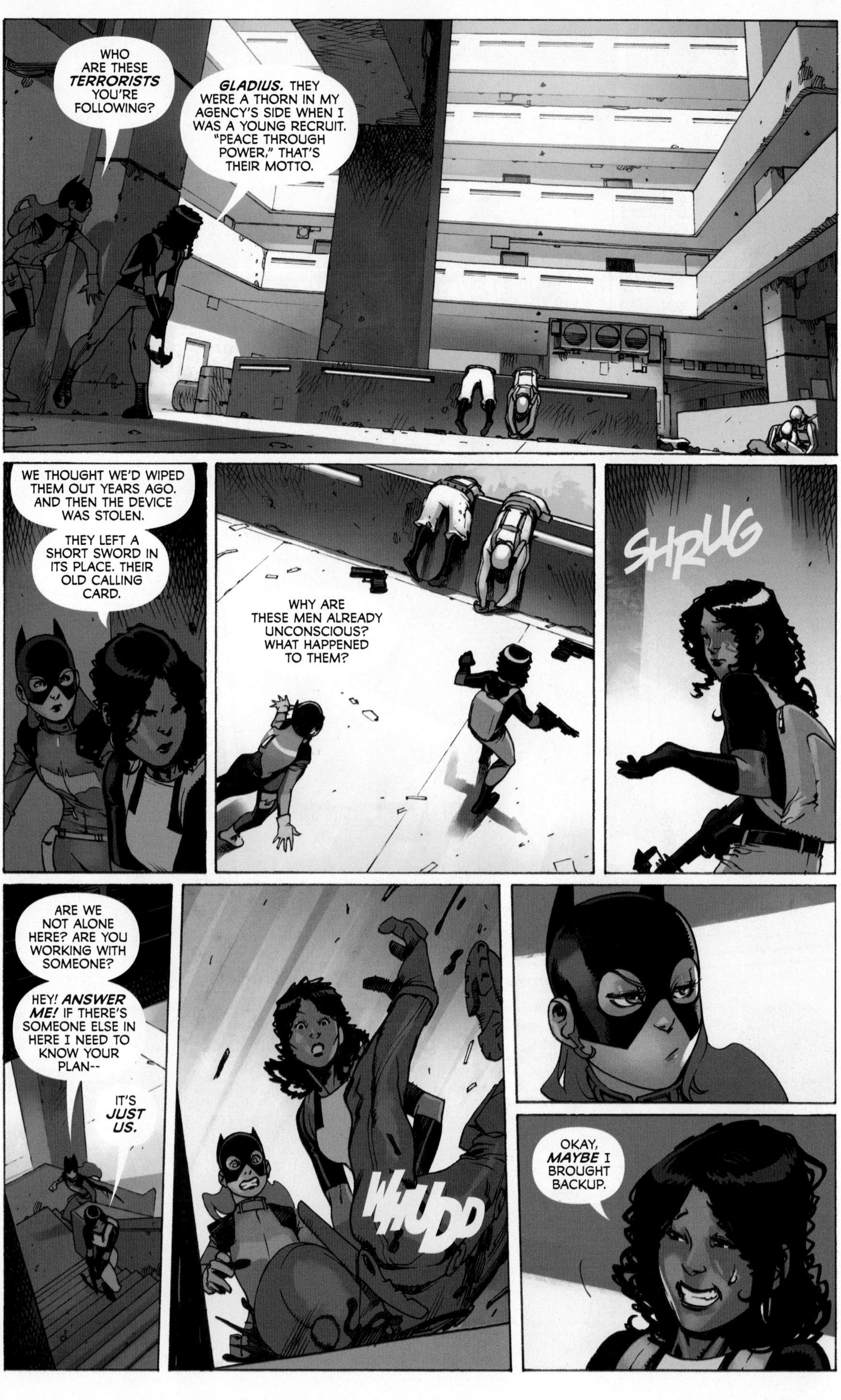
WHO ARE THESE TERRORISTS YOU'RE FOLLOWING?
GLADIUS. THEY WERE A THORN IN MY AGENCY'S SIDE WHEN I WAS A YOUNG RECRUIT. "PEACE THROUGH POWER," THAT'S THEIR MOTTO.
WE THOUGHT WE'D WIPED THEM OUT YEARS AGO. AND THEN THE DEVICE WAS STOLEN.
THEY LEFT A SHORT SWORD IN ITS PLACE. THEIR OLD CALLING CARD.
WHY ARE THESE MEN ALREADY UNCONSCIOUS? WHAT HAPPENED TO THEM?
SHRUG
ARE WE NOT ALONE HERE? ARE YOU WORKING WITH SOMEONE?
HEY! ANSWER ME! IF THERE'S SOMEONE ELSE IN HERE I NEED TO KNOW YOUR PLAN--
IT'S JUST US.
WHUDD
OKAY, MAYBE I BROUGHT BACKUP.

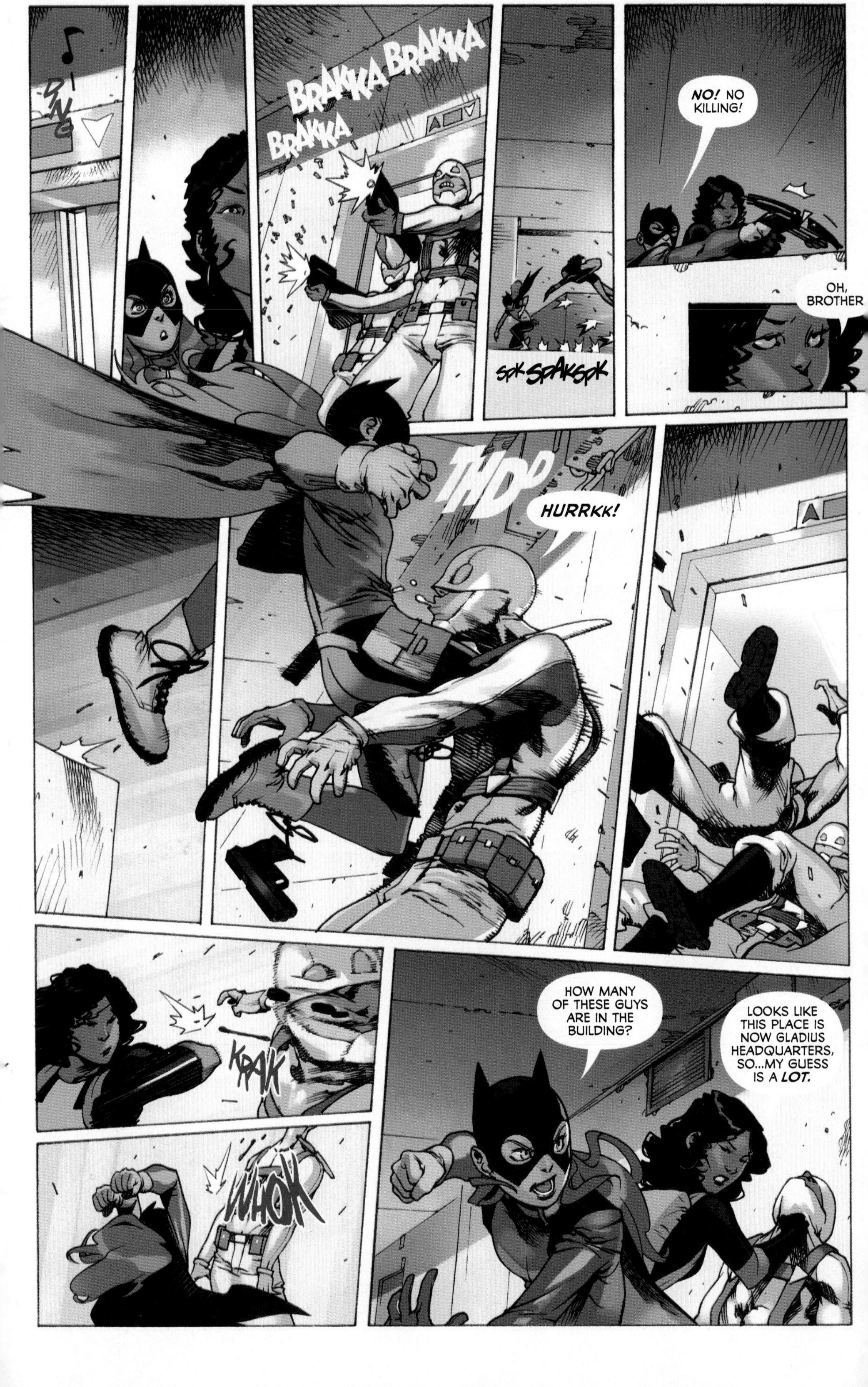
DING
BRAKKA BRAKKA
BRAKKA
NO! NO KILLING!
SPK SPAKSPK
OH, BROTHER
THDD
HURRKK!
KRAK
WHOK
HOW MANY OF THESE GUYS ARE IN THE BUILDING?
LOOKS LIKE THIS PLACE IS NOW GLADIUS HEADQUARTERS, SO...MY GUESS IS A *LOT.*

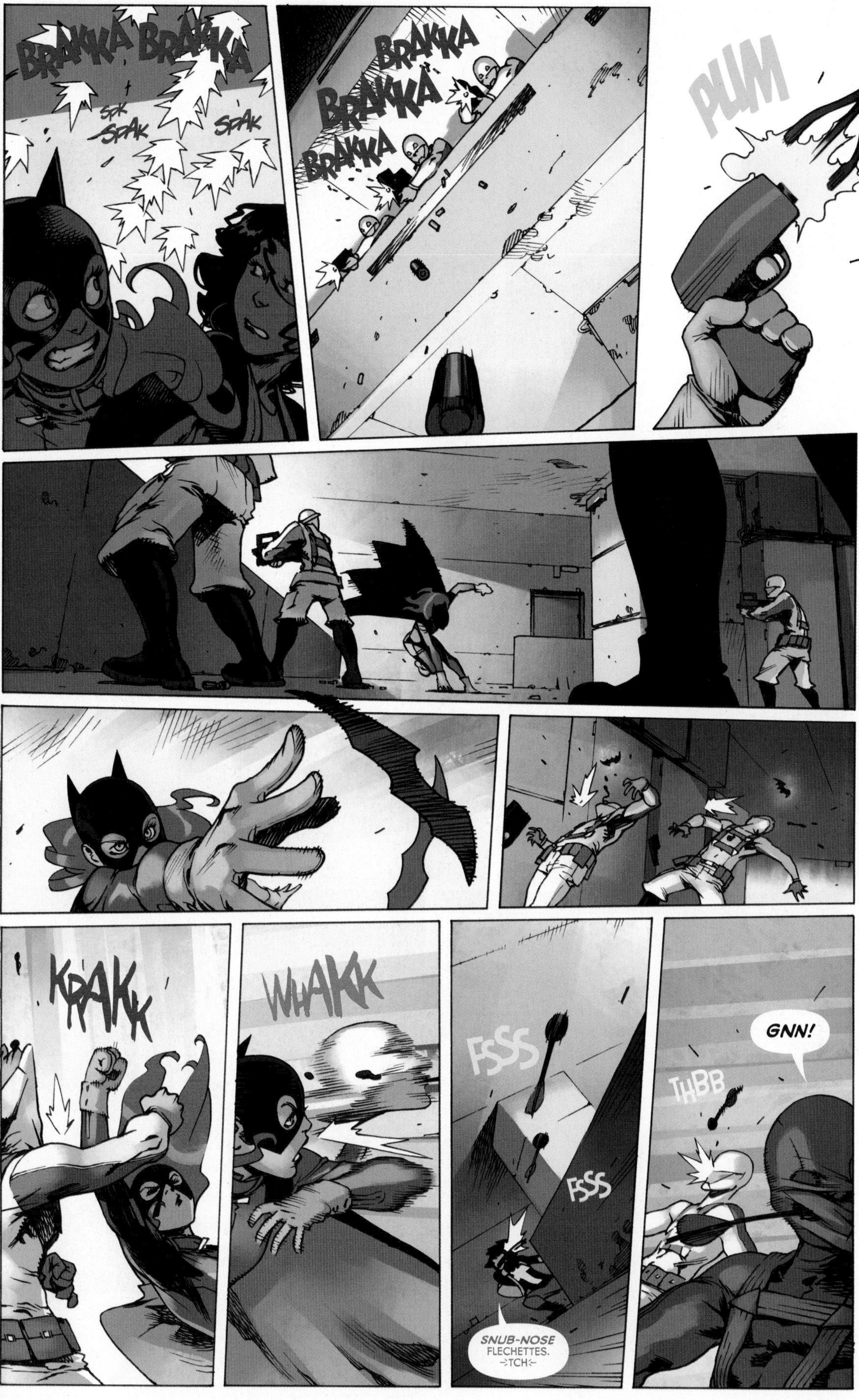
BRAKKA BRAKKA
SPAK
SPAK
SPAK
BRAKKA
BRAKKA
BRAKKA
PUM
KRAKK
WHAKK
FSSS
FSSS
SNUB-NOSE FLECHETTES. -TCH-
THBB
GNN!

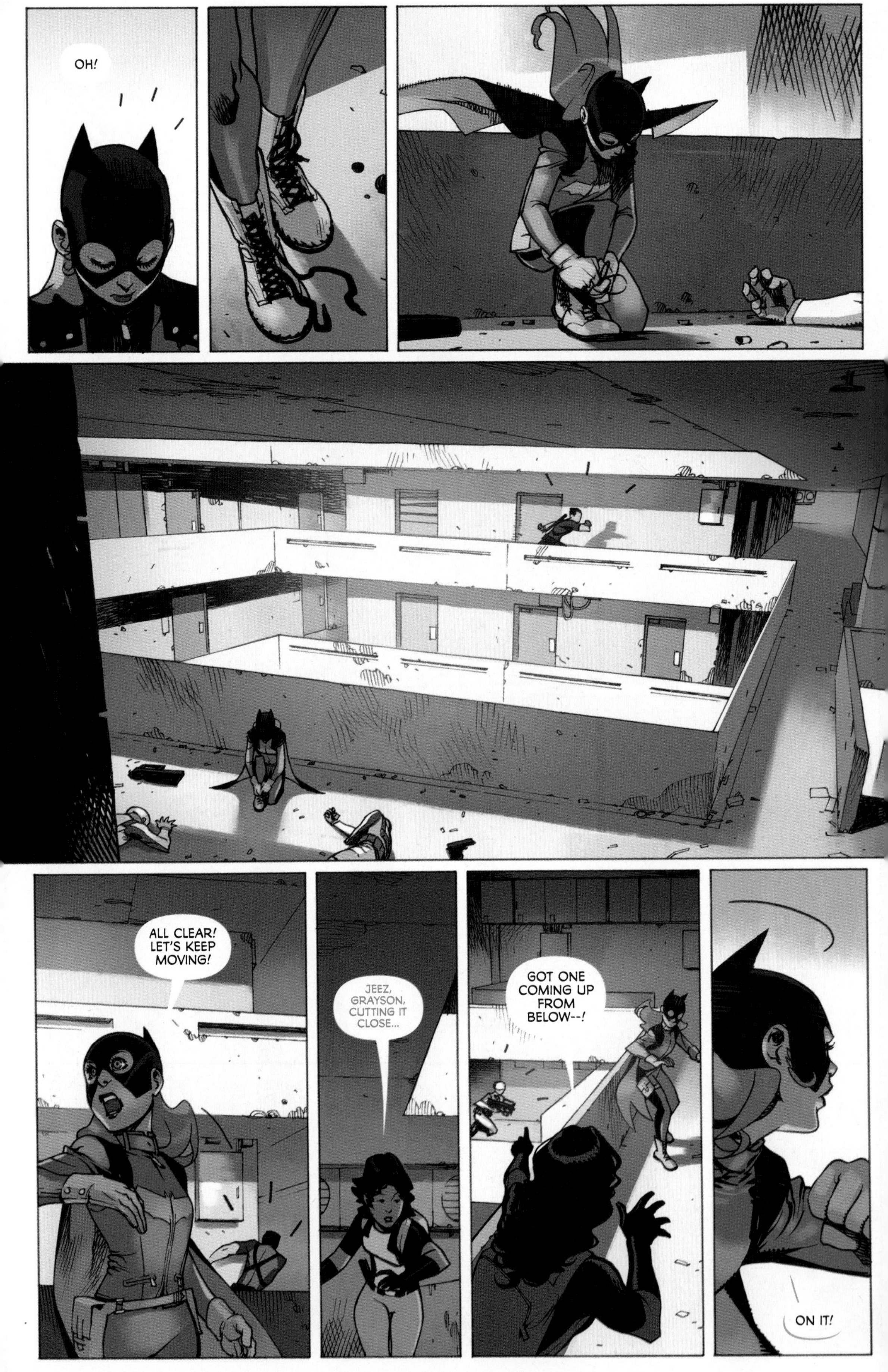
OH!
ALL CLEAR! LET'S KEEP MOVING!
JEEZ, GRAYSON, CUTTING IT CLOSE...
GOT ONE COMING UP FROM BELOW--!
ON IT!

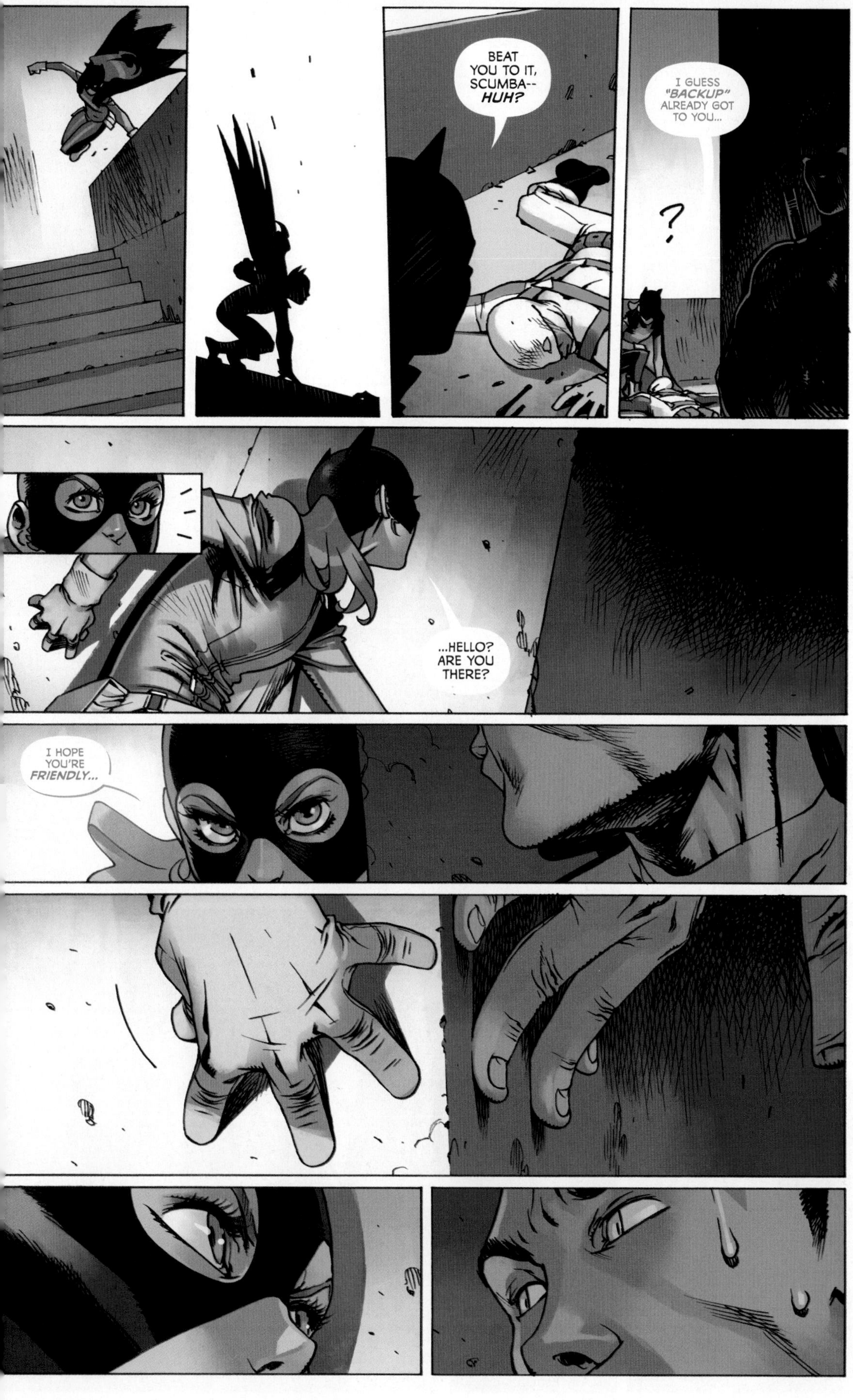
BEAT YOU TO IT, SCUMBA-- HUH?
I GUESS "BACKUP" ALREADY GOT TO YOU...
?
...HELLO? ARE YOU THERE?
I HOPE YOU'RE FRIENDLY...

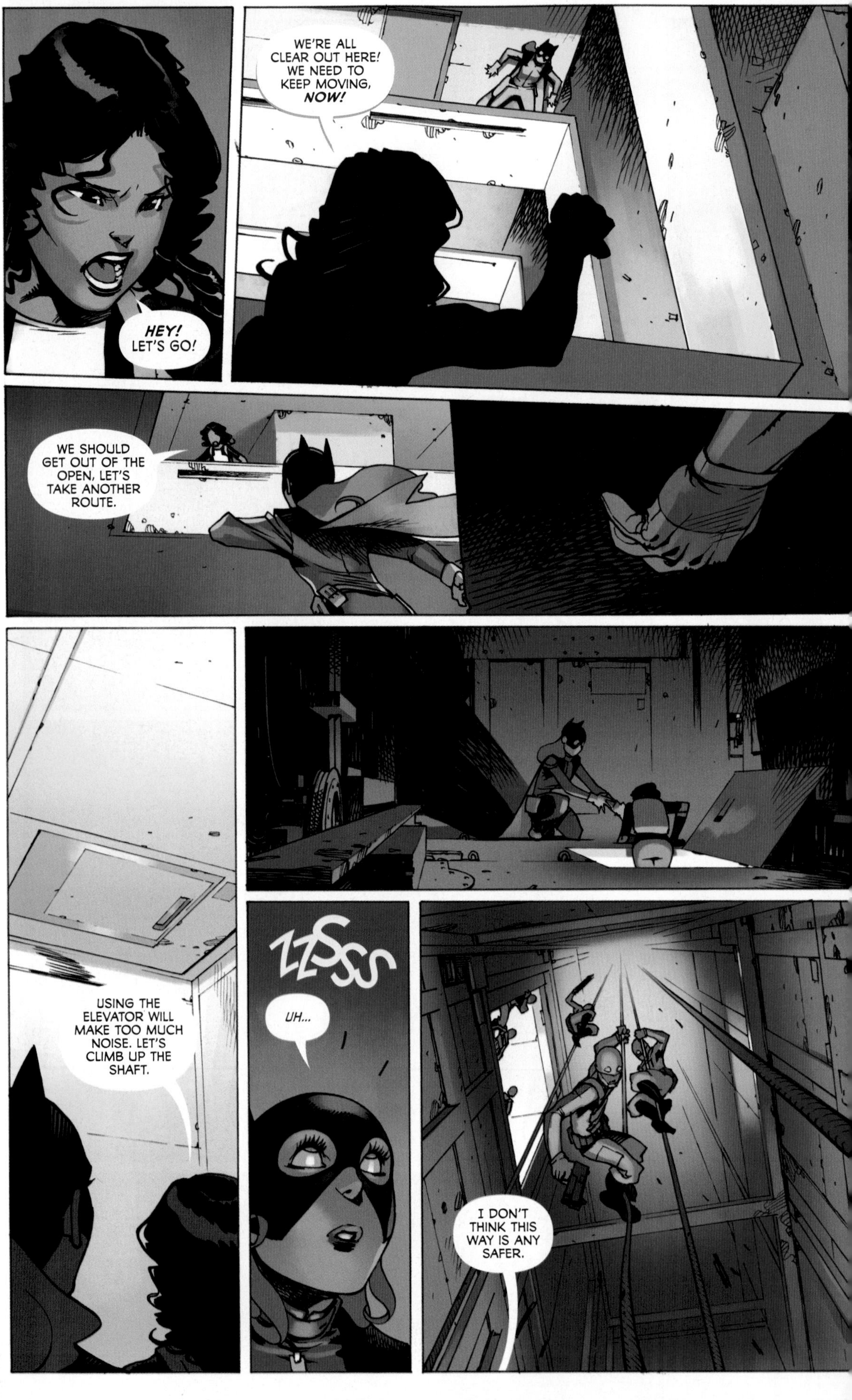
HEY! LET'S GO!
WE'RE ALL CLEAR OUT HERE! WE NEED TO KEEP MOVING, NOW!
WE SHOULD GET OUT OF THE OPEN, LET'S TAKE ANOTHER ROUTE.
USING THE ELEVATOR WILL MAKE TOO MUCH NOISE. LET'S CLIMB UP THE SHAFT.
ZZSSS
UH...
I DON'T THINK THIS WAY IS ANY SAFER.

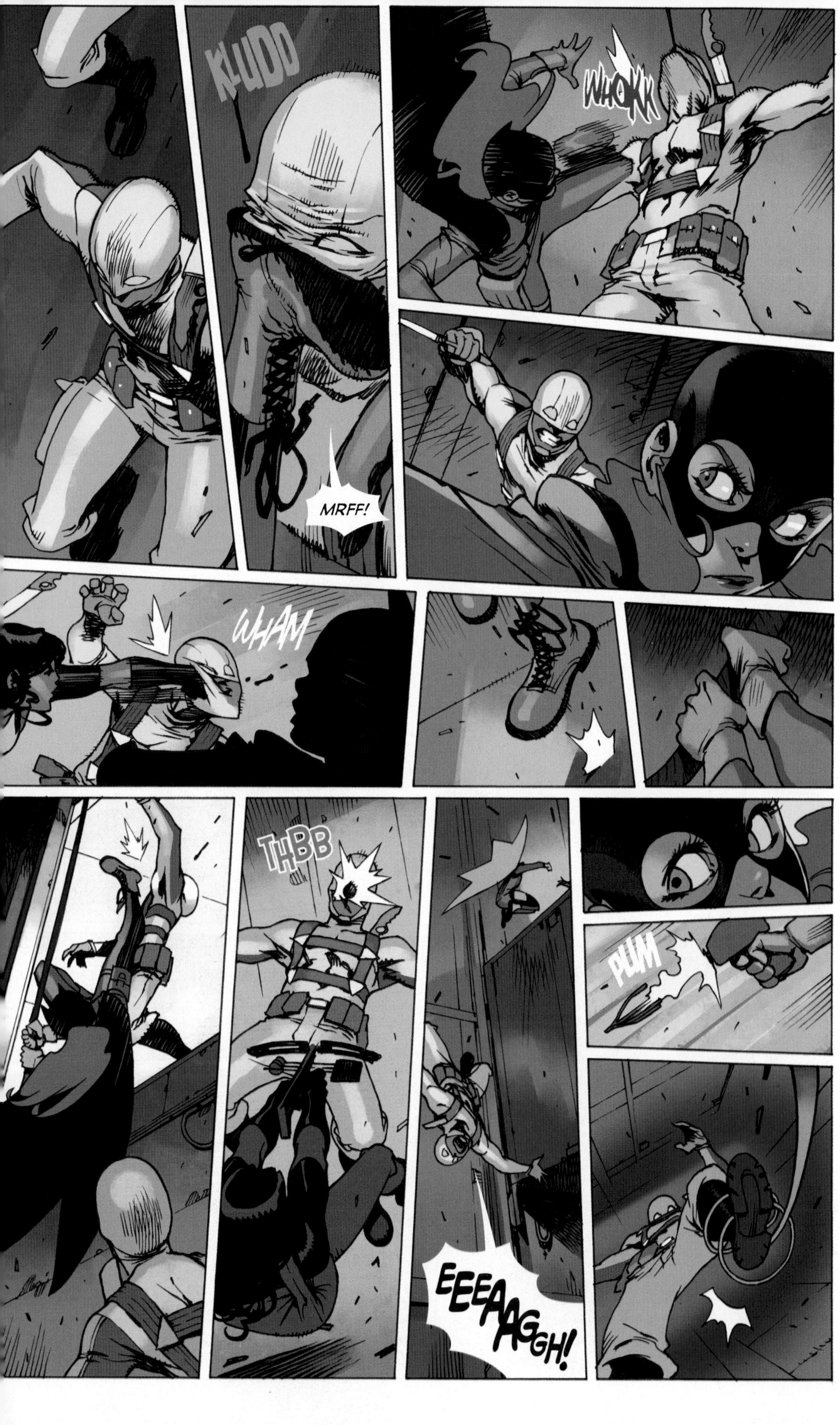

KLUDD
WHOKK
MRFF!
WHAM
THBB
PLUM
EEEAAAGGH!

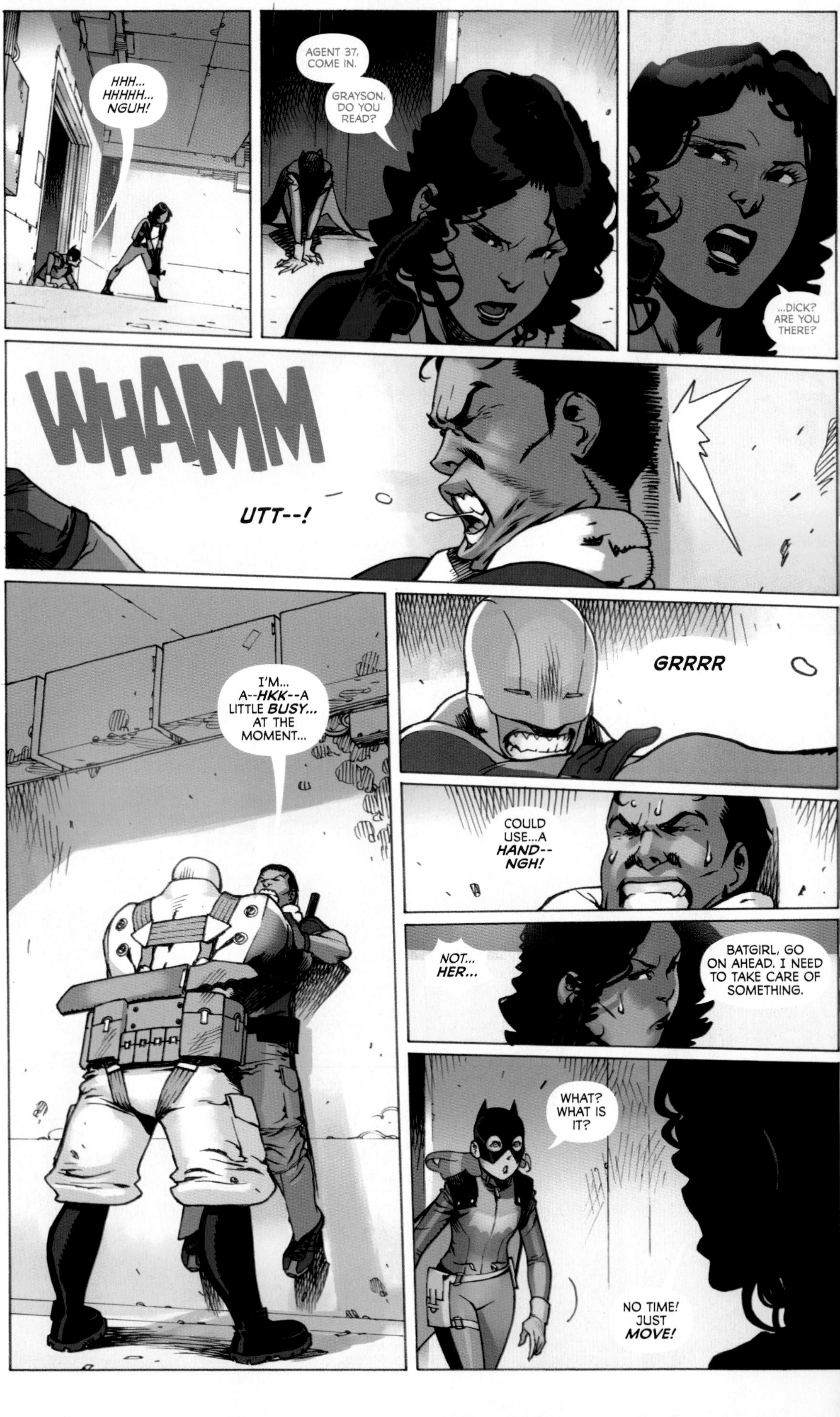
HHH... HHHHH... NGUH!
AGENT 37, COME IN.
GRAYSON, DO YOU READ?
...DICK? ARE YOU THERE?
WHAMM
UTT--!
I'M... A--HKK--A LITTLE BUSY... AT THE MOMENT...
GRRRR
COULD USE...A HAND--NGH!
NOT... HER...
BATGIRL, GO ON AHEAD. I NEED TO TAKE CARE OF SOMETHING.
WHAT? WHAT IS IT?
NO TIME! JUST MOVE!

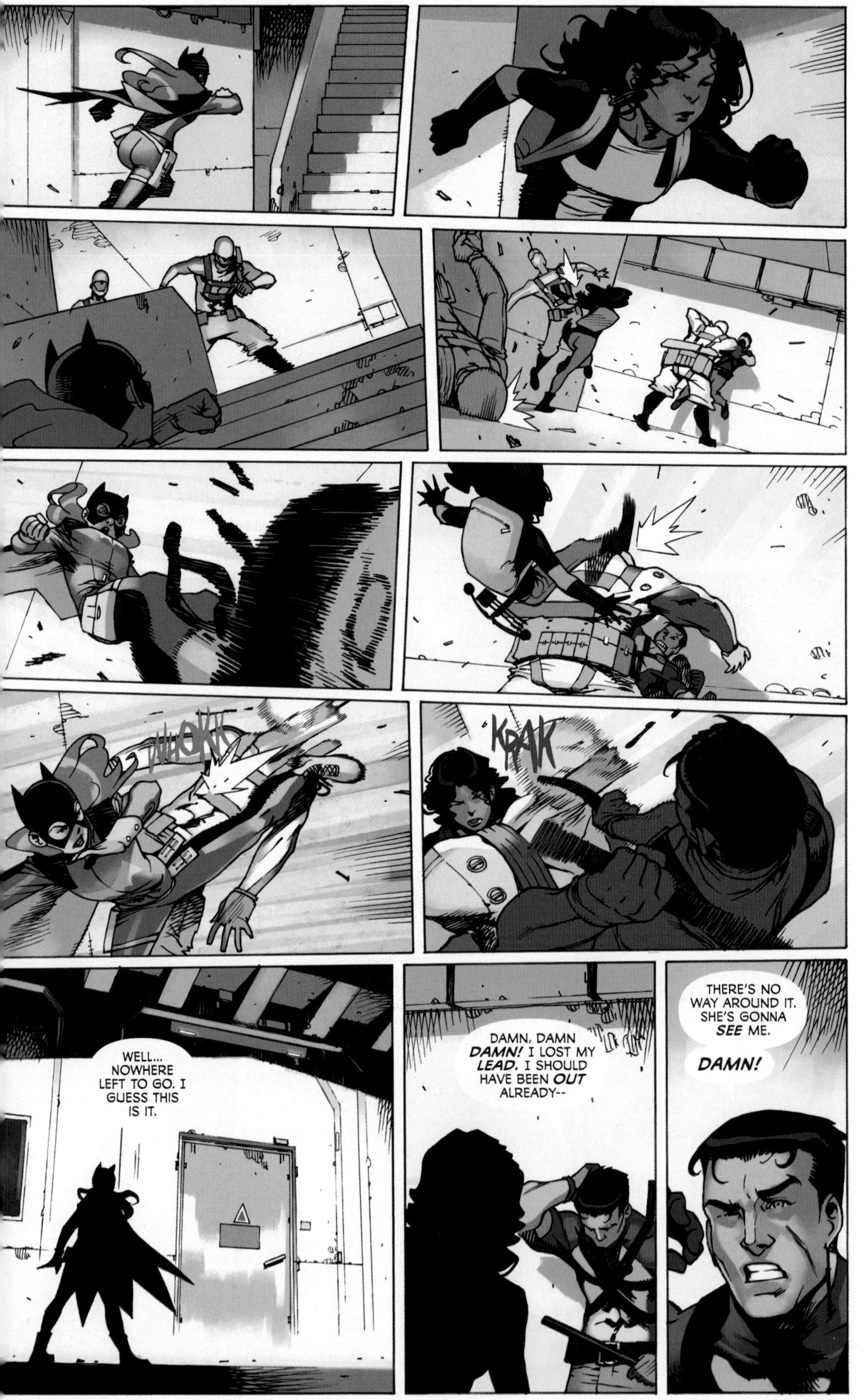
WHOKK
KRAK
WELL... NOWHERE LEFT TO GO. I GUESS THIS IS IT.
DAMN, DAMN *DAMN!* I LOST MY *LEAD.* I SHOULD HAVE BEEN *OUT* ALREADY--
THERE'S NO WAY AROUND IT. SHE'S GONNA *SEE* ME.
DAMN!

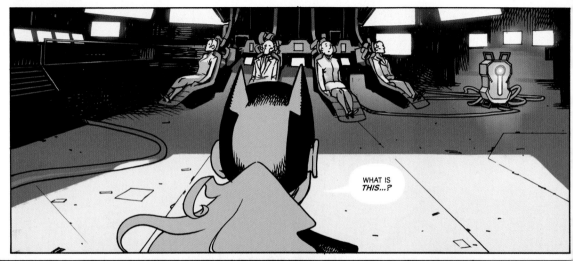

WHAT IS *THIS...?*

HEY!

TKATIKTAKTIK

KCHIK

NOT SO *FAST!*

YOU CAN STOP ME OR YOU CAN *SAVE* THEM! THAT DEVICE IS RIGGED TO EXPLODE, AND IT WILL TAKE *ALL* OF US WITH IT!

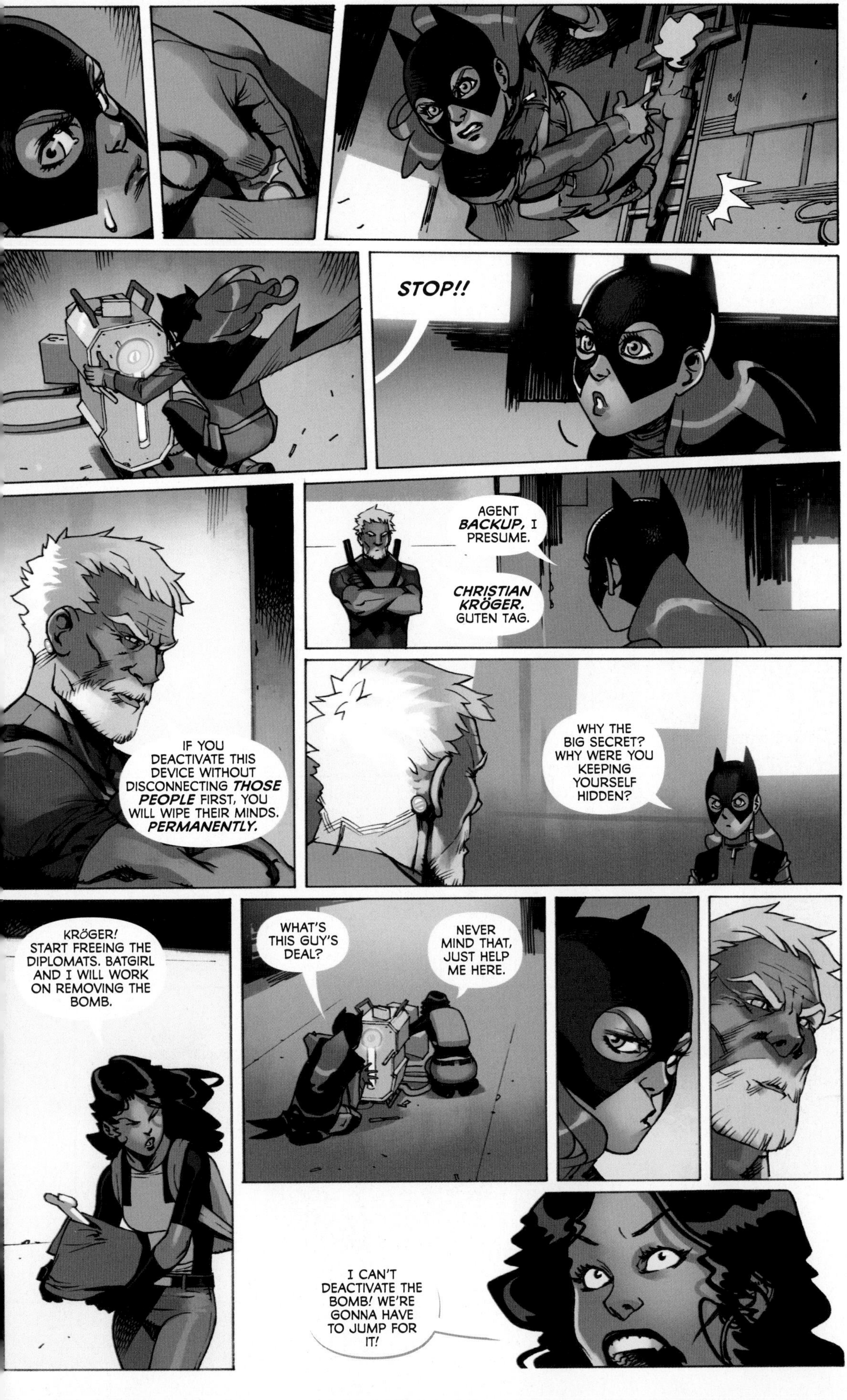
STOP!!
AGENT BACKUP, I PRESUME.
CHRISTIAN KRÖGER. GUTEN TAG.
IF YOU DEACTIVATE THIS DEVICE WITHOUT DISCONNECTING THOSE PEOPLE FIRST, YOU WILL WIPE THEIR MINDS. PERMANENTLY.
WHY THE BIG SECRET? WHY WERE YOU KEEPING YOURSELF HIDDEN?
KRÖGER! START FREEING THE DIPLOMATS. BATGIRL AND I WILL WORK ON REMOVING THE BOMB.
WHAT'S THIS GUY'S DEAL?
NEVER MIND THAT, JUST HELP ME HERE.
I CAN'T DEACTIVATE THE BOMB! WE'RE GONNA HAVE TO JUMP FOR IT!

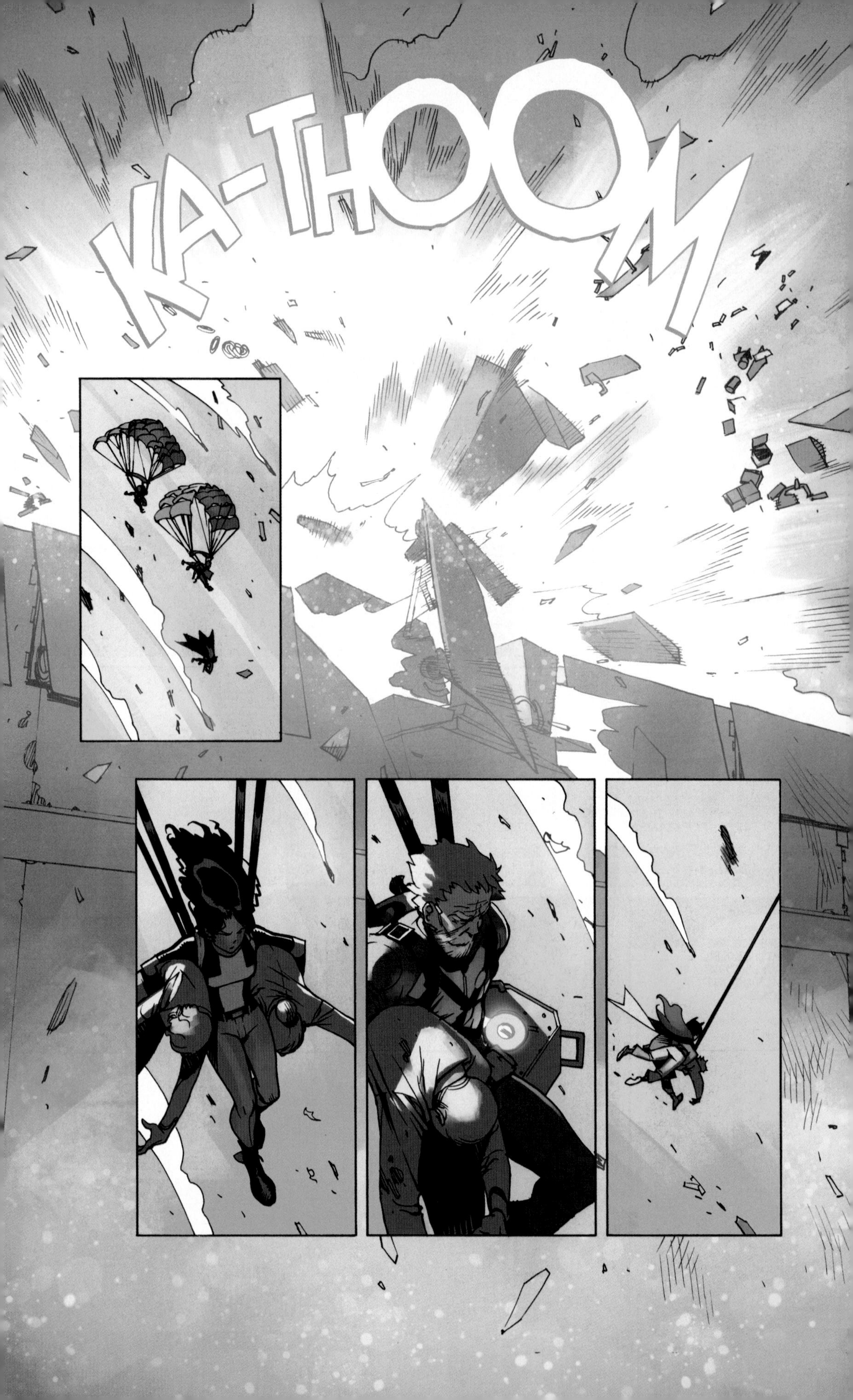
KA-THOOM

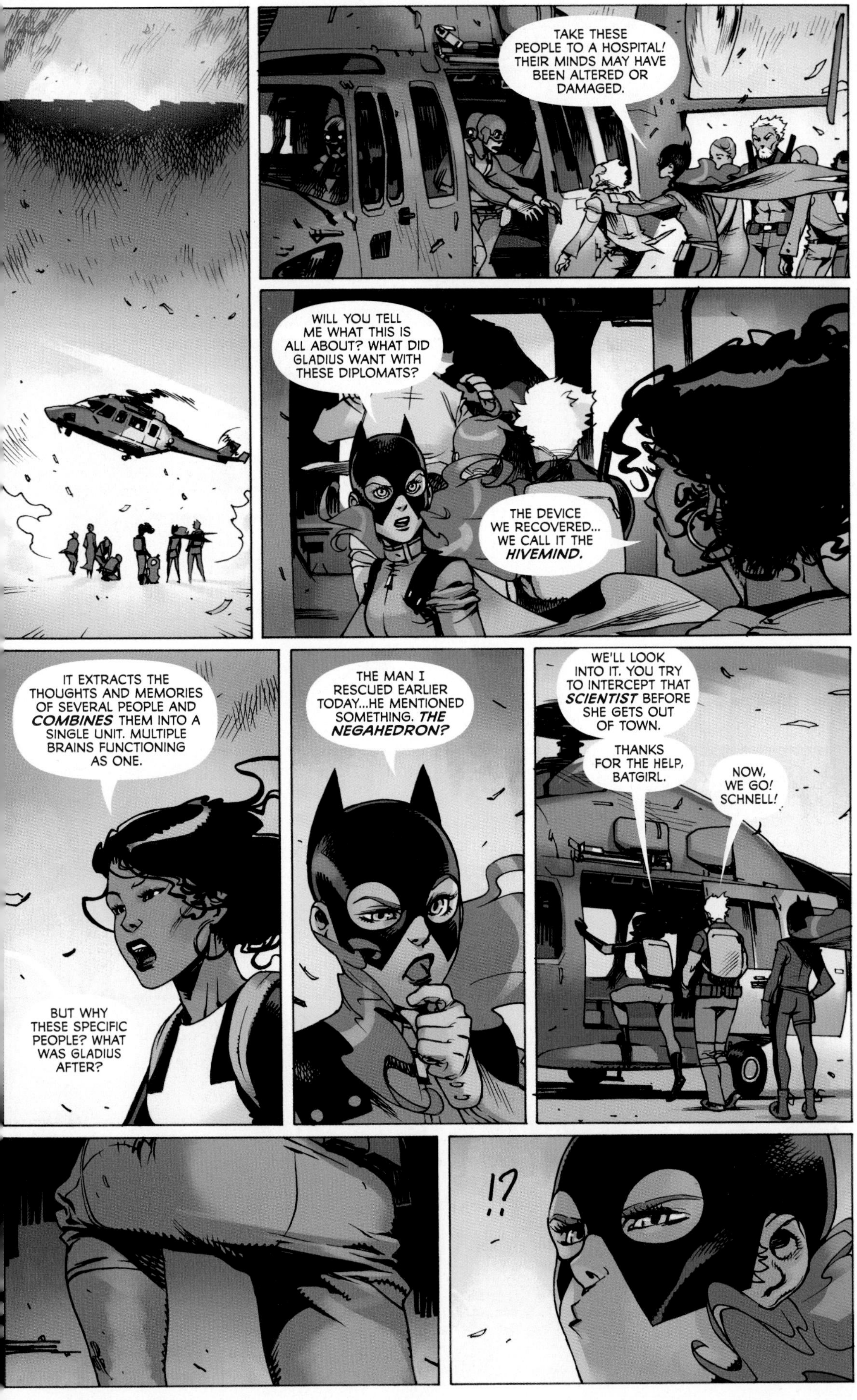
TAKE THESE PEOPLE TO A HOSPITAL! THEIR MINDS MAY HAVE BEEN ALTERED OR DAMAGED.
WILL YOU TELL ME WHAT THIS IS ALL ABOUT? WHAT DID GLADIUS WANT WITH THESE DIPLOMATS?
THE DEVICE WE RECOVERED... WE CALL IT THE HIVEMIND.
IT EXTRACTS THE THOUGHTS AND MEMORIES OF SEVERAL PEOPLE AND COMBINES THEM INTO A SINGLE UNIT. MULTIPLE BRAINS FUNCTIONING AS ONE.
BUT WHY THESE SPECIFIC PEOPLE? WHAT WAS GLADIUS AFTER?
THE MAN I RESCUED EARLIER TODAY...HE MENTIONED SOMETHING. THE NEGAHEDRON?
WE'LL LOOK INTO IT. YOU TRY TO INTERCEPT THAT SCIENTIST BEFORE SHE GETS OUT OF TOWN.
THANKS FOR THE HELP, BATGIRL.
NOW, WE GO! SCHNELL!
!?

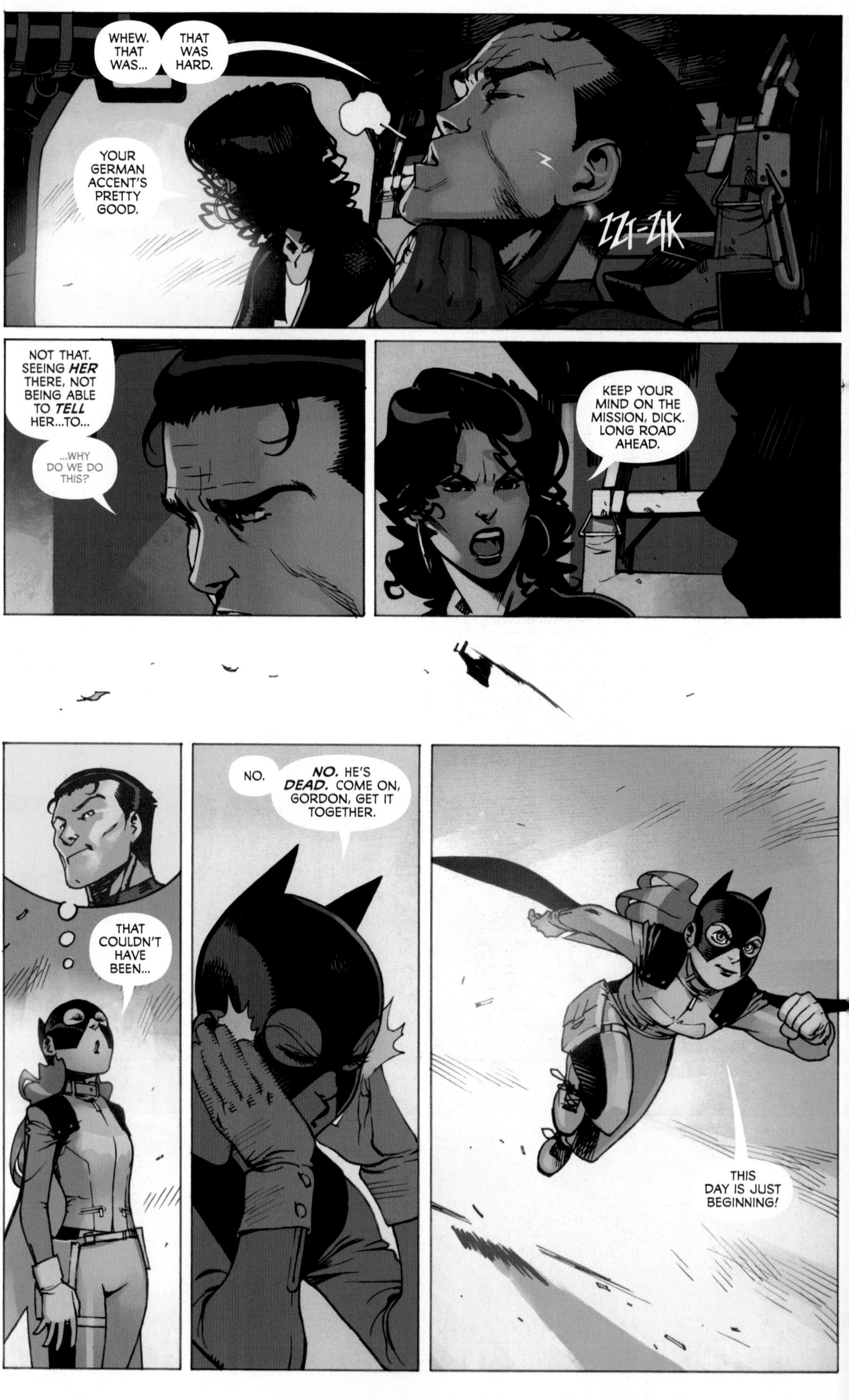

WHEW. THAT WAS...
THAT WAS HARD.
YOUR GERMAN ACCENT'S PRETTY GOOD.
ZZT-ZIK
NOT THAT. SEEING *HER* THERE, NOT BEING ABLE TO *TELL* HER...TO...
...WHY DO WE DO THIS?
KEEP YOUR MIND ON THE MISSION, DICK. LONG ROAD AHEAD.
THAT COULDN'T HAVE BEEN...
NO.
NO. HE'S *DEAD.* COME ON, GORDON, GET IT TOGETHER.
THIS DAY IS JUST BEGINNING!

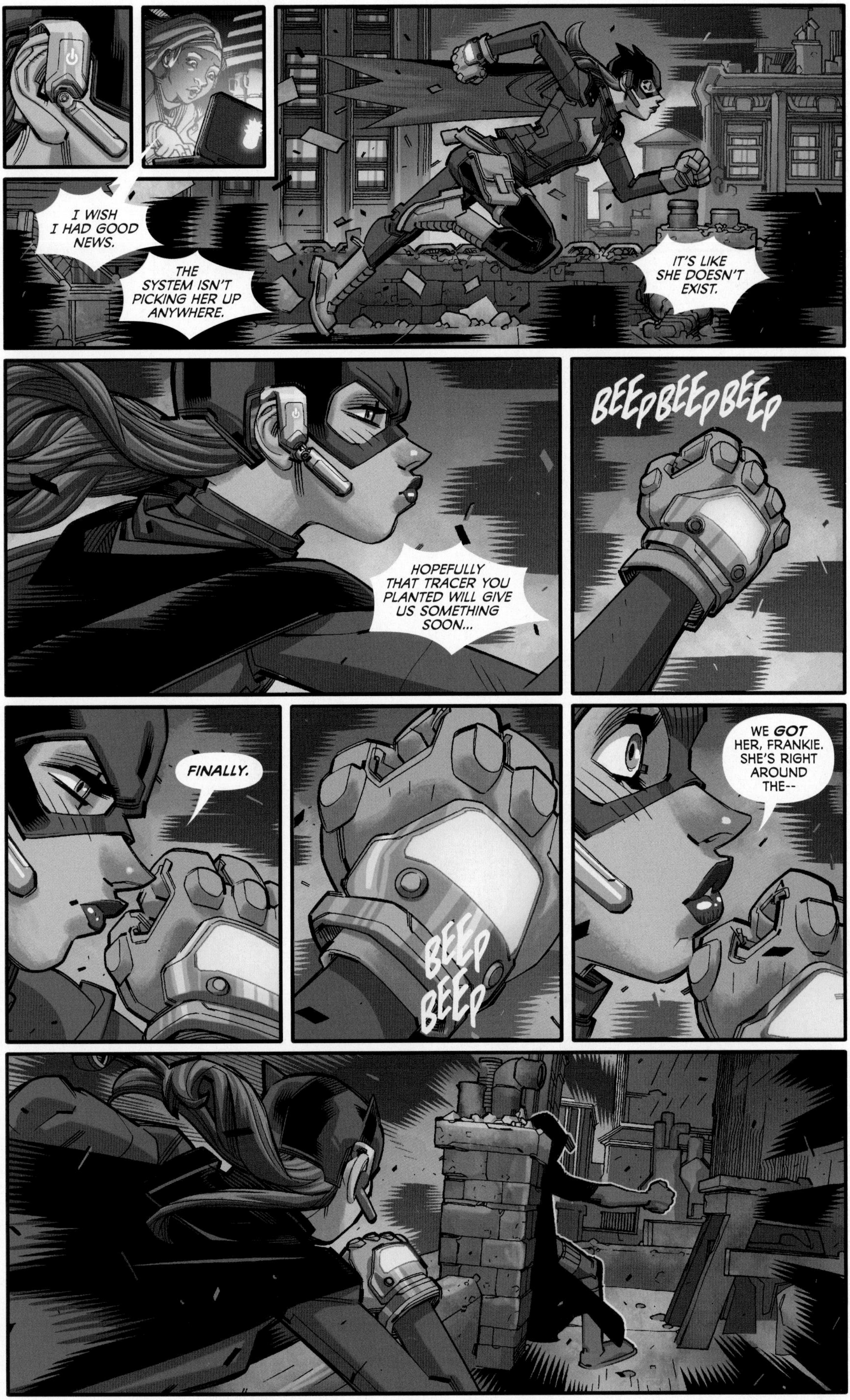
I WISH I HAD GOOD NEWS.
THE SYSTEM ISN'T PICKING HER UP ANYWHERE.
IT'S LIKE SHE DOESN'T EXIST.
HOPEFULLY THAT TRACER YOU PLANTED WILL GIVE US SOMETHING SOON...
BEEP BEEP BEEP
FINALLY.
BEEP BEEP
WE GOT HER, FRANKIE. SHE'S RIGHT AROUND THE--

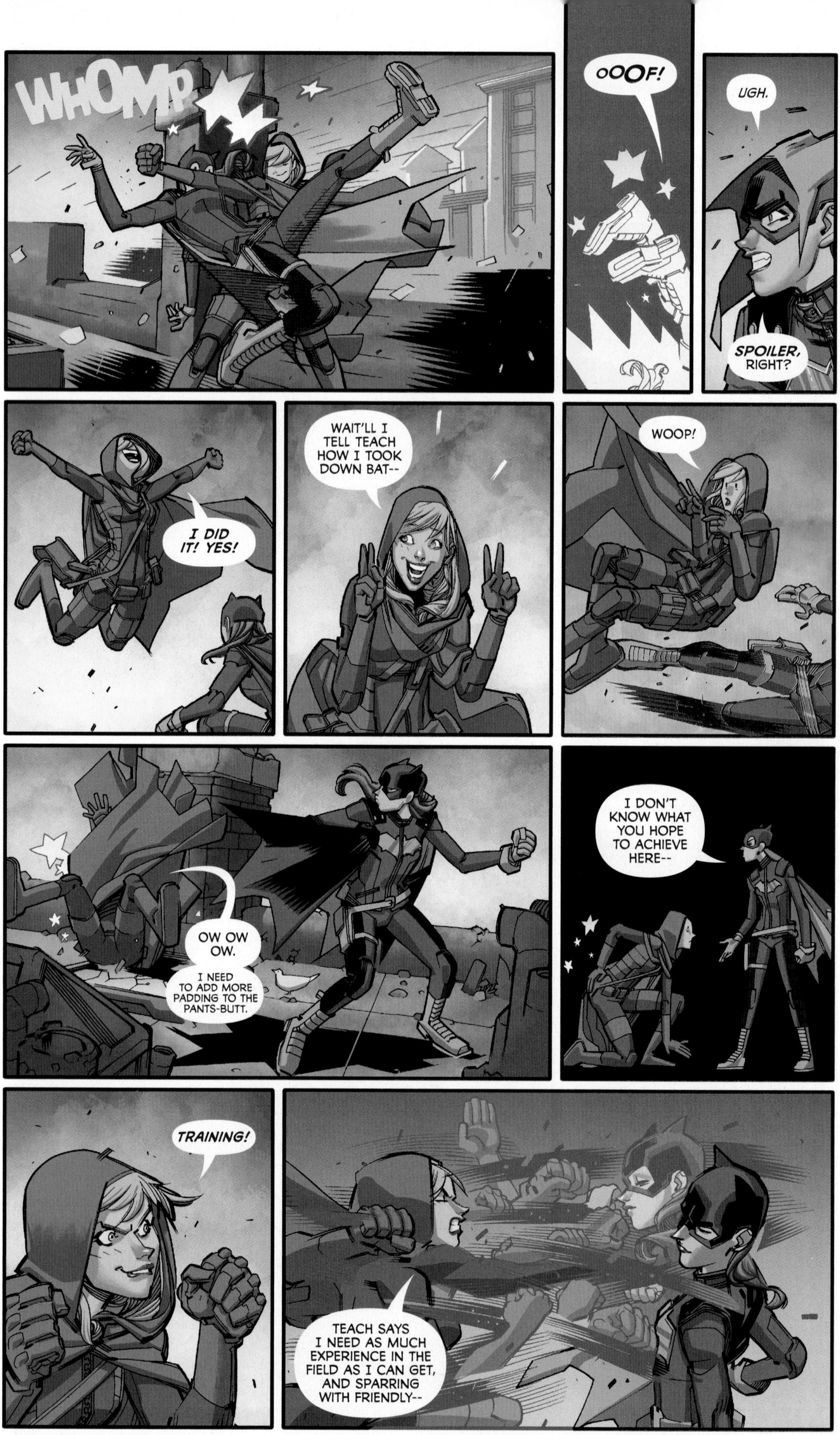
WHOMP
OOOF!
UGH.
SPOILER, RIGHT?
I DID IT! YES!
WAIT'LL I TELL TEACH HOW I TOOK DOWN BAT--
WOOP!
OW OW OW.
I NEED TO ADD MORE PADDING TO THE PANTS-BUTT.
I DON'T KNOW WHAT YOU HOPE TO ACHIEVE HERE--
TRAINING!
TEACH SAYS I NEED AS MUCH EXPERIENCE IN THE FIELD AS I CAN GET, AND SPARRING WITH FRIENDLY--

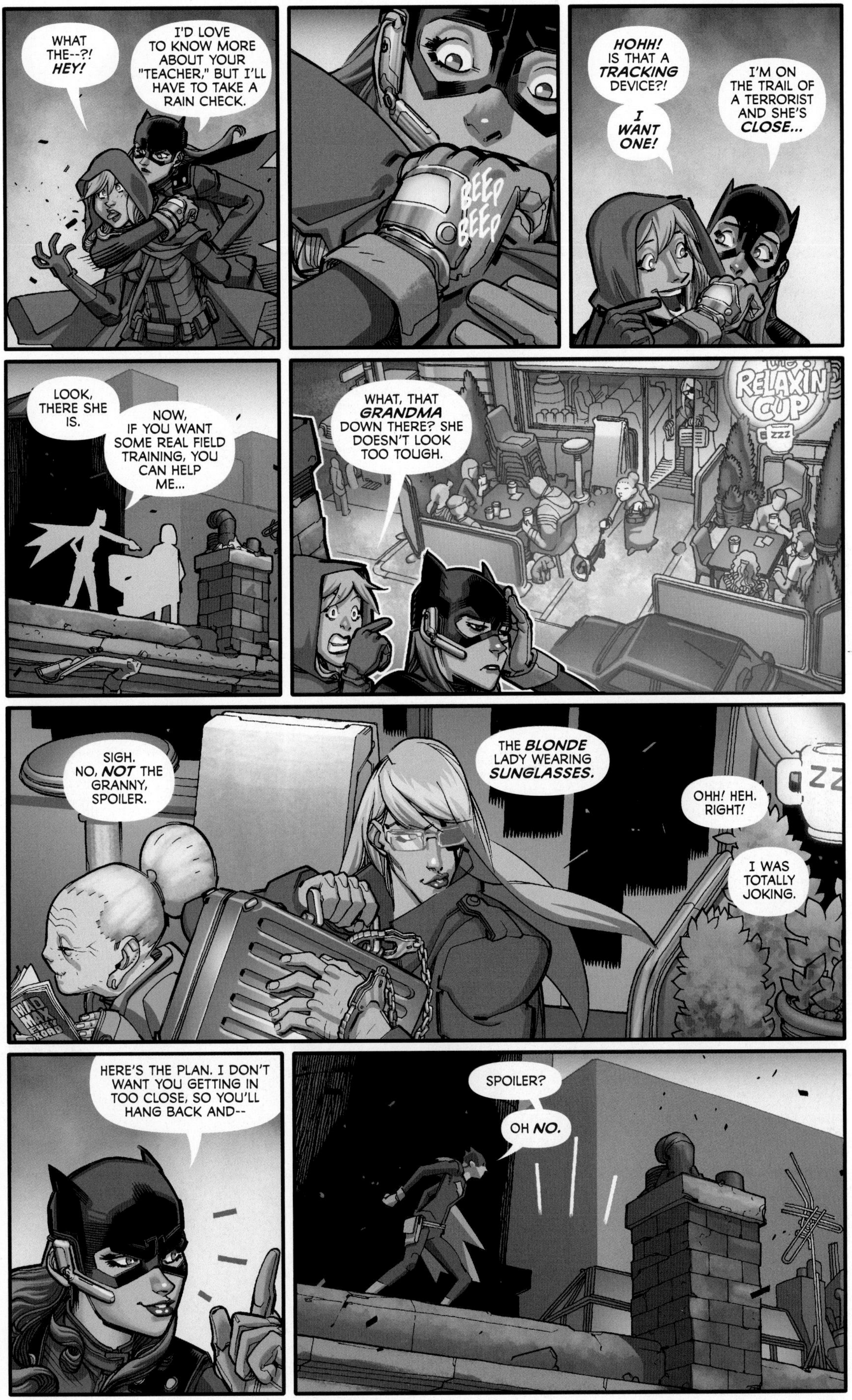
WHAT THE--?! HEY!
I'D LOVE TO KNOW MORE ABOUT YOUR "TEACHER," BUT I'LL HAVE TO TAKE A RAIN CHECK.
BEEP BEEP
HOHH! IS THAT A TRACKING DEVICE?!
I WANT ONE!
I'M ON THE TRAIL OF A TERRORIST AND SHE'S CLOSE...
LOOK, THERE SHE IS.
NOW, IF YOU WANT SOME REAL FIELD TRAINING, YOU CAN HELP ME...
WHAT, THAT GRANDMA DOWN THERE? SHE DOESN'T LOOK TOO TOUGH.
RELAXIN CUP
SIGH. NO, NOT THE GRANNY, SPOILER.
THE BLONDE LADY WEARING SUNGLASSES.
OHH! HEH. RIGHT!
I WAS TOTALLY JOKING.
HERE'S THE PLAN. I DON'T WANT YOU GETTING IN TOO CLOSE, SO YOU'LL HANG BACK AND--
SPOILER?
OH NO.

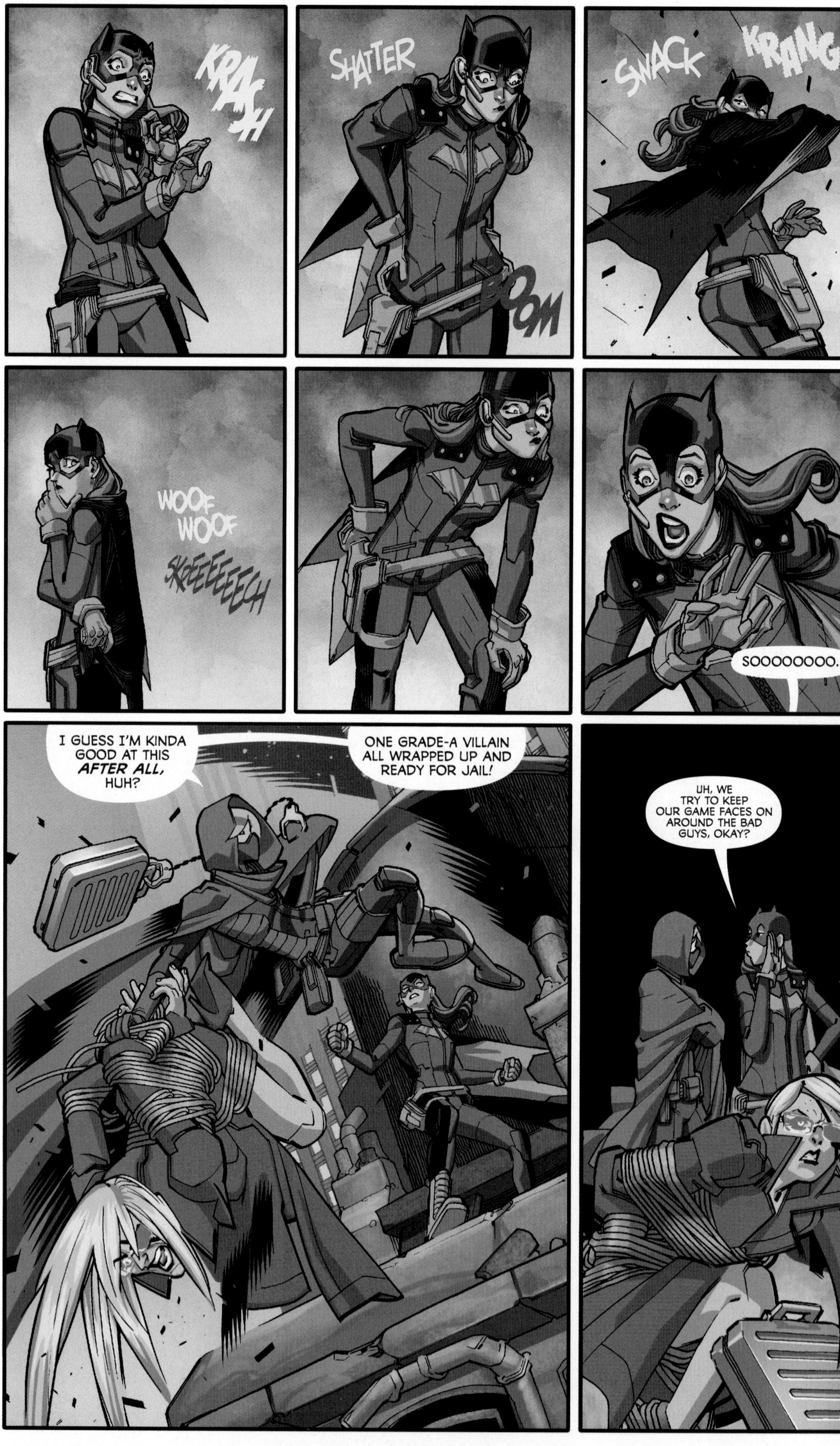
KRASH
SHATTER
BOOM
SWACK
KRANG
WOOF WOOF
SKREEEEEEECH
SOOOOOOOO...
I GUESS I'M KINDA GOOD AT THIS *AFTER ALL*, HUH?
ONE GRADE-A VILLAIN ALL WRAPPED UP AND READY FOR JAIL!
UH, WE TRY TO KEEP OUR GAME FACES ON AROUND THE BAD GUYS, OKAY?

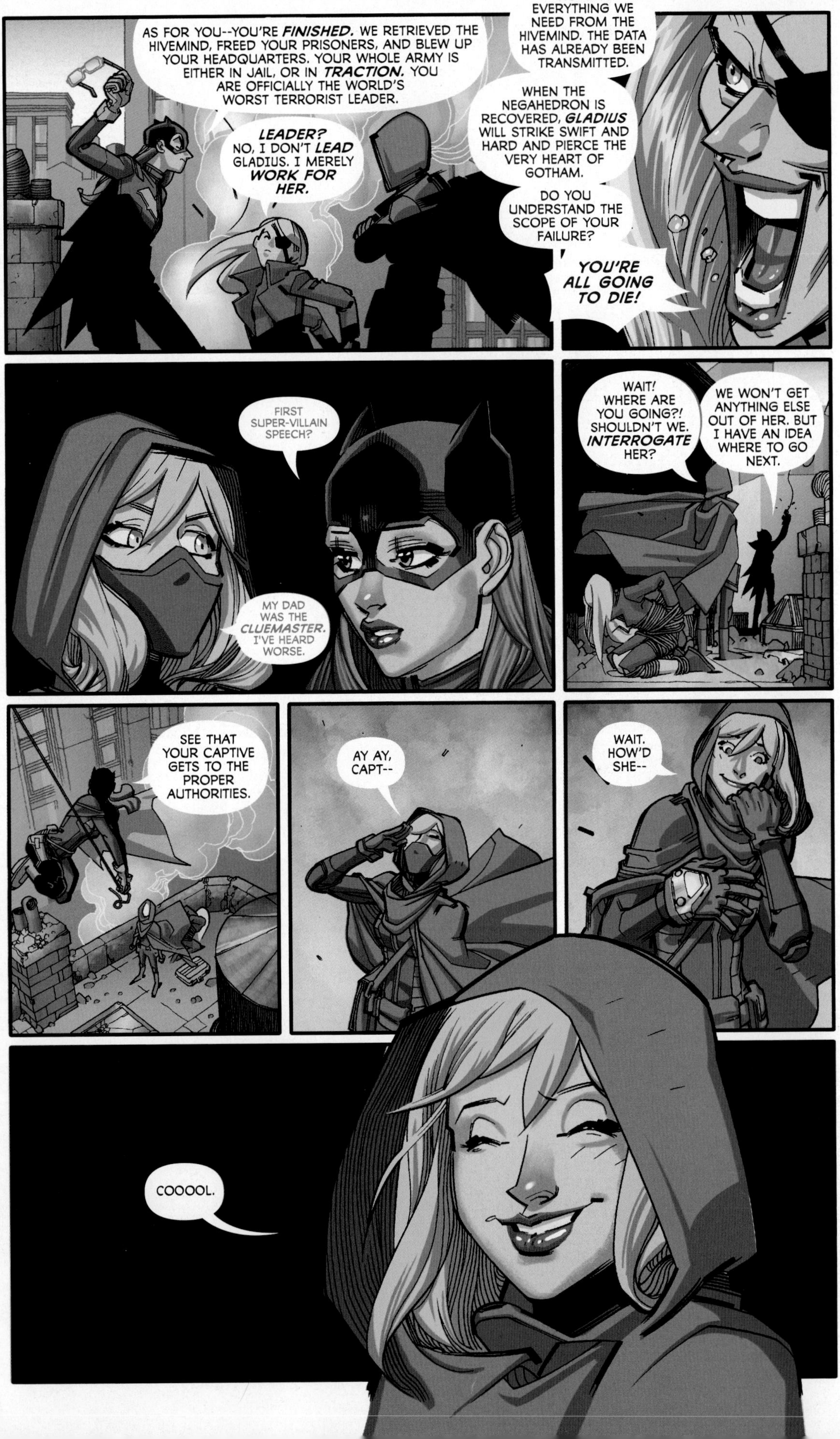
AS FOR YOU--YOU'RE FINISHED. WE RETRIEVED THE HIVEMIND, FREED YOUR PRISONERS, AND BLEW UP YOUR HEADQUARTERS. YOUR WHOLE ARMY IS EITHER IN JAIL, OR IN TRACTION. YOU ARE OFFICIALLY THE WORLD'S WORST TERRORIST LEADER.
LEADER? NO, I DON'T LEAD GLADIUS. I MERELY WORK FOR HER.
WE HAVE EVERYTHING WE NEED FROM THE HIVEMIND. THE DATA HAS ALREADY BEEN TRANSMITTED.
WHEN THE NEGAHEDRON IS RECOVERED, GLADIUS WILL STRIKE SWIFT AND HARD AND PIERCE THE VERY HEART OF GOTHAM.
DO YOU UNDERSTAND THE SCOPE OF YOUR FAILURE?
YOU'RE ALL GOING TO DIE!
FIRST SUPER-VILLAIN SPEECH?
MY DAD WAS THE CLUEMASTER. I'VE HEARD WORSE.
WAIT! WHERE ARE YOU GOING?! SHOULDN'T WE. INTERROGATE HER?
WE WON'T GET ANYTHING ELSE OUT OF HER. BUT I HAVE AN IDEA WHERE TO GO NEXT.
SEE THAT YOUR CAPTIVE GETS TO THE PROPER AUTHORITIES.
AY AY, CAPT--
WAIT. HOW'D SHE--
COOOOL.

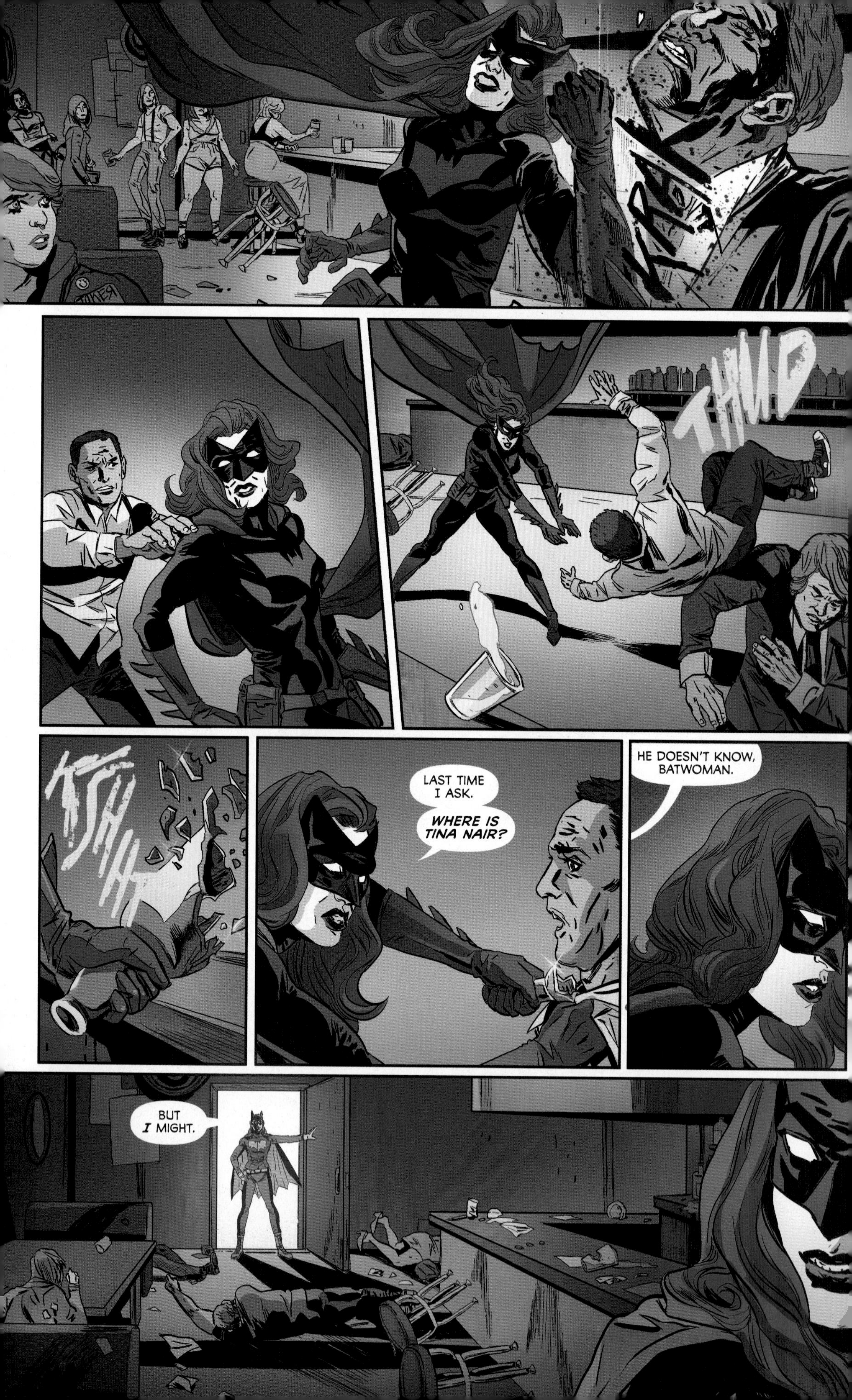
THUD
LAST TIME I ASK.
WHERE IS TINA NAIR?
HE DOESN'T KNOW, BATWOMAN.
BUT I MIGHT.

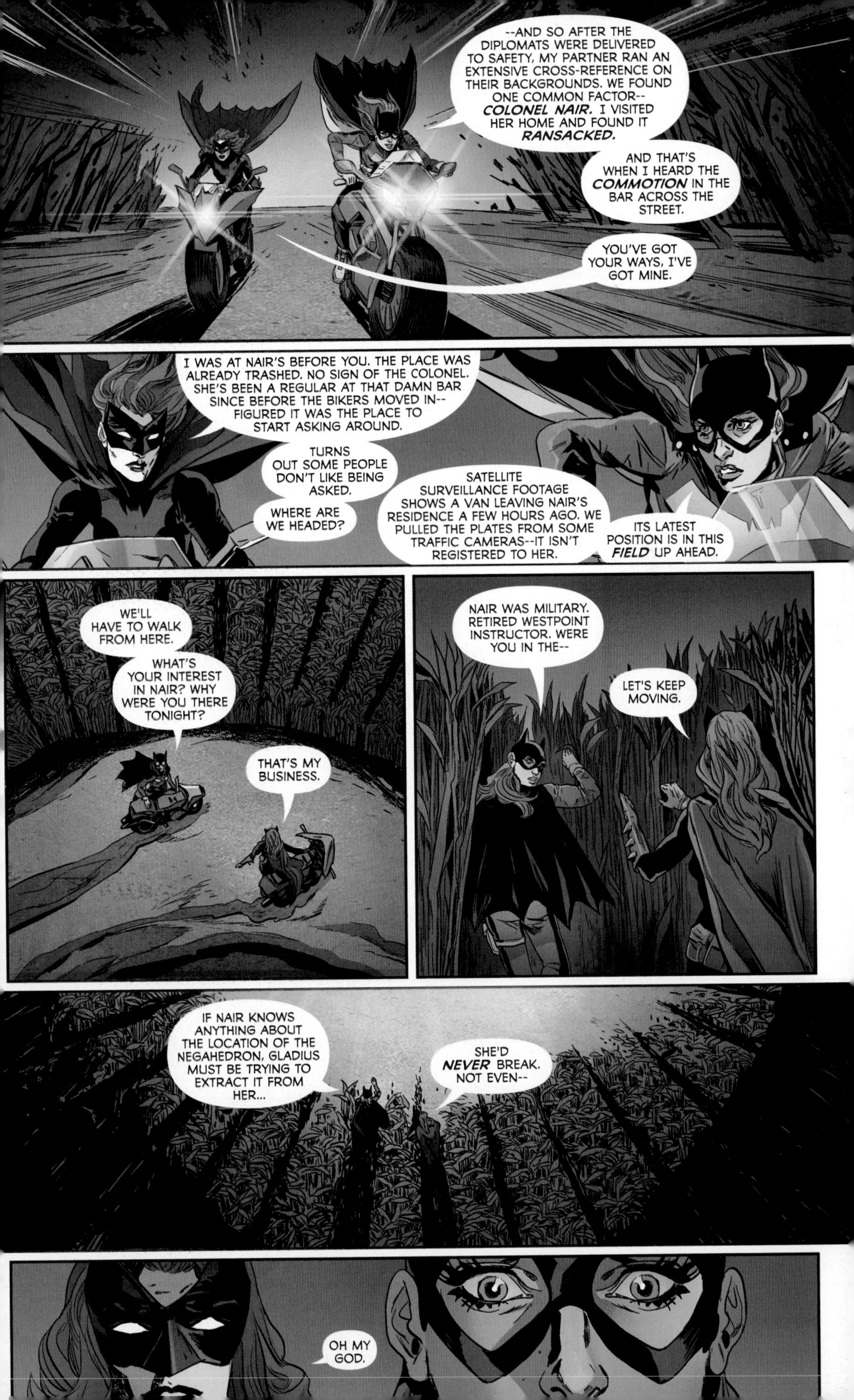

--AND SO AFTER THE DIPLOMATS WERE DELIVERED TO SAFETY, MY PARTNER RAN AN EXTENSIVE CROSS-REFERENCE ON THEIR BACKGROUNDS. WE FOUND ONE COMMON FACTOR-- COLONEL NAIR. I VISITED HER HOME AND FOUND IT RANSACKED.
AND THAT'S WHEN I HEARD THE COMMOTION IN THE BAR ACROSS THE STREET.
YOU'VE GOT YOUR WAYS, I'VE GOT MINE.
I WAS AT NAIR'S BEFORE YOU. THE PLACE WAS ALREADY TRASHED. NO SIGN OF THE COLONEL. SHE'S BEEN A REGULAR AT THAT DAMN BAR SINCE BEFORE THE BIKERS MOVED IN-- FIGURED IT WAS THE PLACE TO START ASKING AROUND.
TURNS OUT SOME PEOPLE DON'T LIKE BEING ASKED.
WHERE ARE WE HEADED?
SATELLITE SURVEILLANCE FOOTAGE SHOWS A VAN LEAVING NAIR'S RESIDENCE A FEW HOURS AGO. WE PULLED THE PLATES FROM SOME TRAFFIC CAMERAS--IT ISN'T REGISTERED TO HER.
ITS LATEST POSITION IS IN THIS FIELD UP AHEAD.
WE'LL HAVE TO WALK FROM HERE.
WHAT'S YOUR INTEREST IN NAIR? WHY WERE YOU THERE TONIGHT?
THAT'S MY BUSINESS.
NAIR WAS MILITARY. RETIRED WESTPOINT INSTRUCTOR. WERE YOU IN THE--
LET'S KEEP MOVING.
IF NAIR KNOWS ANYTHING ABOUT THE LOCATION OF THE NEGAHEDRON, GLADIUS MUST BE TRYING TO EXTRACT IT FROM HER...
SHE'D NEVER BREAK. NOT EVEN--
OH MY GOD.

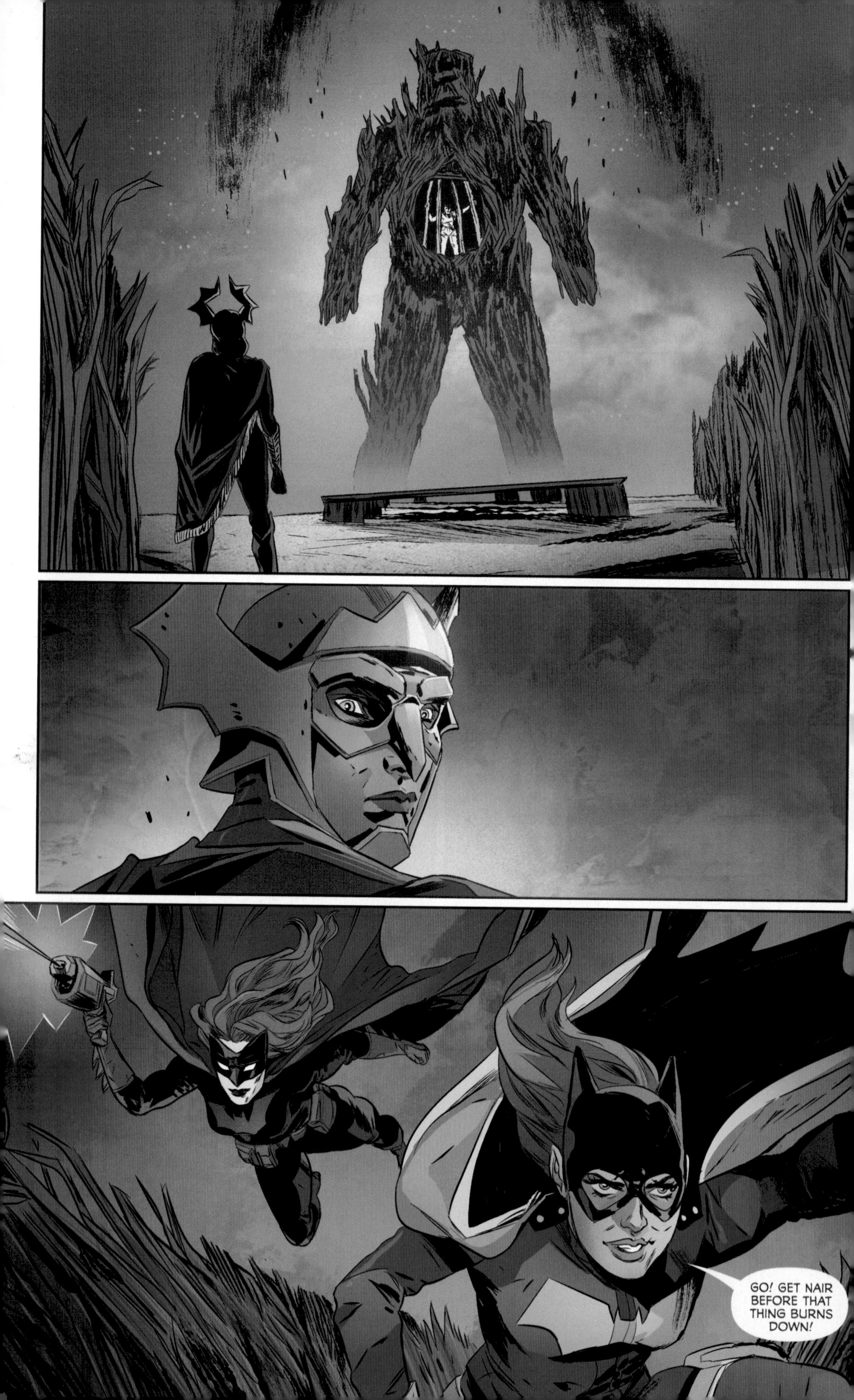
GO! GET NAIR BEFORE THAT THING BURNS DOWN!

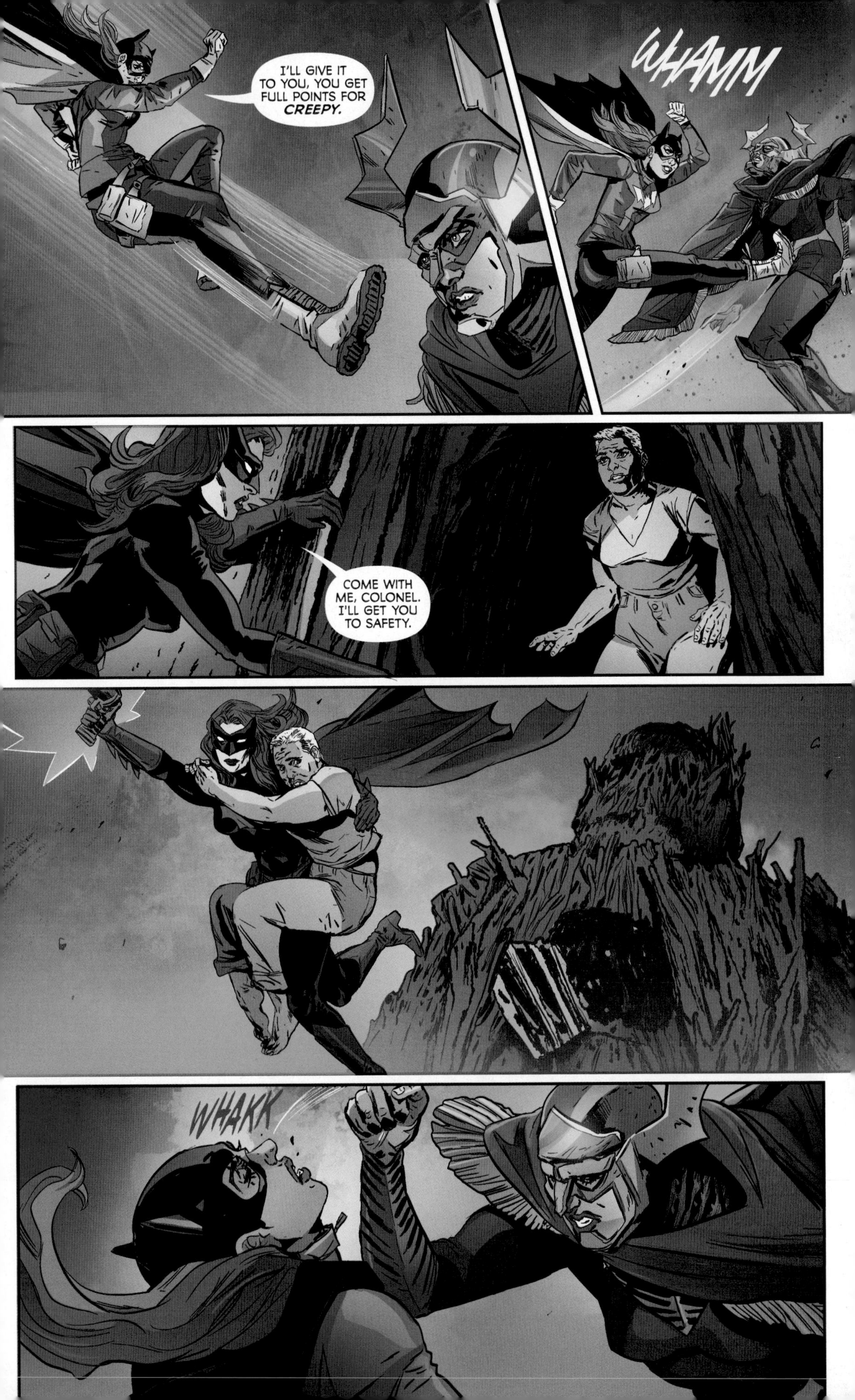
I'LL GIVE IT TO YOU, YOU GET FULL POINTS FOR *CREEPY.*
WHAMM
COME WITH ME, COLONEL. I'LL GET YOU TO SAFETY.
WHAKK

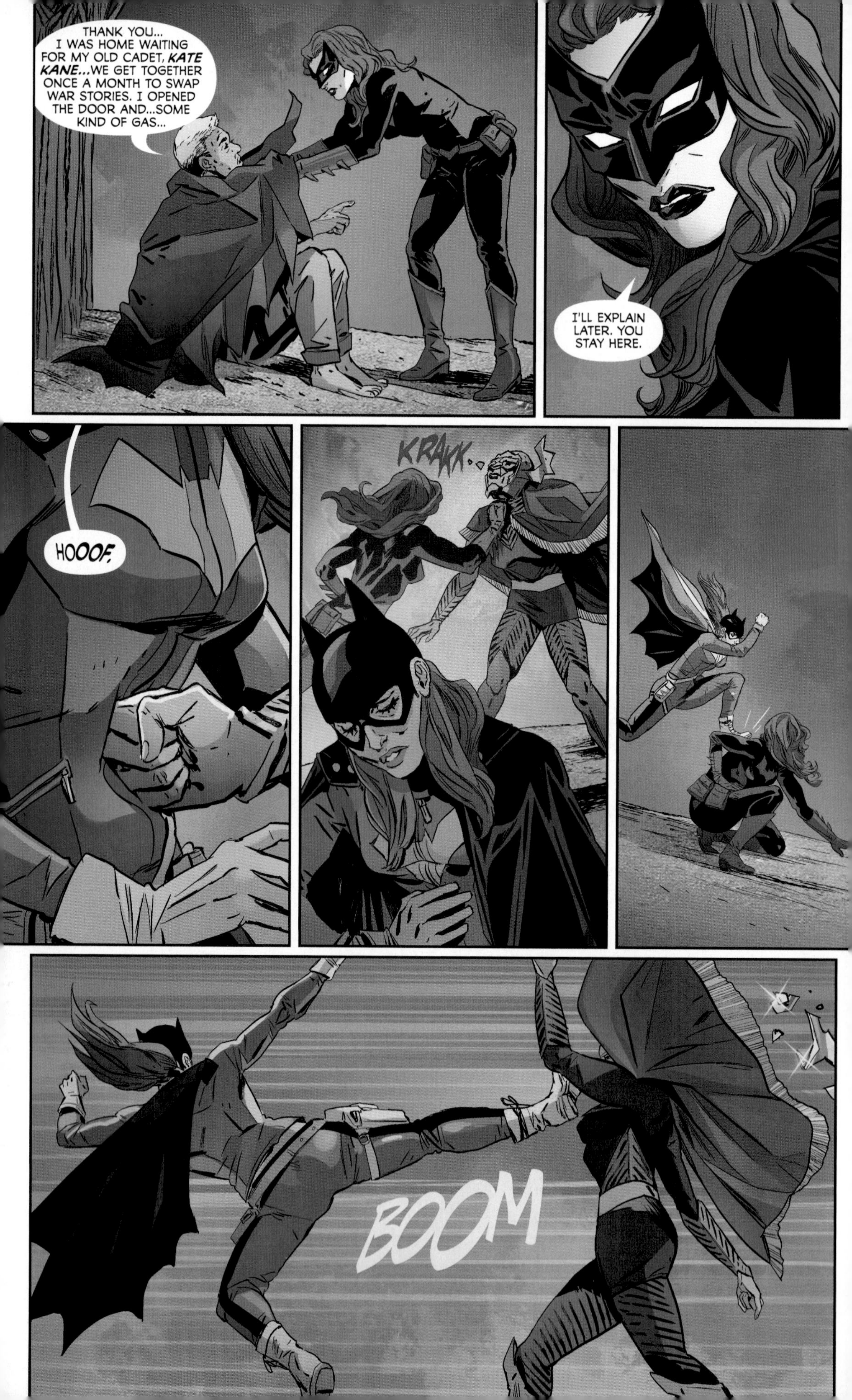
THANK YOU... I WAS HOME WAITING FOR MY OLD CADET, KATE KANE...WE GET TOGETHER ONCE A MONTH TO SWAP WAR STORIES. I OPENED THE DOOR AND...SOME KIND OF GAS...
I'LL EXPLAIN LATER. YOU STAY HERE.
HOOOF.
KRAKK
BOOM

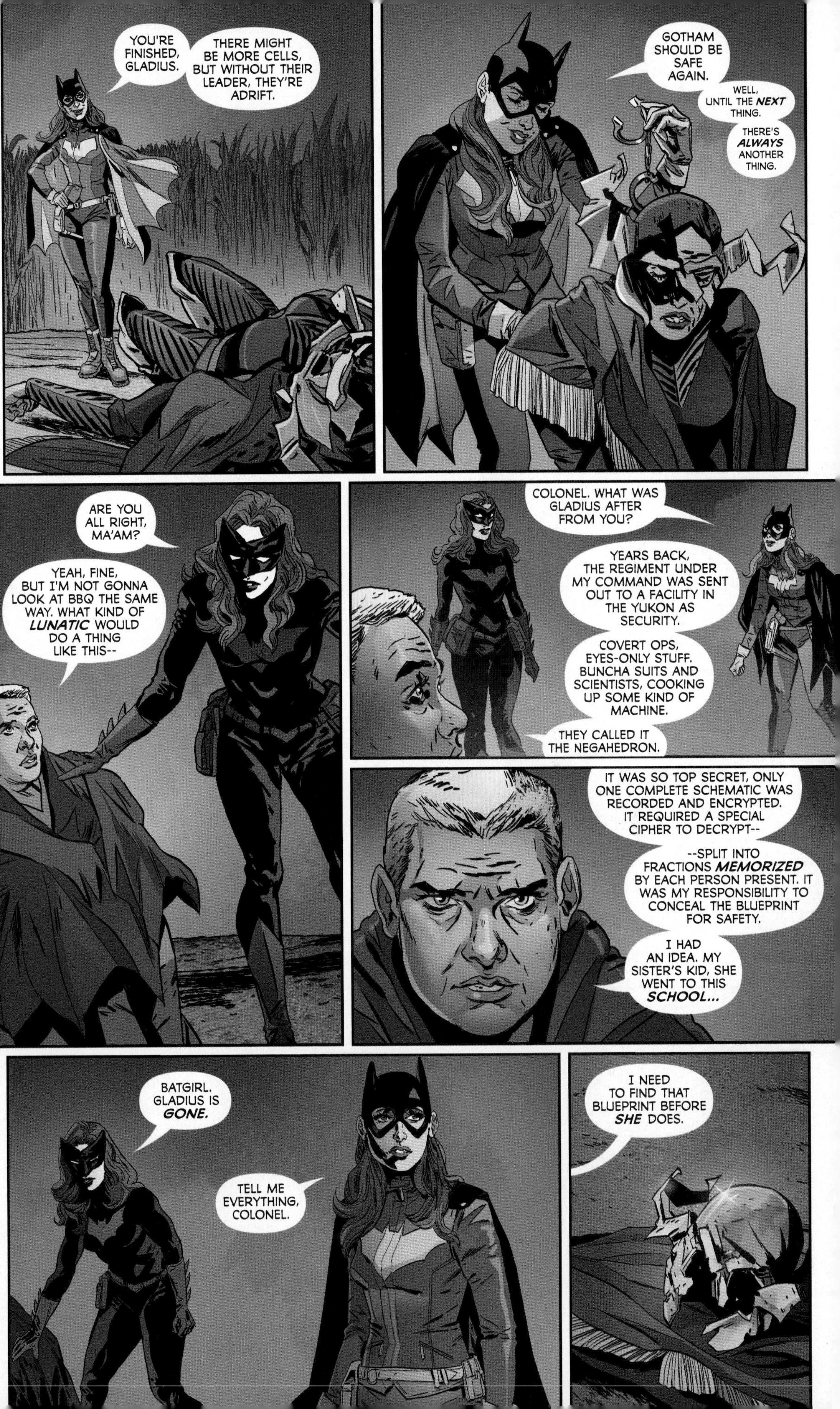
YOU'RE FINISHED, GLADIUS.
THERE MIGHT BE MORE CELLS, BUT WITHOUT THEIR LEADER, THEY'RE ADRIFT.
GOTHAM SHOULD BE SAFE AGAIN.
WELL, UNTIL THE NEXT THING.
THERE'S ALWAYS ANOTHER THING.
ARE YOU ALL RIGHT, MA'AM?
YEAH, FINE, BUT I'M NOT GONNA LOOK AT BBQ THE SAME WAY. WHAT KIND OF LUNATIC WOULD DO A THING LIKE THIS--
COLONEL. WHAT WAS GLADIUS AFTER FROM YOU?
YEARS BACK, THE REGIMENT UNDER MY COMMAND WAS SENT OUT TO A FACILITY IN THE YUKON AS SECURITY.
COVERT OPS, EYES-ONLY STUFF. BUNCHA SUITS AND SCIENTISTS, COOKING UP SOME KIND OF MACHINE.
THEY CALLED IT THE NEGAHEDRON.
IT WAS SO TOP SECRET, ONLY ONE COMPLETE SCHEMATIC WAS RECORDED AND ENCRYPTED. IT REQUIRED A SPECIAL CIPHER TO DECRYPT--
--SPLIT INTO FRACTIONS MEMORIZED BY EACH PERSON PRESENT. IT WAS MY RESPONSIBILITY TO CONCEAL THE BLUEPRINT FOR SAFETY.
I HAD AN IDEA. MY SISTER'S KID, SHE WENT TO THIS SCHOOL...
BATGIRL. GLADIUS IS GONE.
TELL ME EVERYTHING, COLONEL.
I NEED TO FIND THAT BLUEPRINT BEFORE SHE DOES.

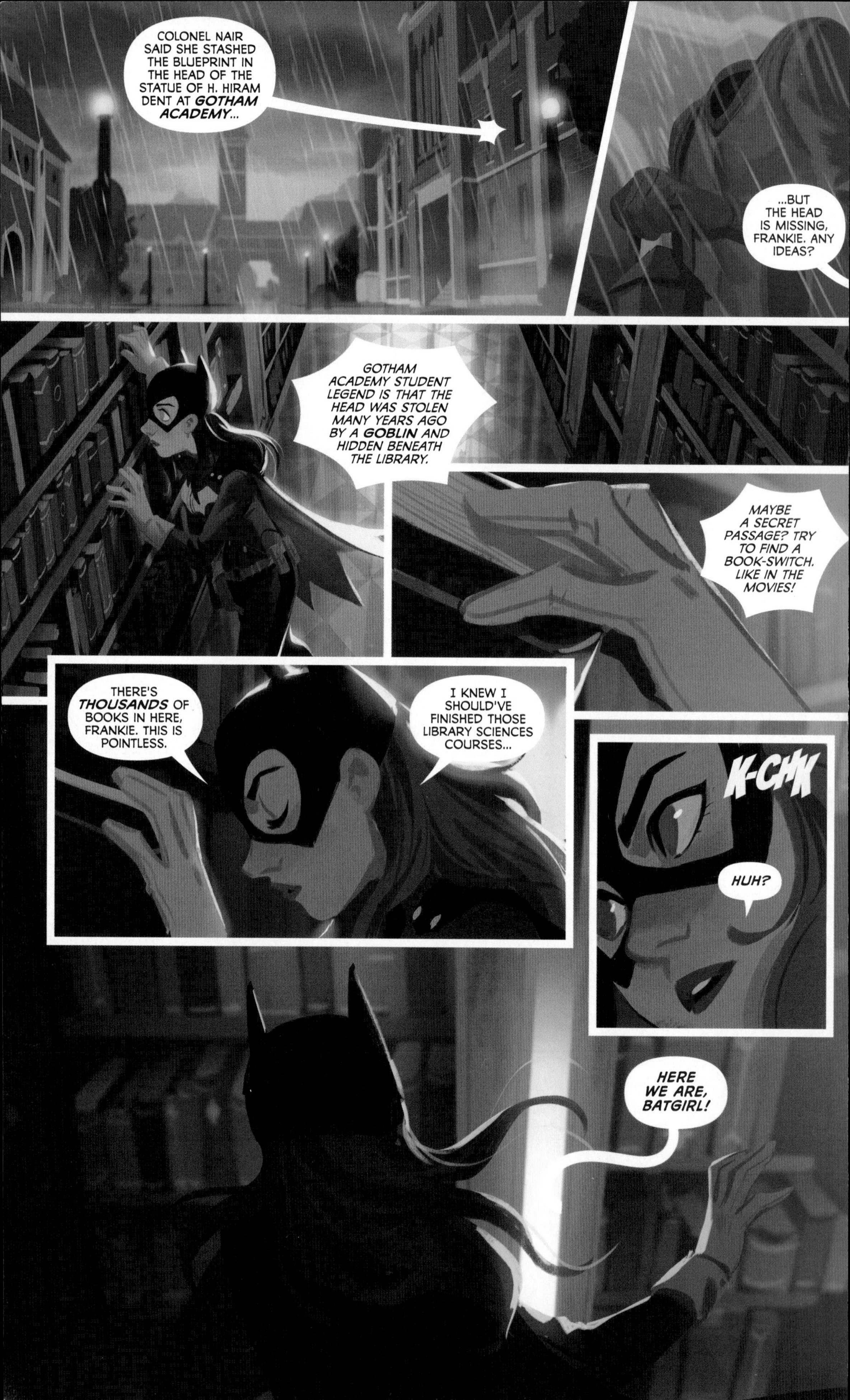
COLONEL NAIR SAID SHE STASHED THE BLUEPRINT IN THE HEAD OF THE STATUE OF H. HIRAM DENT AT GOTHAM ACADEMY...
...BUT THE HEAD IS MISSING, FRANKIE. ANY IDEAS?
GOTHAM ACADEMY STUDENT LEGEND IS THAT THE HEAD WAS STOLEN MANY YEARS AGO BY A GOBLIN AND HIDDEN BENEATH THE LIBRARY.
MAYBE A SECRET PASSAGE? TRY TO FIND A BOOK-SWITCH. LIKE IN THE MOVIES!
THERE'S THOUSANDS OF BOOKS IN HERE, FRANKIE. THIS IS POINTLESS.
I KNEW I SHOULD'VE FINISHED THOSE LIBRARY SCIENCES COURSES...
K-CHK
HUH?
HERE WE ARE, BATGIRL!

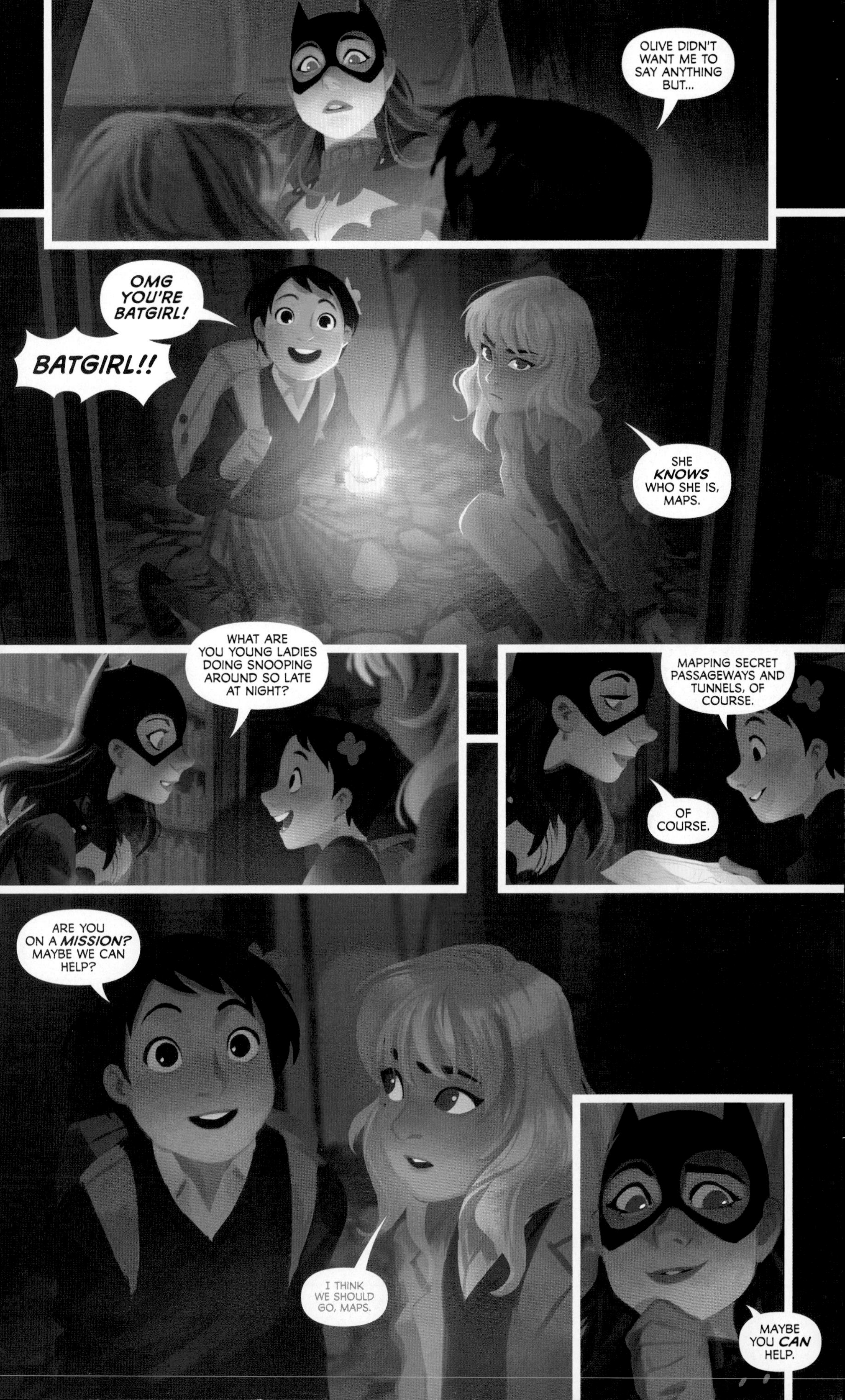
OLIVE DIDN'T WANT ME TO SAY ANYTHING BUT...
OMG YOU'RE BATGIRL!
BATGIRL!!
SHE KNOWS WHO SHE IS, MAPS.
WHAT ARE YOU YOUNG LADIES DOING SNOOPING AROUND SO LATE AT NIGHT?
MAPPING SECRET PASSAGEWAYS AND TUNNELS, OF COURSE.
OF COURSE.
ARE YOU ON A MISSION? MAYBE WE CAN HELP?
I THINK WE SHOULD GO, MAPS.
MAYBE YOU CAN HELP.

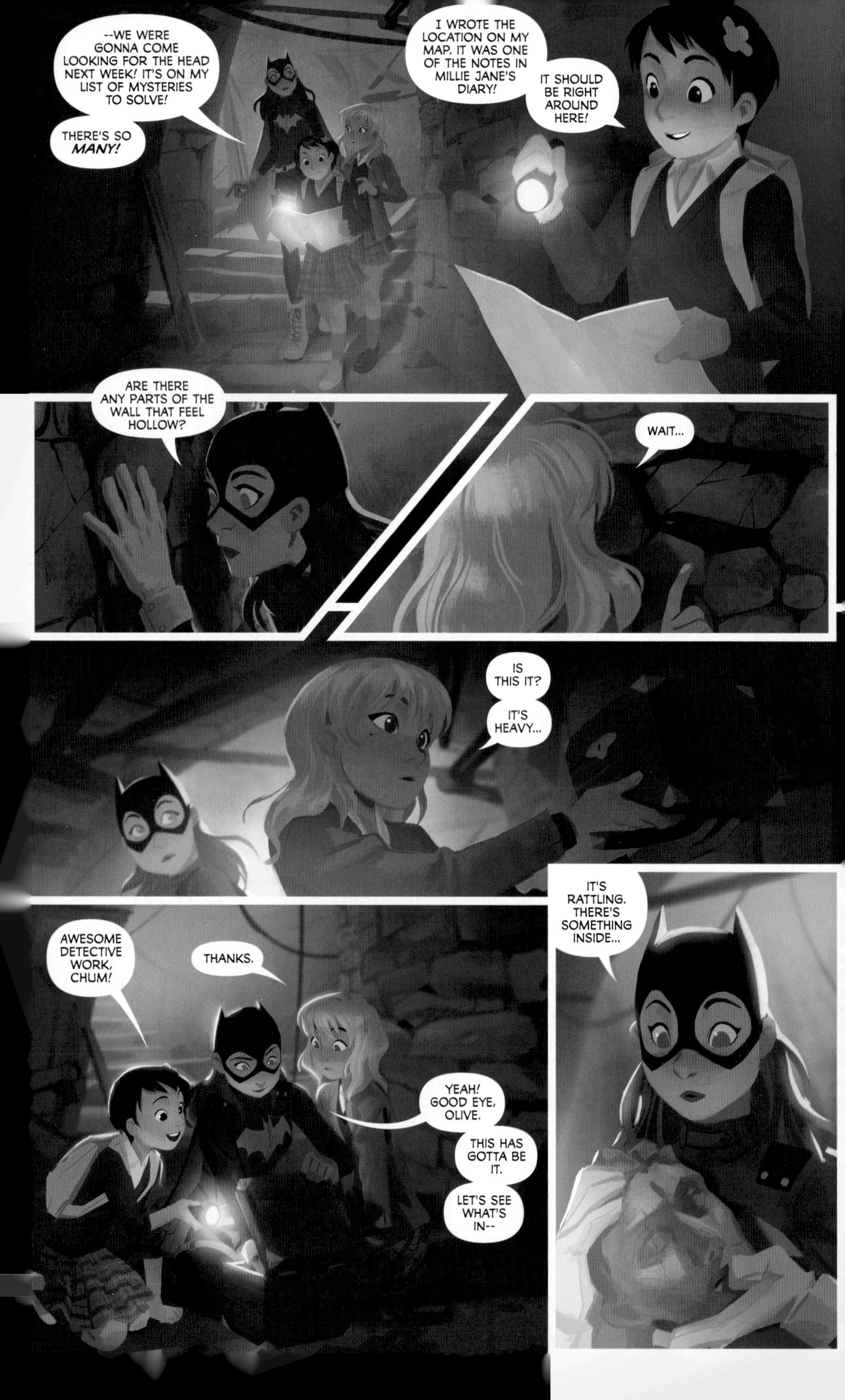
--WE WERE GONNA COME LOOKING FOR THE HEAD NEXT WEEK! IT'S ON MY LIST OF MYSTERIES TO SOLVE!
THERE'S SO *MANY!*
I WROTE THE LOCATION ON MY MAP. IT WAS ONE OF THE NOTES IN MILLIE JANE'S DIARY!
IT SHOULD BE RIGHT AROUND HERE!
ARE THERE ANY PARTS OF THE WALL THAT FEEL HOLLOW?
WAIT...
IS THIS IT?
IT'S HEAVY...
AWESOME DETECTIVE WORK, CHUM!
THANKS.
YEAH! GOOD EYE, OLIVE.
THIS HAS GOTTA BE IT.
LET'S SEE WHAT'S IN--
IT'S RATTLING. THERE'S SOMETHING INSIDE...

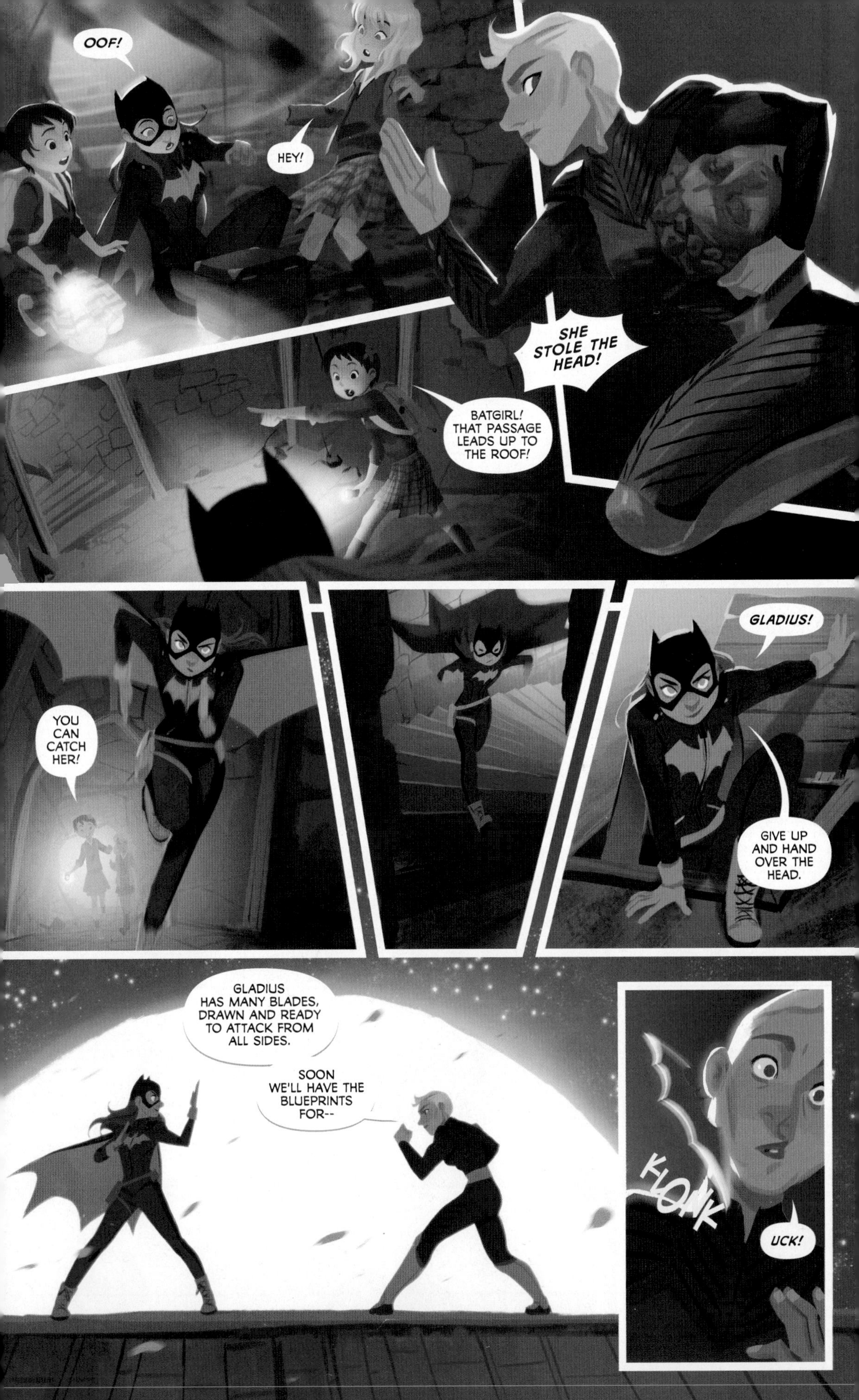
OOF!
HEY!
SHE STOLE THE HEAD!
BATGIRL! THAT PASSAGE LEADS UP TO THE ROOF!
YOU CAN CATCH HER!
GLADIUS!
GIVE UP AND HAND OVER THE HEAD.
GLADIUS HAS MANY BLADES, DRAWN AND READY TO ATTACK FROM ALL SIDES.
SOON WE'LL HAVE THE BLUEPRINTS FOR--
KLONK
UCK!

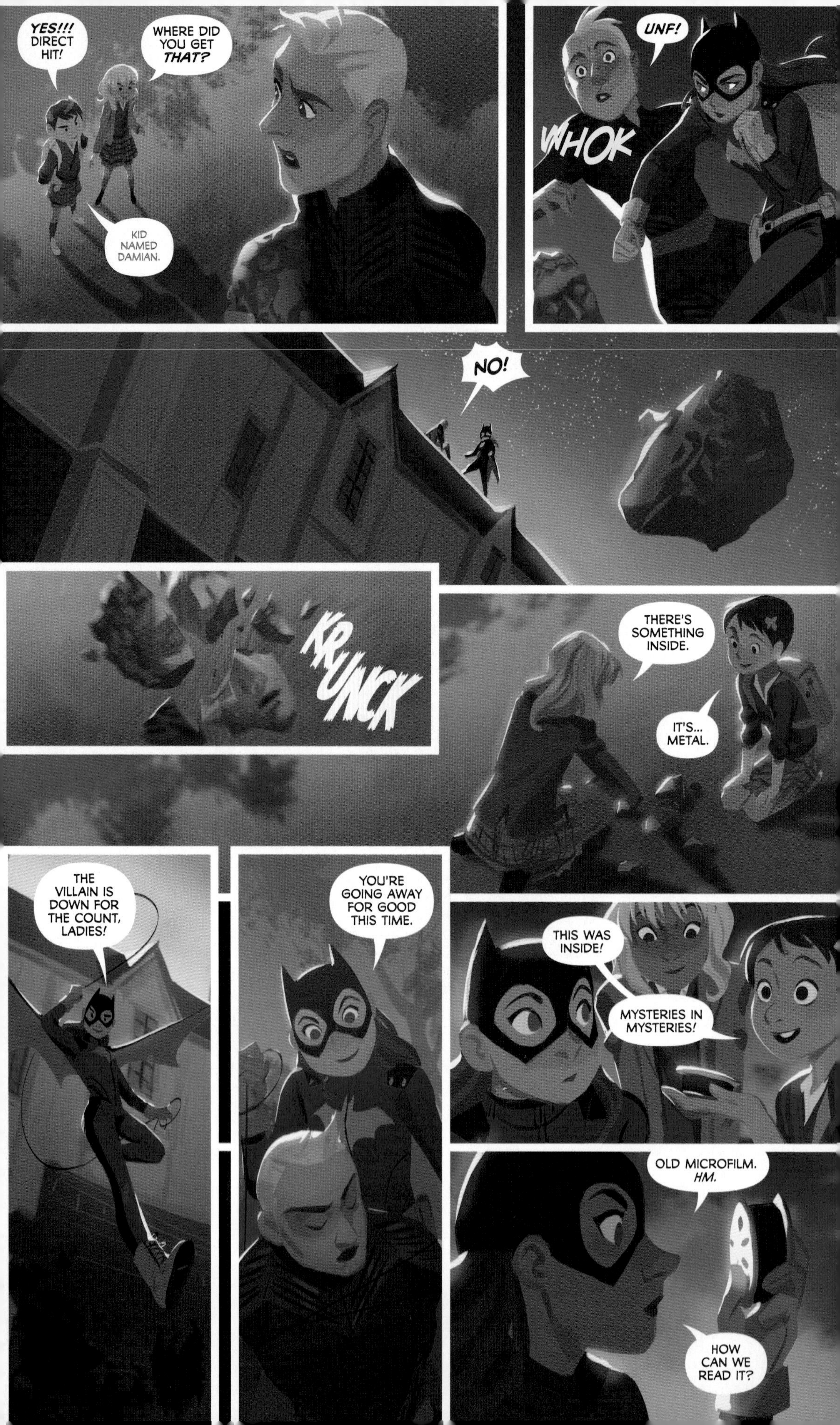
YES!!! DIRECT HIT!
WHERE DID YOU GET THAT?
KID NAMED DAMIAN.
UNF!
WHOK
NO!
KRUNCK
THERE'S SOMETHING INSIDE.
IT'S... METAL.
THE VILLAIN IS DOWN FOR THE COUNT, LADIES!
YOU'RE GOING AWAY FOR GOOD THIS TIME.
THIS WAS INSIDE!
MYSTERIES IN MYSTERIES!
OLD MICROFILM. HM.
HOW CAN WE READ IT?

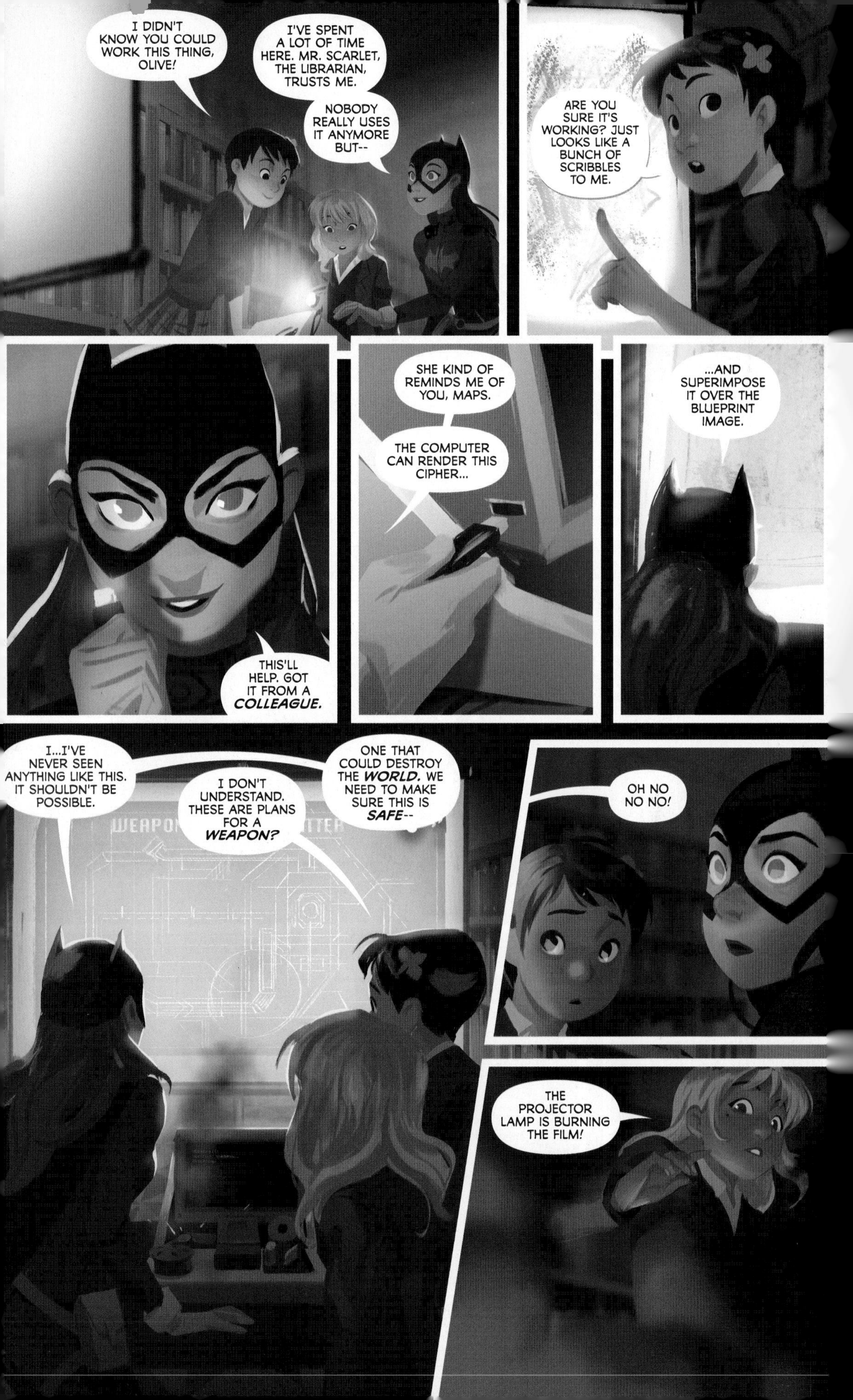
I DIDN'T KNOW YOU COULD WORK THIS THING, OLIVE!
I'VE SPENT A LOT OF TIME HERE. MR. SCARLET, THE LIBRARIAN, TRUSTS ME.
NOBODY REALLY USES IT ANYMORE BUT--
ARE YOU SURE IT'S WORKING? JUST LOOKS LIKE A BUNCH OF SCRIBBLES TO ME.
THIS'LL HELP. GOT IT FROM A *COLLEAGUE.*
SHE KIND OF REMINDS ME OF YOU, MAPS.
THE COMPUTER CAN RENDER THIS CIPHER...
...AND SUPERIMPOSE IT OVER THE BLUEPRINT IMAGE.
I...I'VE NEVER SEEN ANYTHING LIKE THIS. IT SHOULDN'T BE POSSIBLE.
I DON'T UNDERSTAND. THESE ARE PLANS FOR A *WEAPON?*
ONE THAT COULD DESTROY THE *WORLD.* WE NEED TO MAKE SURE THIS IS *SAFE*--
OH NO NO NO!
THE PROJECTOR LAMP IS BURNING THE FILM!

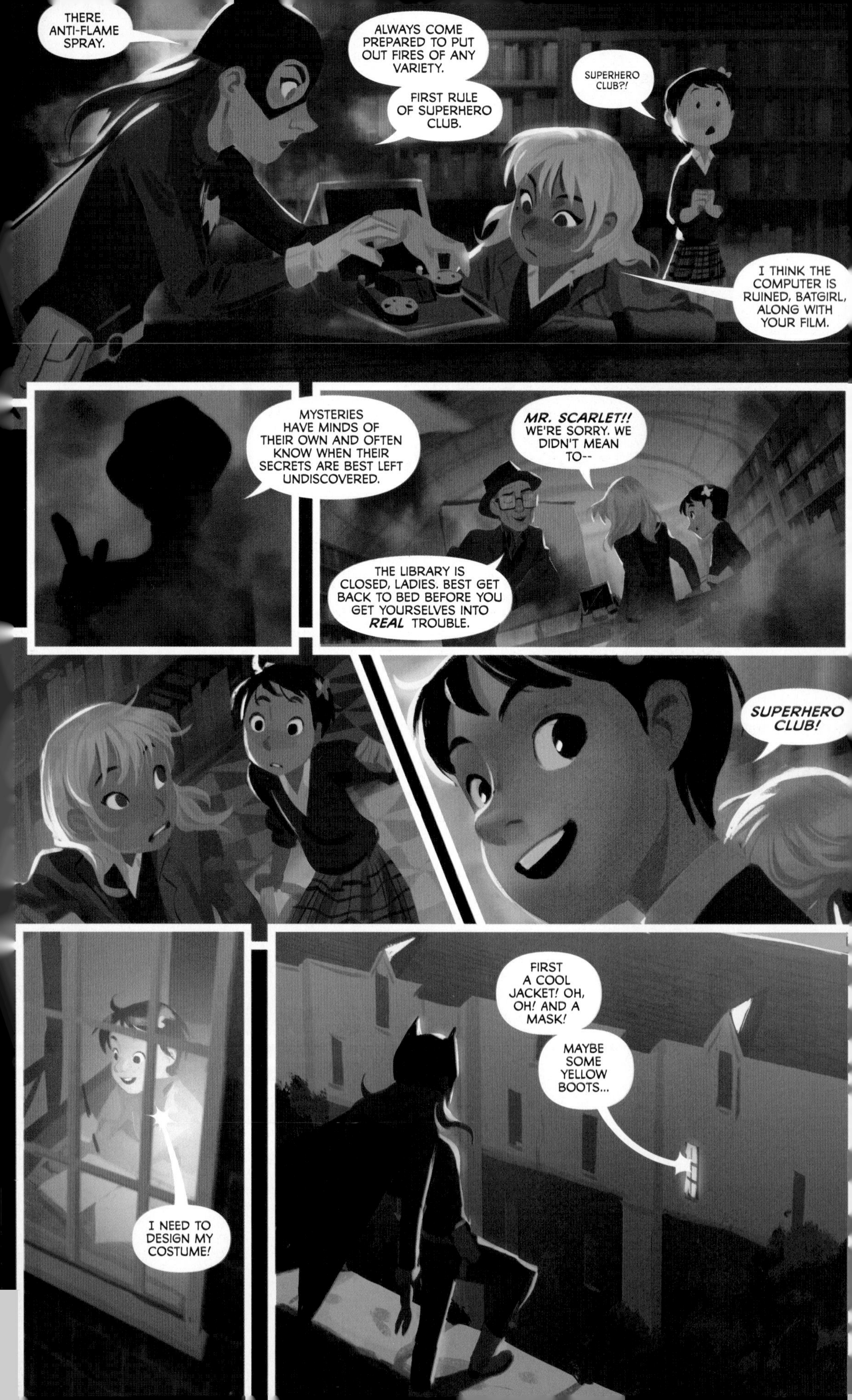
THERE. ANTI-FLAME SPRAY.
ALWAYS COME PREPARED TO PUT OUT FIRES OF ANY VARIETY.
FIRST RULE OF SUPERHERO CLUB.
SUPERHERO CLUB?!
I THINK THE COMPUTER IS RUINED, BATGIRL, ALONG WITH YOUR FILM.
MYSTERIES HAVE MINDS OF THEIR OWN AND OFTEN KNOW WHEN THEIR SECRETS ARE BEST LEFT UNDISCOVERED.
MR. SCARLET!! WE'RE SORRY. WE DIDN'T MEAN TO--
THE LIBRARY IS CLOSED, LADIES. BEST GET BACK TO BED BEFORE YOU GET YOURSELVES INTO REAL TROUBLE.
SUPERHERO CLUB!
I NEED TO DESIGN MY COSTUME!
FIRST A COOL JACKET! OH, OH! AND A MASK!
MAYBE SOME YELLOW BOOTS...

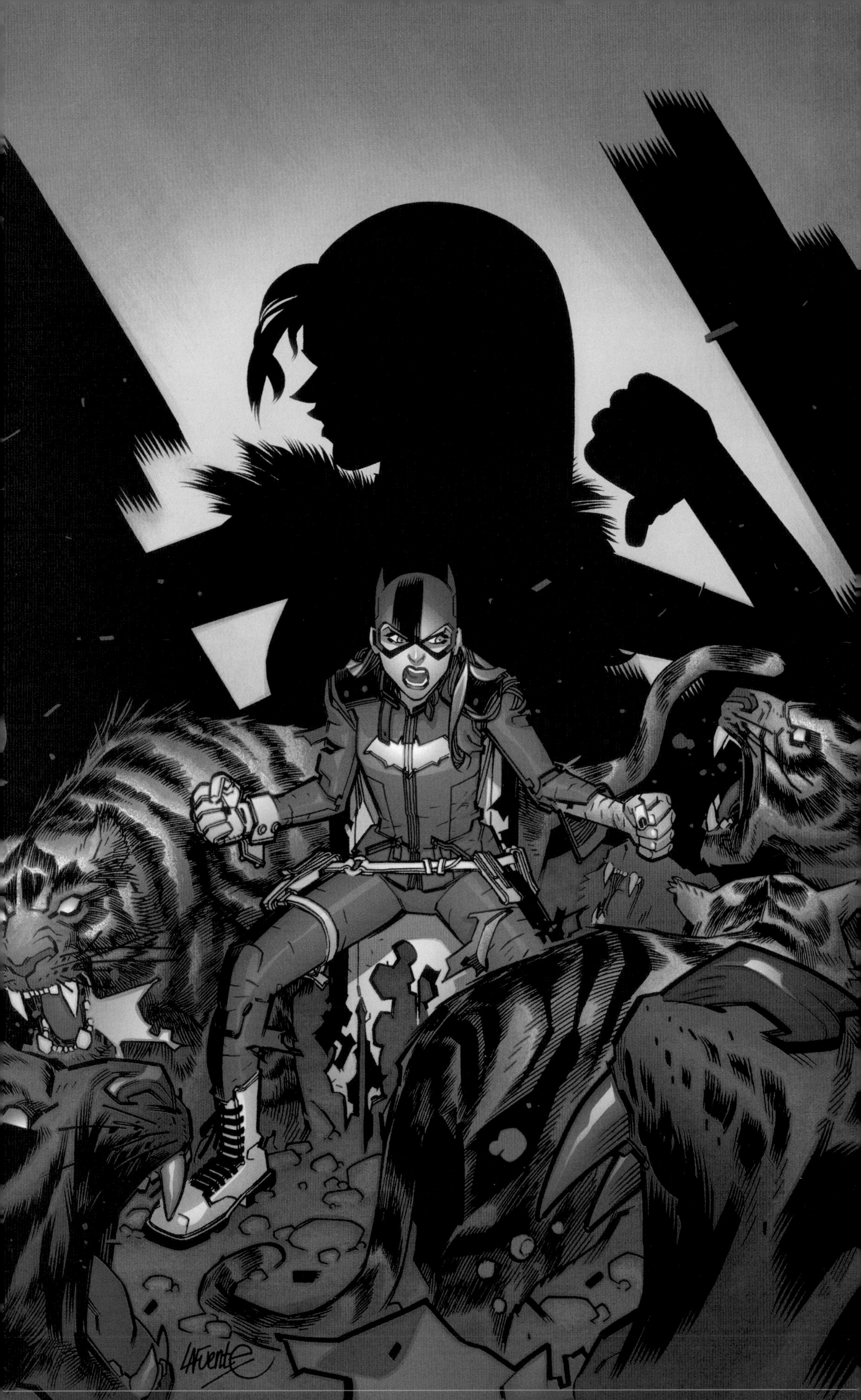

TOOTH AND CLAW

CAMERON STEWART & BRENDEN FLETCHER writers BABS TARR artist JUAN CASTRO additional inks
BABS TARR MICHEL LACOMBE breakdown artists SERGE LAPOINTE colorist STEVE WANDS letterer cover by DAVID LAFUENTE & JOHN RAUCH

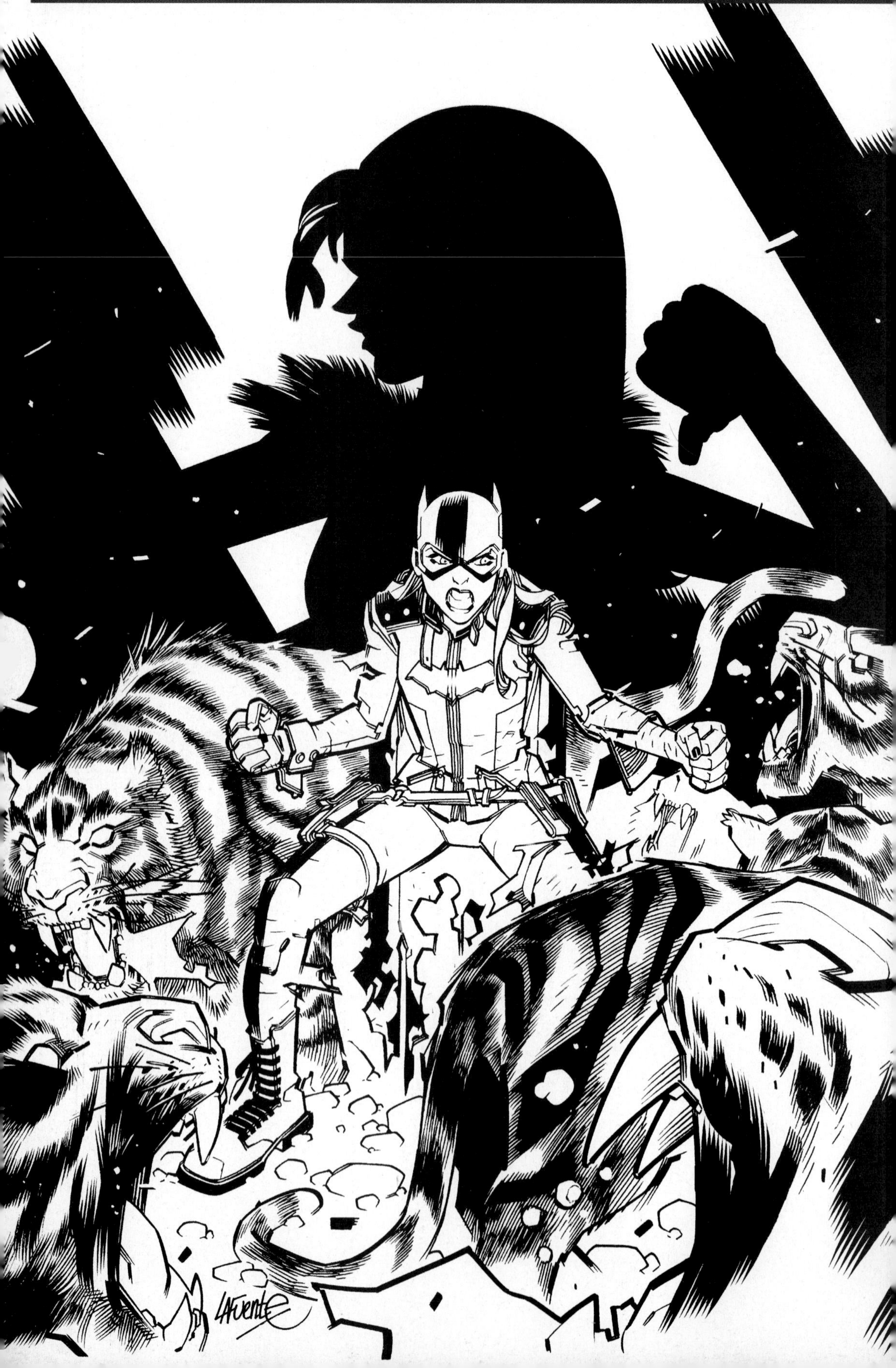

TOOTH AND CLAW

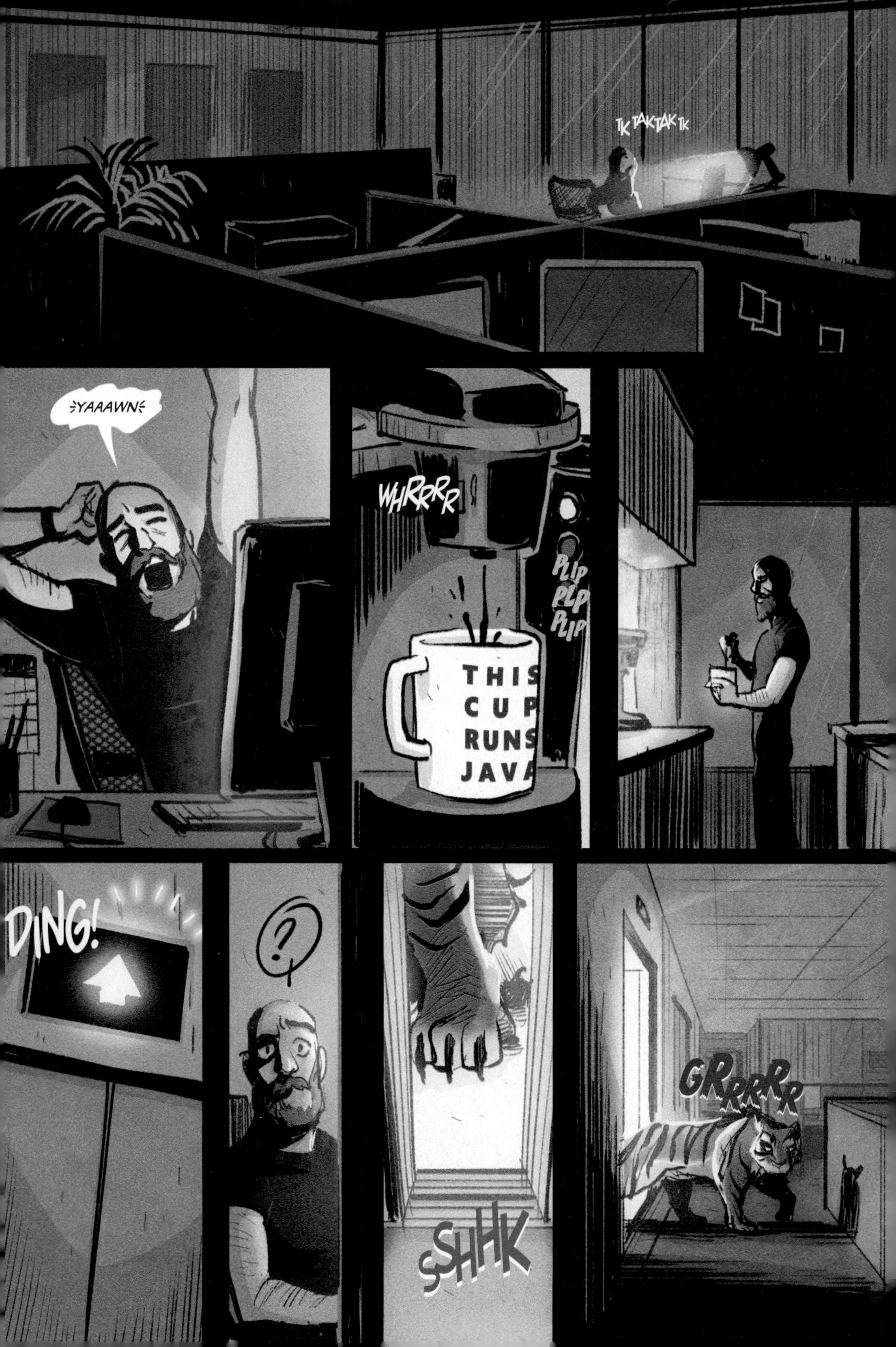

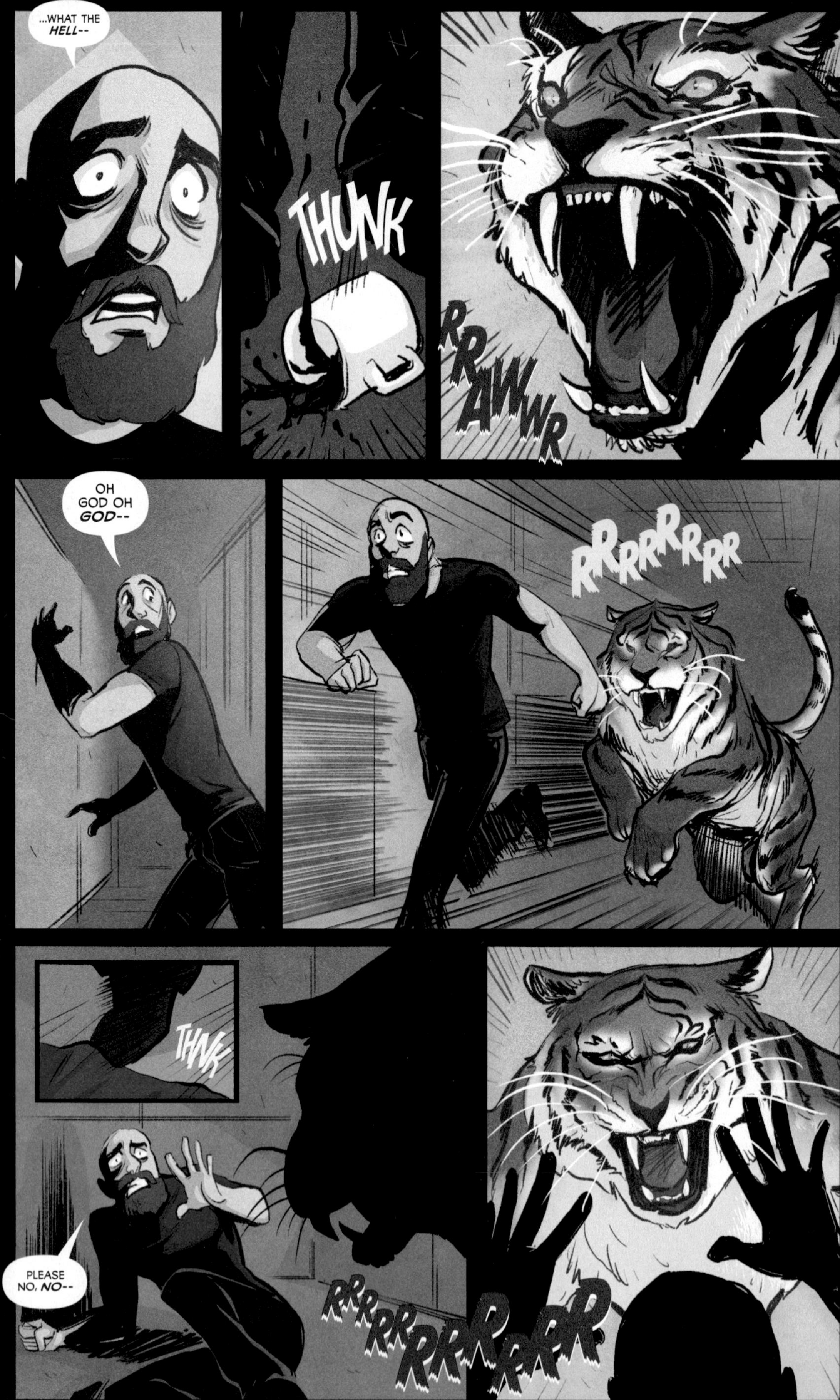
...WHAT THE HELL--
THUNK
RRAWWR
OH GOD OH GOD--
RRRRRRRRR
THNK
PLEASE NO, NO--
RRRRRRRRRRRR

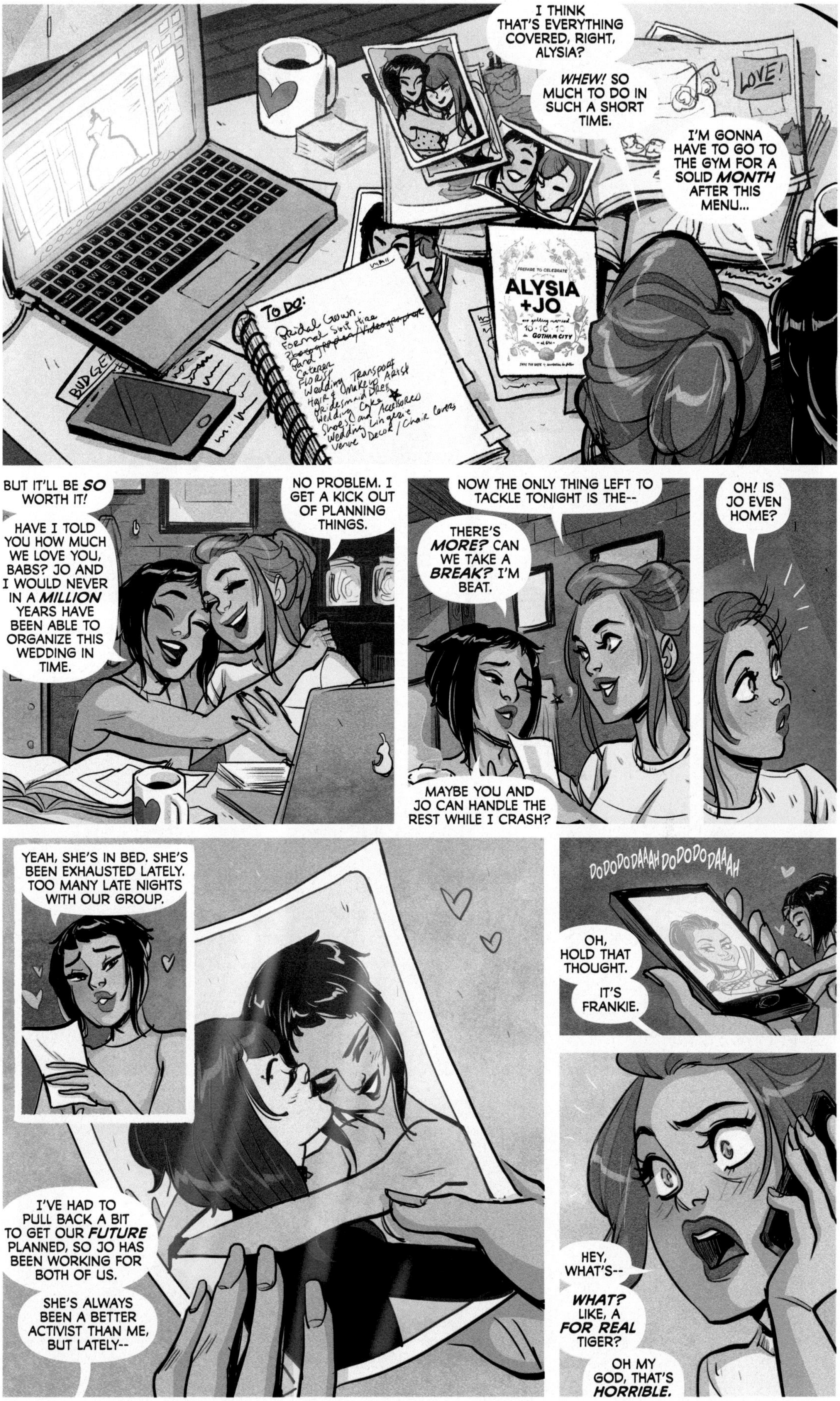
I THINK THAT'S EVERYTHING COVERED, RIGHT, ALYSIA?
WHEW! SO MUCH TO DO IN SUCH A SHORT TIME.
I'M GONNA HAVE TO GO TO THE GYM FOR A SOLID *MONTH* AFTER THIS MENU...
LOVE!
BUDGET
TO DO:
Bridal Gown
Formal Suit Hire
Band
Caterer
Florist
Wedding Transport
Hair & Makeup Artist
Bridesmaid Dress
Wedding Cake
Shoes and Accessories
Wedding Lingerie
Venue Decor / Chair Covers
PREPARE TO CELEBRATE
ALYSIA +JO
GOTHAM CITY
BUT IT'LL BE *SO* WORTH IT!
HAVE I TOLD YOU HOW MUCH WE LOVE YOU, BABS? JO AND I WOULD NEVER IN A *MILLION* YEARS HAVE BEEN ABLE TO ORGANIZE THIS WEDDING IN TIME.
NO PROBLEM. I GET A KICK OUT OF PLANNING THINGS.
NOW THE ONLY THING LEFT TO TACKLE TONIGHT IS THE--
THERE'S *MORE?* CAN WE TAKE A *BREAK?* I'M BEAT.
MAYBE YOU AND JO CAN HANDLE THE REST WHILE I CRASH?
OH! IS JO EVEN HOME?
YEAH, SHE'S IN BED. SHE'S BEEN EXHAUSTED LATELY. TOO MANY LATE NIGHTS WITH OUR GROUP.
I'VE HAD TO PULL BACK A BIT TO GET OUR *FUTURE* PLANNED, SO JO HAS BEEN WORKING FOR BOTH OF US.
SHE'S ALWAYS BEEN A BETTER ACTIVIST THAN ME, BUT LATELY--
DODODODAAAH DODODODAAAH
OH, HOLD THAT THOUGHT.
IT'S FRANKIE.
HEY, WHAT'S--
WHAT? LIKE, A *FOR REAL* TIGER?
OH MY GOD, THAT'S *HORRIBLE.*

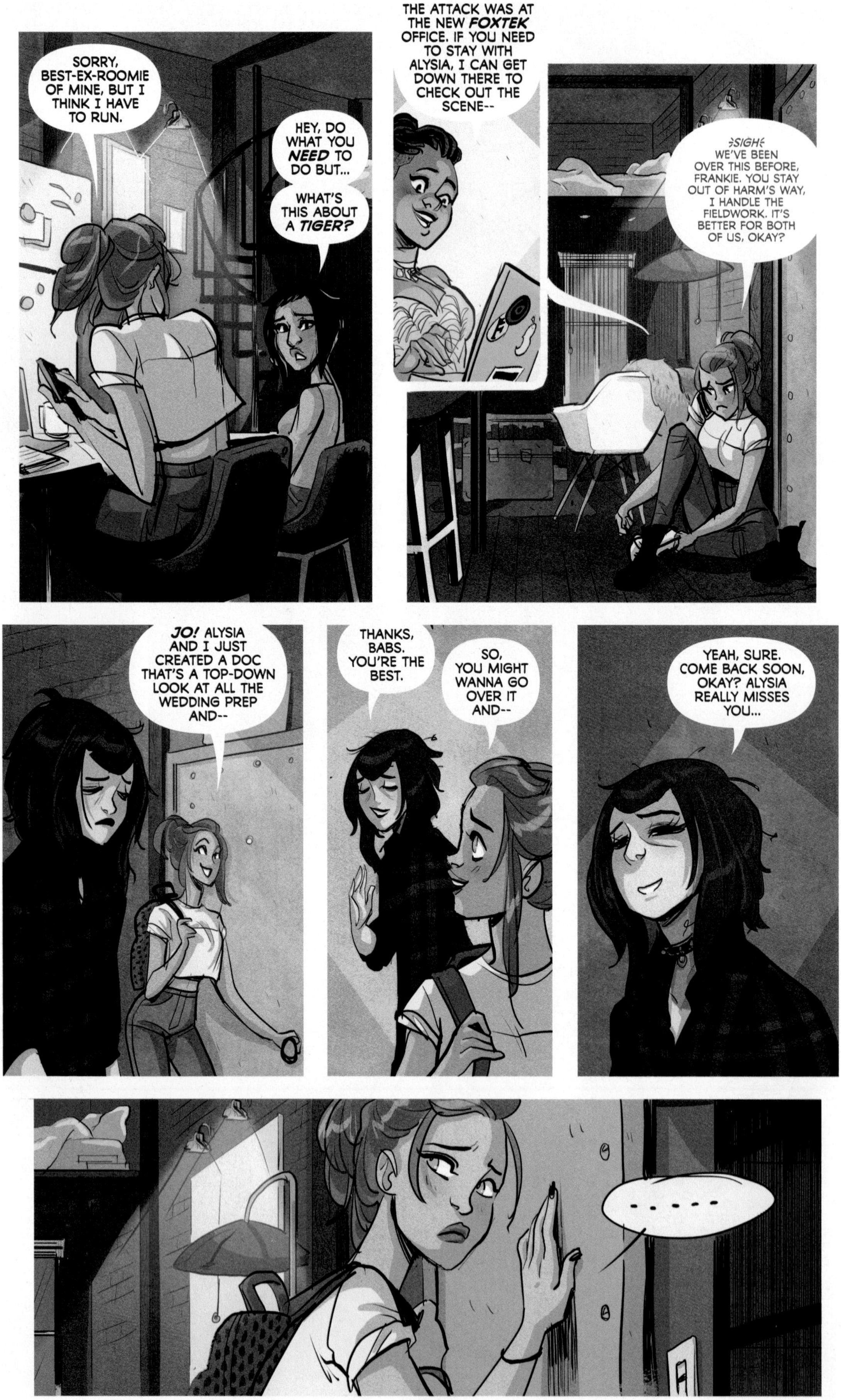
SORRY, BEST-EX-ROOMIE OF MINE, BUT I THINK I HAVE TO RUN.
HEY, DO WHAT YOU NEED TO DO BUT...
WHAT'S THIS ABOUT A TIGER?
THE ATTACK WAS AT THE NEW FOXTEK OFFICE. IF YOU NEED TO STAY WITH ALYSIA, I CAN GET DOWN THERE TO CHECK OUT THE SCENE--
SIGH
WE'VE BEEN OVER THIS BEFORE, FRANKIE. YOU STAY OUT OF HARM'S WAY, I HANDLE THE FIELDWORK. IT'S BETTER FOR BOTH OF US, OKAY?
JO! ALYSIA AND I JUST CREATED A DOC THAT'S A TOP-DOWN LOOK AT ALL THE WEDDING PREP AND--
THANKS, BABS. YOU'RE THE BEST.
SO, YOU MIGHT WANNA GO OVER IT AND--
YEAH, SURE. COME BACK SOON, OKAY? ALYSIA REALLY MISSES YOU...
. . . . .

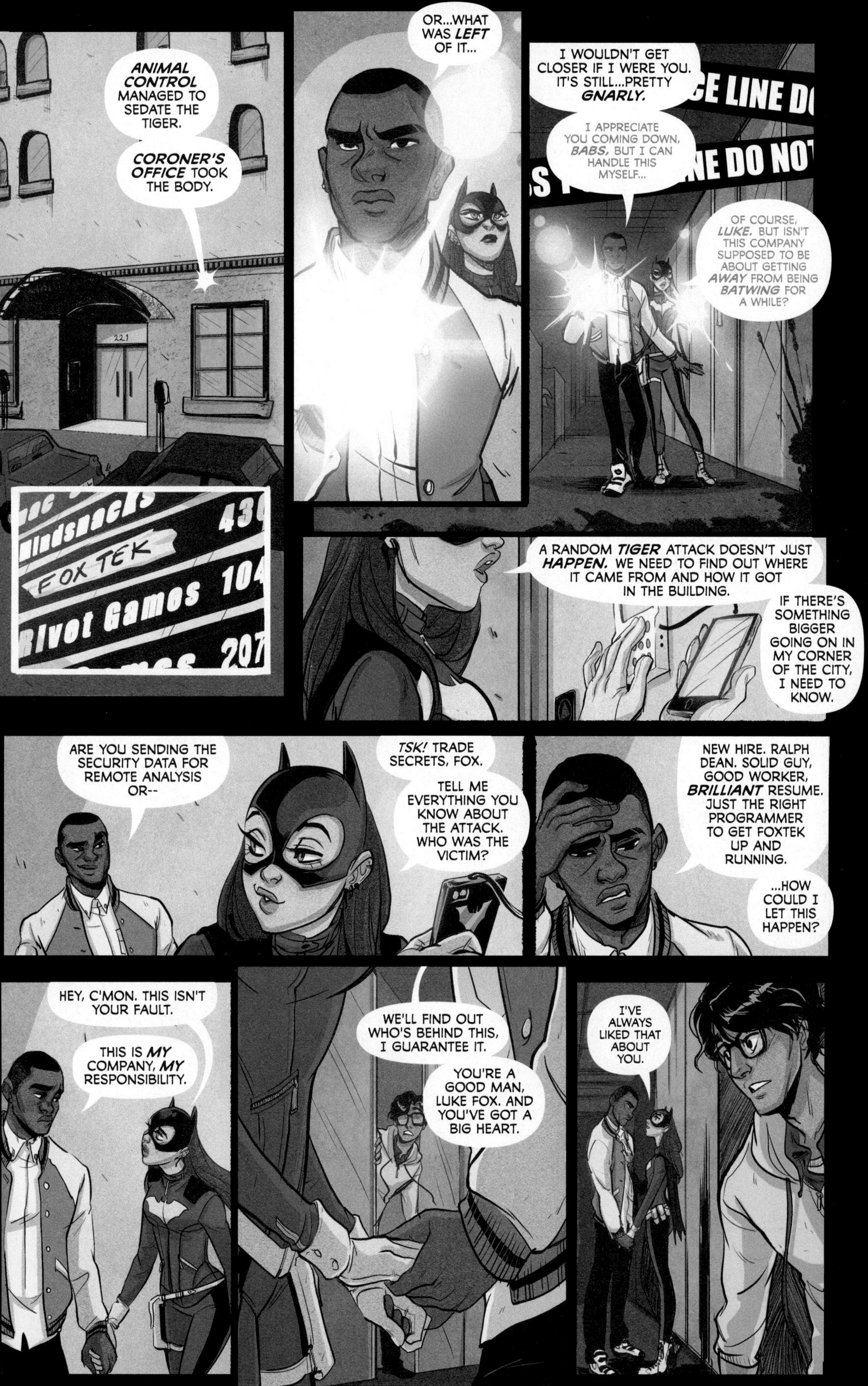

ANIMAL CONTROL MANAGED TO SEDATE THE TIGER.
CORONER'S OFFICE TOOK THE BODY.
221
OR...WHAT WAS LEFT OF IT...
I WOULDN'T GET CLOSER IF I WERE YOU. IT'S STILL...PRETTY GNARLY.
I APPRECIATE YOU COMING DOWN, BABS, BUT I CAN HANDLE THIS MYSELF...
OF COURSE, LUKE. BUT ISN'T THIS COMPANY SUPPOSED TO BE ABOUT GETTING AWAY FROM BEING BATWING FOR A WHILE?
Mindsnacks 430
FOX TEK
Rivot Games 104
A RANDOM TIGER ATTACK DOESN'T JUST HAPPEN. WE NEED TO FIND OUT WHERE IT CAME FROM AND HOW IT GOT IN THE BUILDING.
IF THERE'S SOMETHING BIGGER GOING ON IN MY CORNER OF THE CITY, I NEED TO KNOW.
ARE YOU SENDING THE SECURITY DATA FOR REMOTE ANALYSIS OR--
TSK! TRADE SECRETS, FOX.
TELL ME EVERYTHING YOU KNOW ABOUT THE ATTACK. WHO WAS THE VICTIM?
NEW HIRE. RALPH DEAN. SOLID GUY, GOOD WORKER, BRILLIANT RESUME. JUST THE RIGHT PROGRAMMER TO GET FOXTEK UP AND RUNNING.
...HOW COULD I LET THIS HAPPEN?
HEY, C'MON. THIS ISN'T YOUR FAULT.
THIS IS MY COMPANY, MY RESPONSIBILITY.
WE'LL FIND OUT WHO'S BEHIND THIS, I GUARANTEE IT.
YOU'RE A GOOD MAN, LUKE FOX. AND YOU'VE GOT A BIG HEART.
I'VE ALWAYS LIKED THAT ABOUT YOU.

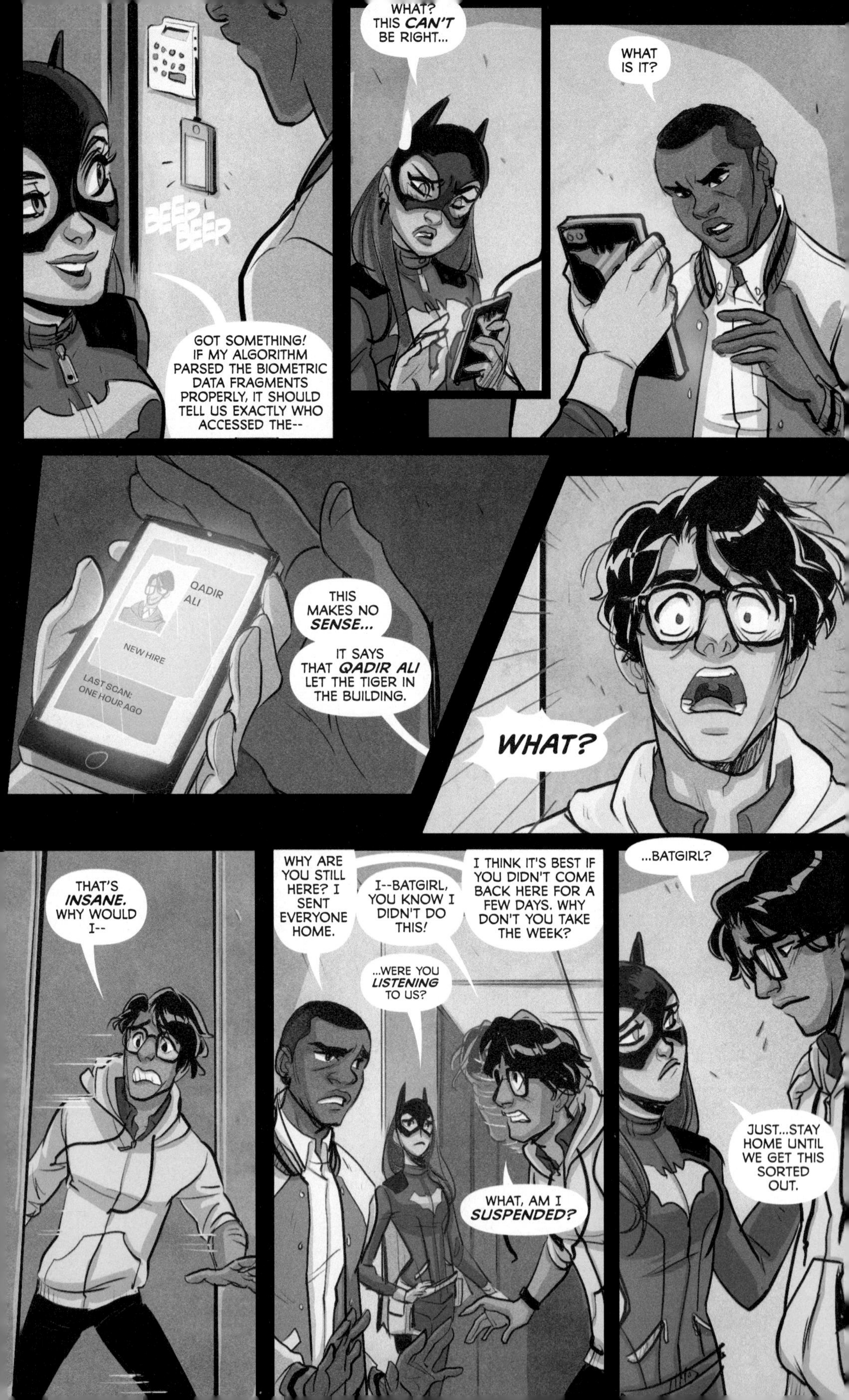
BEEP BEEP
GOT SOMETHING! IF MY ALGORITHM PARSED THE BIOMETRIC DATA FRAGMENTS PROPERLY, IT SHOULD TELL US EXACTLY WHO ACCESSED THE--
WHAT? THIS CAN'T BE RIGHT...
WHAT IS IT?
QADIR ALI
NEW HIRE
LAST SCAN: ONE HOUR AGO
THIS MAKES NO SENSE...
IT SAYS THAT QADIR ALI LET THE TIGER IN THE BUILDING.
WHAT?
THAT'S INSANE. WHY WOULD I--
WHY ARE YOU STILL HERE? I SENT EVERYONE HOME.
I--BATGIRL, YOU KNOW I DIDN'T DO THIS!
I THINK IT'S BEST IF YOU DIDN'T COME BACK HERE FOR A FEW DAYS. WHY DON'T YOU TAKE THE WEEK?
...WERE YOU LISTENING TO US?
WHAT, AM I SUSPENDED?
...BATGIRL?
JUST...STAY HOME UNTIL WE GET THIS SORTED OUT.

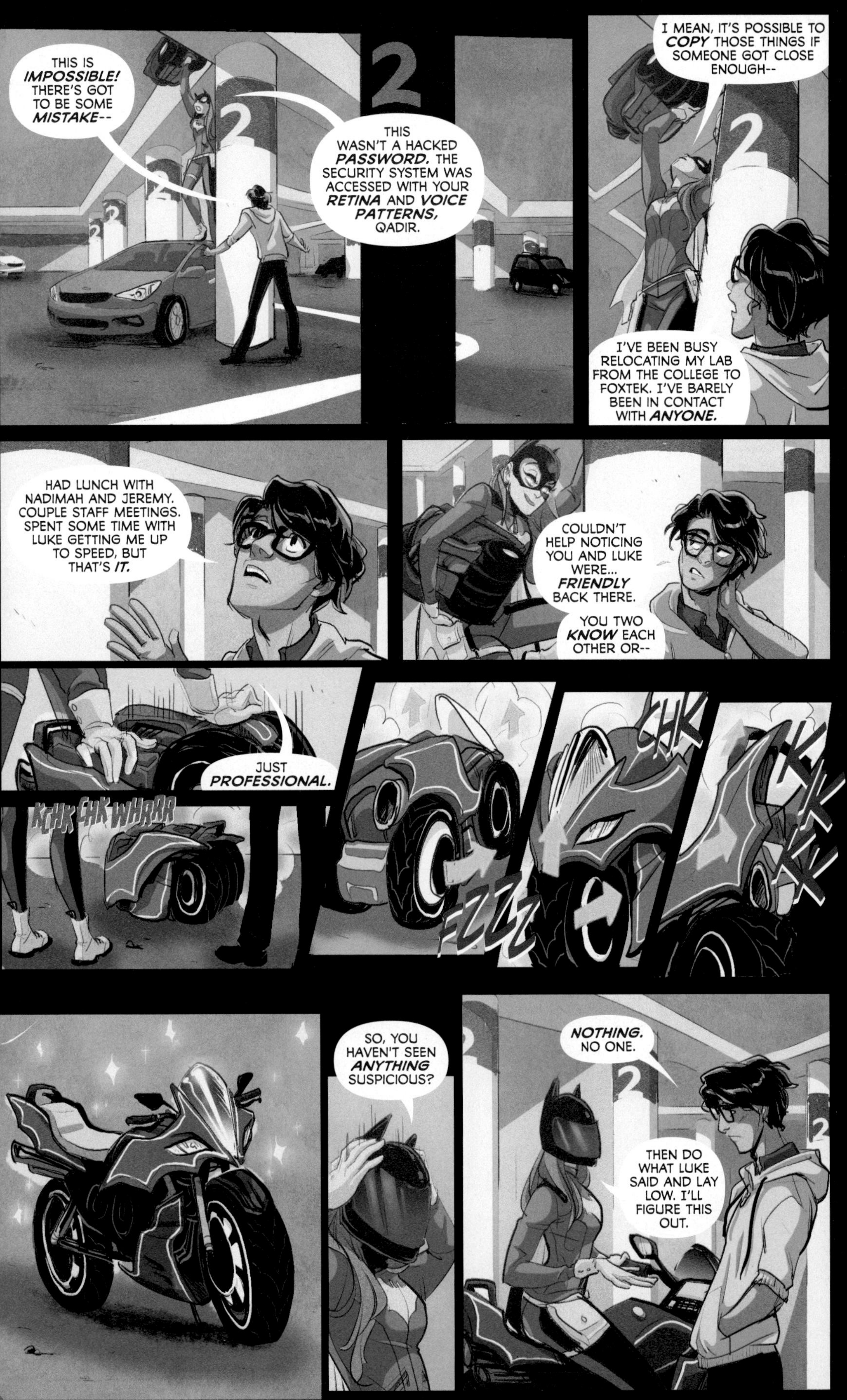

THIS IS IMPOSSIBLE! THERE'S GOT TO BE SOME MISTAKE--
THIS WASN'T A HACKED PASSWORD. THE SECURITY SYSTEM WAS ACCESSED WITH YOUR RETINA AND VOICE PATTERNS, QADIR.
I MEAN, IT'S POSSIBLE TO COPY THOSE THINGS IF SOMEONE GOT CLOSE ENOUGH--
I'VE BEEN BUSY RELOCATING MY LAB FROM THE COLLEGE TO FOXTEK. I'VE BARELY BEEN IN CONTACT WITH ANYONE.
HAD LUNCH WITH NADIMAH AND JEREMY. COUPLE STAFF MEETINGS. SPENT SOME TIME WITH LUKE GETTING ME UP TO SPEED, BUT THAT'S IT.
COULDN'T HELP NOTICING YOU AND LUKE WERE... FRIENDLY BACK THERE.
YOU TWO KNOW EACH OTHER OR--
JUST PROFESSIONAL.
KCHK CHK WHRRR
CHK
FZZZ
SO, YOU HAVEN'T SEEN ANYTHING SUSPICIOUS?
NOTHING. NO ONE.
THEN DO WHAT LUKE SAID AND LAY LOW. I'LL FIGURE THIS OUT.

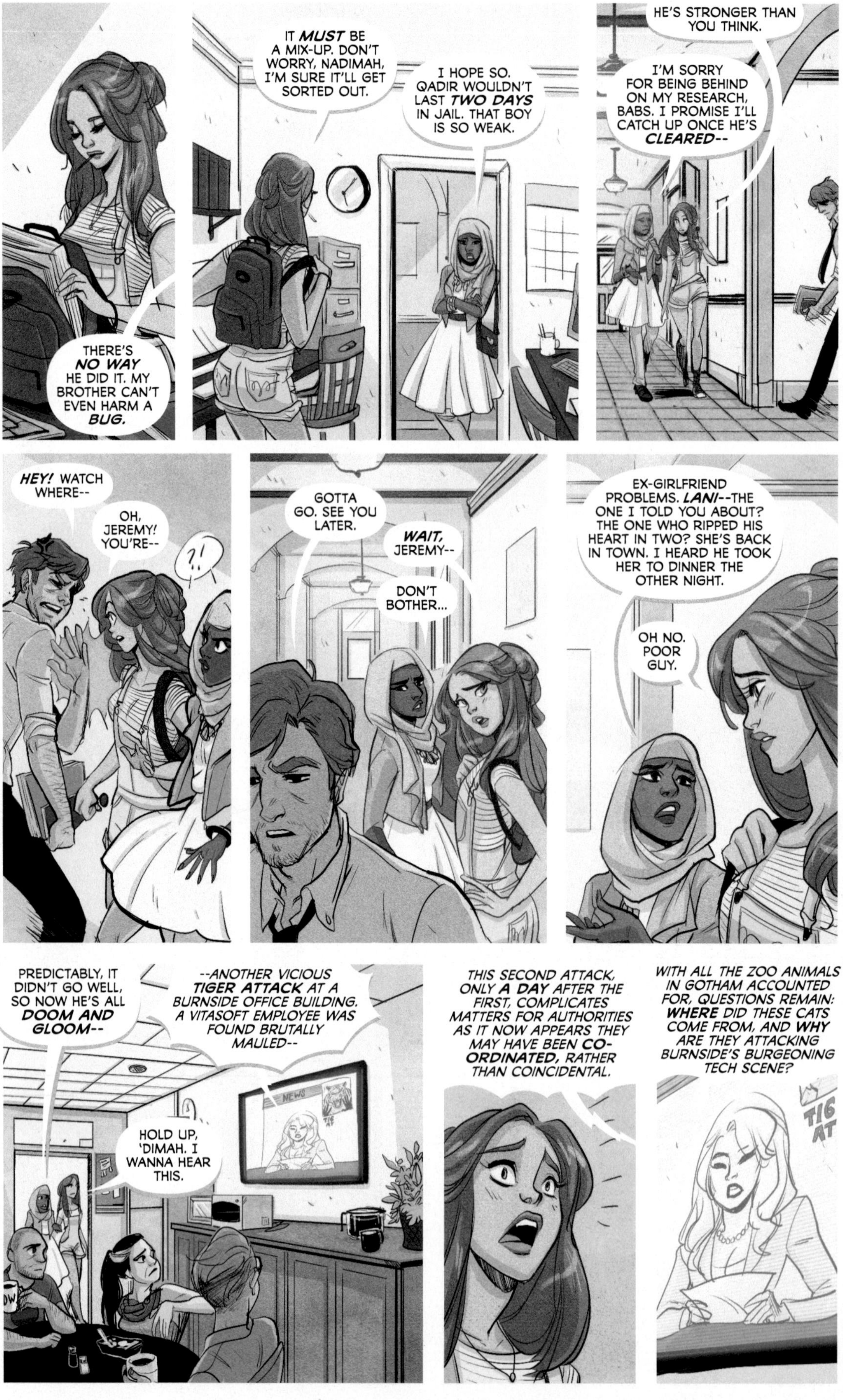
THERE'S NO WAY HE DID IT. MY BROTHER CAN'T EVEN HARM A BUG.
IT MUST BE A MIX-UP. DON'T WORRY, NADIMAH, I'M SURE IT'LL GET SORTED OUT.
I HOPE SO. QADIR WOULDN'T LAST TWO DAYS IN JAIL. THAT BOY IS SO WEAK.
HE'S STRONGER THAN YOU THINK.
I'M SORRY FOR BEING BEHIND ON MY RESEARCH, BABS. I PROMISE I'LL CATCH UP ONCE HE'S CLEARED--
HEY! WATCH WHERE--
OH, JEREMY! YOU'RE--
?!
GOTTA GO. SEE YOU LATER.
WAIT, JEREMY--
DON'T BOTHER...
EX-GIRLFRIEND PROBLEMS. LANI--THE ONE I TOLD YOU ABOUT? THE ONE WHO RIPPED HIS HEART IN TWO? SHE'S BACK IN TOWN. I HEARD HE TOOK HER TO DINNER THE OTHER NIGHT.
OH NO. POOR GUY.
PREDICTABLY, IT DIDN'T GO WELL, SO NOW HE'S ALL DOOM AND GLOOM--
--ANOTHER VICIOUS TIGER ATTACK AT A BURNSIDE OFFICE BUILDING. A VITASOFT EMPLOYEE WAS FOUND BRUTALLY MAULED--
NEWS
HOLD UP, 'DIMAH. I WANNA HEAR THIS.
THIS SECOND ATTACK, ONLY A DAY AFTER THE FIRST, COMPLICATES MATTERS FOR AUTHORITIES AS IT NOW APPEARS THEY MAY HAVE BEEN CO-ORDINATED, RATHER THAN COINCIDENTAL.
WITH ALL THE ZOO ANIMALS IN GOTHAM ACCOUNTED FOR, QUESTIONS REMAIN: WHERE DID THESE CATS COME FROM, AND WHY ARE THEY ATTACKING BURNSIDE'S BURGEONING TECH SCENE?
TIG AT

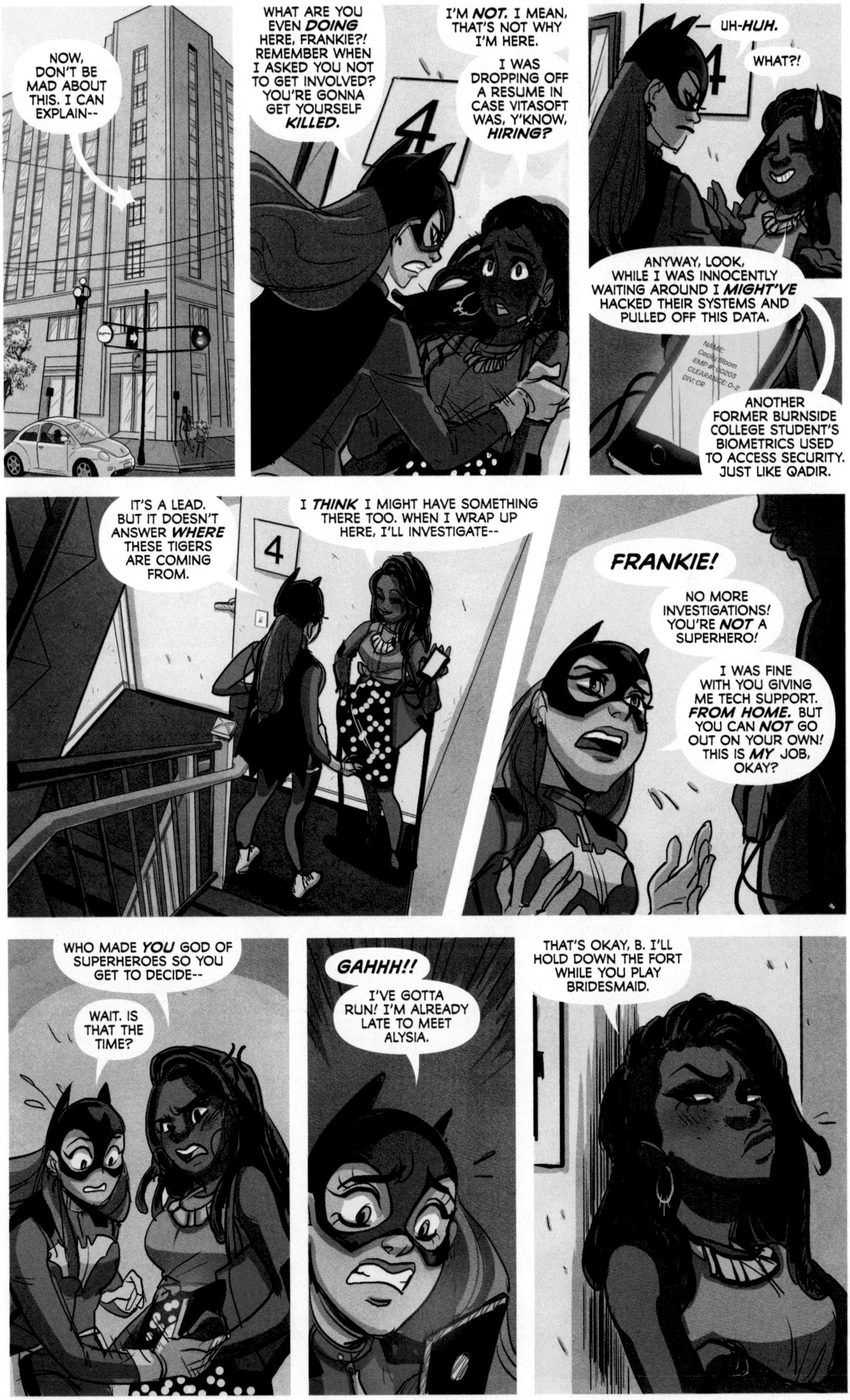
NOW, DON'T BE MAD ABOUT THIS. I CAN EXPLAIN--
WHAT ARE YOU EVEN DOING HERE, FRANKIE?! REMEMBER WHEN I ASKED YOU NOT TO GET INVOLVED? YOU'RE GONNA GET YOURSELF KILLED.
I'M NOT. I MEAN, THAT'S NOT WHY I'M HERE.
I WAS DROPPING OFF A RESUME IN CASE VITASOFT WAS, Y'KNOW, HIRING?
4
UH-HUH.
WHAT?!
ANYWAY, LOOK, WHILE I WAS INNOCENTLY WAITING AROUND I MIGHT'VE HACKED THEIR SYSTEMS AND PULLED OFF THIS DATA.
NAME: Cecily Bloom
EMP #: 00203
CLEARANCE: 0-2
DIV: CR
ANOTHER FORMER BURNSIDE COLLEGE STUDENT'S BIOMETRICS USED TO ACCESS SECURITY. JUST LIKE QADIR.
IT'S A LEAD. BUT IT DOESN'T ANSWER WHERE THESE TIGERS ARE COMING FROM.
I THINK I MIGHT HAVE SOMETHING THERE TOO. WHEN I WRAP UP HERE, I'LL INVESTIGATE--
FRANKIE!
NO MORE INVESTIGATIONS! YOU'RE NOT A SUPERHERO!
I WAS FINE WITH YOU GIVING ME TECH SUPPORT. FROM HOME. BUT YOU CAN NOT GO OUT ON YOUR OWN! THIS IS MY JOB, OKAY?
WHO MADE YOU GOD OF SUPERHEROES SO YOU GET TO DECIDE--
WAIT. IS THAT THE TIME?
GAHHH!!
I'VE GOTTA RUN! I'M ALREADY LATE TO MEET ALYSIA.
THAT'S OKAY, B. I'LL HOLD DOWN THE FORT WHILE YOU PLAY BRIDESMAID.

OKAY, I DON'T WANNA JINX IT, BUT I THINK THIS MIGHT BE THE ONE.

TRY IT ON BEFORE YOU CHANGE YOUR MIND *AGAIN!*

I'M SO GLAD YOU COULD DO THIS WITH ME, GBG.

ZAK

ZAK

SEARCH CRITERIA:
+ Former student - Burnside College
+ Recent hire at Burnside company
+ Company in technology business

I MEAN, I KNOW HOW BUSY YOU ARE WITH SCHOOL AND EVERYTHING...

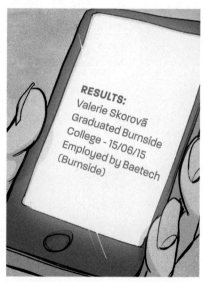

RESULTS:
Valerie Skorová
Graduated Burnside College - 15/06/15
Employed by Baetech (Burnside)

*UM...*ALYSIA. SPEAK OF THE DEVIL--*SCHOOL EMERGENCY.* I'M SO SORRY BUT I'VE GOTTA RUN...

‡SIGH‡ I'VE *ALWAYS* GOTTA RUN.

HEY, DON'T WORRY ABOUT IT. IT WAS GREAT TO HANG FOR A BIT. WE CAN CATCH UP LATER. I'M SURE IT'S IMPORTANT, RIGHT?

LISTEN, I'M STILL HERE FOR YOU. TAKE PHOTOS OF THE DRESSES AND TEXT THEM TO ME--I'LL GIVE YOU MY OPINION TO NARROW DOWN THE LIST. LATER WE'LL GO FOR DINNER AND PICK ONE. SOUND GOOD?

PERFECT! *GO!*

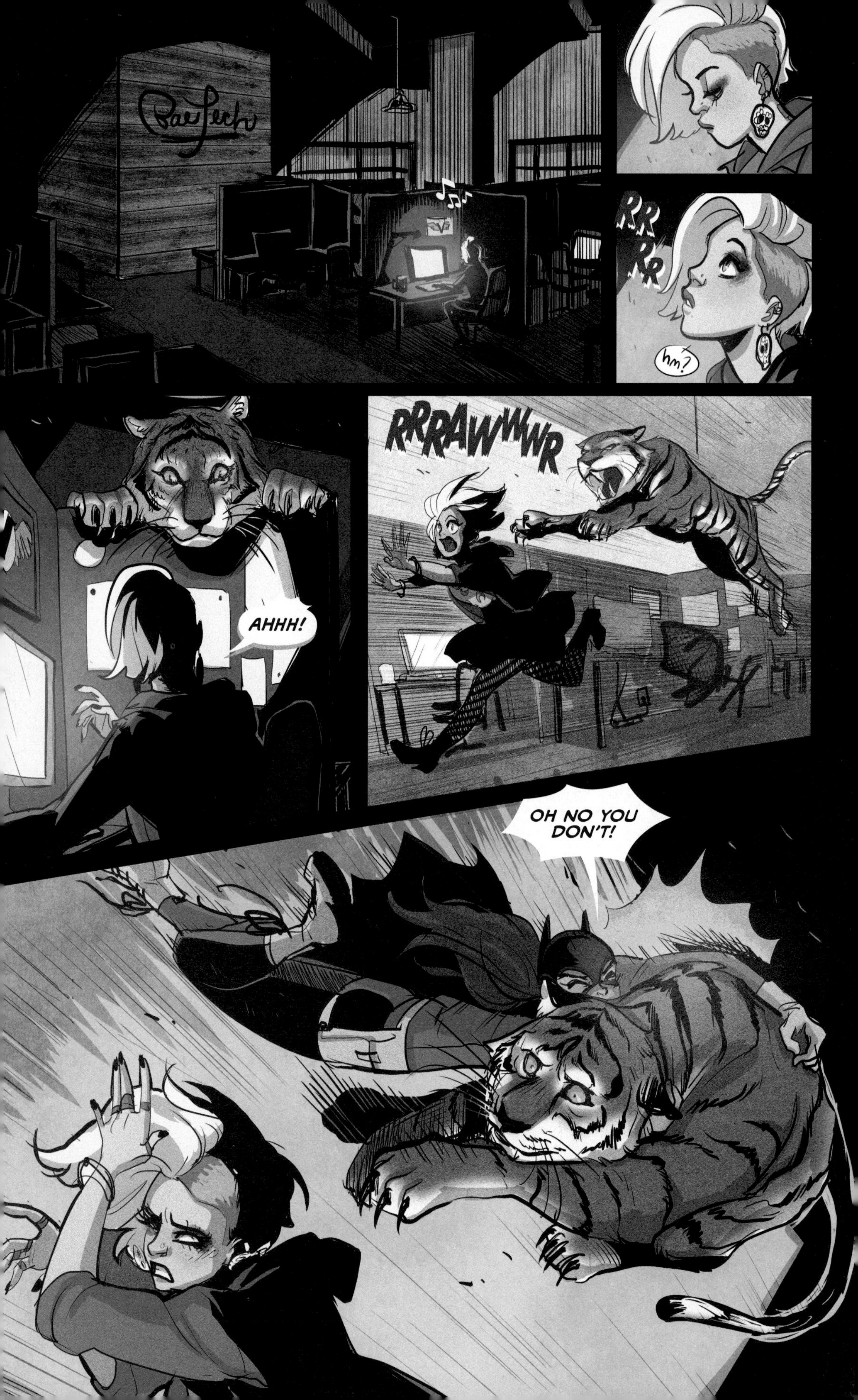
RR
RR
hm?
AHHH!
RRRAWWWR
OH NO YOU DON'T!

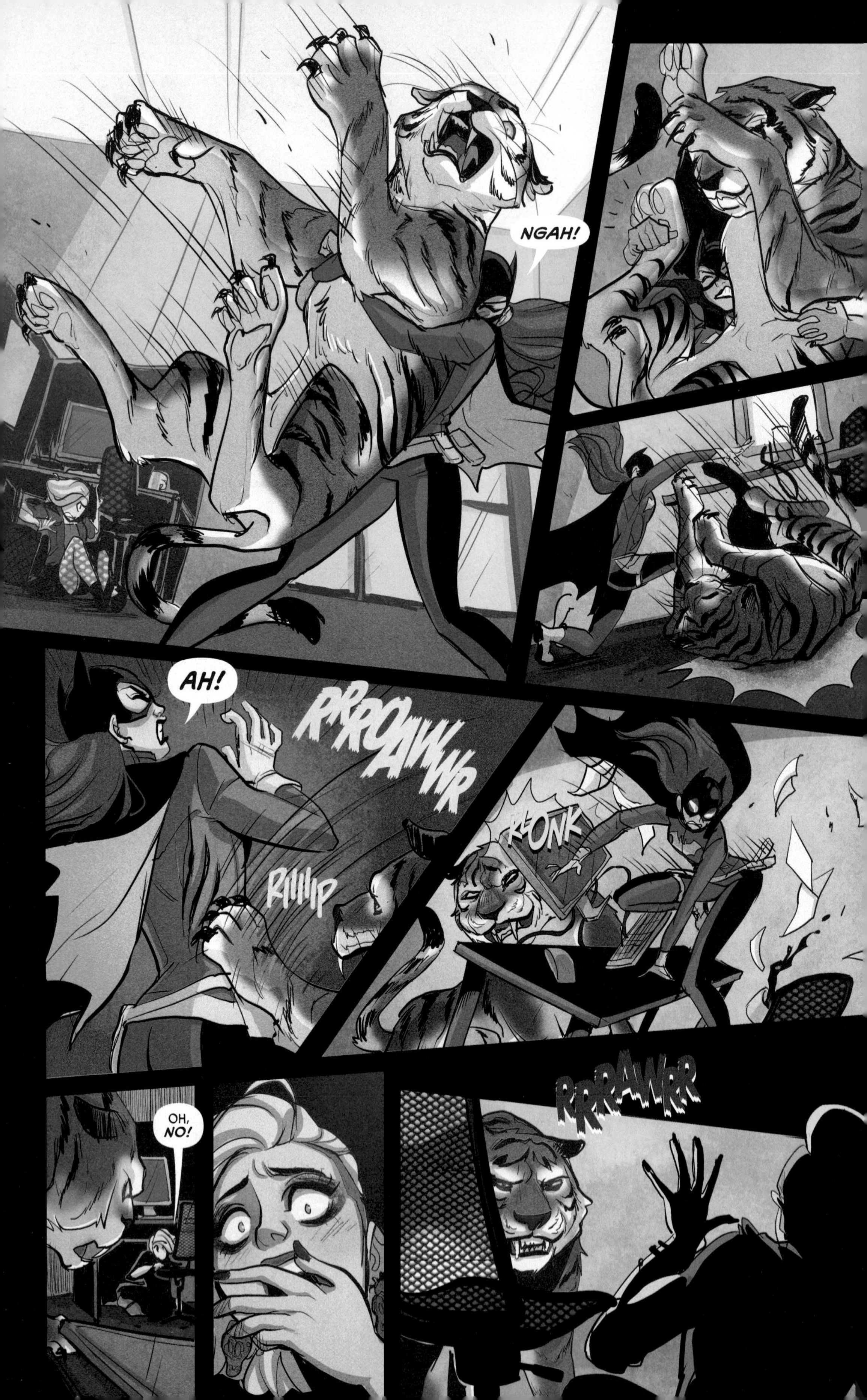
NGAH!
AH!
RRRROAWR
RIIIIP
KLONK
OH, NO!
RRRAWRR

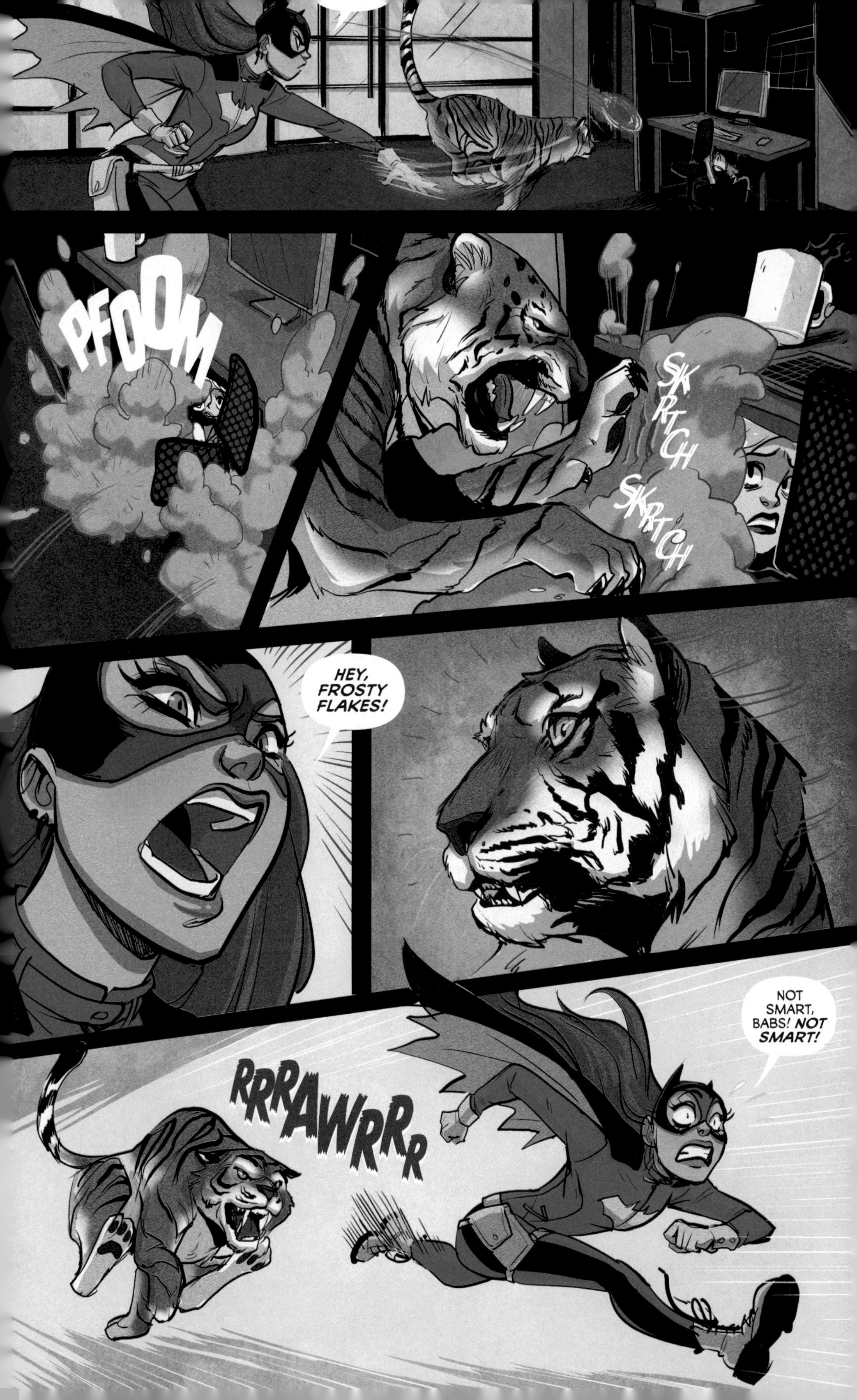
PFOOM
SKRTCH
SKRTCH
HEY, FROSTY FLAKES!
RRRAWRRR
NOT SMART, BABS! NOT SMART!

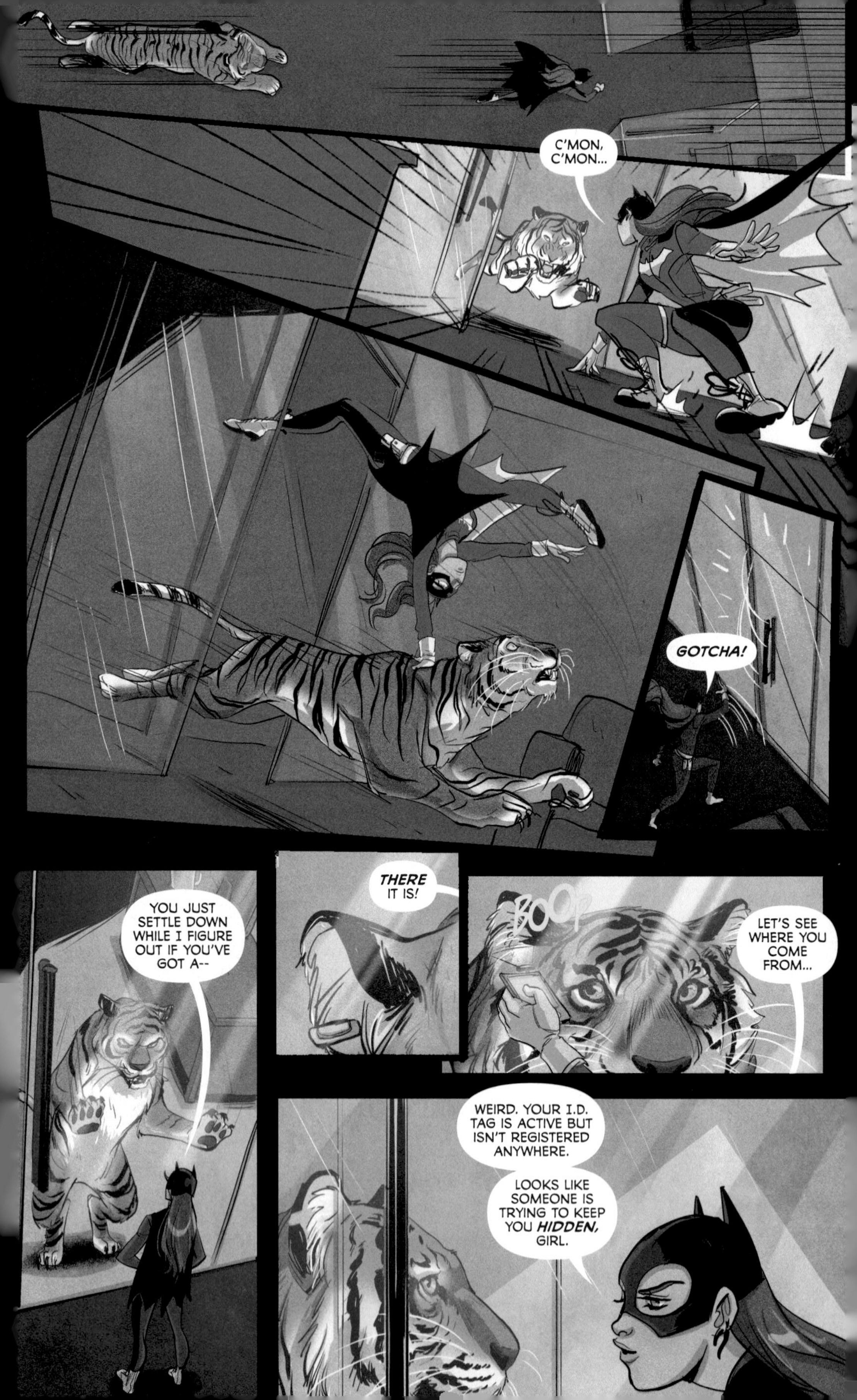
C'MON, C'MON...
GOTCHA!
YOU JUST SETTLE DOWN WHILE I FIGURE OUT IF YOU'VE GOT A--
THERE IT IS!
BOOP
LET'S SEE WHERE YOU COME FROM...
WEIRD. YOUR I.D. TAG IS ACTIVE BUT ISN'T REGISTERED ANYWHERE.
LOOKS LIKE SOMEONE IS TRYING TO KEEP YOU *HIDDEN,* GIRL.

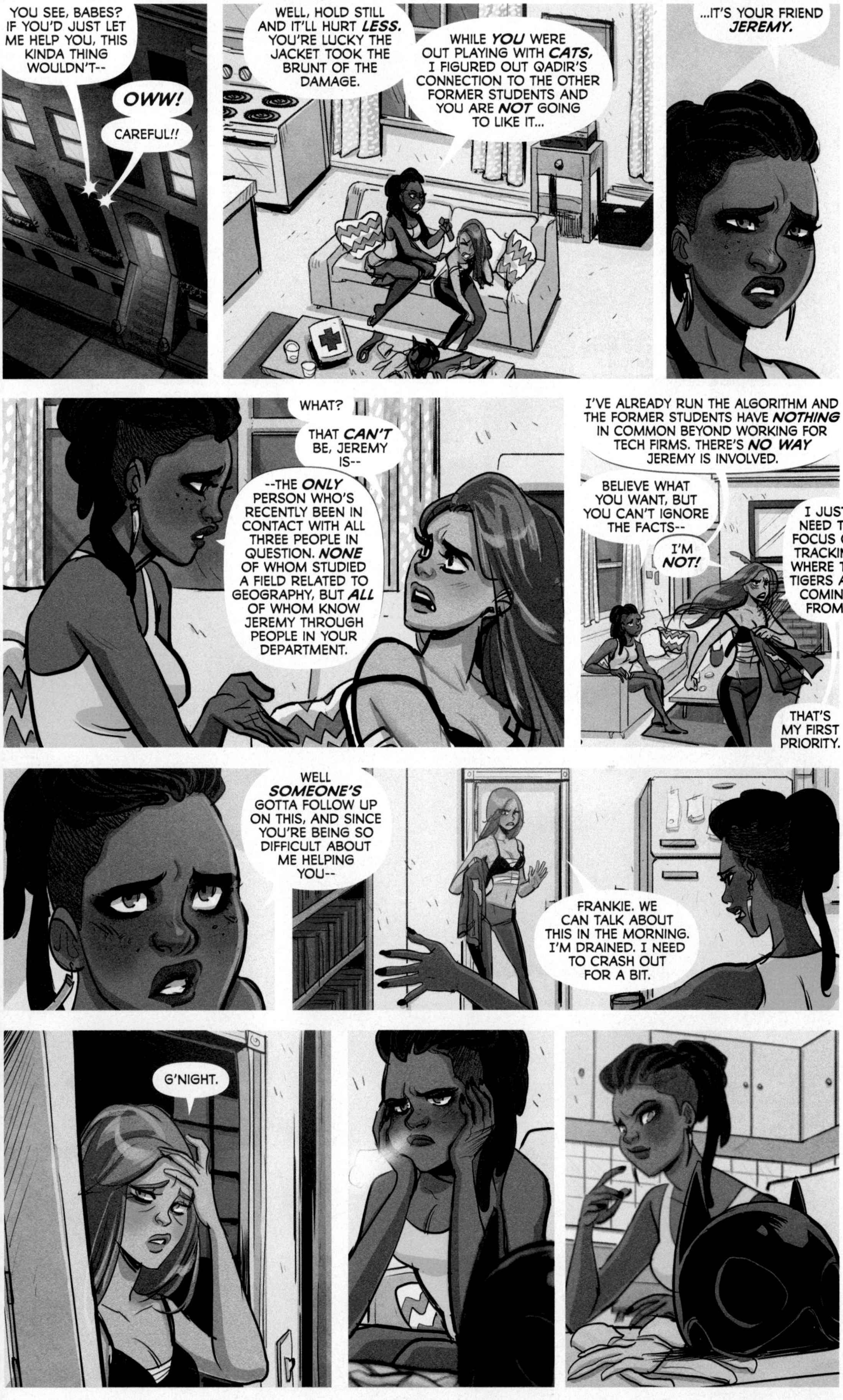
YOU SEE, BABES? IF YOU'D JUST LET ME HELP YOU, THIS KINDA THING WOULDN'T--
OWW!
CAREFUL!!
WELL, HOLD STILL AND IT'LL HURT LESS. YOU'RE LUCKY THE JACKET TOOK THE BRUNT OF THE DAMAGE.
WHILE YOU WERE OUT PLAYING WITH CATS, I FIGURED OUT QADIR'S CONNECTION TO THE OTHER FORMER STUDENTS AND YOU ARE NOT GOING TO LIKE IT...
...IT'S YOUR FRIEND JEREMY.
WHAT?
THAT CAN'T BE, JEREMY IS--
--THE ONLY PERSON WHO'S RECENTLY BEEN IN CONTACT WITH ALL THREE PEOPLE IN QUESTION. NONE OF WHOM STUDIED A FIELD RELATED TO GEOGRAPHY, BUT ALL OF WHOM KNOW JEREMY THROUGH PEOPLE IN YOUR DEPARTMENT.
I'VE ALREADY RUN THE ALGORITHM AND THE FORMER STUDENTS HAVE NOTHING IN COMMON BEYOND WORKING FOR TECH FIRMS. THERE'S NO WAY JEREMY IS INVOLVED.
BELIEVE WHAT YOU WANT, BUT YOU CAN'T IGNORE THE FACTS--
I'M NOT!
I JUST NEED TO FOCUS ON TRACKING WHERE THE TIGERS ARE COMING FROM.
THAT'S MY FIRST PRIORITY.
WELL SOMEONE'S GOTTA FOLLOW UP ON THIS, AND SINCE YOU'RE BEING SO DIFFICULT ABOUT ME HELPING YOU--
FRANKIE. WE CAN TALK ABOUT THIS IN THE MORNING. I'M DRAINED. I NEED TO CRASH OUT FOR A BIT.
G'NIGHT.

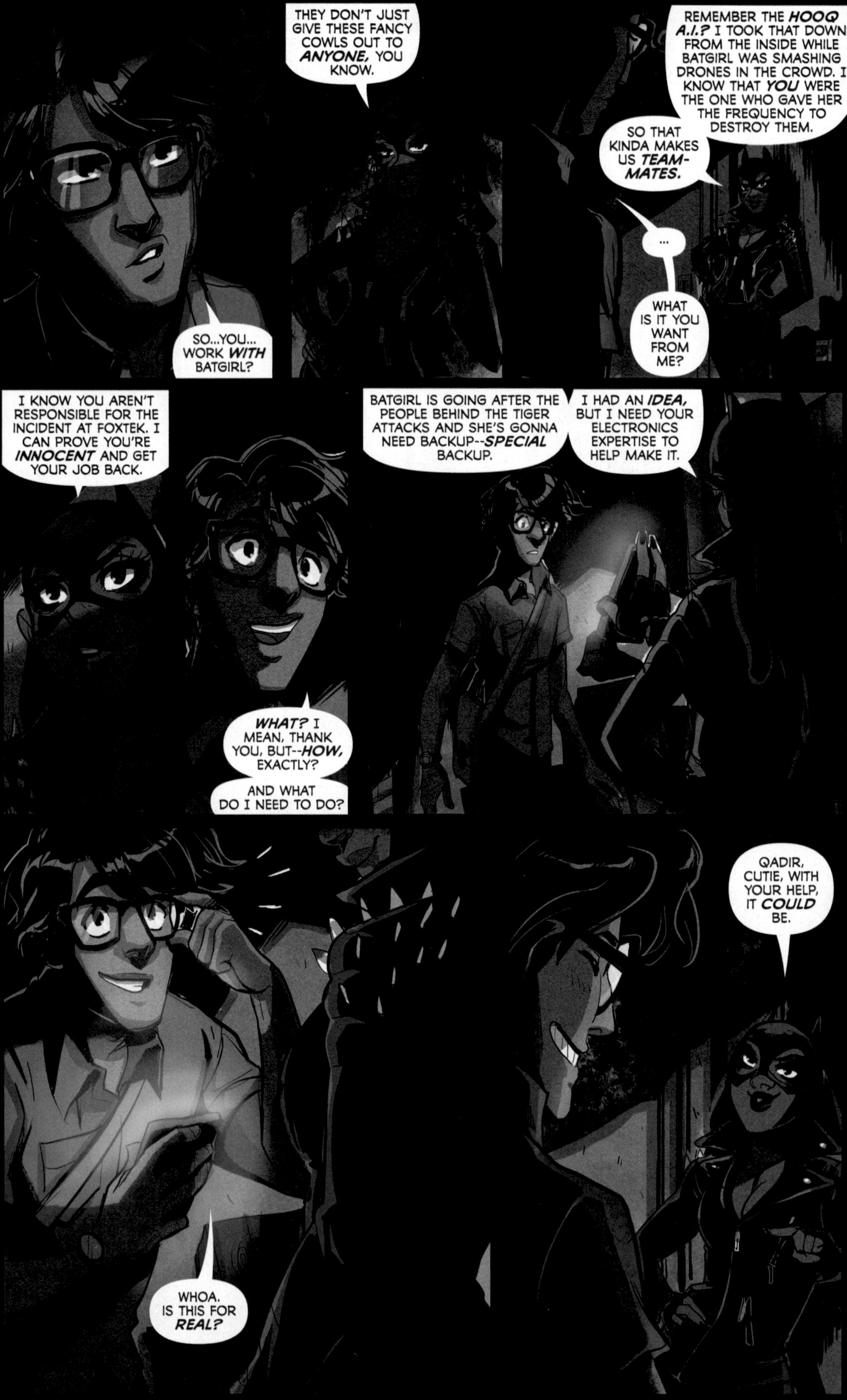
THEY DON'T JUST GIVE THESE FANCY COWLS OUT TO ANYONE, YOU KNOW.
SO...YOU... WORK WITH BATGIRL?
REMEMBER THE HOOQ A.I.? I TOOK THAT DOWN FROM THE INSIDE WHILE BATGIRL WAS SMASHING DRONES IN THE CROWD. I KNOW THAT YOU WERE THE ONE WHO GAVE HER THE FREQUENCY TO DESTROY THEM.
SO THAT KINDA MAKES US TEAM-MATES.
...
WHAT IS IT YOU WANT FROM ME?
I KNOW YOU AREN'T RESPONSIBLE FOR THE INCIDENT AT FOXTEK. I CAN PROVE YOU'RE INNOCENT AND GET YOUR JOB BACK.
WHAT? I MEAN, THANK YOU, BUT--HOW, EXACTLY?
AND WHAT DO I NEED TO DO?
BATGIRL IS GOING AFTER THE PEOPLE BEHIND THE TIGER ATTACKS AND SHE'S GONNA NEED BACKUP--SPECIAL BACKUP.
I HAD AN IDEA, BUT I NEED YOUR ELECTRONICS EXPERTISE TO HELP MAKE IT.
WHOA. IS THIS FOR REAL?
QADIR, CUTIE, WITH YOUR HELP, IT COULD BE.

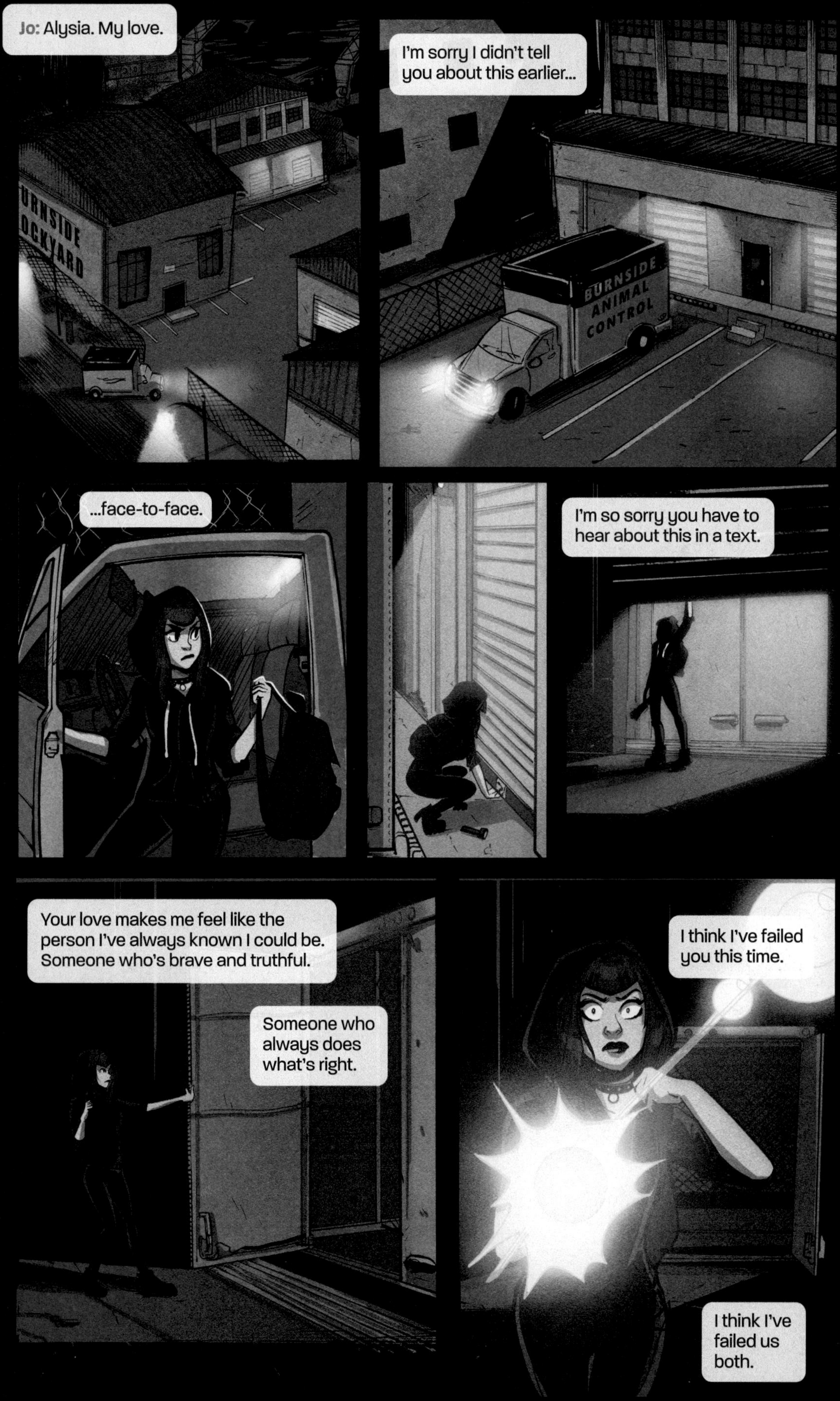
Jo: Alysia. My love.
I'm sorry I didn't tell you about this earlier...
BURNSIDE DOCKYARD
BURNSIDE ANIMAL CONTROL
...face-to-face.
I'm so sorry you have to hear about this in a text.
Your love makes me feel like the person I've always known I could be. Someone who's brave and truthful.
Someone who always does what's right.
I think I've failed you this time.
I think I've failed us both.

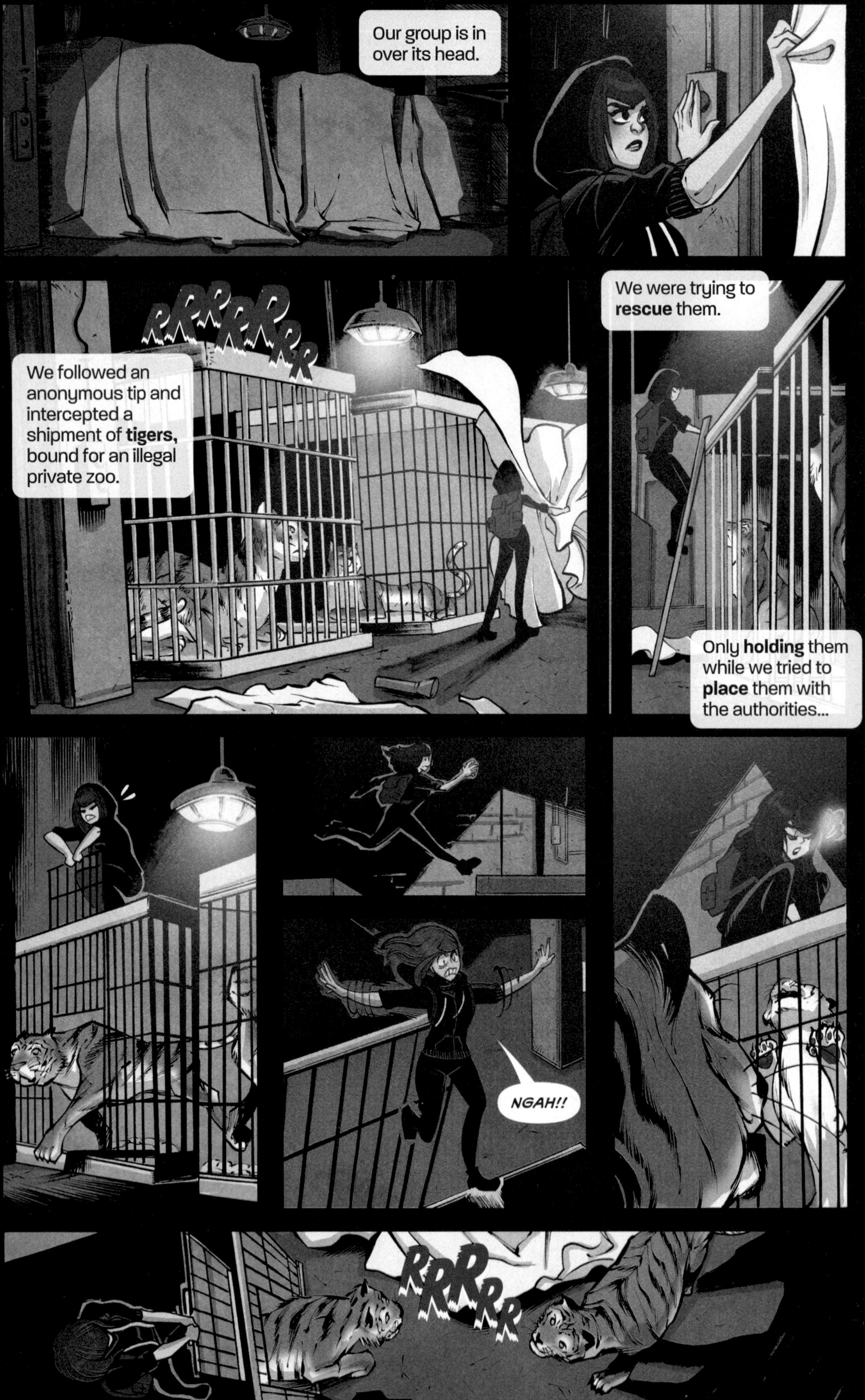
Our group is in over its head.
RRRRRRRR
We followed an anonymous tip and intercepted a shipment of **tigers,** bound for an illegal private zoo.
We were trying to **rescue** them.
Only **holding** them while we tried to **place** them with the authorities...
NGAH!!
RRRRR

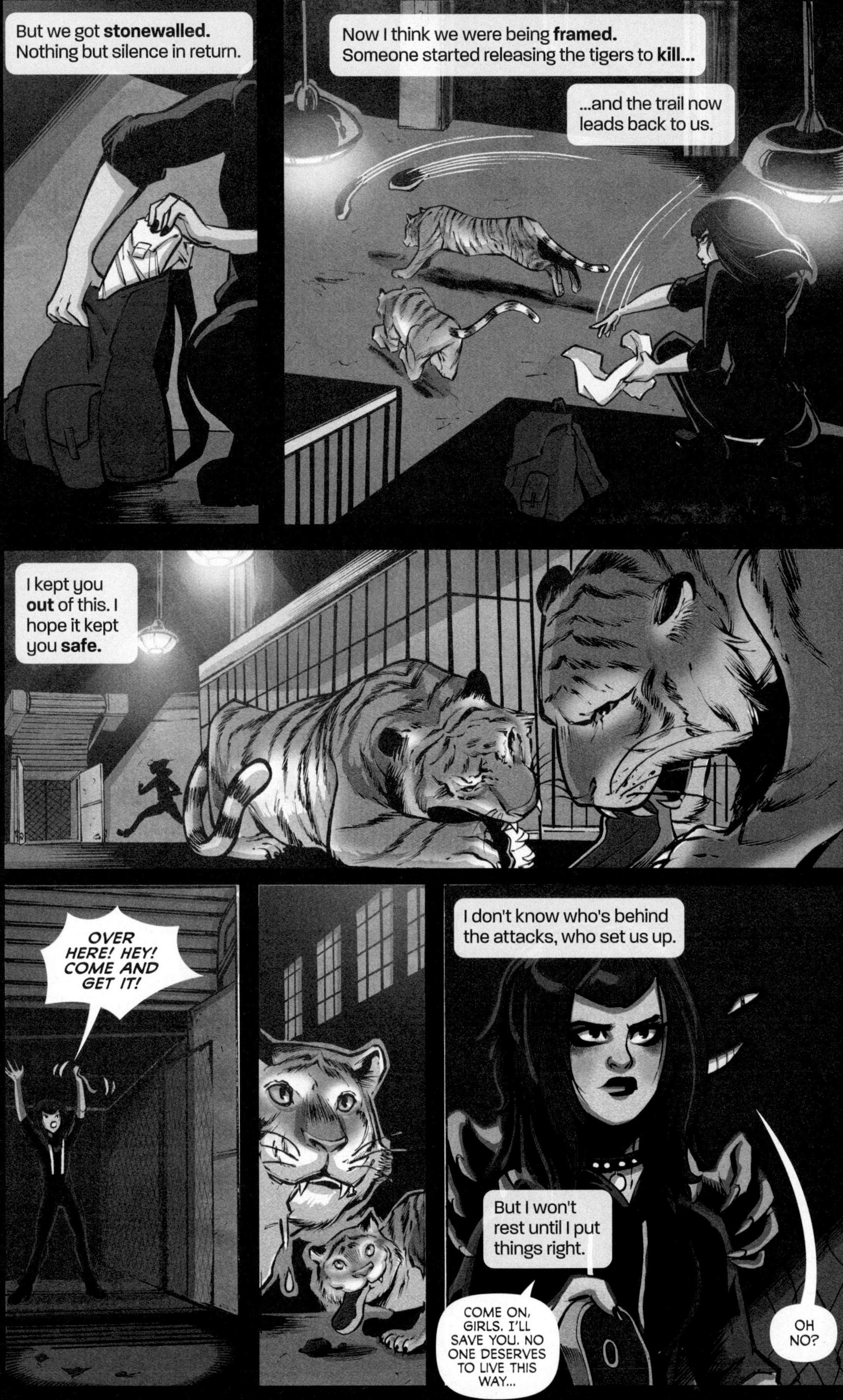
But we got **stonewalled.** Nothing but silence in return.
Now I think we were being **framed.** Someone started releasing the tigers to **kill...**
...and the trail now leads back to us.
I kept you **out** of this. I hope it kept you **safe.**
OVER HERE! HEY! COME AND GET IT!
I don't know who's behind the attacks, who set us up.
But I won't rest until I put things right.
COME ON, GIRLS. I'LL SAVE YOU. NO ONE DESERVES TO LIVE THIS WAY...
OH NO?

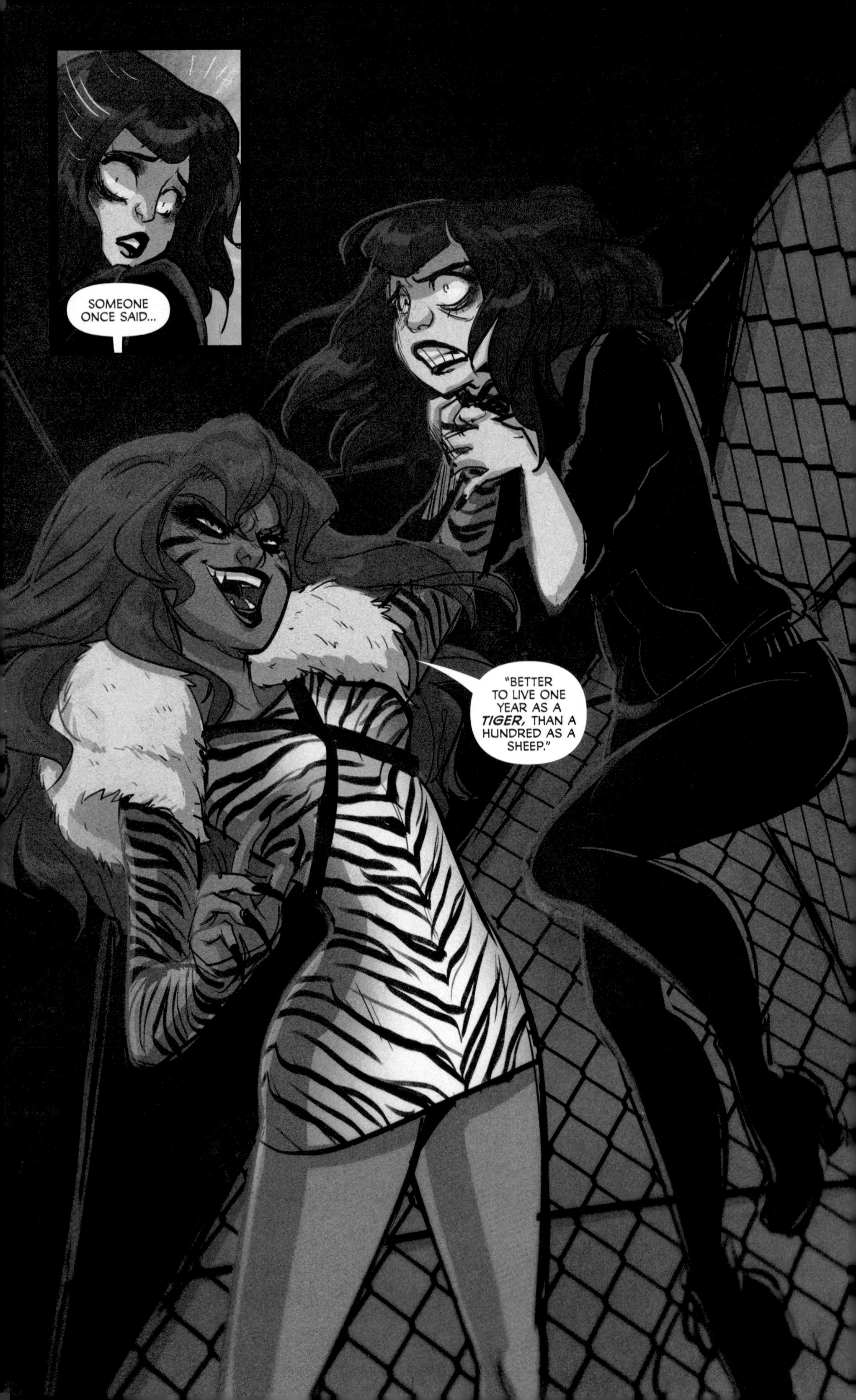
SOMEONE ONCE SAID...
"BETTER TO LIVE ONE YEAR AS A *TIGER,* THAN A HUNDRED AS A SHEEP."

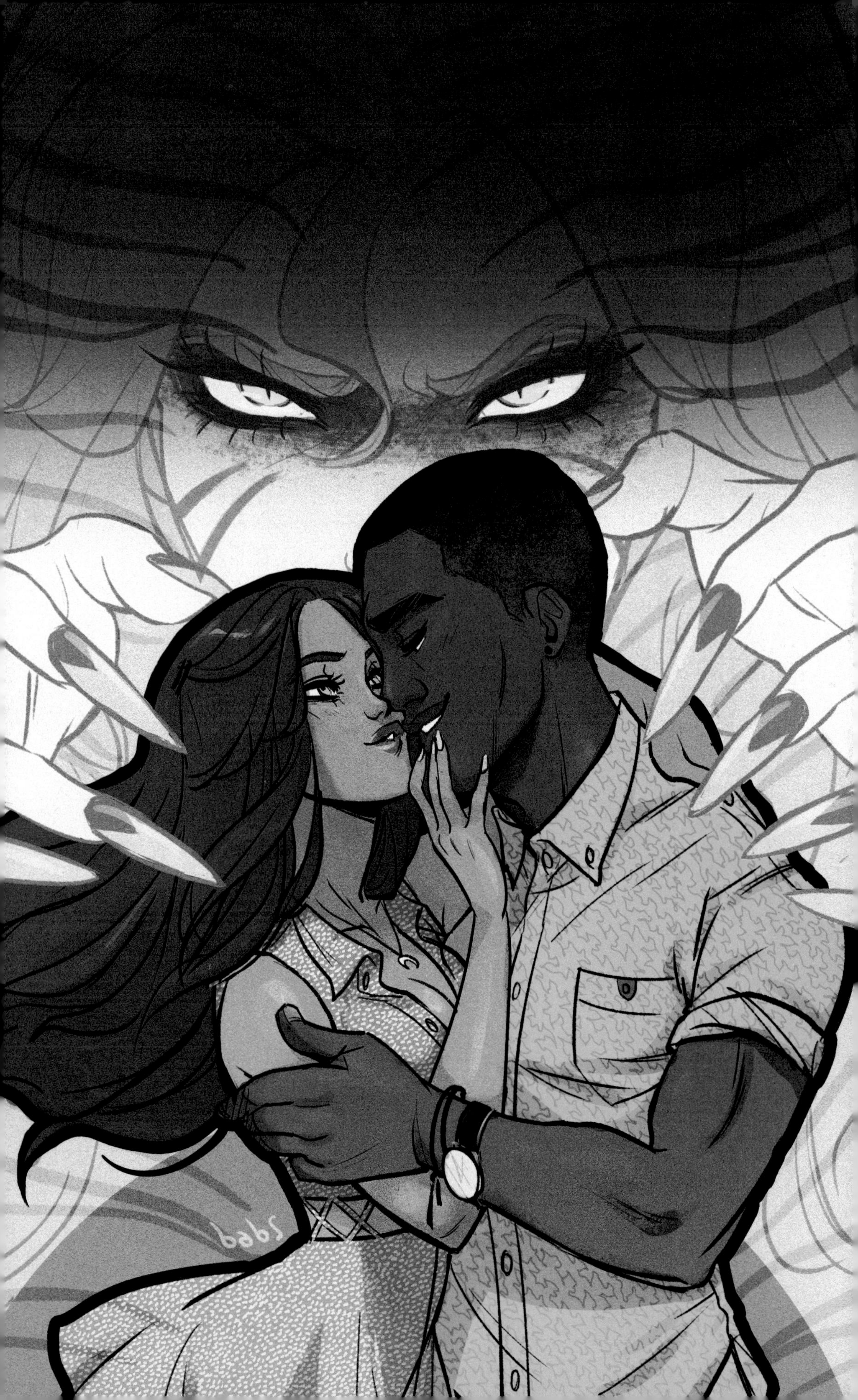
babs

CAMERON STEWART & BRENDEN FLETCHER writers BENGAL artist SERGE LAPOINTE colorist STEVE WANDS letterer cover by BABS TARR

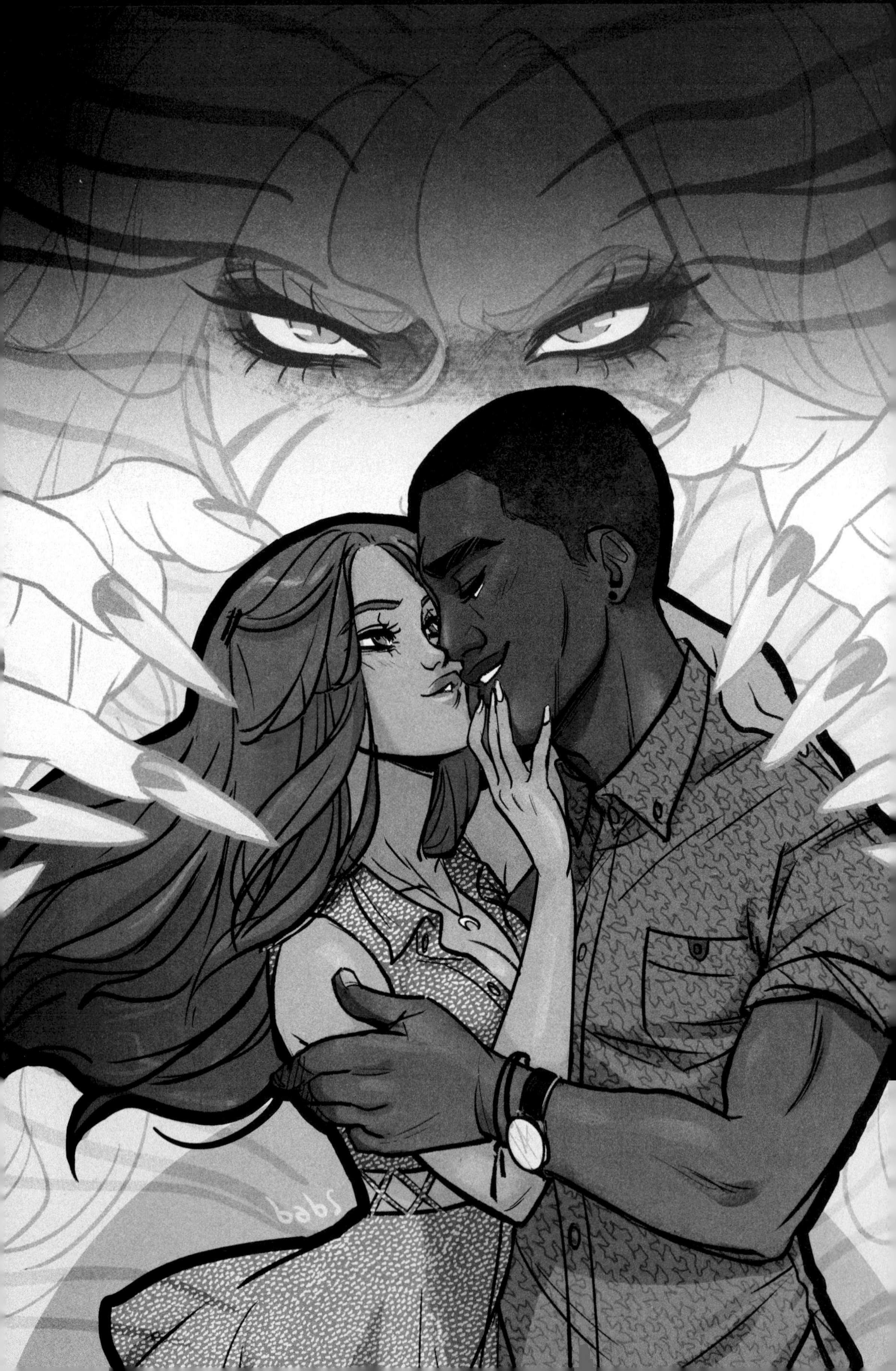
babs

AN AMBUSH OF TIGERS

"JO'S BEEN MISSING FOR *OVER TWENTY-FOUR HOURS,* BARBARA! OH MY GOD, I'M GOING OUT OF MY MIND!"

"LET'S TRY TO KEEP *CALM,* ALYSIA. WHERE WAS SHE LAST?"

TRACKING SIGNAL...!

GOTHAM SHIPYARD

Found user: 134.456
Last report : 32 hours ago

JO'S MESSAGE SAID OUR ACTIVIST GROUP WAS FED AN *ANONYMOUS TIP* ABOUT *ANIMAL TRAFFICKING.*

BUT SHE SAID SHE'D BEEN *MANIPULATED,* DELIVERING THE TIGERS TO SOMEONE WHO USED THEM TO *HURT* PEOPLE. SHE WENT TO THE WAREHOUSE TO TRANSFER THEM SOMEWHERE SAFE...

SHE WAS TRYING TO *FIX* THINGS. AND NOW SHE'S...OH, *GOD...*

I'LL CALL MY *FATHER.* THE *GCPD* CAN--

NO. NO, YOU CAN'T.

"I BELIEVE IN OUR GROUP, BUT ACTING WITHIN THE LAW...HASN'T ALWAYS WORKED FOR US."

"MAYBE...WE CAN TRY TO CONTACT *BATGIRL?*"

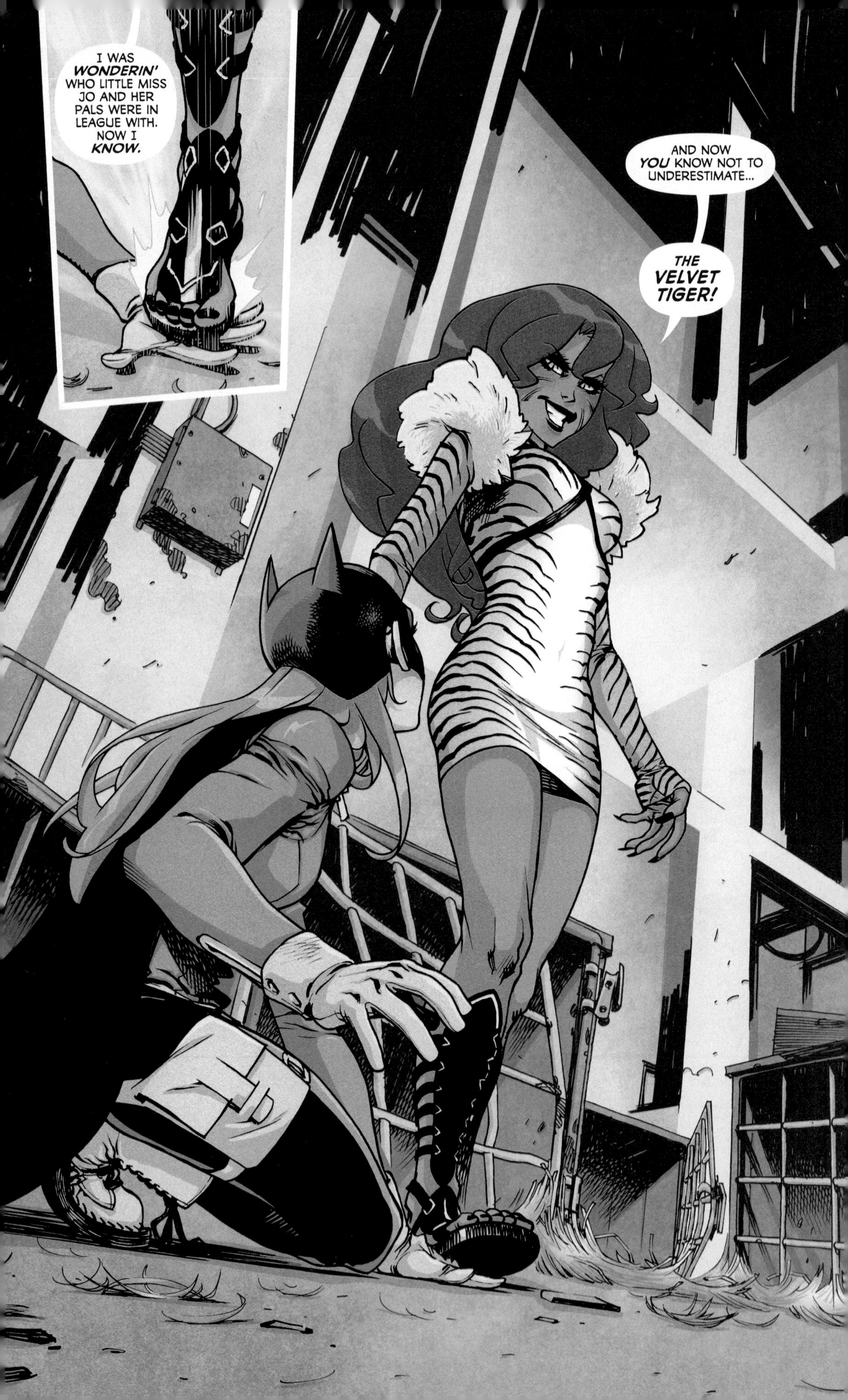
I WAS WONDERIN' WHO LITTLE MISS JO AND HER PALS WERE IN LEAGUE WITH. NOW I KNOW.
AND NOW YOU KNOW NOT TO UNDERESTIMATE...
THE VELVET TIGER!

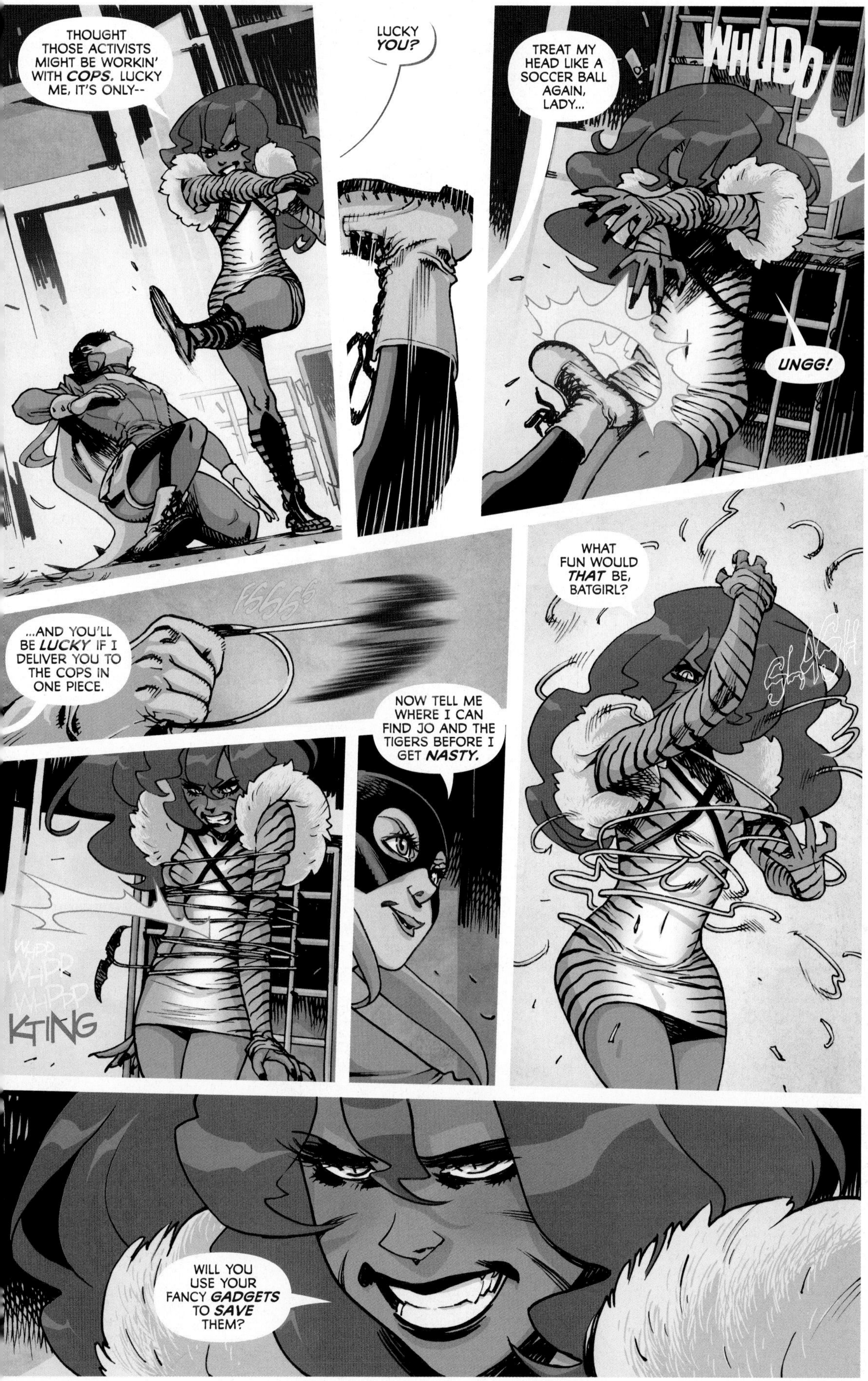
THOUGHT THOSE ACTIVISTS MIGHT BE WORKIN' WITH COPS. LUCKY ME, IT'S ONLY--
LUCKY YOU?
TREAT MY HEAD LIKE A SOCCER BALL AGAIN, LADY...
WHUDD
UNGG!
...AND YOU'LL BE LUCKY IF I DELIVER YOU TO THE COPS IN ONE PIECE.
WHAT FUN WOULD THAT BE, BATGIRL?
NOW TELL ME WHERE I CAN FIND JO AND THE TIGERS BEFORE I GET NASTY.
KTING
WILL YOU USE YOUR FANCY GADGETS TO SAVE THEM?

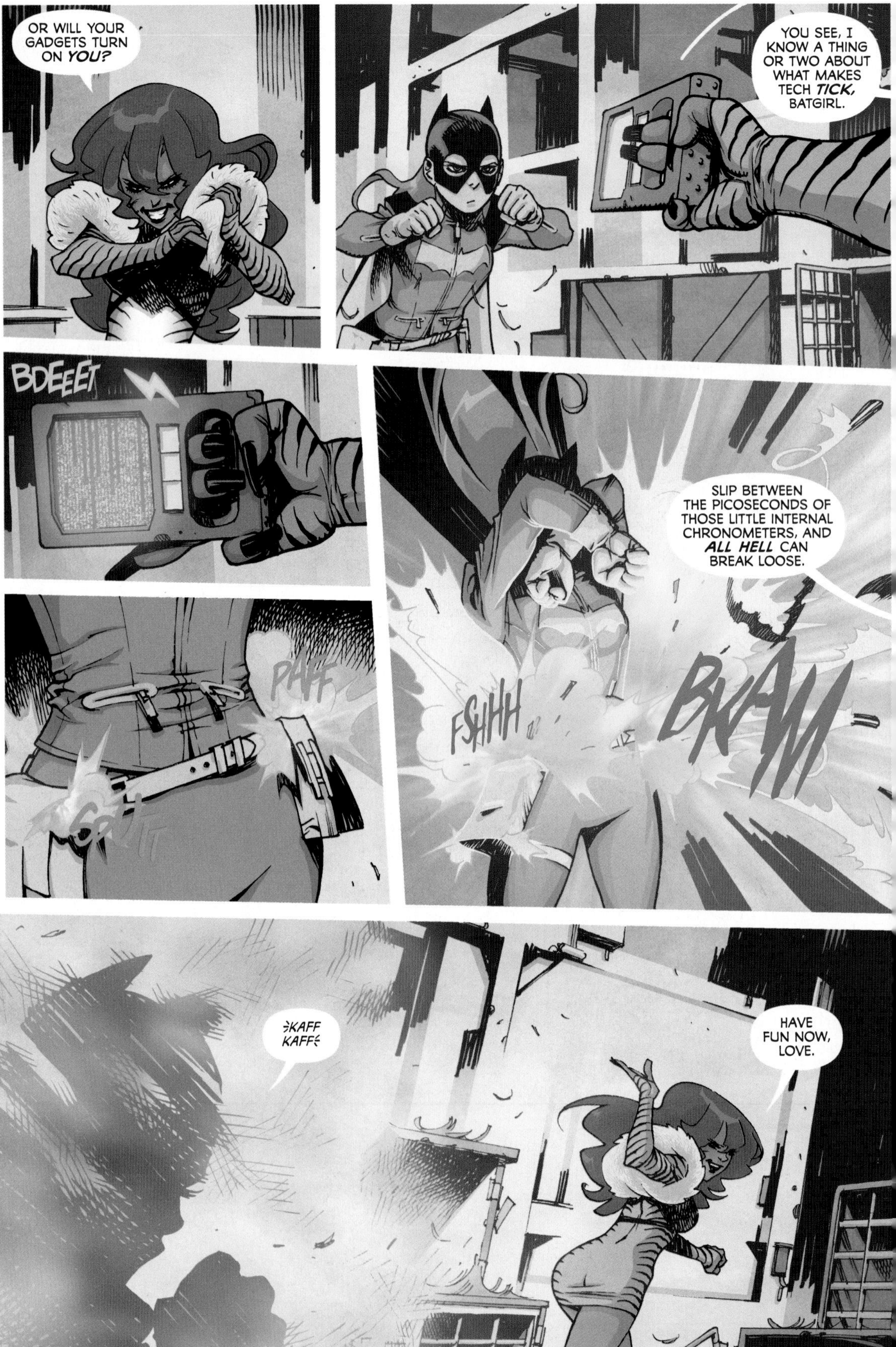
OR WILL YOUR GADGETS TURN ON *YOU?*
YOU SEE, I KNOW A THING OR TWO ABOUT WHAT MAKES TECH *TICK,* BATGIRL.
BDEEEET
PAFF
SLIP BETWEEN THE PICOSECONDS OF THOSE LITTLE INTERNAL CHRONOMETERS, AND ***ALL HELL*** CAN BREAK LOOSE.
FSHHH
KAFF KAFF
HAVE FUN NOW, LOVE.

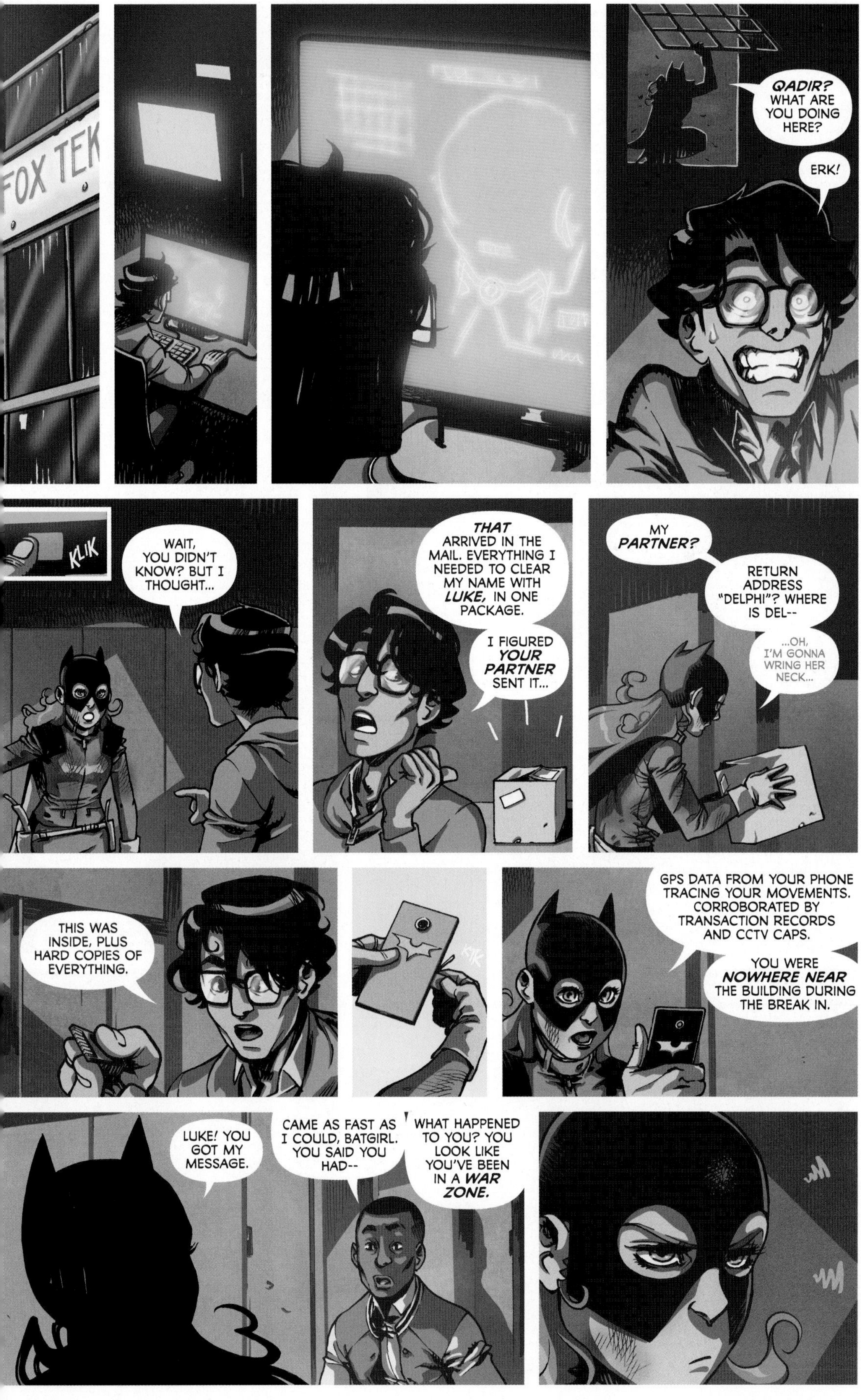

FOX TEK
QADIR? WHAT ARE YOU DOING HERE?
ERK!
KLIK
WAIT, YOU DIDN'T KNOW? BUT I THOUGHT...
THAT ARRIVED IN THE MAIL. EVERYTHING I NEEDED TO CLEAR MY NAME WITH LUKE, IN ONE PACKAGE.
I FIGURED YOUR PARTNER SENT IT...
MY PARTNER?
RETURN ADDRESS "DELPHI"? WHERE IS DEL--
...OH, I'M GONNA WRING HER NECK...
THIS WAS INSIDE, PLUS HARD COPIES OF EVERYTHING.
KTK
GPS DATA FROM YOUR PHONE TRACING YOUR MOVEMENTS. CORROBORATED BY TRANSACTION RECORDS AND CCTV CAPS.
YOU WERE NOWHERE NEAR THE BUILDING DURING THE BREAK IN.
LUKE! YOU GOT MY MESSAGE.
CAME AS FAST AS I COULD, BATGIRL. YOU SAID YOU HAD--
WHAT HAPPENED TO YOU? YOU LOOK LIKE YOU'VE BEEN IN A WAR ZONE.

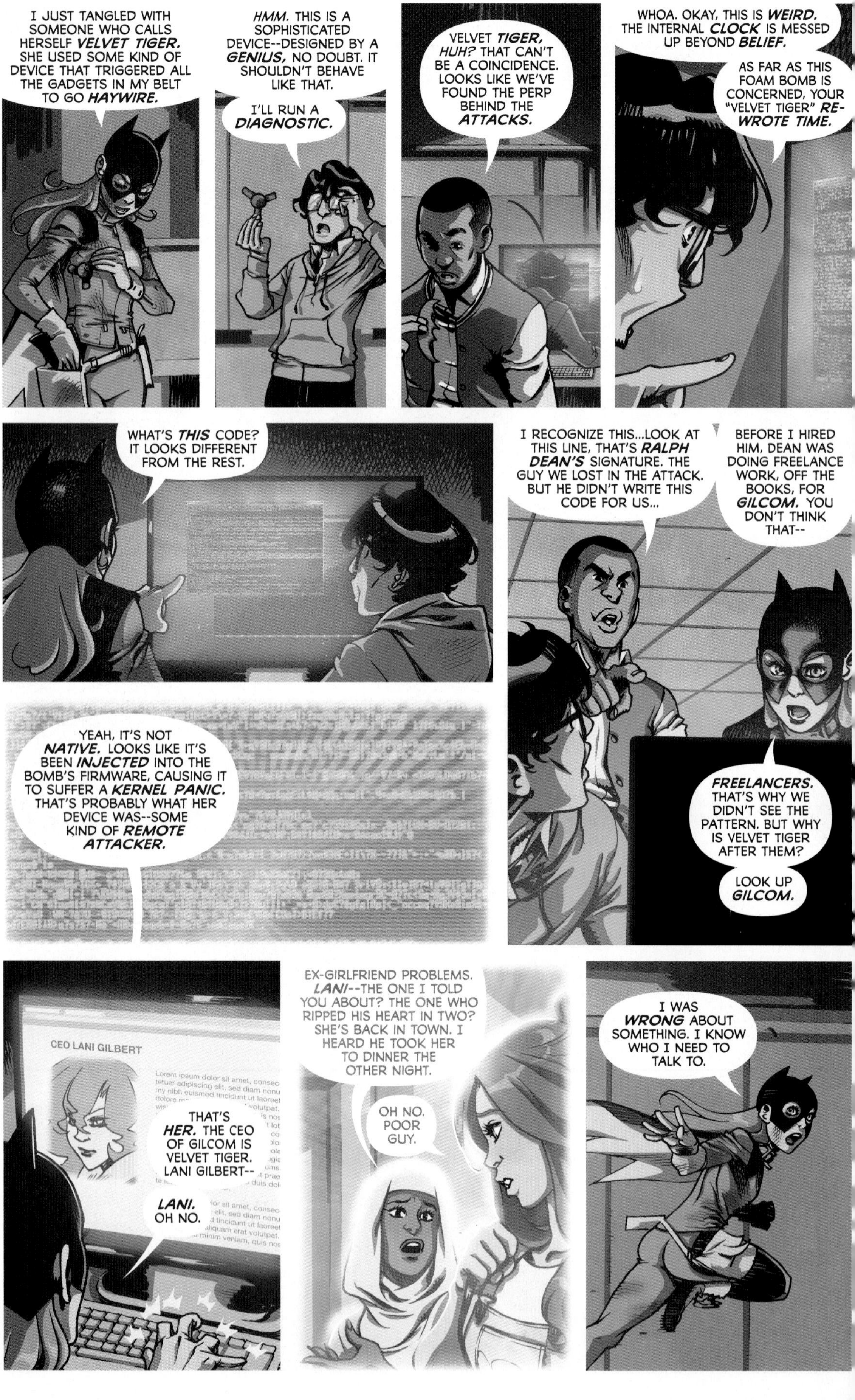
I JUST TANGLED WITH SOMEONE WHO CALLS HERSELF VELVET TIGER. SHE USED SOME KIND OF DEVICE THAT TRIGGERED ALL THE GADGETS IN MY BELT TO GO HAYWIRE.
HMM. THIS IS A SOPHISTICATED DEVICE--DESIGNED BY A GENIUS, NO DOUBT. IT SHOULDN'T BEHAVE LIKE THAT.
I'LL RUN A DIAGNOSTIC.
VELVET TIGER, HUH? THAT CAN'T BE A COINCIDENCE. LOOKS LIKE WE'VE FOUND THE PERP BEHIND THE ATTACKS.
WHOA. OKAY, THIS IS WEIRD. THE INTERNAL CLOCK IS MESSED UP BEYOND BELIEF.
AS FAR AS THIS FOAM BOMB IS CONCERNED, YOUR "VELVET TIGER" RE-WROTE TIME.
WHAT'S THIS CODE? IT LOOKS DIFFERENT FROM THE REST.
YEAH, IT'S NOT NATIVE. LOOKS LIKE IT'S BEEN INJECTED INTO THE BOMB'S FIRMWARE, CAUSING IT TO SUFFER A KERNEL PANIC. THAT'S PROBABLY WHAT HER DEVICE WAS--SOME KIND OF REMOTE ATTACKER.
I RECOGNIZE THIS...LOOK AT THIS LINE, THAT'S RALPH DEAN'S SIGNATURE. THE GUY WE LOST IN THE ATTACK. BUT HE DIDN'T WRITE THIS CODE FOR US...
BEFORE I HIRED HIM, DEAN WAS DOING FREELANCE WORK, OFF THE BOOKS, FOR GILCOM. YOU DON'T THINK THAT--
FREELANCERS. THAT'S WHY WE DIDN'T SEE THE PATTERN. BUT WHY IS VELVET TIGER AFTER THEM?
LOOK UP GILCOM.
CEO LANI GILBERT
THAT'S HER. THE CEO OF GILCOM IS VELVET TIGER. LANI GILBERT--
LANI. OH NO.
EX-GIRLFRIEND PROBLEMS. LANI--THE ONE I TOLD YOU ABOUT? THE ONE WHO RIPPED HIS HEART IN TWO? SHE'S BACK IN TOWN. I HEARD HE TOOK HER TO DINNER THE OTHER NIGHT.
OH NO. POOR GUY.
I WAS WRONG ABOUT SOMETHING. I KNOW WHO I NEED TO TALK TO.

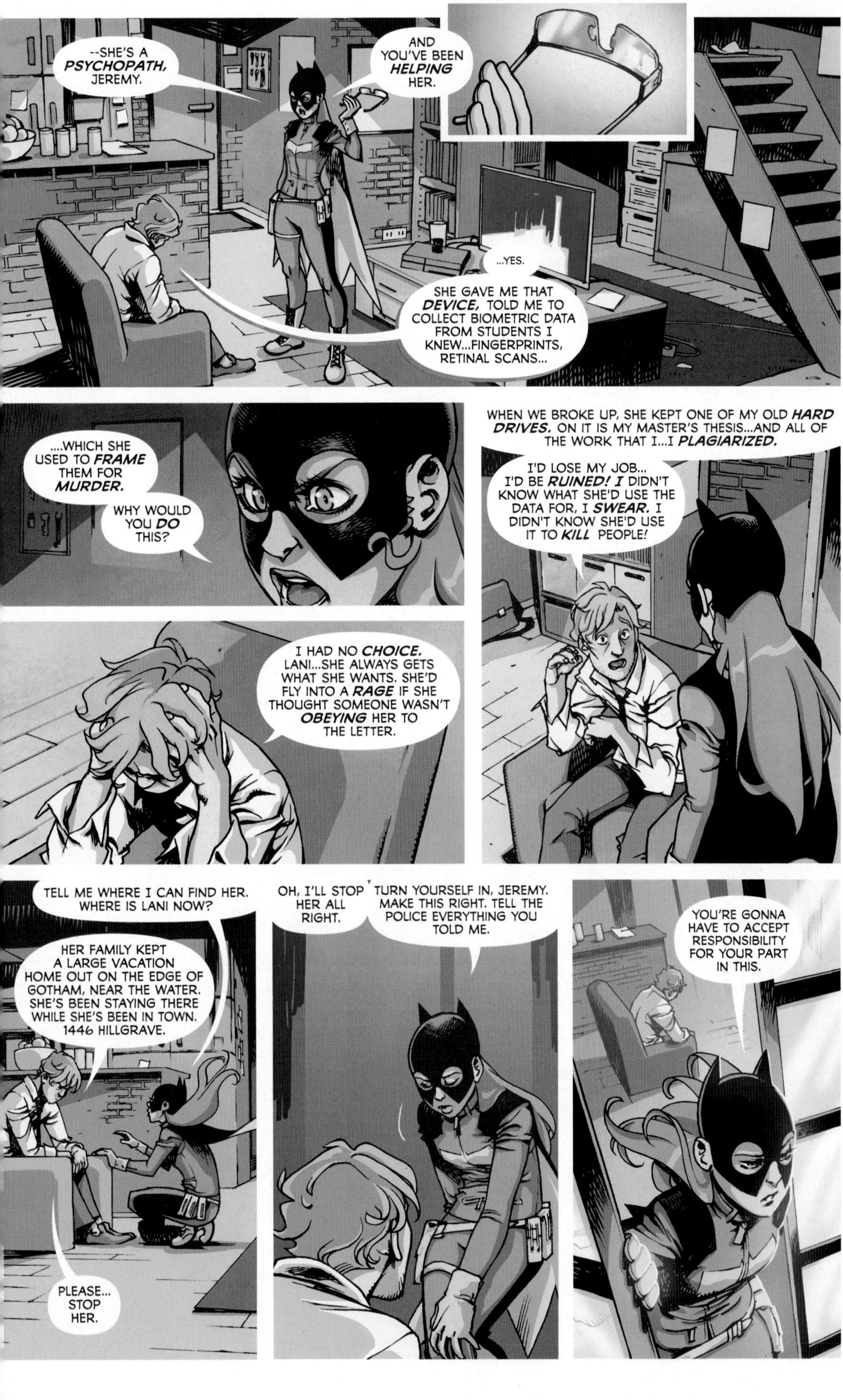
--SHE'S A PSYCHOPATH, JEREMY.
AND YOU'VE BEEN HELPING HER.
...YES.
SHE GAVE ME THAT DEVICE, TOLD ME TO COLLECT BIOMETRIC DATA FROM STUDENTS I KNEW...FINGERPRINTS, RETINAL SCANS...
....WHICH SHE USED TO FRAME THEM FOR MURDER.
WHY WOULD YOU DO THIS?
I HAD NO CHOICE. LANI...SHE ALWAYS GETS WHAT SHE WANTS. SHE'D FLY INTO A RAGE IF SHE THOUGHT SOMEONE WASN'T OBEYING HER TO THE LETTER.
WHEN WE BROKE UP, SHE KEPT ONE OF MY OLD HARD DRIVES. ON IT IS MY MASTER'S THESIS...AND ALL OF THE WORK THAT I...I PLAGIARIZED.
I'D LOSE MY JOB... I'D BE RUINED! I DIDN'T KNOW WHAT SHE'D USE THE DATA FOR, I SWEAR. I DIDN'T KNOW SHE'D USE IT TO KILL PEOPLE!
TELL ME WHERE I CAN FIND HER. WHERE IS LANI NOW?
HER FAMILY KEPT A LARGE VACATION HOME OUT ON THE EDGE OF GOTHAM, NEAR THE WATER. SHE'S BEEN STAYING THERE WHILE SHE'S BEEN IN TOWN. 1446 HILLGRAVE.
PLEASE... STOP HER.
OH, I'LL STOP HER ALL RIGHT.
TURN YOURSELF IN, JEREMY. MAKE THIS RIGHT. TELL THE POLICE EVERYTHING YOU TOLD ME.
YOU'RE GONNA HAVE TO ACCEPT RESPONSIBILITY FOR YOUR PART IN THIS.

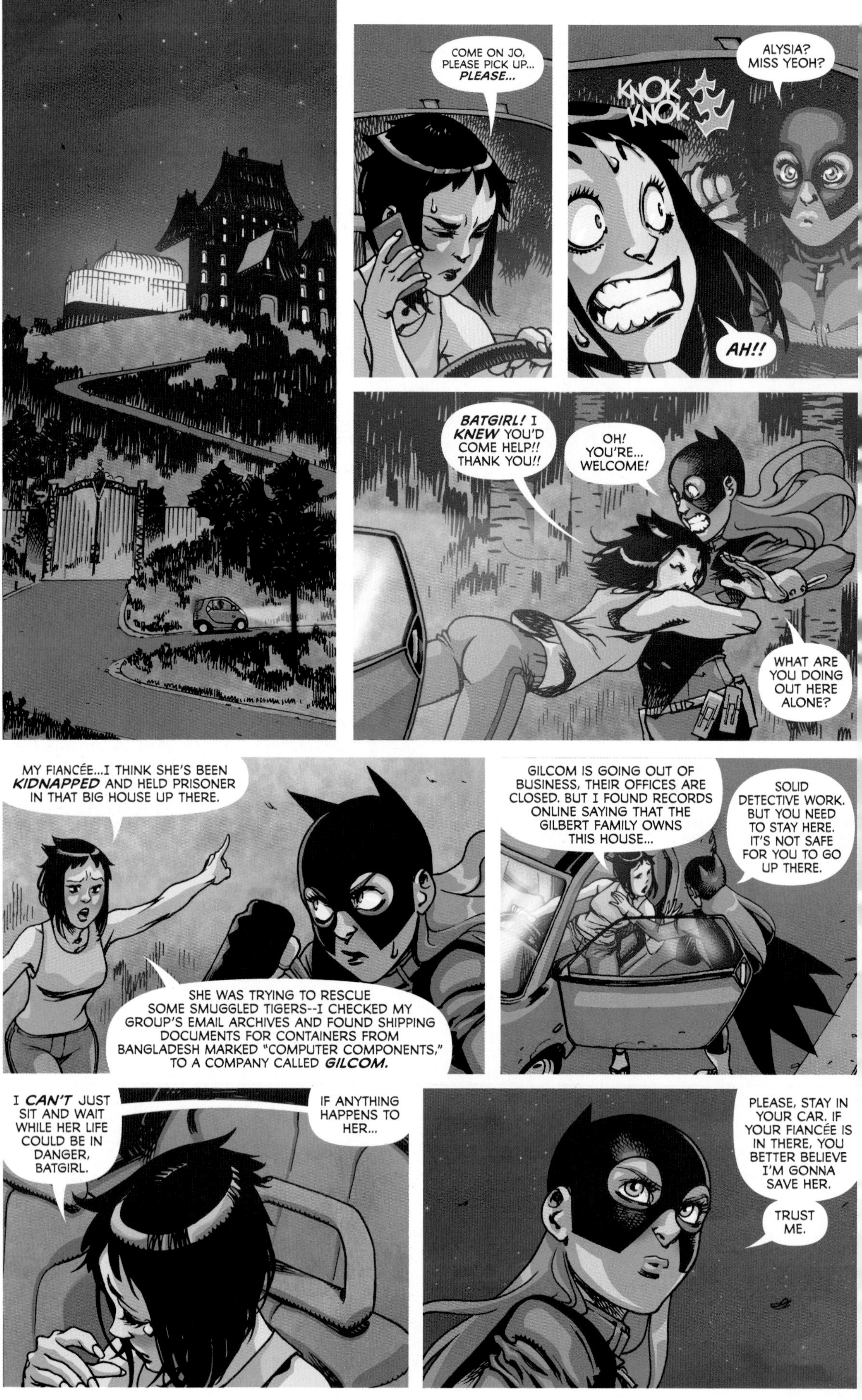
COME ON JO, PLEASE PICK UP... PLEASE...
ALYSIA? MISS YEOH?
KNOK KNOK
AH!!
BATGIRL! I KNEW YOU'D COME HELP!! THANK YOU!!
OH! YOU'RE... WELCOME!
WHAT ARE YOU DOING OUT HERE ALONE?
MY FIANCÉE...I THINK SHE'S BEEN KIDNAPPED AND HELD PRISONER IN THAT BIG HOUSE UP THERE.
SHE WAS TRYING TO RESCUE SOME SMUGGLED TIGERS--I CHECKED MY GROUP'S EMAIL ARCHIVES AND FOUND SHIPPING DOCUMENTS FOR CONTAINERS FROM BANGLADESH MARKED "COMPUTER COMPONENTS," TO A COMPANY CALLED GILCOM.
GILCOM IS GOING OUT OF BUSINESS, THEIR OFFICES ARE CLOSED. BUT I FOUND RECORDS ONLINE SAYING THAT THE GILBERT FAMILY OWNS THIS HOUSE...
SOLID DETECTIVE WORK. BUT YOU NEED TO STAY HERE. IT'S NOT SAFE FOR YOU TO GO UP THERE.
I CAN'T JUST SIT AND WAIT WHILE HER LIFE COULD BE IN DANGER, BATGIRL.
IF ANYTHING HAPPENS TO HER...
PLEASE, STAY IN YOUR CAR. IF YOUR FIANCÉE IS IN THERE, YOU BETTER BELIEVE I'M GONNA SAVE HER.
TRUST ME.

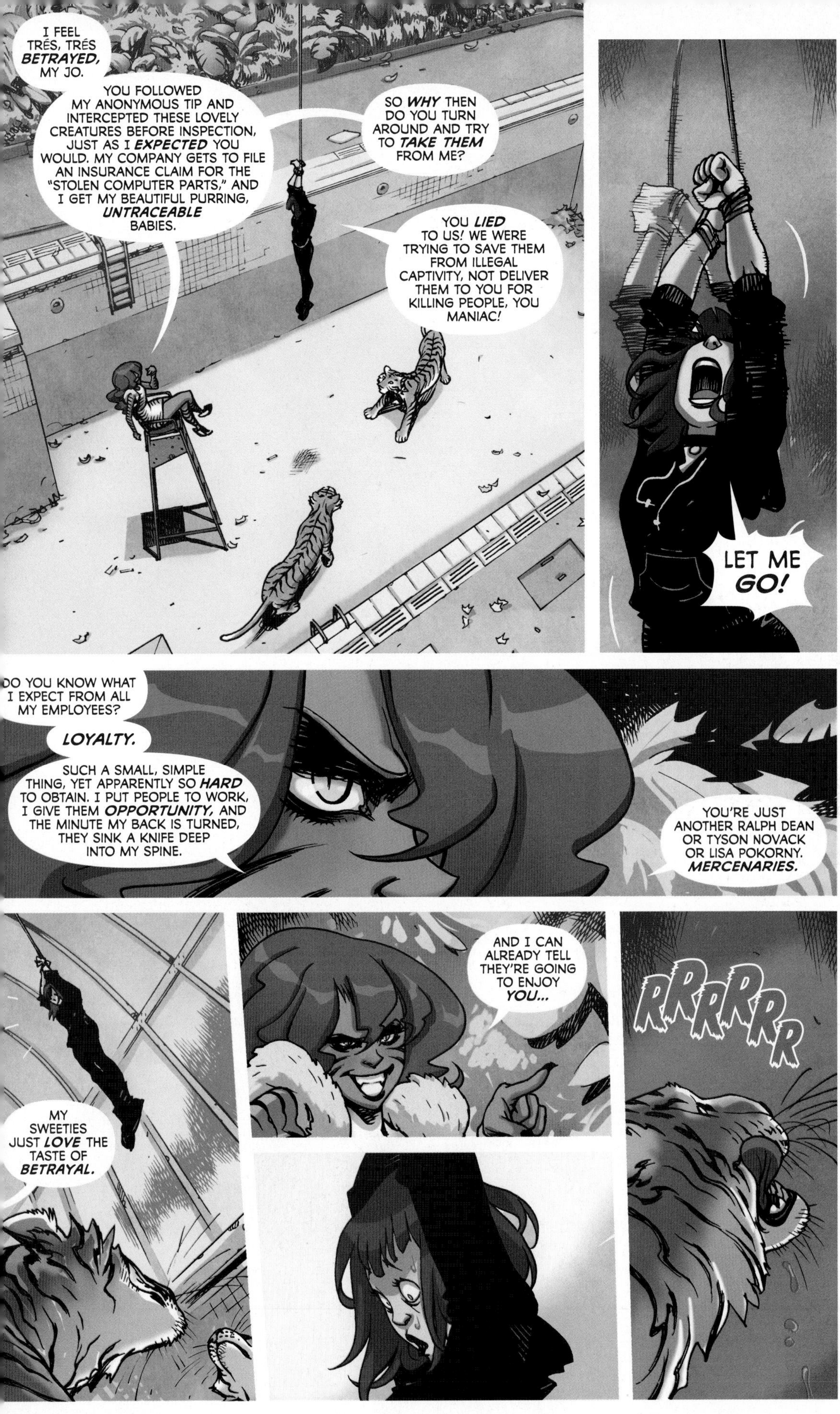
I FEEL TRÉS, TRÉS BETRAYED, MY JO.
YOU FOLLOWED MY ANONYMOUS TIP AND INTERCEPTED THESE LOVELY CREATURES BEFORE INSPECTION, JUST AS I EXPECTED YOU WOULD. MY COMPANY GETS TO FILE AN INSURANCE CLAIM FOR THE "STOLEN COMPUTER PARTS," AND I GET MY BEAUTIFUL PURRING, UNTRACEABLE BABIES.
SO WHY THEN DO YOU TURN AROUND AND TRY TO TAKE THEM FROM ME?
YOU LIED TO US! WE WERE TRYING TO SAVE THEM FROM ILLEGAL CAPTIVITY, NOT DELIVER THEM TO YOU FOR KILLING PEOPLE, YOU MANIAC!
LET ME GO!
DO YOU KNOW WHAT I EXPECT FROM ALL MY EMPLOYEES?
LOYALTY.
SUCH A SMALL, SIMPLE THING, YET APPARENTLY SO HARD TO OBTAIN. I PUT PEOPLE TO WORK, I GIVE THEM OPPORTUNITY, AND THE MINUTE MY BACK IS TURNED, THEY SINK A KNIFE DEEP INTO MY SPINE.
YOU'RE JUST ANOTHER RALPH DEAN OR TYSON NOVACK OR LISA POKORNY. MERCENARIES.
MY SWEETIES JUST LOVE THE TASTE OF BETRAYAL.
AND I CAN ALREADY TELL THEY'RE GOING TO ENJOY YOU...
RRRRRRR

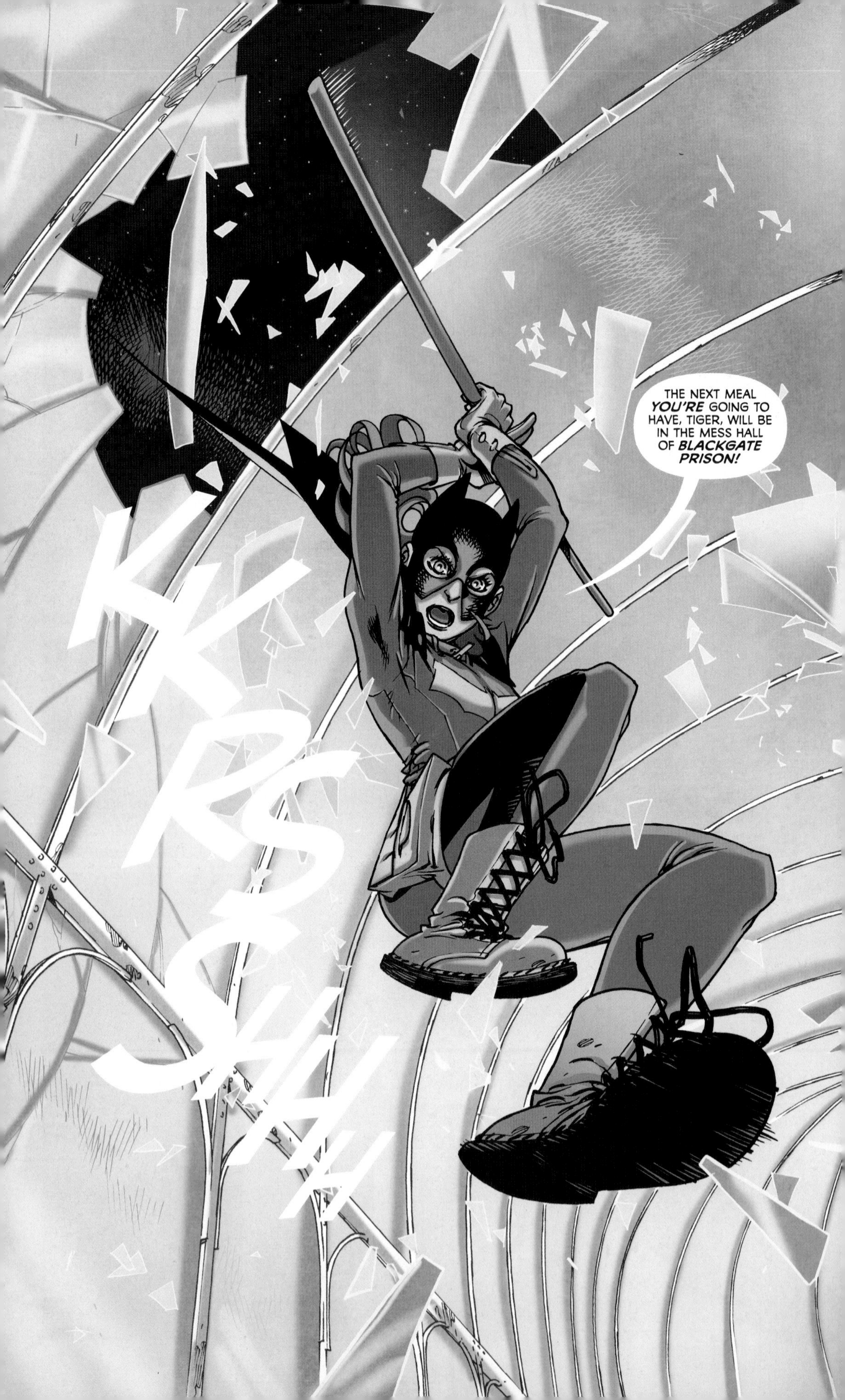
THE NEXT MEAL *YOU'RE* GOING TO HAVE, TIGER, WILL BE IN THE MESS HALL OF ***BLACKGATE PRISON!***
KKRSSHH

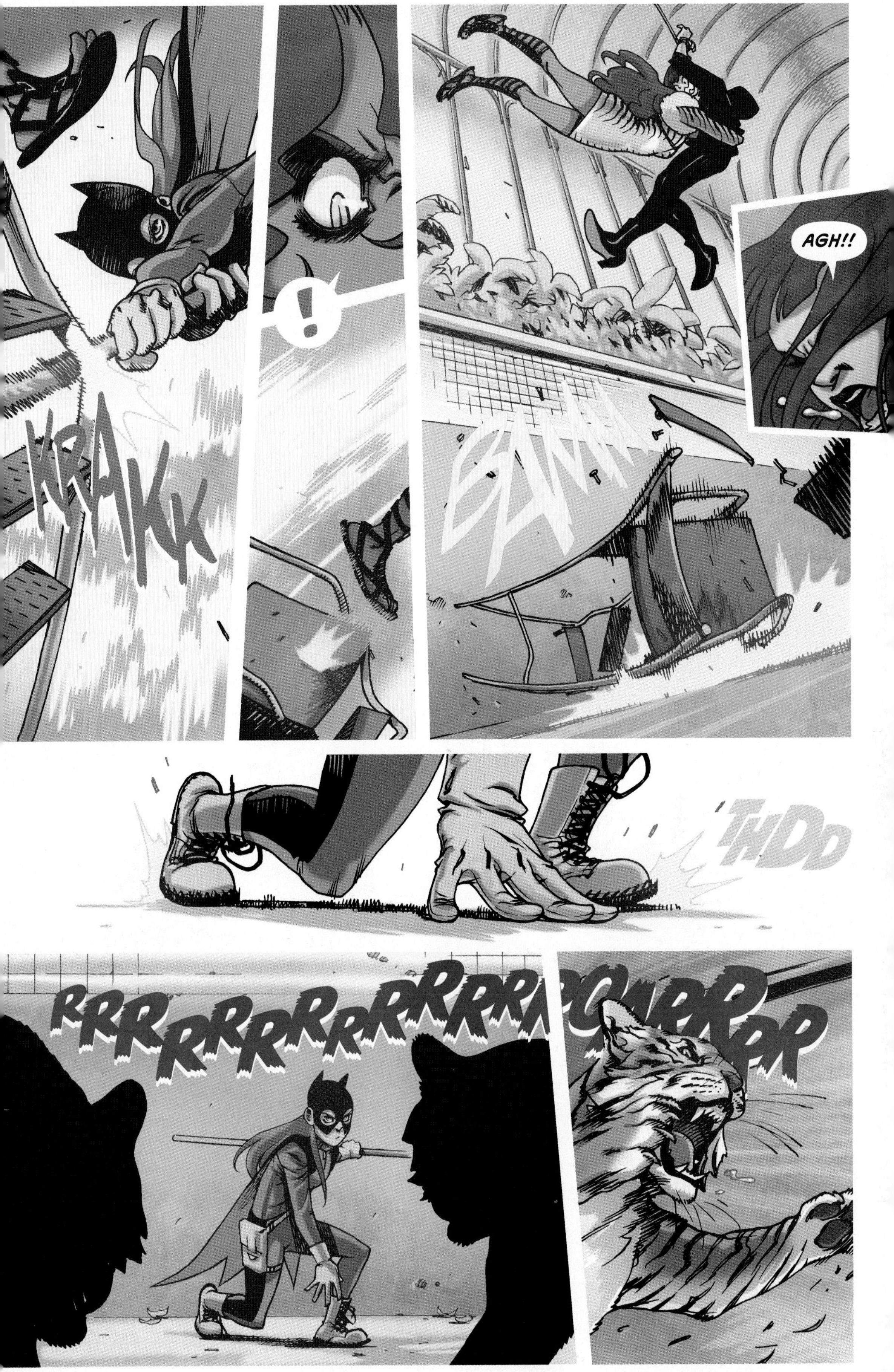

KRAKK
!
BAMM
AGH!!
THDD
RRRRRRRRRRRRRROARRRR

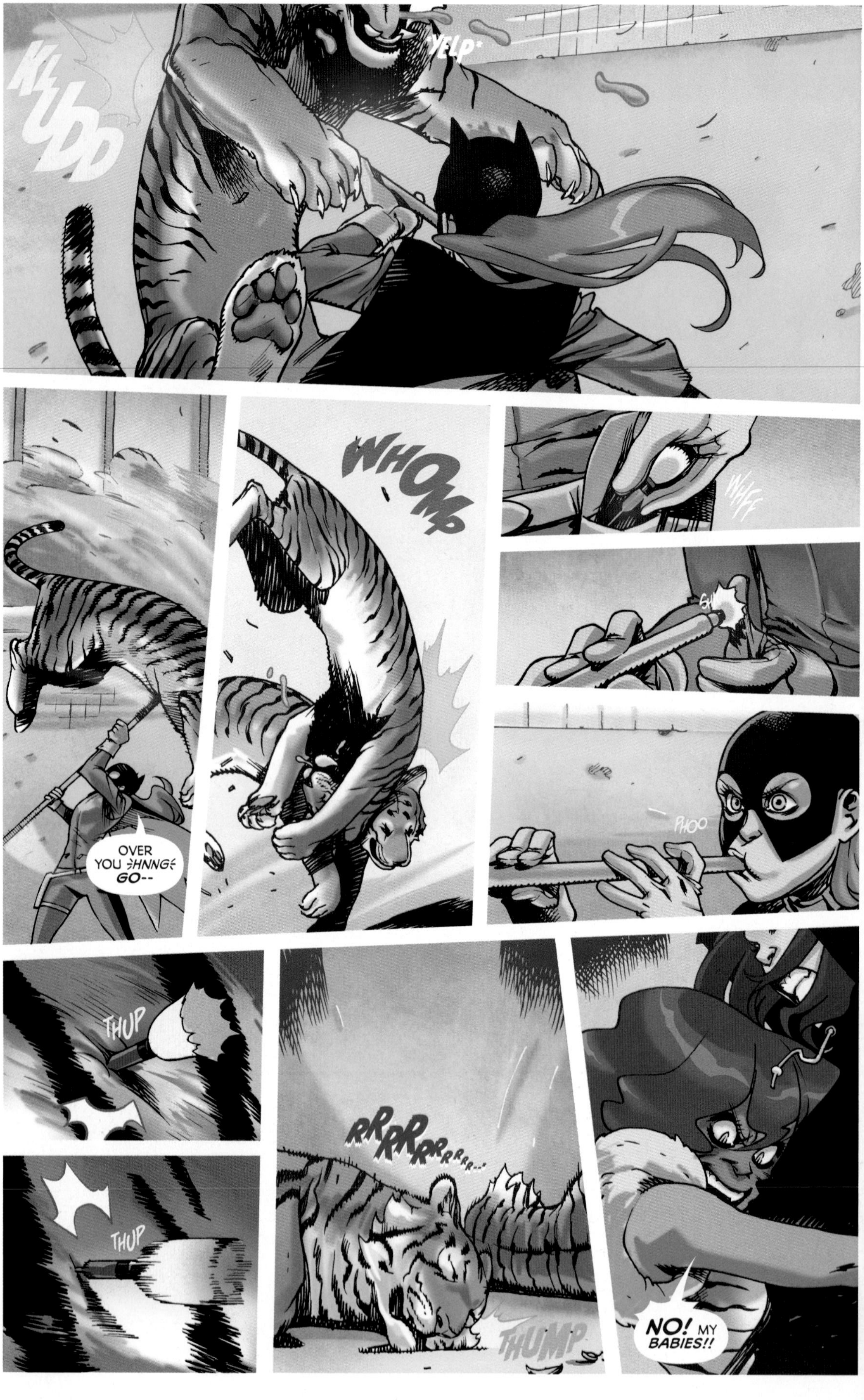

KLUDD
YELP
OVER YOU ⟨HNNG⟩ GO--
WHOMP
WHFF
PHOO
THUP
THUP
RRRRRrrrr...
THUMP
NO! MY BABIES!!

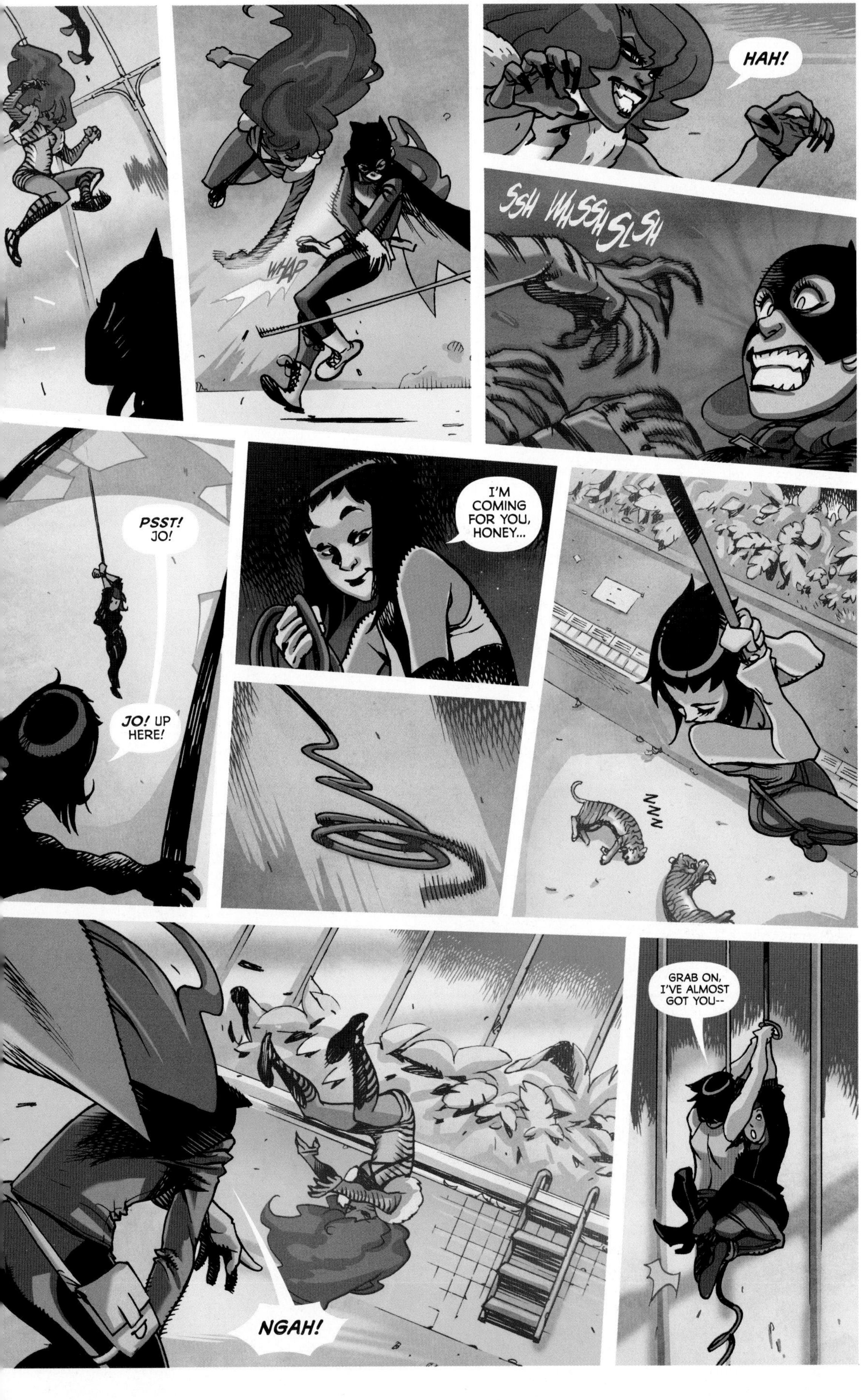
WHAP
HAH!
SSH WHSSH SLSH
PSST! JO!
JO! UP HERE!
I'M COMING FOR YOU, HONEY...
NNN
NGAH!
GRAB ON, I'VE ALMOST GOT YOU--

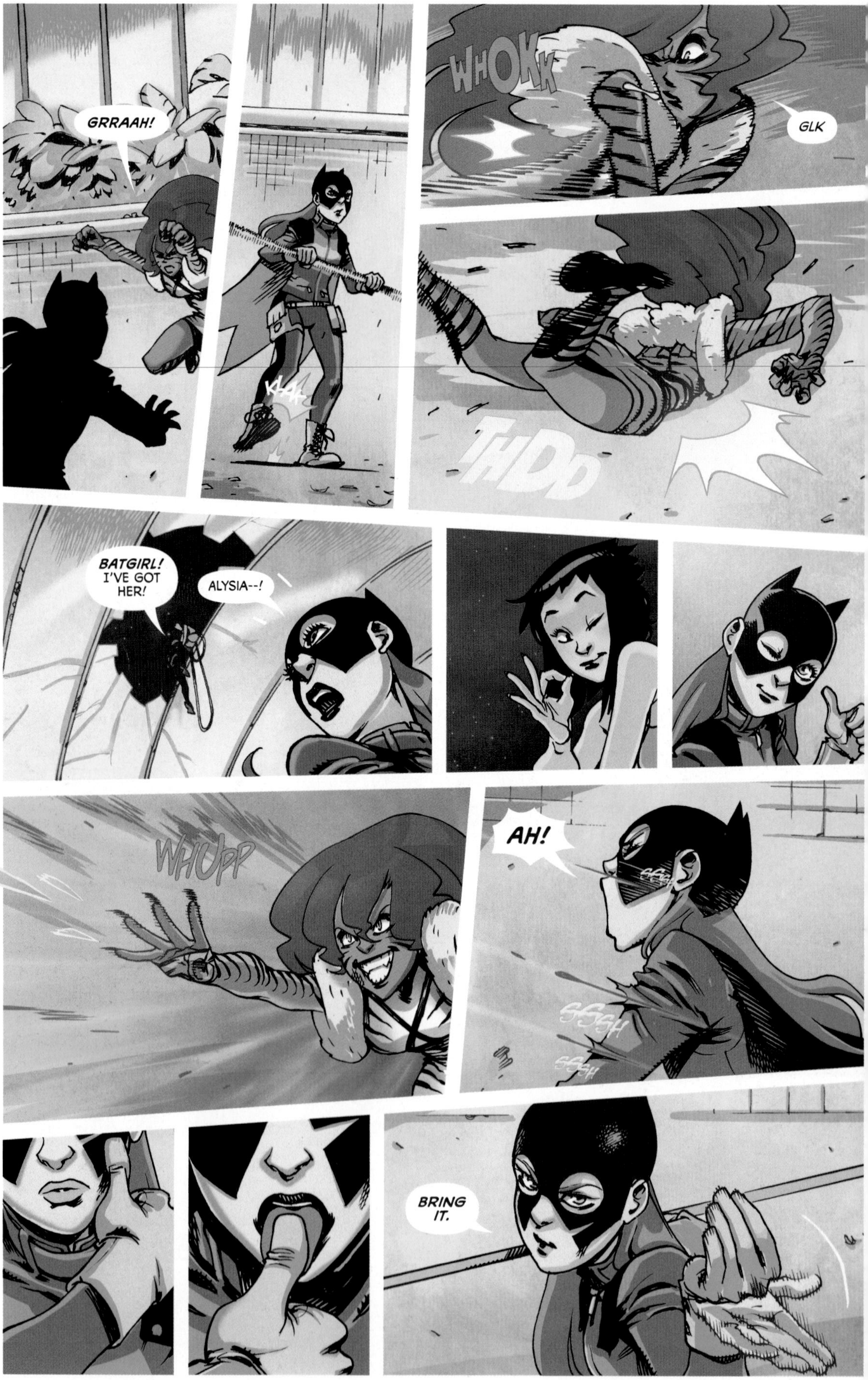
GRRAAH!
KLAK
WHOKK
GLK
THDD
BATGIRL! I'VE GOT HER!
ALYSIA--!
WHUPP
AH!
SSSH
SSSH
BRING IT.

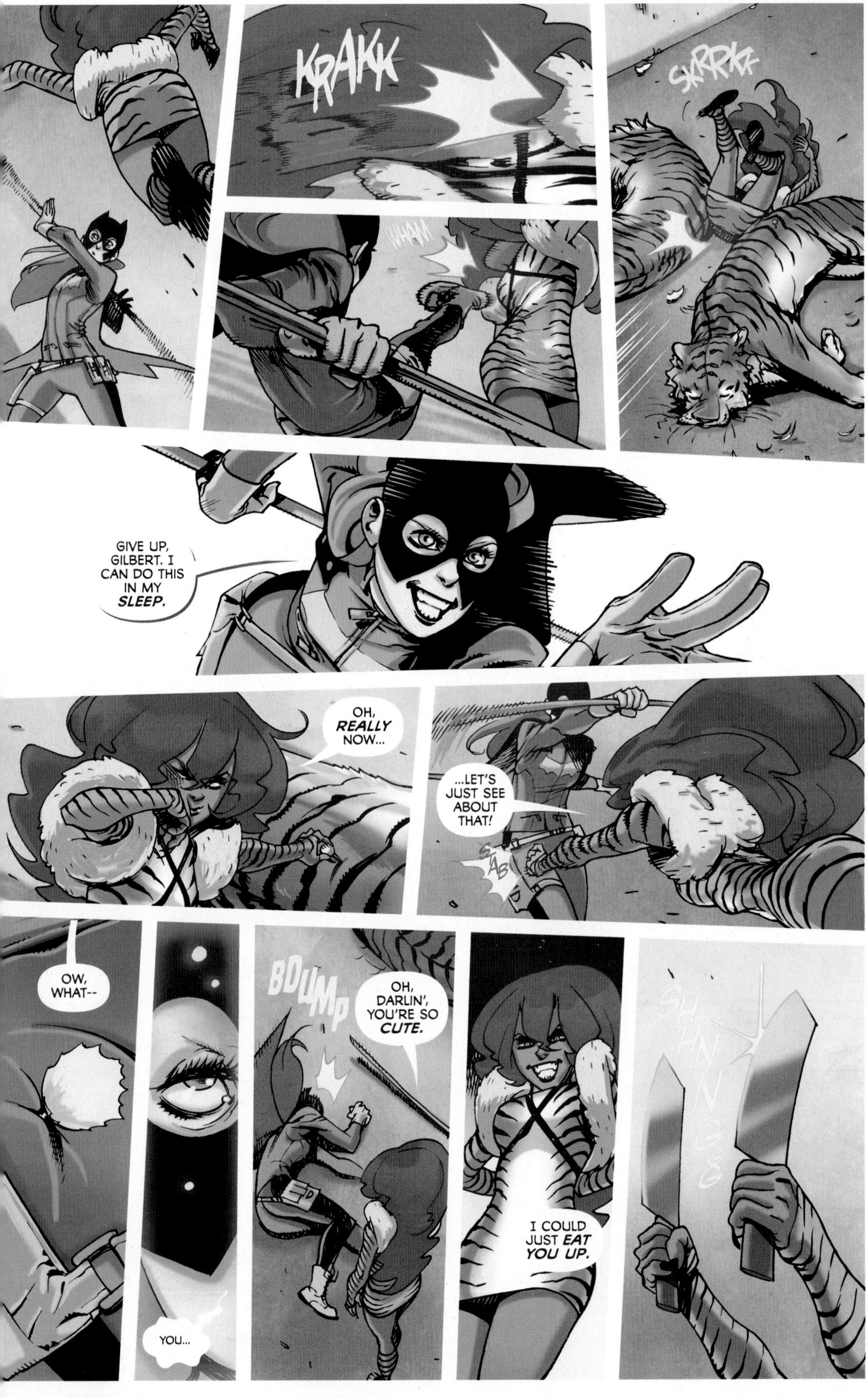
KRAKK
SKRRKK
WHAM
GIVE UP, GILBERT. I CAN DO THIS IN MY *SLEEP.*
OH, *REALLY* NOW...
...LET'S JUST SEE ABOUT THAT!
STAB
OW, WHAT--
YOU...
BDUMP
OH, DARLIN', YOU'RE SO *CUTE.*
I COULD JUST *EAT YOU UP.*
SHHNNGG

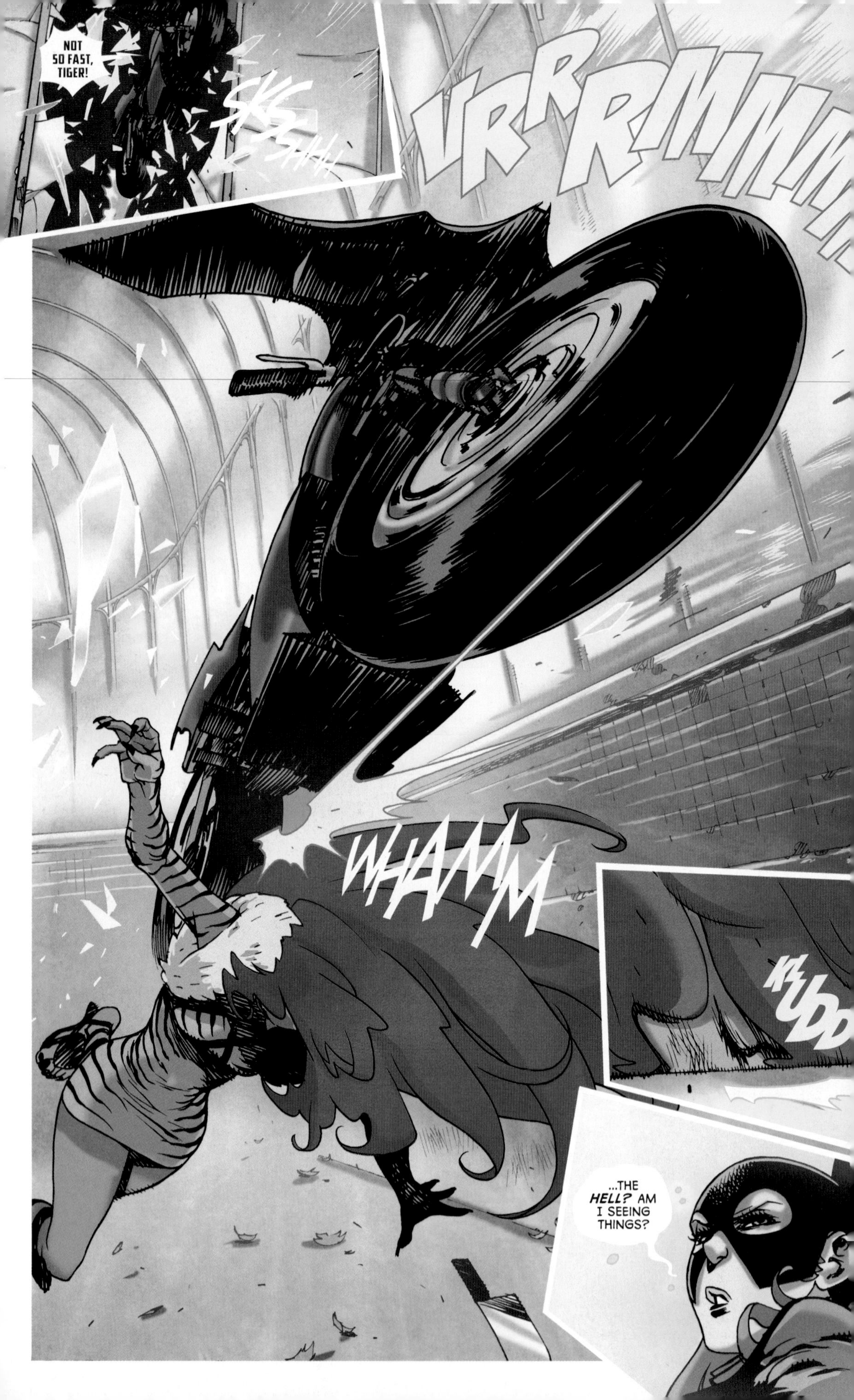
NOT SO FAST, TIGER!
SKSSHH!
VRRRMMMM
WHAMM
KRUDD
...THE HELL? AM I SEEING THINGS?

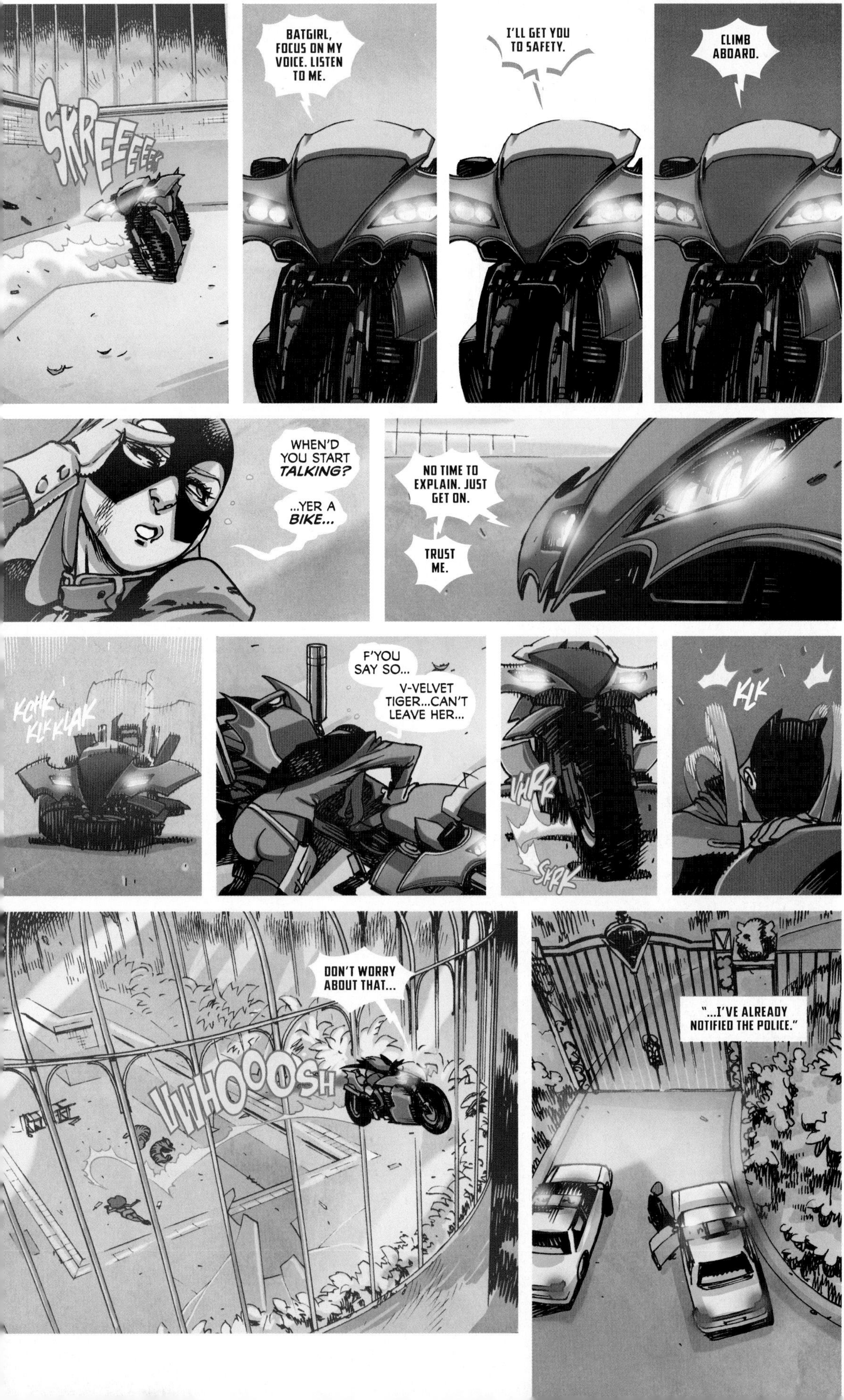
SKREEEEEEE
BATGIRL, FOCUS ON MY VOICE. LISTEN TO ME.
I'LL GET YOU TO SAFETY.
CLIMB ABOARD.
WHEN'D YOU START *TALKING?*
...YER A *BIKE...*
NO TIME TO EXPLAIN. JUST GET ON.
TRUST ME.
KCHK KLIKKLAK
F'YOU SAY SO...
V-VELVET TIGER...CAN'T LEAVE HER...
VHRR
SKRK
KLIK
DON'T WORRY ABOUT THAT...
WHOOOSH
"...I'VE ALREADY NOTIFIED THE POLICE."

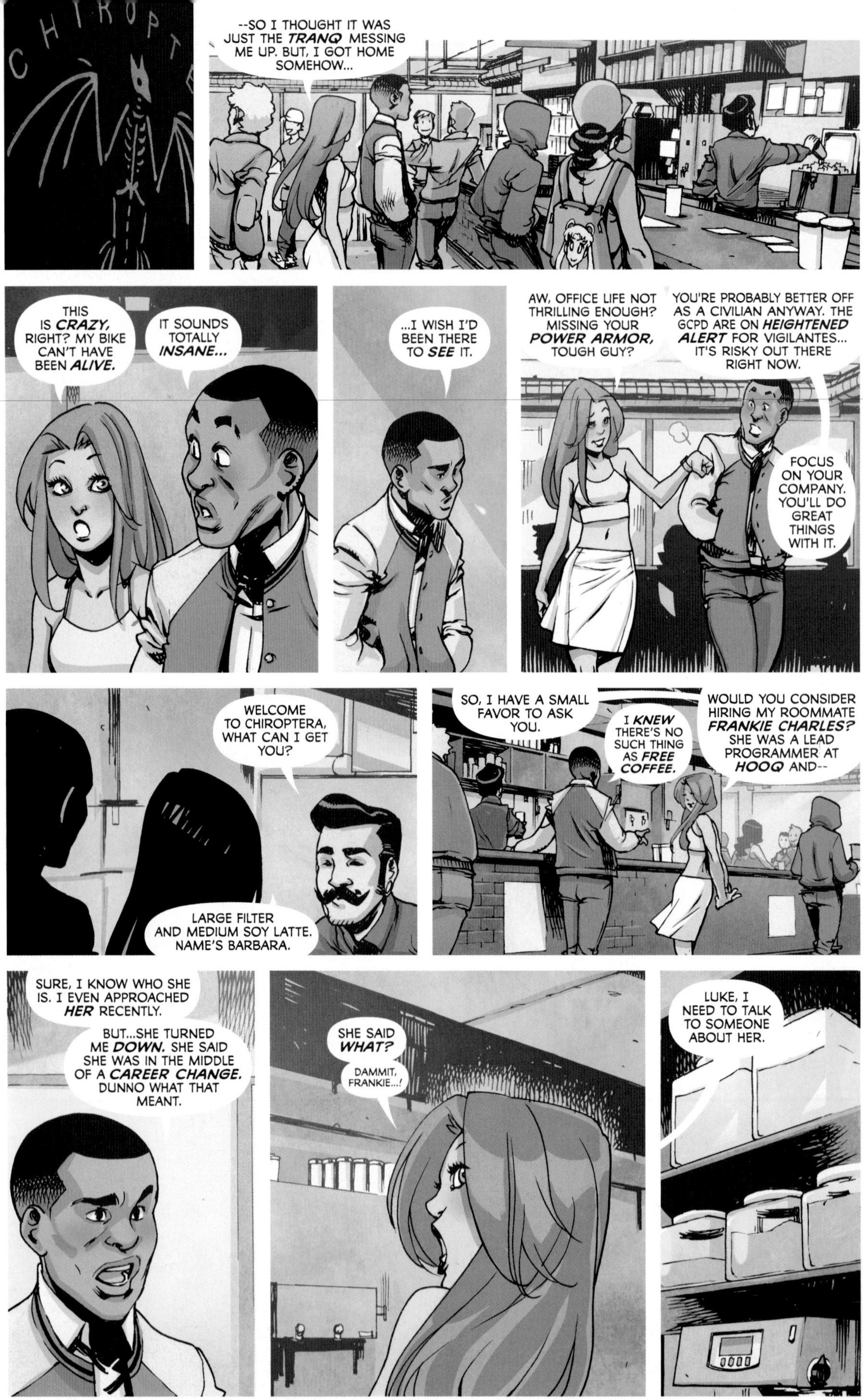
CHIROPTE
--SO I THOUGHT IT WAS JUST THE TRANQ MESSING ME UP. BUT, I GOT HOME SOMEHOW...
THIS IS CRAZY, RIGHT? MY BIKE CAN'T HAVE BEEN ALIVE.
IT SOUNDS TOTALLY INSANE...
...I WISH I'D BEEN THERE TO SEE IT.
AW, OFFICE LIFE NOT THRILLING ENOUGH? MISSING YOUR POWER ARMOR, TOUGH GUY?
YOU'RE PROBABLY BETTER OFF AS A CIVILIAN ANYWAY. THE GCPD ARE ON HEIGHTENED ALERT FOR VIGILANTES... IT'S RISKY OUT THERE RIGHT NOW.
FOCUS ON YOUR COMPANY. YOU'LL DO GREAT THINGS WITH IT.
WELCOME TO CHIROPTERA, WHAT CAN I GET YOU?
LARGE FILTER AND MEDIUM SOY LATTE. NAME'S BARBARA.
SO, I HAVE A SMALL FAVOR TO ASK YOU.
I KNEW THERE'S NO SUCH THING AS FREE COFFEE.
WOULD YOU CONSIDER HIRING MY ROOMMATE FRANKIE CHARLES? SHE WAS A LEAD PROGRAMMER AT HOOQ AND--
SURE, I KNOW WHO SHE IS. I EVEN APPROACHED HER RECENTLY.
BUT...SHE TURNED ME DOWN. SHE SAID SHE WAS IN THE MIDDLE OF A CAREER CHANGE. DUNNO WHAT THAT MEANT.
SHE SAID WHAT?
DAMMIT, FRANKIE...!
LUKE, I NEED TO TALK TO SOMEONE ABOUT HER.

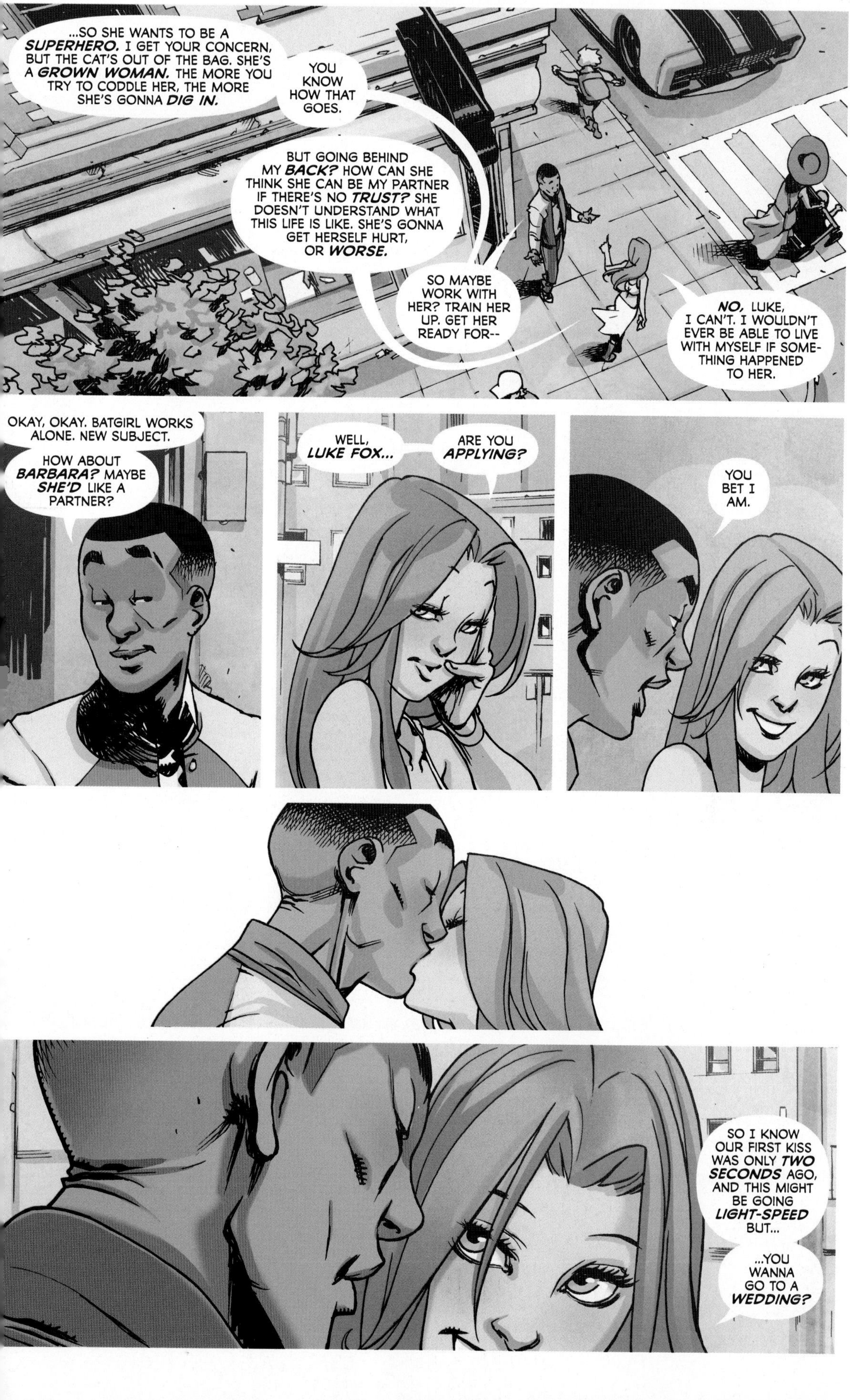
...SO SHE WANTS TO BE A SUPERHERO. I GET YOUR CONCERN, BUT THE CAT'S OUT OF THE BAG. SHE'S A GROWN WOMAN. THE MORE YOU TRY TO CODDLE HER, THE MORE SHE'S GONNA DIG IN.
YOU KNOW HOW THAT GOES.
BUT GOING BEHIND MY BACK? HOW CAN SHE THINK SHE CAN BE MY PARTNER IF THERE'S NO TRUST? SHE DOESN'T UNDERSTAND WHAT THIS LIFE IS LIKE. SHE'S GONNA GET HERSELF HURT, OR WORSE.
SO MAYBE WORK WITH HER? TRAIN HER UP. GET HER READY FOR--
NO, LUKE, I CAN'T. I WOULDN'T EVER BE ABLE TO LIVE WITH MYSELF IF SOMETHING HAPPENED TO HER.
OKAY, OKAY. BATGIRL WORKS ALONE. NEW SUBJECT.
HOW ABOUT BARBARA? MAYBE SHE'D LIKE A PARTNER?
WELL, LUKE FOX...
ARE YOU APPLYING?
YOU BET I AM.
SO I KNOW OUR FIRST KISS WAS ONLY TWO SECONDS AGO, AND THIS MIGHT BE GOING LIGHT-SPEED BUT...
...YOU WANNA GO TO A WEDDING?

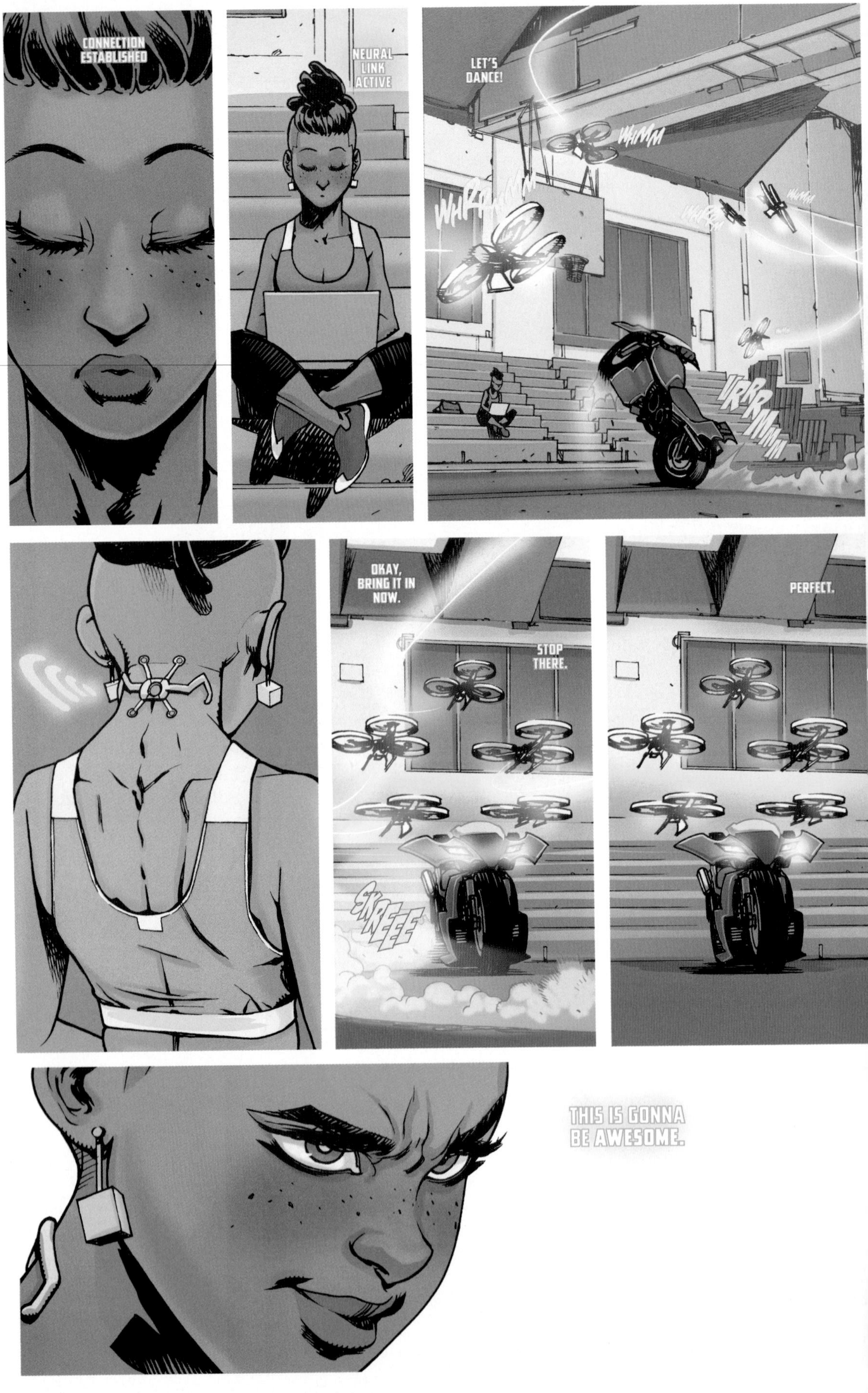
CONNECTION ESTABLISHED
NEURAL LINK ACTIVE
LET'S DANCE!
OKAY, BRING IT IN NOW.
STOP THERE.
SKREEE
PERFECT.
THIS IS GONNA BE AWESOME.

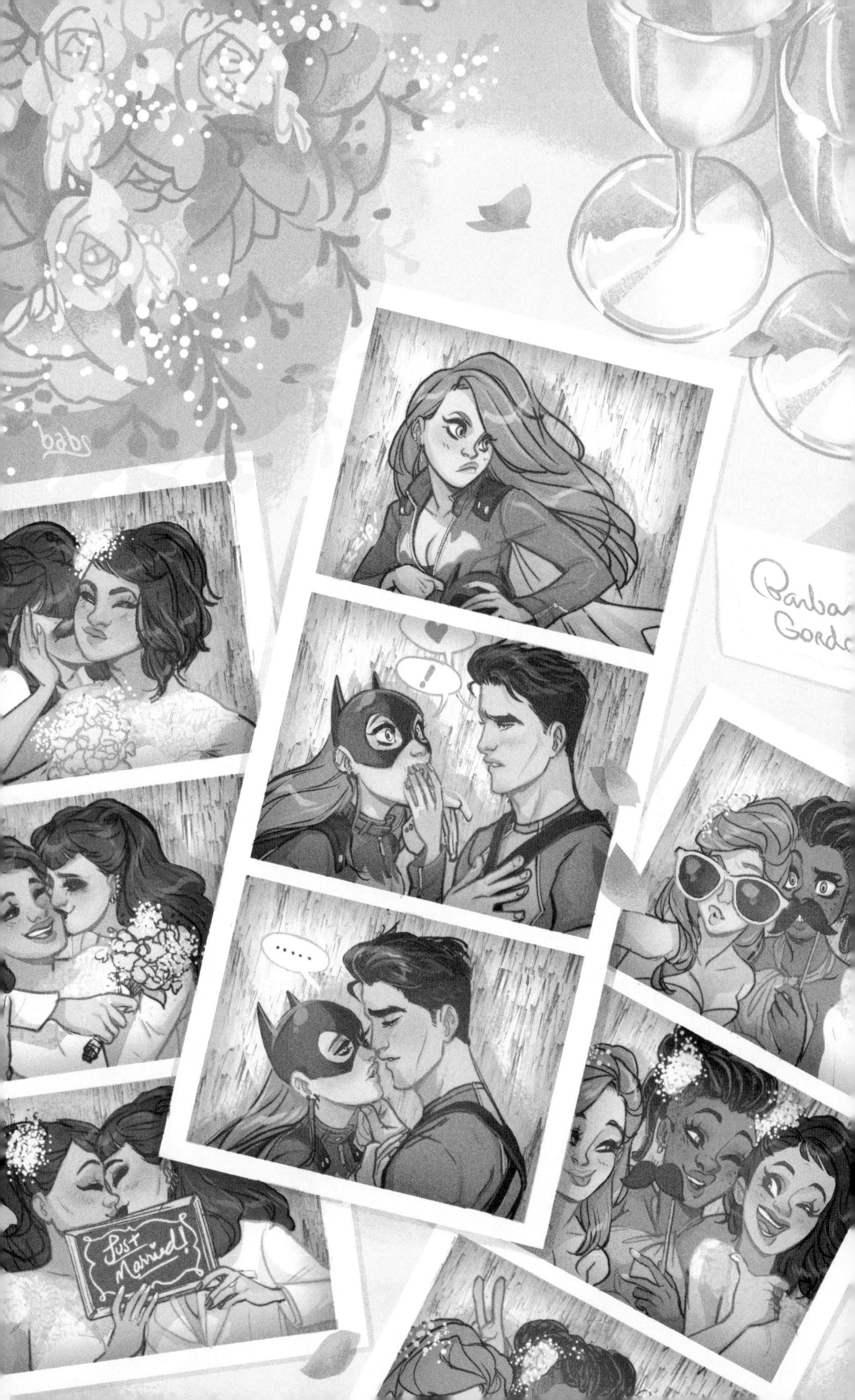

ZIP!
!
.....
Just Married!

CAMERON STEWART & BRENDEN FLETCHER writers BABS TARR artist SERGE LAPOINTE colorist STEVE WANDS letterer cover by BABS TARR

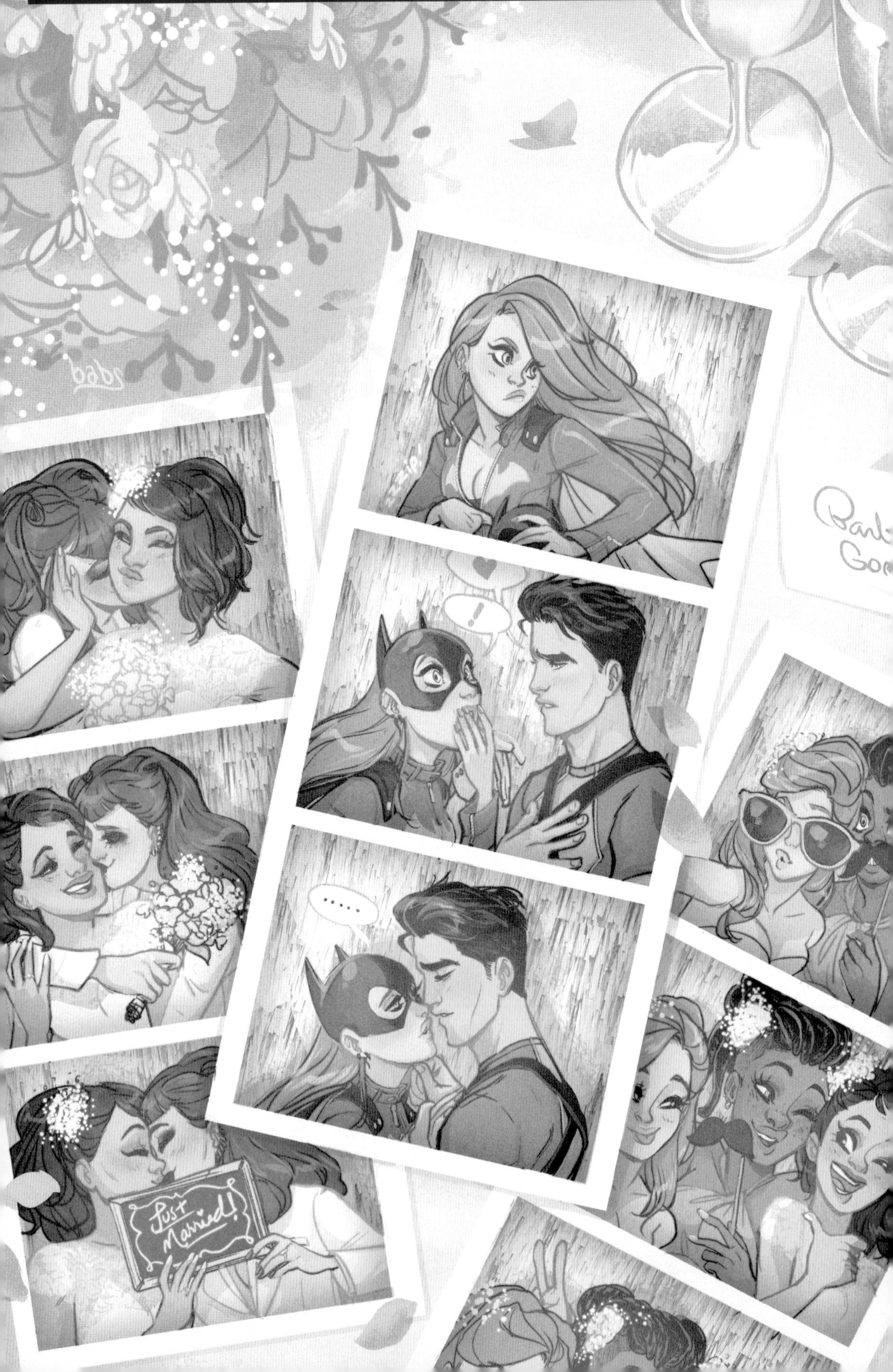
babs
!
.....
Just Married!

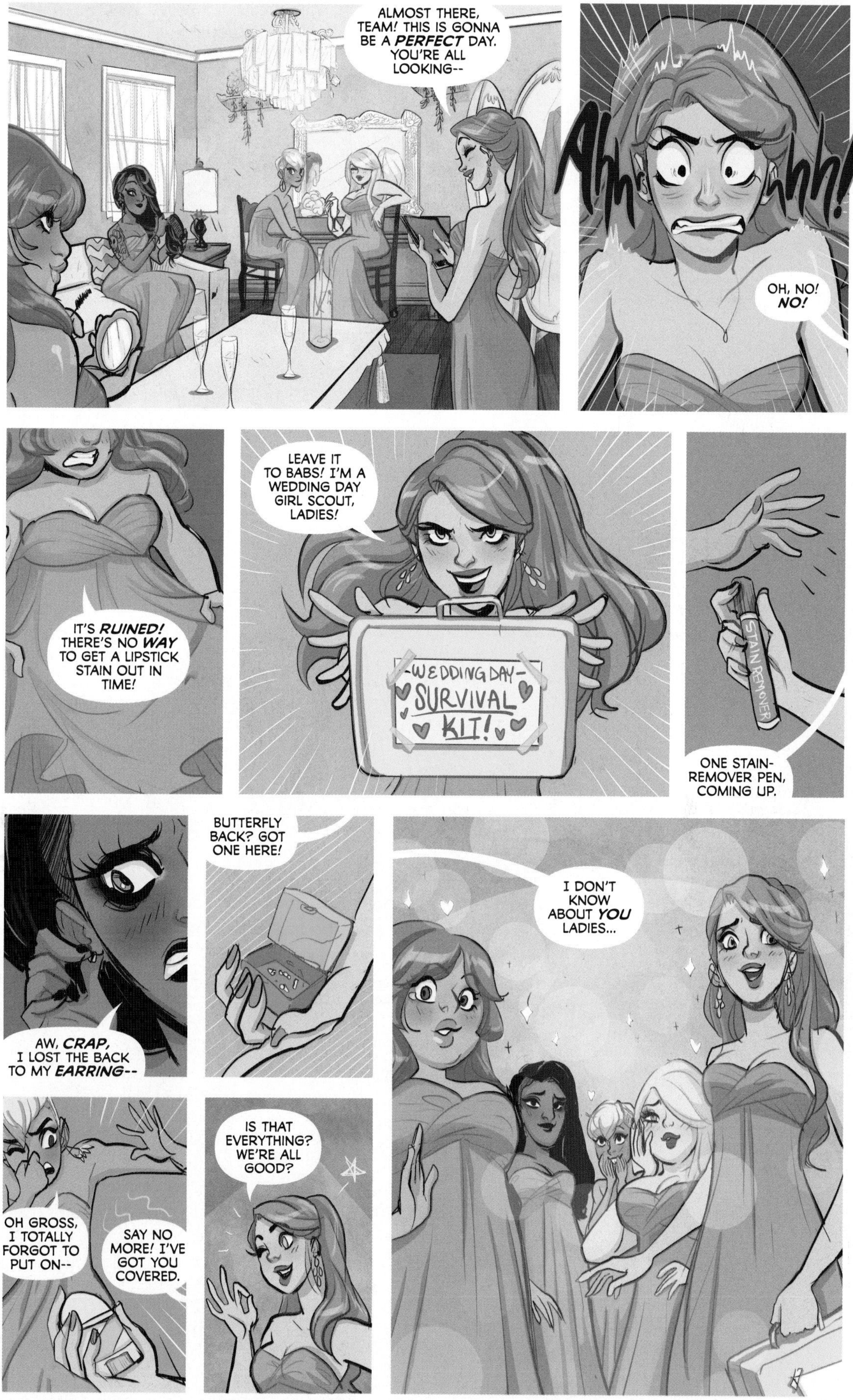

ALMOST THERE, TEAM! THIS IS GONNA BE A *PERFECT* DAY. YOU'RE ALL LOOKING--
Ahhhhh!
OH, NO! *NO!*
IT'S *RUINED!* THERE'S NO *WAY* TO GET A LIPSTICK STAIN OUT IN TIME!
LEAVE IT TO BABS! I'M A WEDDING DAY GIRL SCOUT, LADIES!
-WEDDING DAY- SURVIVAL KIT!
STAIN REMOVER
ONE STAIN-REMOVER PEN, COMING UP.
AW, *CRAP,* I LOST THE BACK TO MY *EARRING*--
BUTTERFLY BACK? GOT ONE HERE!
OH GROSS, I TOTALLY FORGOT TO PUT ON--
SAY NO MORE! I'VE GOT YOU COVERED.
IS THAT EVERYTHING? WE'RE ALL GOOD?
I DON'T KNOW ABOUT *YOU* LADIES...

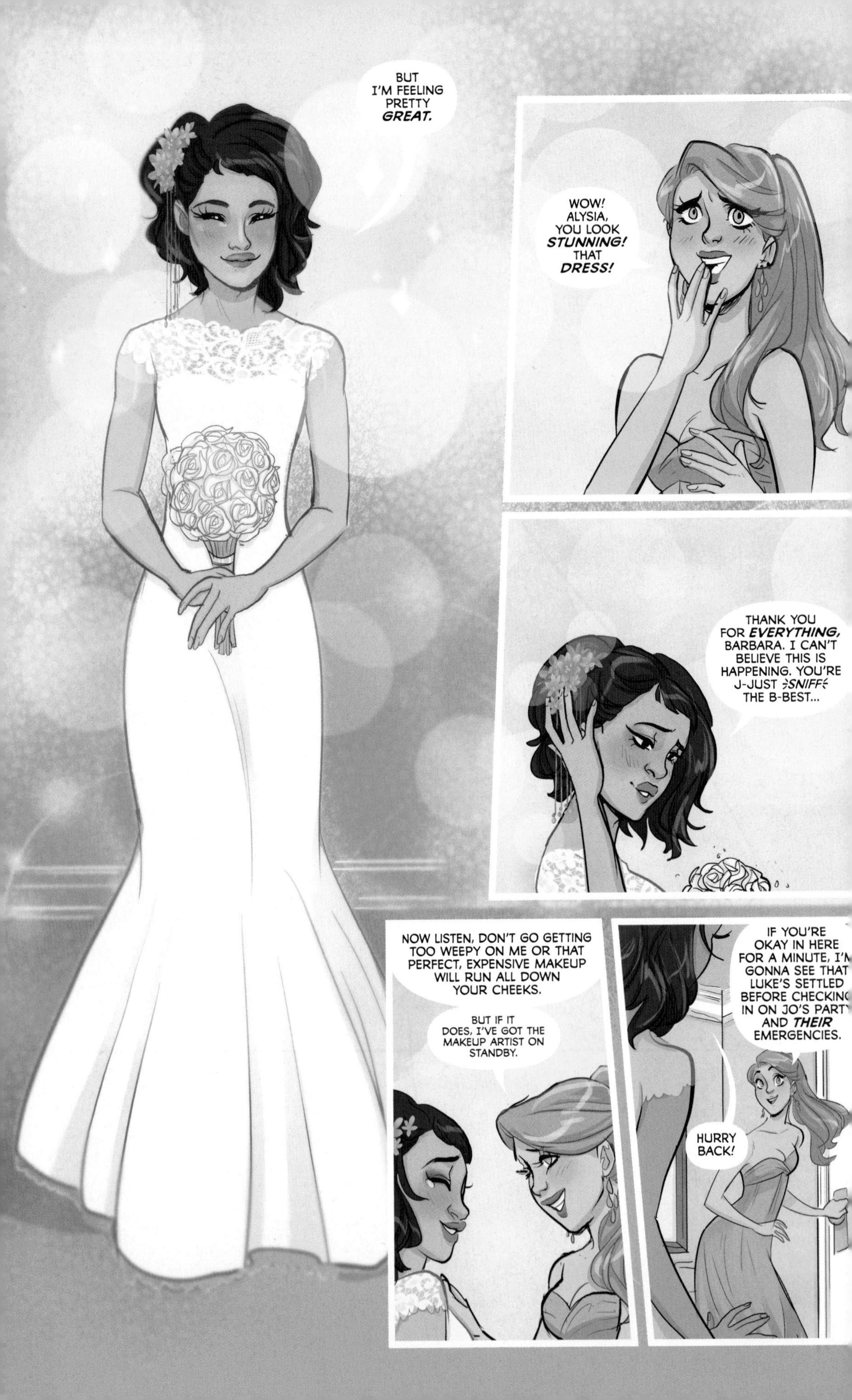
BUT I'M FEELING PRETTY GREAT.
WOW! ALYSIA, YOU LOOK STUNNING! THAT DRESS!
THANK YOU FOR EVERYTHING, BARBARA. I CAN'T BELIEVE THIS IS HAPPENING. YOU'RE J-JUST *SNIFF* THE B-BEST...
NOW LISTEN, DON'T GO GETTING TOO WEEPY ON ME OR THAT PERFECT, EXPENSIVE MAKEUP WILL RUN ALL DOWN YOUR CHEEKS.
BUT IF IT DOES, I'VE GOT THE MAKEUP ARTIST ON STANDBY.
IF YOU'RE OKAY IN HERE FOR A MINUTE, I'M GONNA SEE THAT LUKE'S SETTLED BEFORE CHECKING IN ON JO'S PARTY AND THEIR EMERGENCIES.
HURRY BACK!

BABS: Hey! I don't see you. Where did you go?

LUKE: Bowtie meltdown. In the spare room changing into a tshirt. ;)

HMM. STRANGE. YOU DON'T *LOOK* LIKE A T-SHIRT, FOX.

REALLY? YOU DON'T LOOK LIKE MY *DAD,* BUT YOU SURE HAVE THE SAME STYLE OF COMEDY.

YOU BETTER HOPE I'M *EQUALLY* GIFTED AT ADJUSTING MEN'S FORMALWEAR.

GETTING THIS *PACK* OFF YOU WILL HELP, FOR A START.

I JUST FIGURED WEARING IT WAS THE BEST WAY TO PROTECT THE GOODS INSIDE.

IT *DOES* CARRY THE MOST PRECIOUS CARGO, AFTER ALL.

THE MOST IMPORTANT JOB I'VE GOT TODAY...

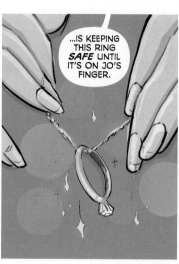

...IS KEEPING THIS RING *SAFE* UNTIL IT'S ON JO'S FINGER.

THERE.

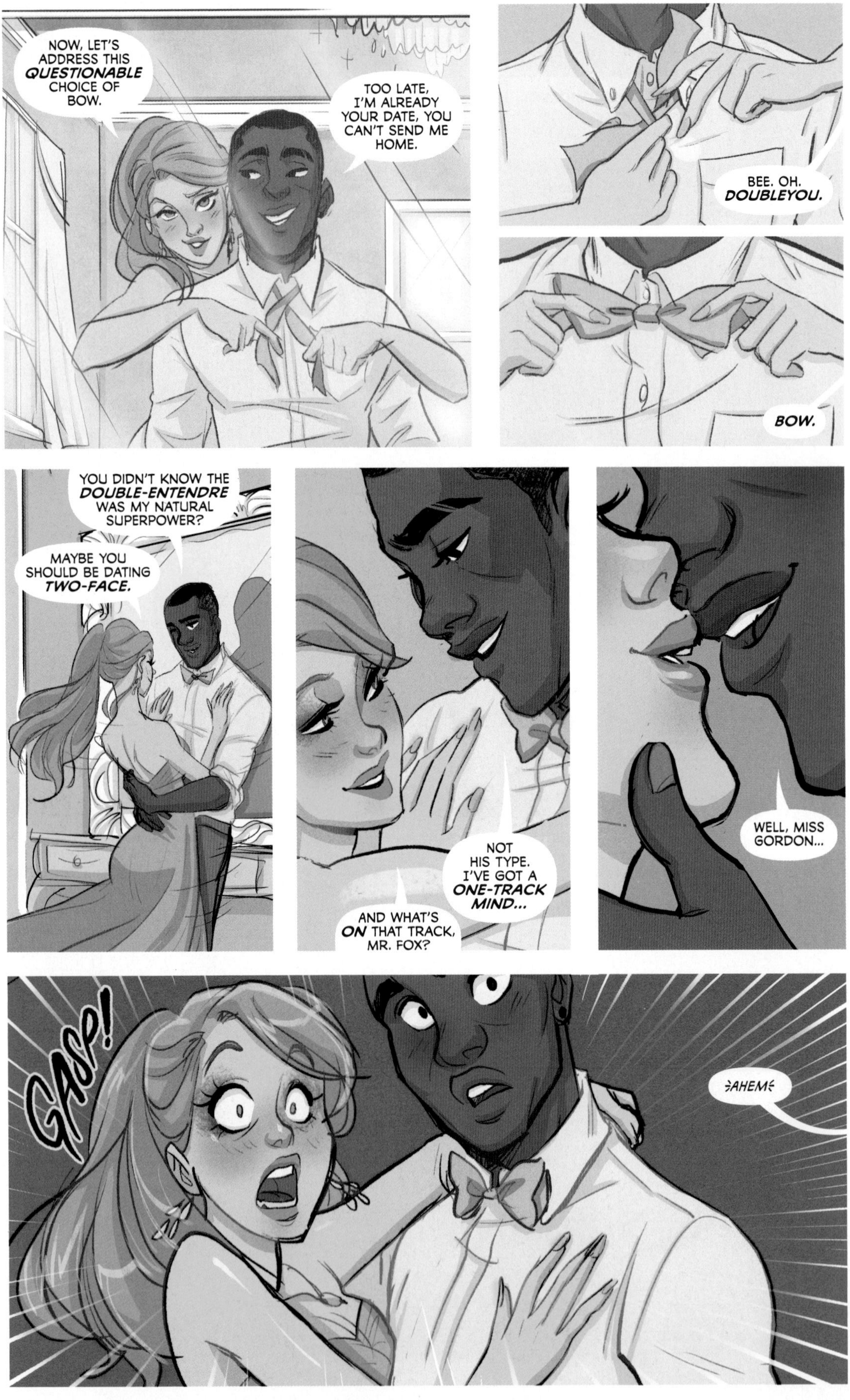
NOW, LET'S ADDRESS THIS *QUESTIONABLE* CHOICE OF BOW.
TOO LATE, I'M ALREADY YOUR DATE, YOU CAN'T SEND ME HOME.
BEE. OH. *DOUBLEYOU.*
BOW.
YOU DIDN'T KNOW THE *DOUBLE-ENTENDRE* WAS MY NATURAL SUPERPOWER?
MAYBE YOU SHOULD BE DATING *TWO-FACE.*
NOT HIS TYPE. I'VE GOT A *ONE-TRACK MIND...*
AND WHAT'S *ON* THAT TRACK, MR. FOX?
WELL, MISS GORDON...
GASP!
AHEM

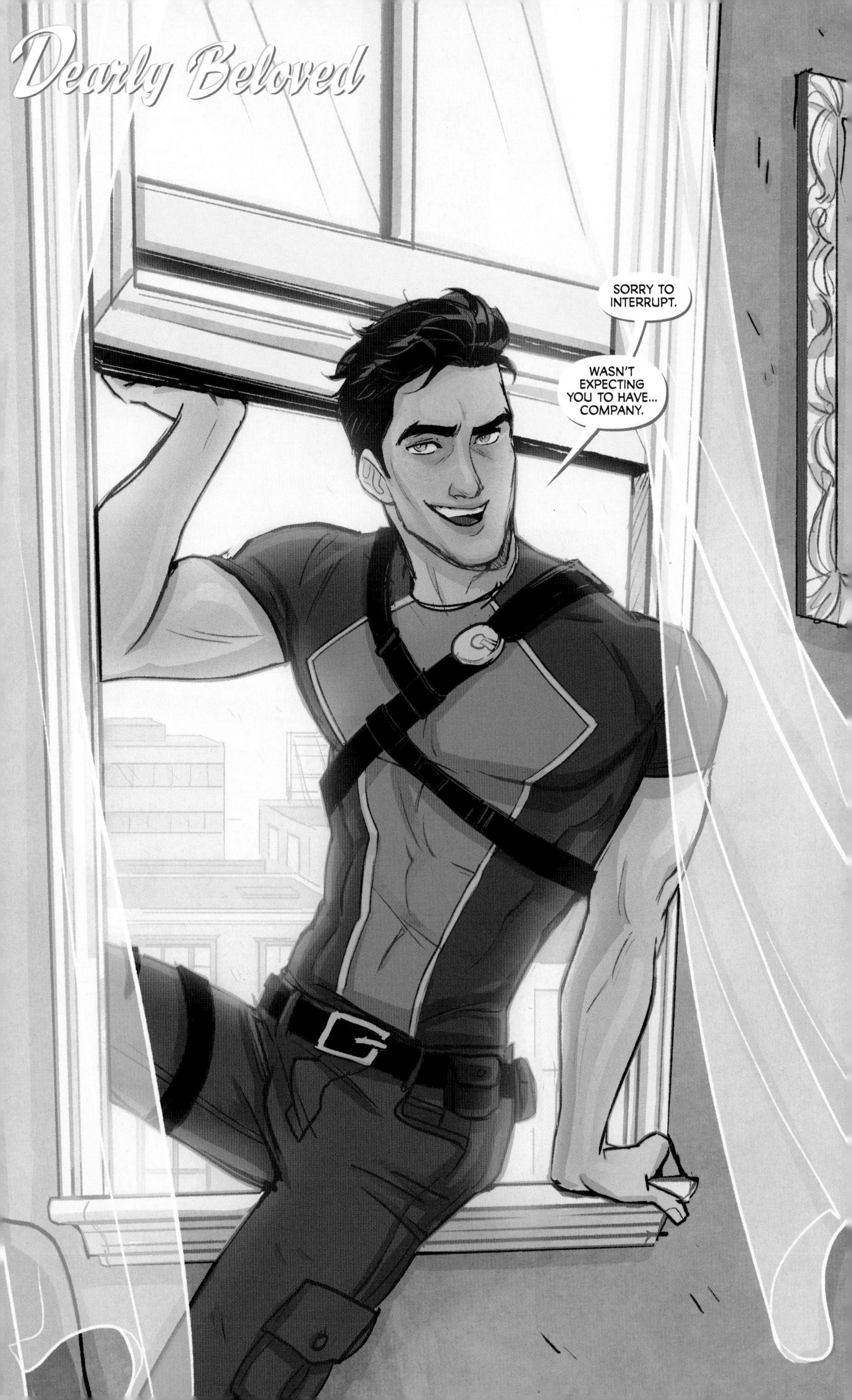
Dearly Beloved
SORRY TO INTERRUPT.
WASN'T EXPECTING YOU TO HAVE... COMPANY.

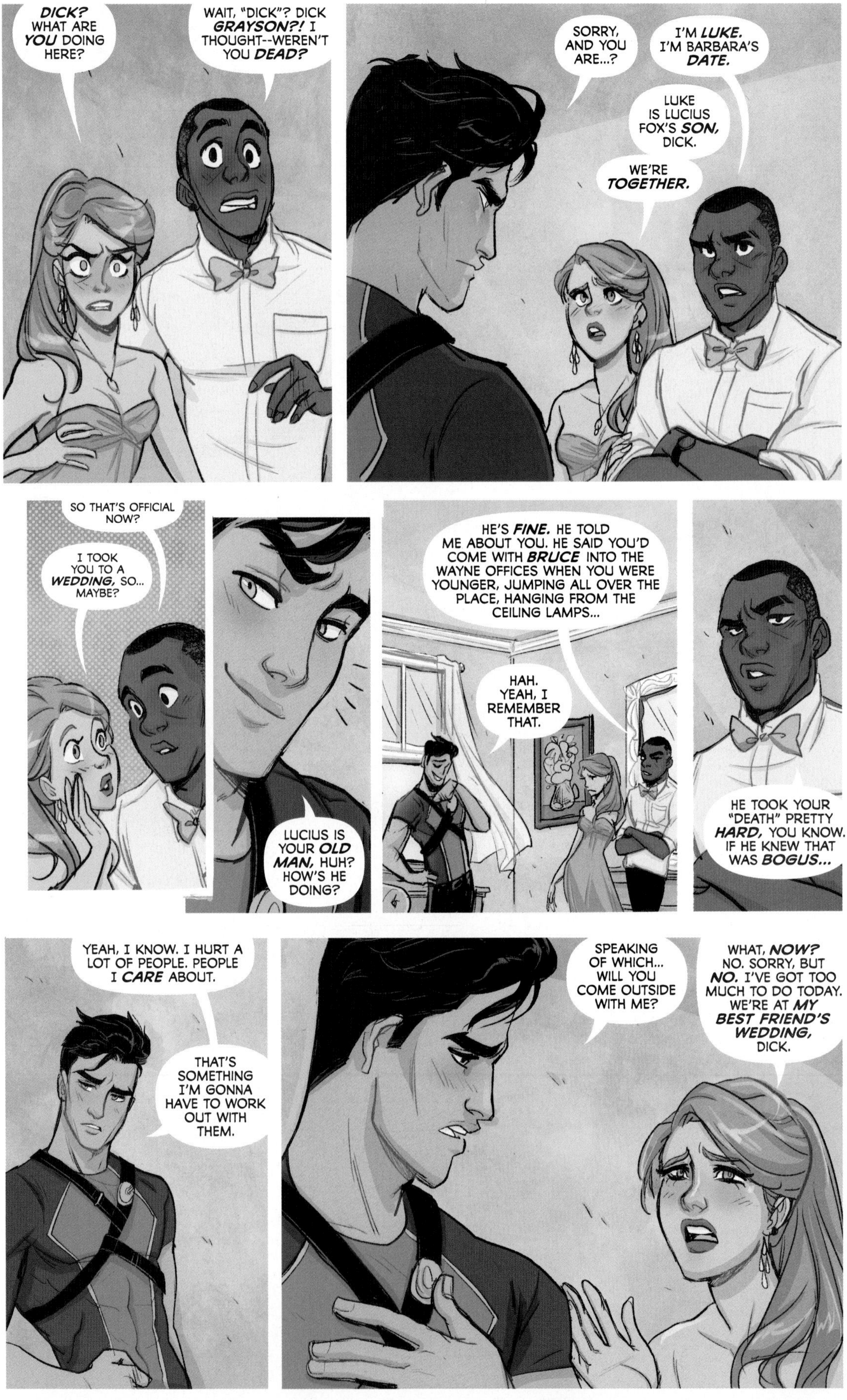
DICK? WHAT ARE YOU DOING HERE?
WAIT, "DICK"? DICK GRAYSON?! I THOUGHT--WEREN'T YOU DEAD?
SORRY, AND YOU ARE...?
I'M LUKE. I'M BARBARA'S DATE.
LUKE IS LUCIUS FOX'S SON, DICK.
WE'RE TOGETHER.
SO THAT'S OFFICIAL NOW?
I TOOK YOU TO A WEDDING, SO... MAYBE?
LUCIUS IS YOUR OLD MAN, HUH? HOW'S HE DOING?
HE'S FINE. HE TOLD ME ABOUT YOU. HE SAID YOU'D COME WITH BRUCE INTO THE WAYNE OFFICES WHEN YOU WERE YOUNGER, JUMPING ALL OVER THE PLACE, HANGING FROM THE CEILING LAMPS...
HAH. YEAH, I REMEMBER THAT.
HE TOOK YOUR "DEATH" PRETTY HARD, YOU KNOW. IF HE KNEW THAT WAS BOGUS...
YEAH, I KNOW. I HURT A LOT OF PEOPLE. PEOPLE I CARE ABOUT.
THAT'S SOMETHING I'M GONNA HAVE TO WORK OUT WITH THEM.
SPEAKING OF WHICH... WILL YOU COME OUTSIDE WITH ME?
WHAT, NOW? NO. SORRY, BUT NO. I'VE GOT TOO MUCH TO DO TODAY. WE'RE AT MY BEST FRIEND'S WEDDING, DICK.

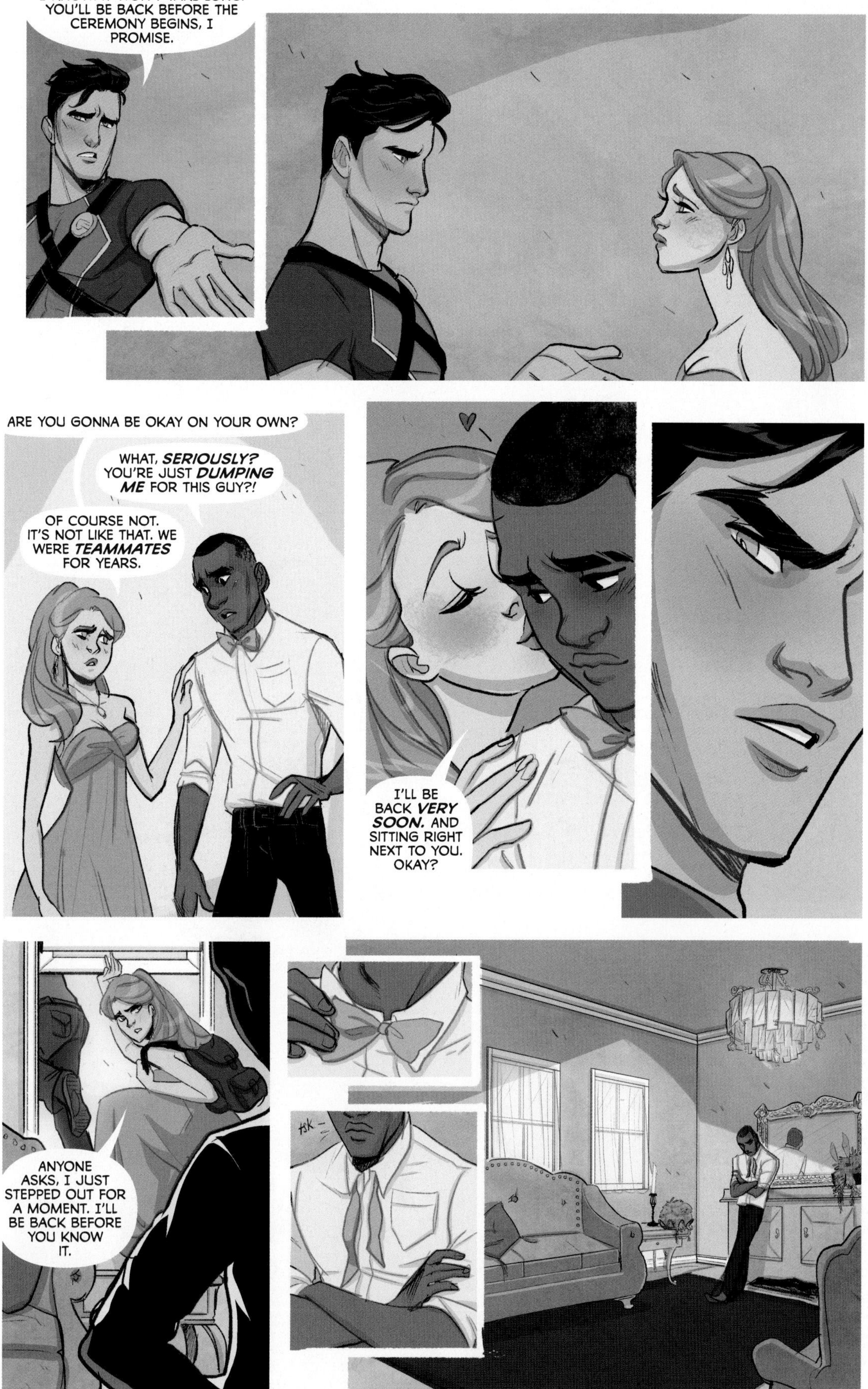
I KNOW. IT WON'T TAKE LONG. YOU'LL BE BACK BEFORE THE CEREMONY BEGINS, I PROMISE.
ARE YOU GONNA BE OKAY ON YOUR OWN?
WHAT, ***SERIOUSLY?*** YOU'RE JUST ***DUMPING ME*** FOR THIS GUY?!
OF COURSE NOT. IT'S NOT LIKE THAT. WE WERE ***TEAMMATES*** FOR YEARS.
I'LL BE BACK ***VERY SOON.*** AND SITTING RIGHT NEXT TO YOU. OKAY?
ANYONE ASKS, I JUST STEPPED OUT FOR A MOMENT. I'LL BE BACK BEFORE YOU KNOW IT.
TSK--

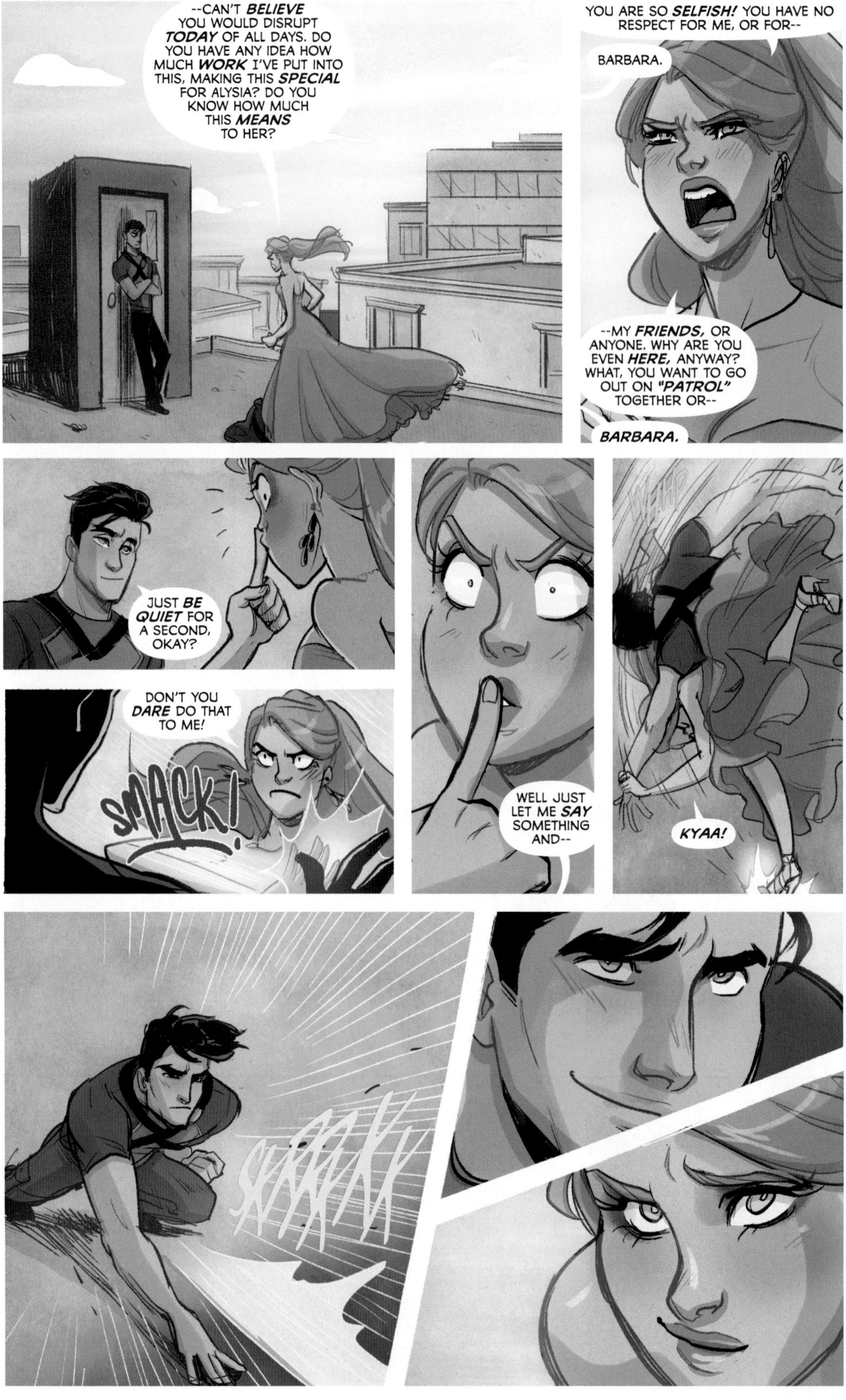

--CAN'T BELIEVE YOU WOULD DISRUPT TODAY OF ALL DAYS. DO YOU HAVE ANY IDEA HOW MUCH WORK I'VE PUT INTO THIS, MAKING THIS SPECIAL FOR ALYSIA? DO YOU KNOW HOW MUCH THIS MEANS TO HER?
YOU ARE SO SELFISH! YOU HAVE NO RESPECT FOR ME, OR FOR--
BARBARA.
--MY FRIENDS, OR ANYONE. WHY ARE YOU EVEN HERE, ANYWAY? WHAT, YOU WANT TO GO OUT ON "PATROL" TOGETHER OR--
BARBARA.
JUST BE QUIET FOR A SECOND, OKAY?
WELL JUST LET ME SAY SOMETHING AND--
DON'T YOU DARE DO THAT TO ME!
SMACK!
KYAA!

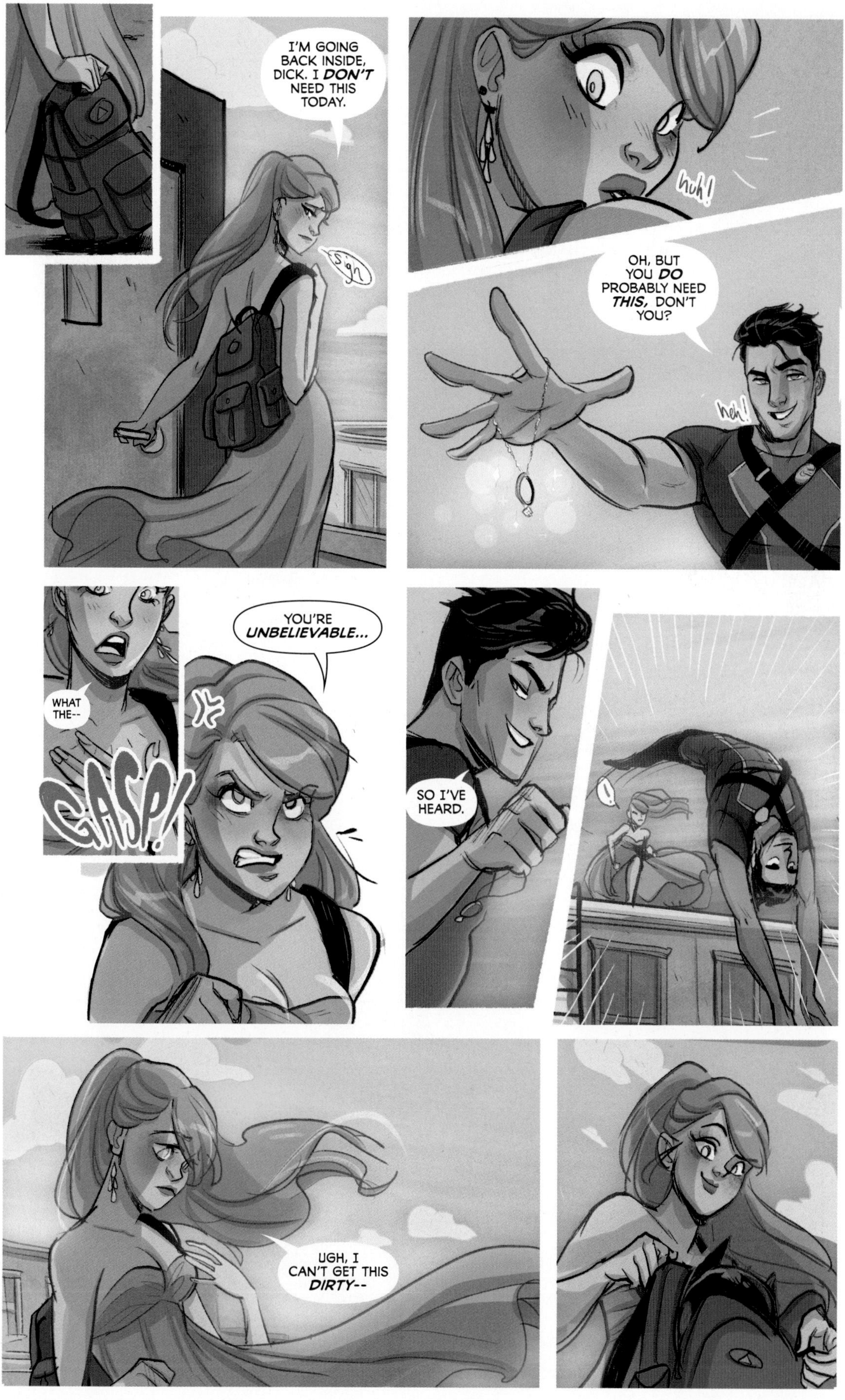
I'M GOING BACK INSIDE, DICK. I DON'T NEED THIS TODAY.
sigh
huh!
OH, BUT YOU DO PROBABLY NEED THIS, DON'T YOU?
heh!
WHAT THE--
GASP!
YOU'RE UNBELIEVABLE...
SO I'VE HEARD.
!
UGH, I CAN'T GET THIS DIRTY--

PLIM

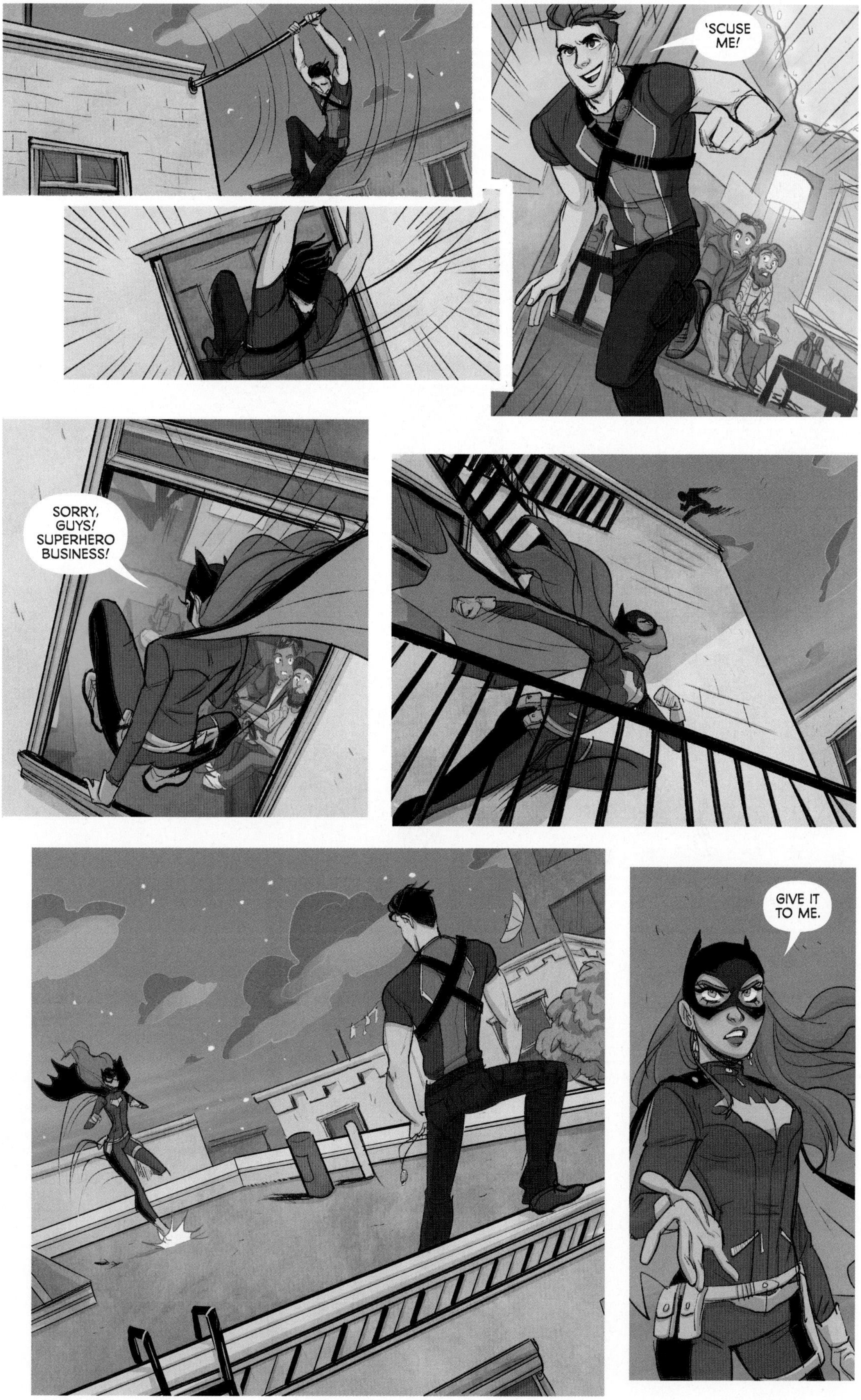
'SCUSE ME!
SORRY, GUYS! SUPERHERO BUSINESS!
GIVE IT TO ME.

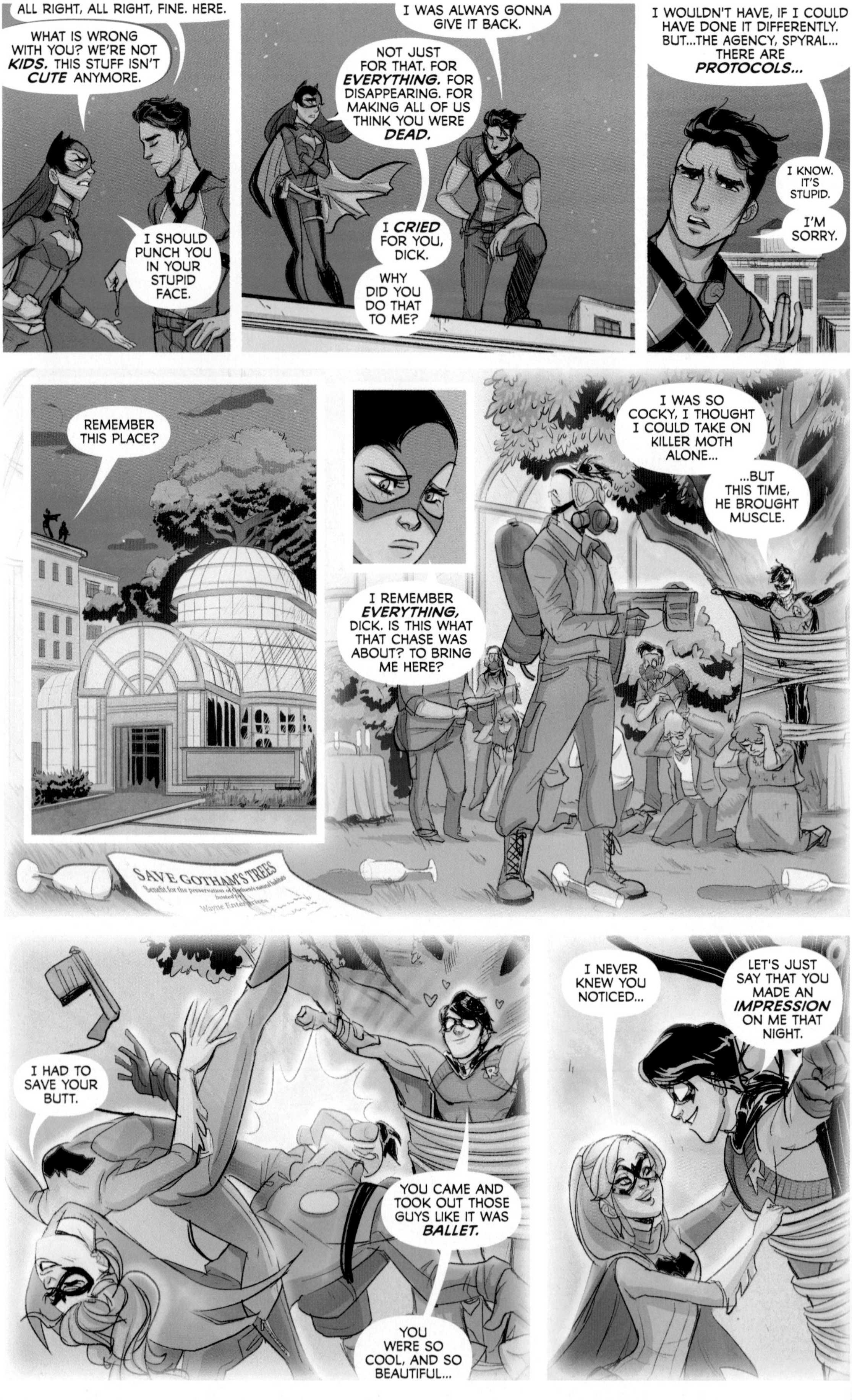
ALL RIGHT, ALL RIGHT, FINE. HERE.
WHAT IS WRONG WITH YOU? WE'RE NOT KIDS. THIS STUFF ISN'T CUTE ANYMORE.
I SHOULD PUNCH YOU IN YOUR STUPID FACE.
I WAS ALWAYS GONNA GIVE IT BACK.
NOT JUST FOR THAT. FOR EVERYTHING. FOR DISAPPEARING. FOR MAKING ALL OF US THINK YOU WERE DEAD.
I CRIED FOR YOU, DICK.
WHY DID YOU DO THAT TO ME?
I WOULDN'T HAVE, IF I COULD HAVE DONE IT DIFFERENTLY. BUT...THE AGENCY, SPYRAL... THERE ARE PROTOCOLS...
I KNOW. IT'S STUPID.
I'M SORRY.
REMEMBER THIS PLACE?
I REMEMBER EVERYTHING, DICK. IS THIS WHAT THAT CHASE WAS ABOUT? TO BRING ME HERE?
I WAS SO COCKY, I THOUGHT I COULD TAKE ON KILLER MOTH ALONE...
...BUT THIS TIME, HE BROUGHT MUSCLE.
SAVE GOTHAM'S TREES
I HAD TO SAVE YOUR BUTT.
YOU CAME AND TOOK OUT THOSE GUYS LIKE IT WAS BALLET.
YOU WERE SO COOL, AND SO BEAUTIFUL...
I NEVER KNEW YOU NOTICED...
LET'S JUST SAY THAT YOU MADE AN IMPRESSION ON ME THAT NIGHT.

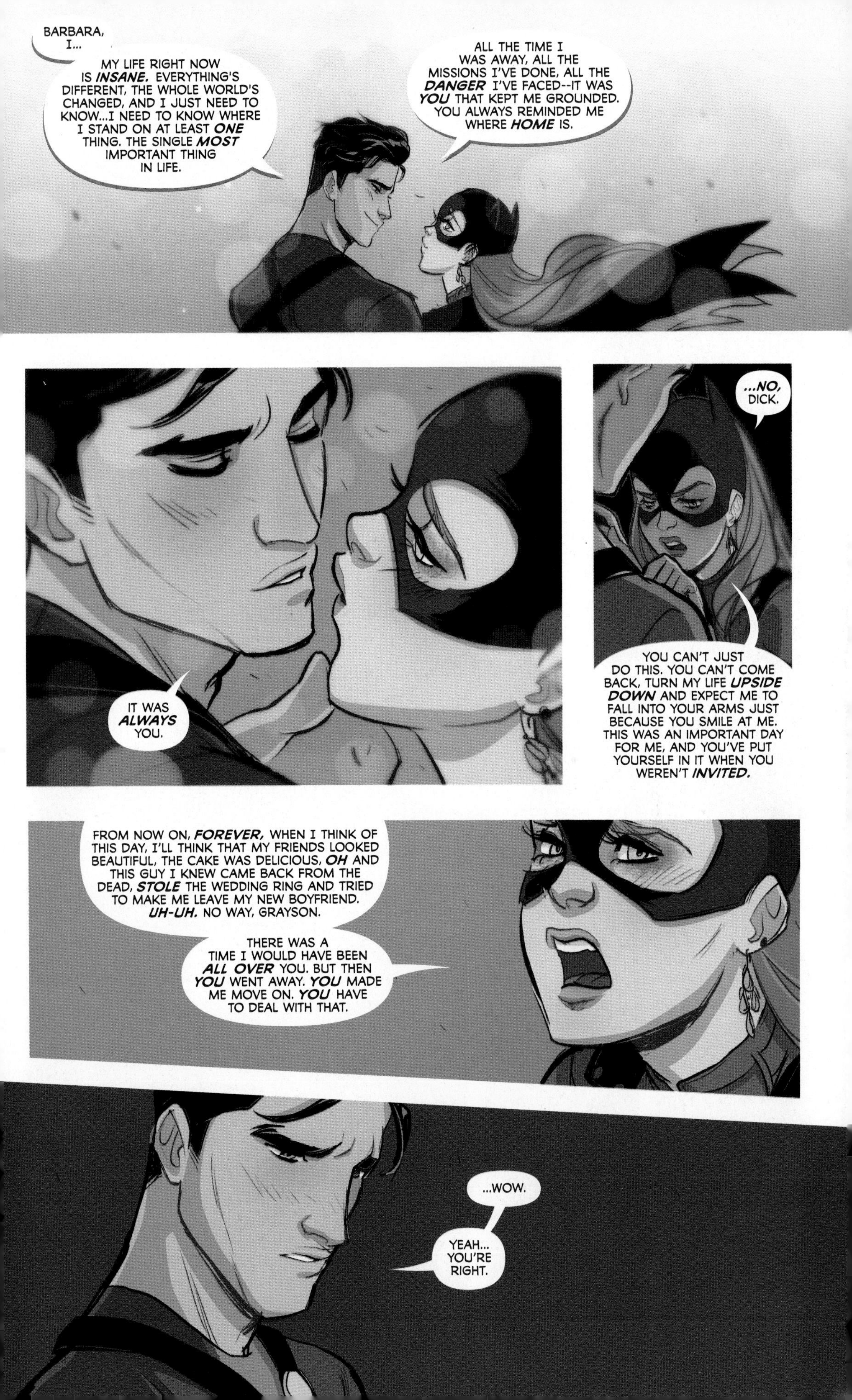
BARBARA, I...
MY LIFE RIGHT NOW IS INSANE. EVERYTHING'S DIFFERENT, THE WHOLE WORLD'S CHANGED, AND I JUST NEED TO KNOW...I NEED TO KNOW WHERE I STAND ON AT LEAST ONE THING. THE SINGLE MOST IMPORTANT THING IN LIFE.
ALL THE TIME I WAS AWAY, ALL THE MISSIONS I'VE DONE, ALL THE DANGER I'VE FACED--IT WAS YOU THAT KEPT ME GROUNDED. YOU ALWAYS REMINDED ME WHERE HOME IS.
IT WAS ALWAYS YOU.
...NO, DICK.
YOU CAN'T JUST DO THIS. YOU CAN'T COME BACK, TURN MY LIFE UPSIDE DOWN AND EXPECT ME TO FALL INTO YOUR ARMS JUST BECAUSE YOU SMILE AT ME. THIS WAS AN IMPORTANT DAY FOR ME, AND YOU'VE PUT YOURSELF IN IT WHEN YOU WEREN'T INVITED.
FROM NOW ON, FOREVER, WHEN I THINK OF THIS DAY, I'LL THINK THAT MY FRIENDS LOOKED BEAUTIFUL, THE CAKE WAS DELICIOUS, OH AND THIS GUY I KNEW CAME BACK FROM THE DEAD, STOLE THE WEDDING RING AND TRIED TO MAKE ME LEAVE MY NEW BOYFRIEND. UH-UH. NO WAY, GRAYSON.
THERE WAS A TIME I WOULD HAVE BEEN ALL OVER YOU. BUT THEN YOU WENT AWAY. YOU MADE ME MOVE ON. YOU HAVE TO DEAL WITH THAT.
...WOW.
YEAH... YOU'RE RIGHT.

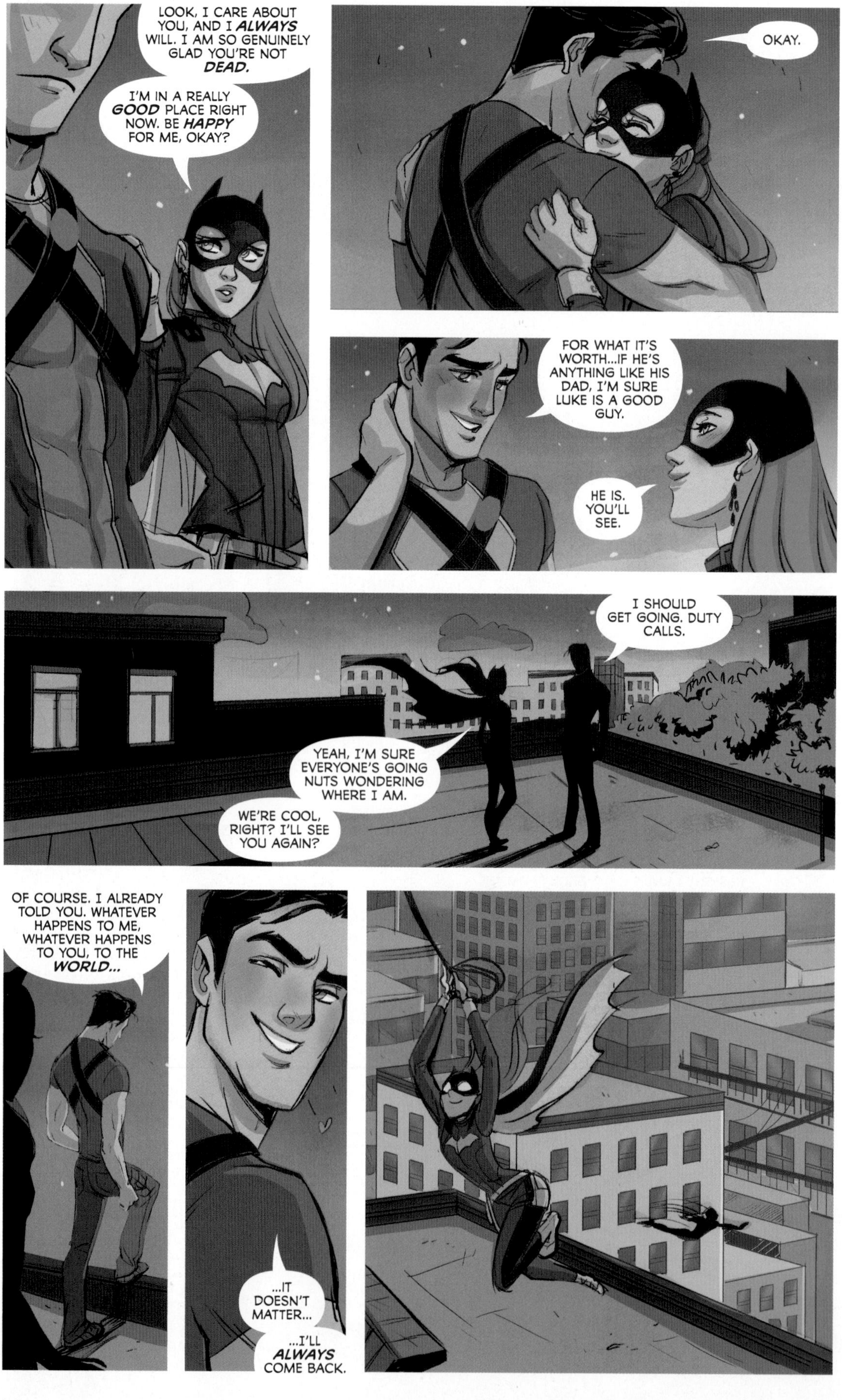

LOOK, I CARE ABOUT YOU, AND I ALWAYS WILL. I AM SO GENUINELY GLAD YOU'RE NOT DEAD.
I'M IN A REALLY GOOD PLACE RIGHT NOW. BE HAPPY FOR ME, OKAY?
OKAY.
FOR WHAT IT'S WORTH...IF HE'S ANYTHING LIKE HIS DAD, I'M SURE LUKE IS A GOOD GUY.
HE IS. YOU'LL SEE.
I SHOULD GET GOING. DUTY CALLS.
YEAH, I'M SURE EVERYONE'S GOING NUTS WONDERING WHERE I AM.
WE'RE COOL, RIGHT? I'LL SEE YOU AGAIN?
OF COURSE. I ALREADY TOLD YOU. WHATEVER HAPPENS TO ME, WHATEVER HAPPENS TO YOU, TO THE WORLD...
...IT DOESN'T MATTER...
...I'LL ALWAYS COME BACK.

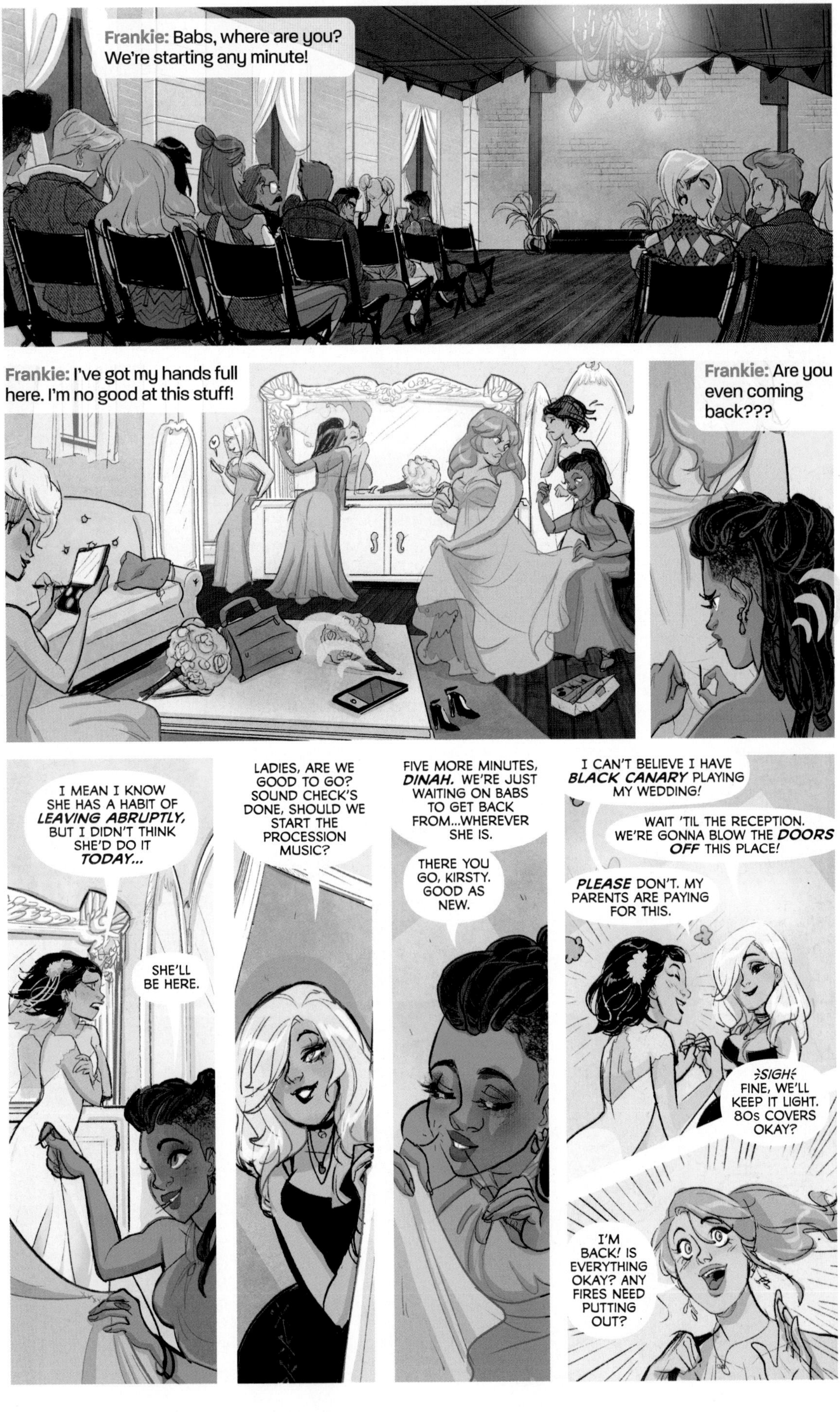
Frankie: Babs, where are you? We're starting any minute!
Frankie: I've got my hands full here. I'm no good at this stuff!
Frankie: Are you even coming back???
I MEAN I KNOW SHE HAS A HABIT OF LEAVING ABRUPTLY, BUT I DIDN'T THINK SHE'D DO IT TODAY...
SHE'LL BE HERE.
LADIES, ARE WE GOOD TO GO? SOUND CHECK'S DONE, SHOULD WE START THE PROCESSION MUSIC?
FIVE MORE MINUTES, DINAH. WE'RE JUST WAITING ON BABS TO GET BACK FROM...WHEREVER SHE IS.
THERE YOU GO, KIRSTY. GOOD AS NEW.
I CAN'T BELIEVE I HAVE BLACK CANARY PLAYING MY WEDDING!
WAIT 'TIL THE RECEPTION. WE'RE GONNA BLOW THE DOORS OFF THIS PLACE!
PLEASE DON'T. MY PARENTS ARE PAYING FOR THIS.
SIGH
FINE, WE'LL KEEP IT LIGHT. 80s COVERS OKAY?
I'M BACK! IS EVERYTHING OKAY? ANY FIRES NEED PUTTING OUT?

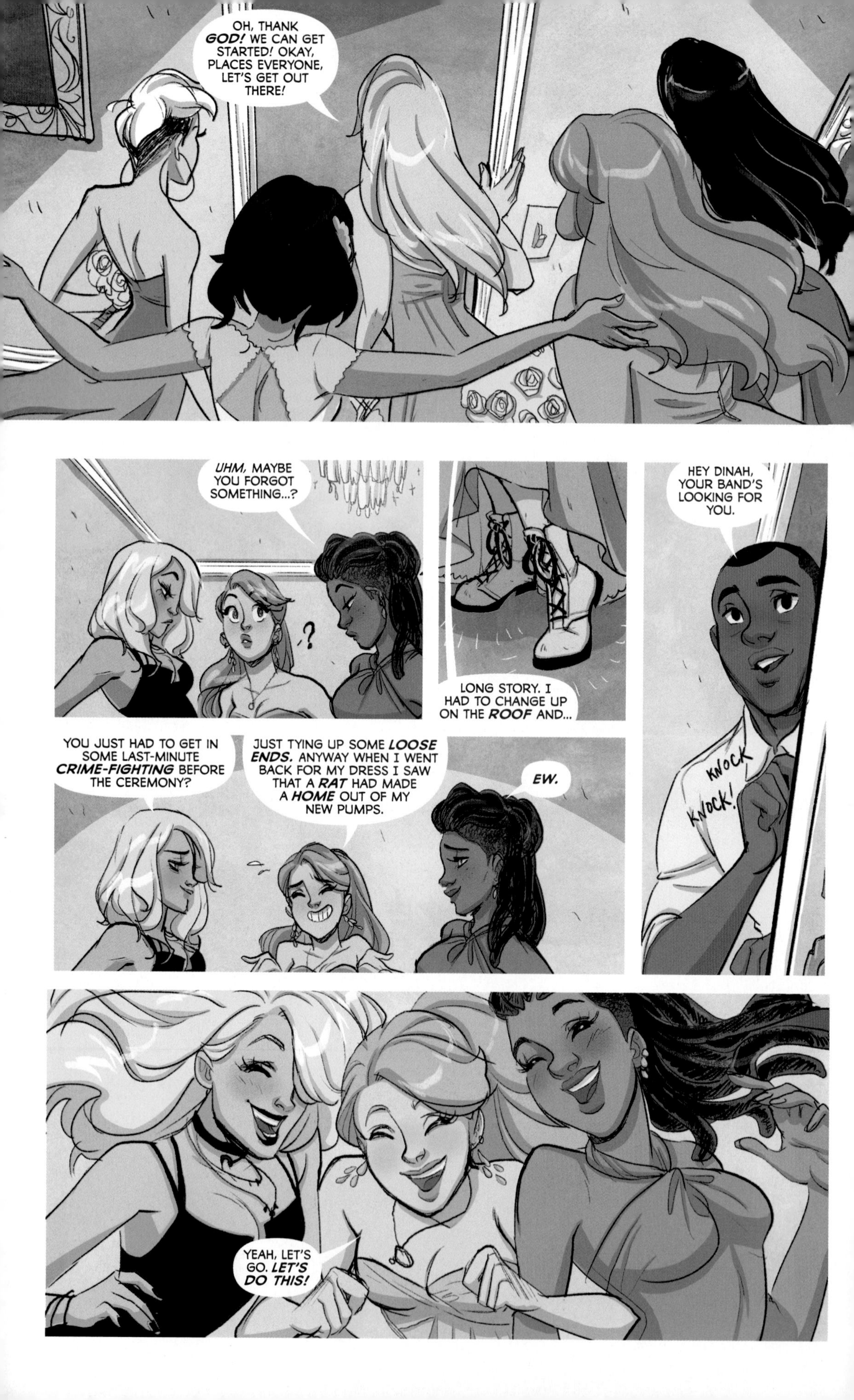
OH, THANK GOD! WE CAN GET STARTED! OKAY, PLACES EVERYONE, LET'S GET OUT THERE!
UHM, MAYBE YOU FORGOT SOMETHING...?
?
LONG STORY. I HAD TO CHANGE UP ON THE ROOF AND...
YOU JUST HAD TO GET IN SOME LAST-MINUTE CRIME-FIGHTING BEFORE THE CEREMONY?
JUST TYING UP SOME LOOSE ENDS. ANYWAY WHEN I WENT BACK FOR MY DRESS I SAW THAT A RAT HAD MADE A HOME OUT OF MY NEW PUMPS.
EW.
HEY DINAH, YOUR BAND'S LOOKING FOR YOU.
KNOCK KNOCK!
YEAH, LET'S GO. LET'S DO THIS!

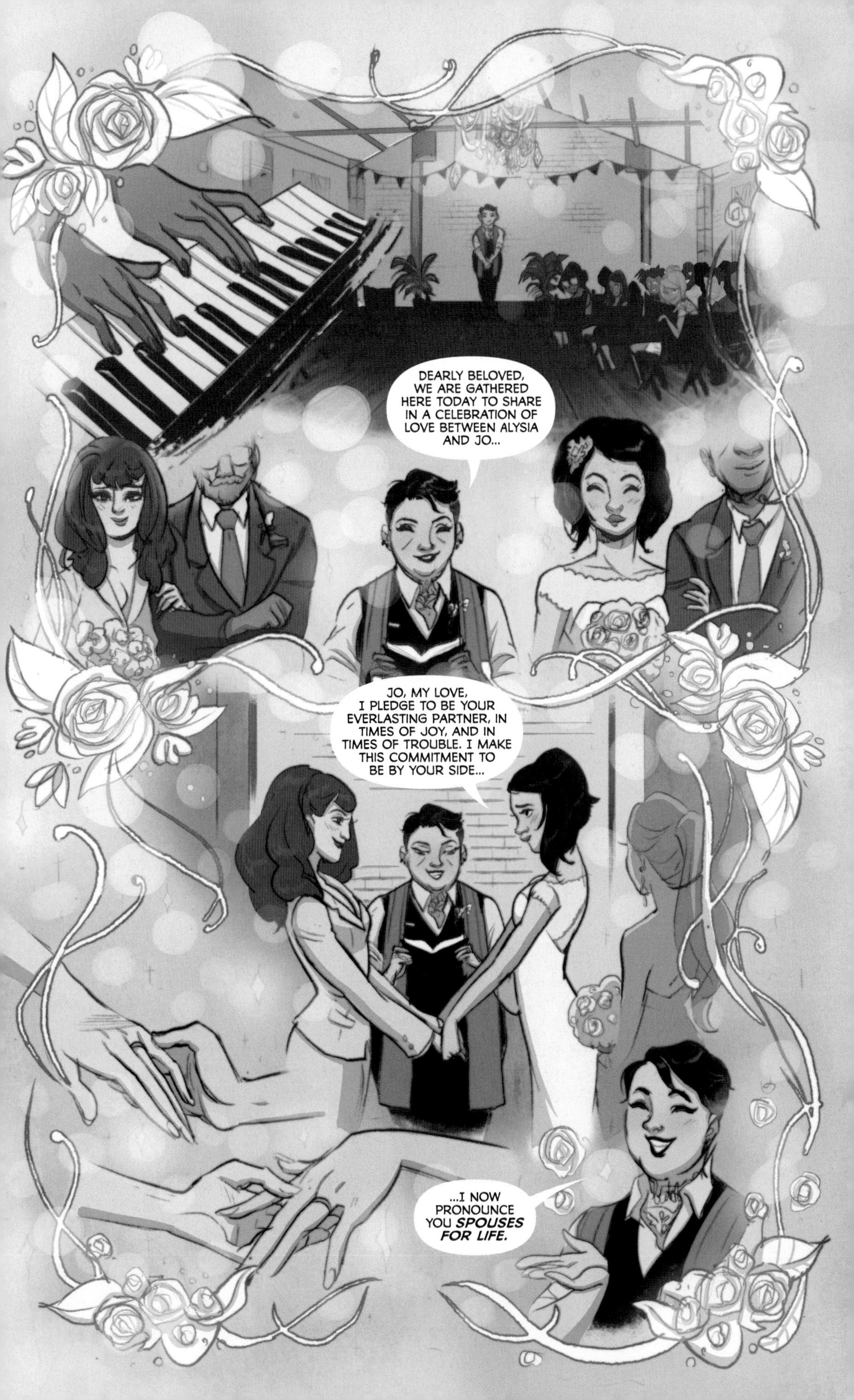
DEARLY BELOVED, WE ARE GATHERED HERE TODAY TO SHARE IN A CELEBRATION OF LOVE BETWEEN ALYSIA AND JO...
JO, MY LOVE, I PLEDGE TO BE YOUR EVERLASTING PARTNER, IN TIMES OF JOY, AND IN TIMES OF TROUBLE. I MAKE THIS COMMITMENT TO BE BY YOUR SIDE...
...I NOW PRONOUNCE YOU ***SPOUSES FOR LIFE.***

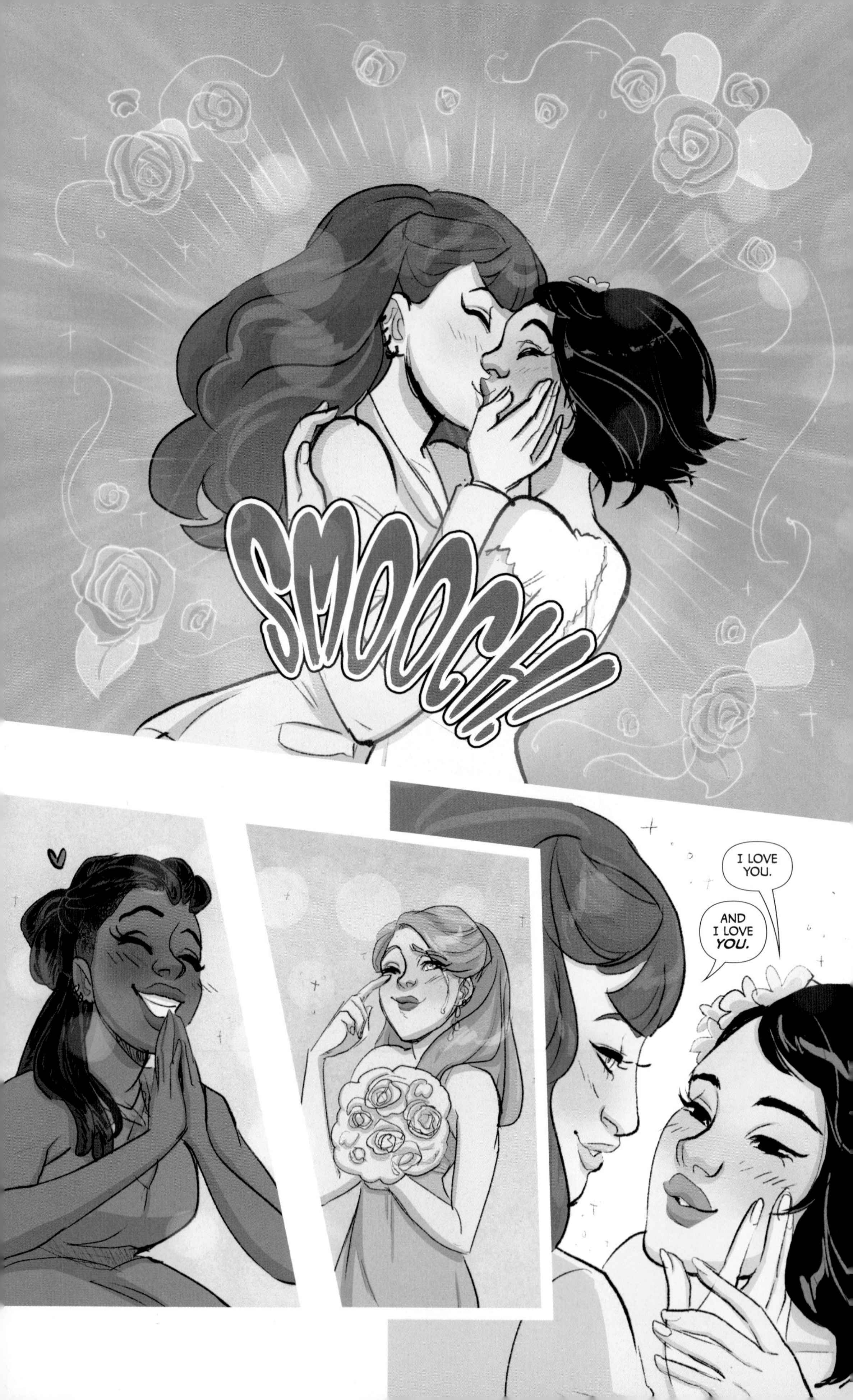
SMOOCH!!
I LOVE YOU.
AND I LOVE YOU.

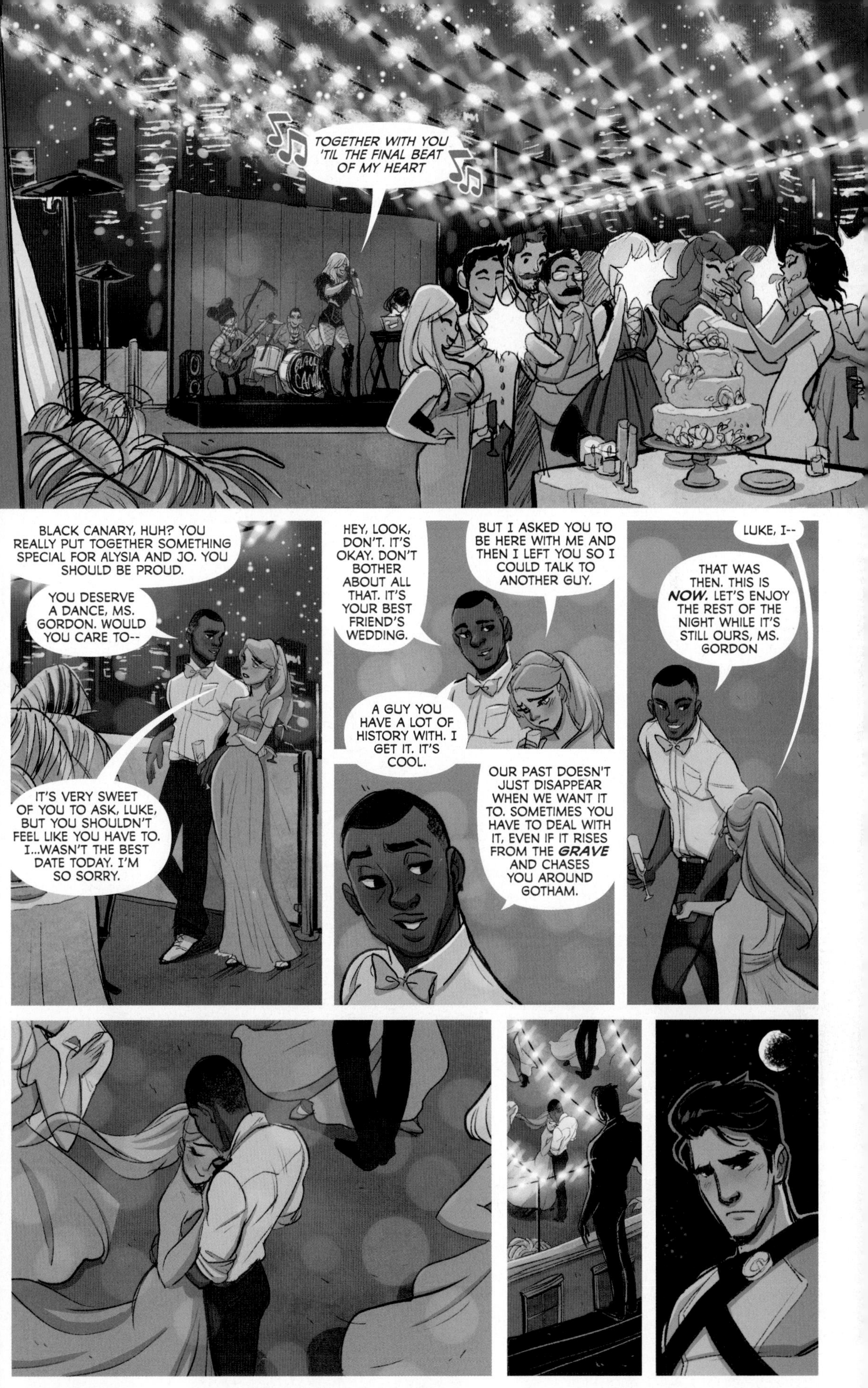
TOGETHER WITH YOU 'TIL THE FINAL BEAT OF MY HEART
BLACK CANARY, HUH? YOU REALLY PUT TOGETHER SOMETHING SPECIAL FOR ALYSIA AND JO. YOU SHOULD BE PROUD.
YOU DESERVE A DANCE, MS. GORDON. WOULD YOU CARE TO--
IT'S VERY SWEET OF YOU TO ASK, LUKE, BUT YOU SHOULDN'T FEEL LIKE YOU HAVE TO. I...WASN'T THE BEST DATE TODAY. I'M SO SORRY.
HEY, LOOK, DON'T. IT'S OKAY. DON'T BOTHER ABOUT ALL THAT. IT'S YOUR BEST FRIEND'S WEDDING.
BUT I ASKED YOU TO BE HERE WITH ME AND THEN I LEFT YOU SO I COULD TALK TO ANOTHER GUY.
A GUY YOU HAVE A LOT OF HISTORY WITH. I GET IT. IT'S COOL.
OUR PAST DOESN'T JUST DISAPPEAR WHEN WE WANT IT TO. SOMETIMES YOU HAVE TO DEAL WITH IT, EVEN IF IT RISES FROM THE GRAVE AND CHASES YOU AROUND GOTHAM.
LUKE, I--
THAT WAS THEN. THIS IS NOW. LET'S ENJOY THE REST OF THE NIGHT WHILE IT'S STILL OURS, MS. GORDON

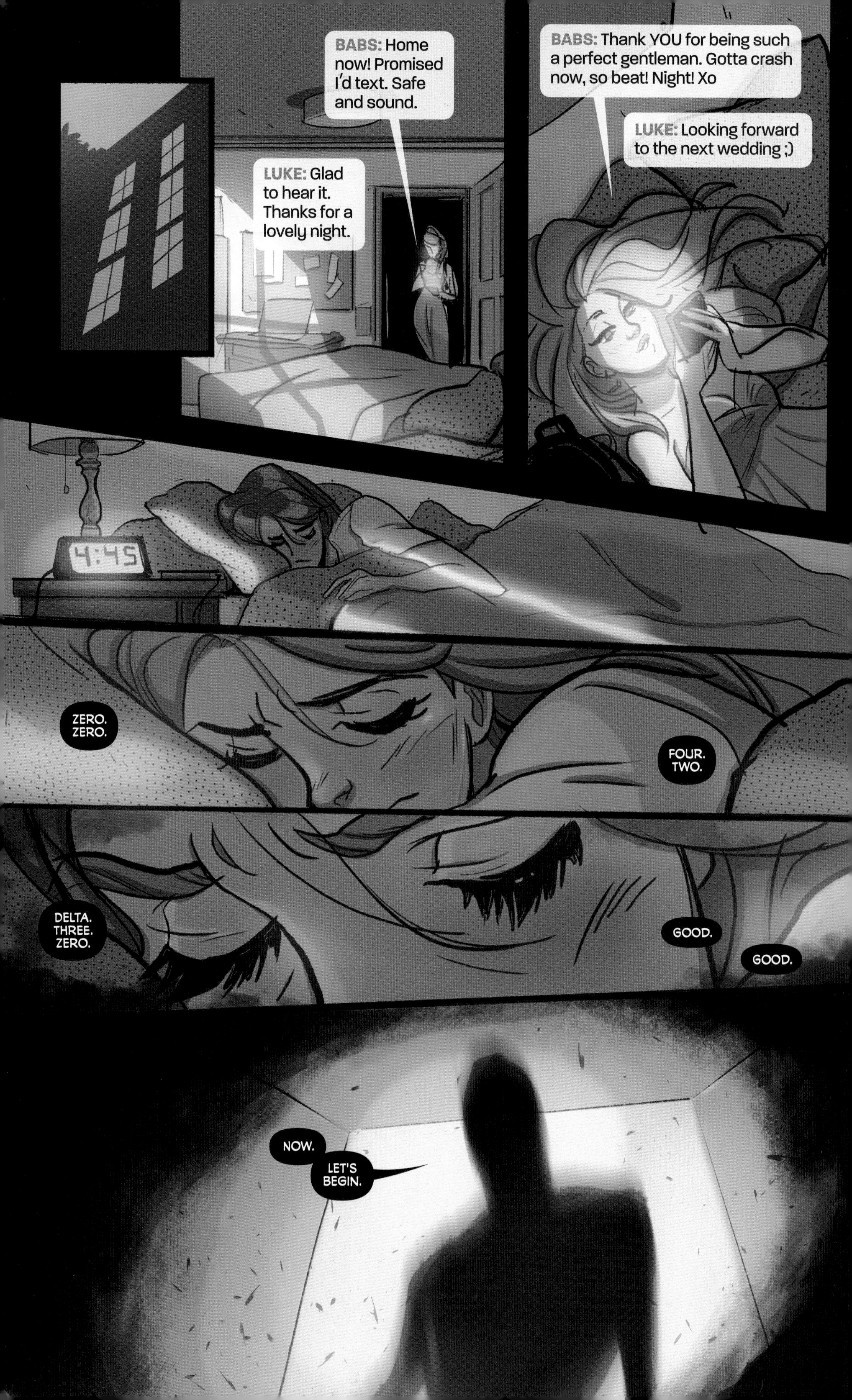
BABS: Home now! Promised I'd text. Safe and sound.
LUKE: Glad to hear it. Thanks for a lovely night.
BABS: Thank YOU for being such a perfect gentleman. Gotta crash now, so beat! Night! Xo
LUKE: Looking forward to the next wedding ;)
4:45
ZERO. ZERO.
FOUR. TWO.
DELTA. THREE. ZERO.
GOOD.
GOOD.
NOW.
LET'S BEGIN.

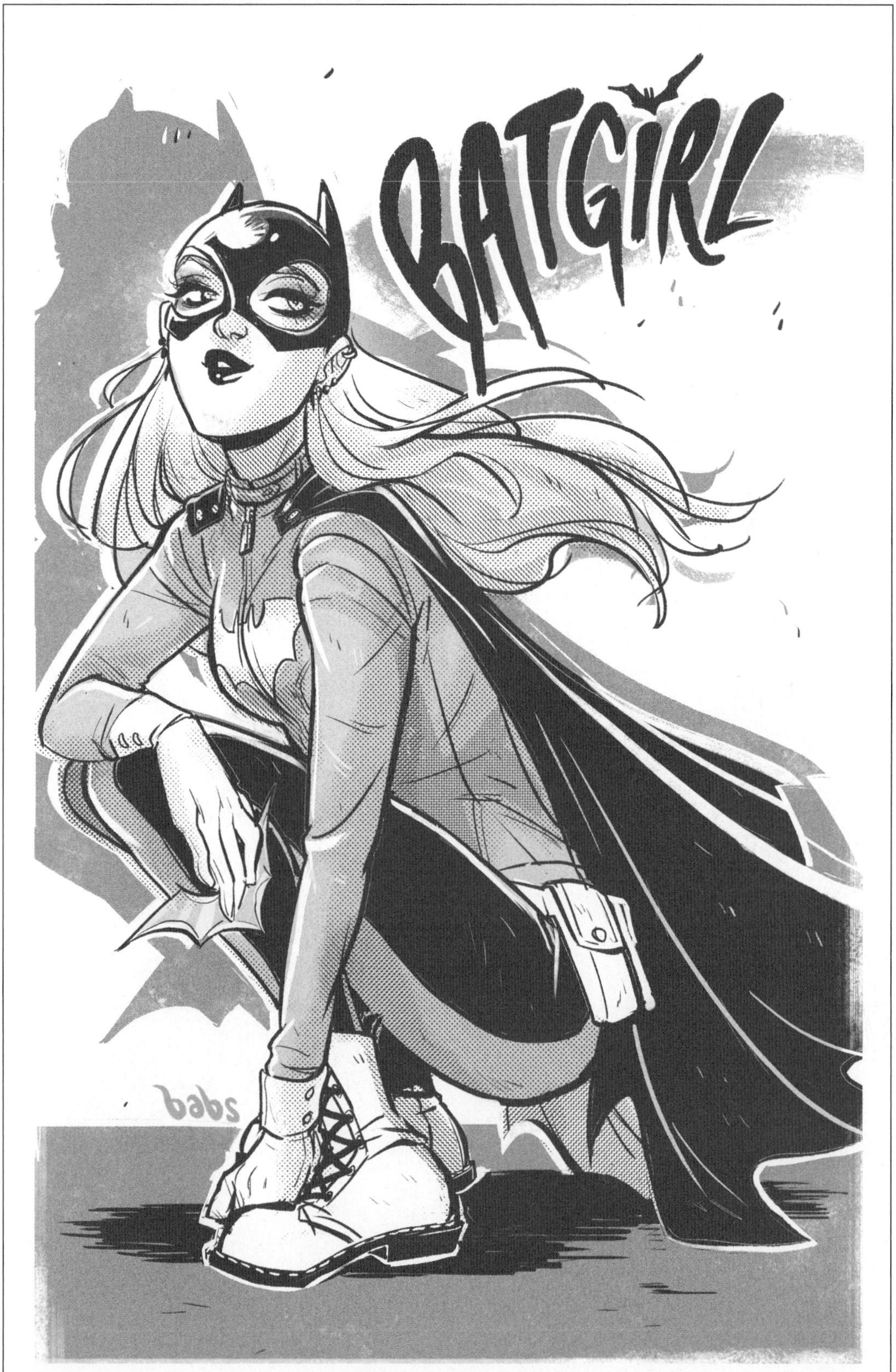
BATGIRL
babs

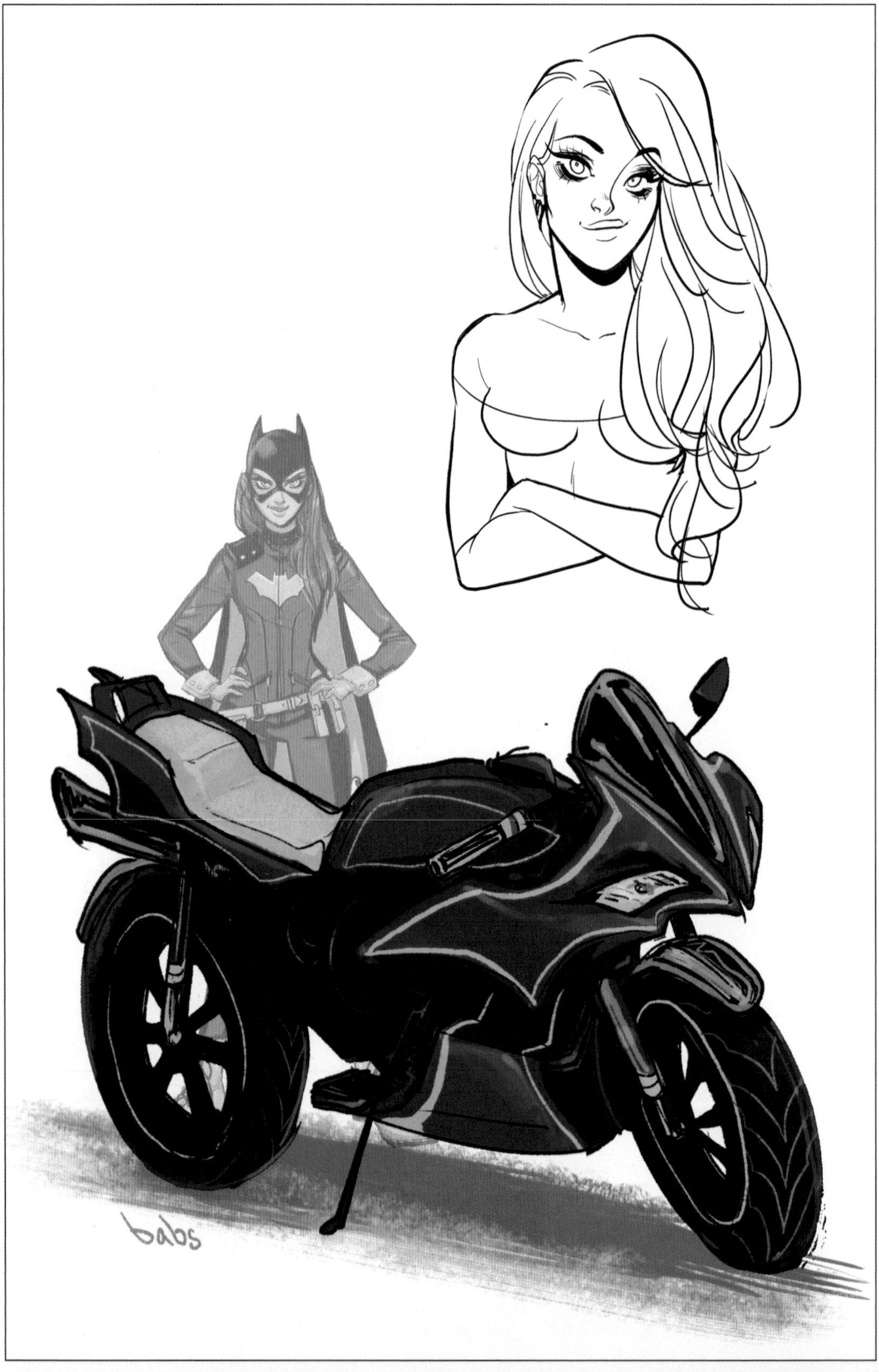
babs

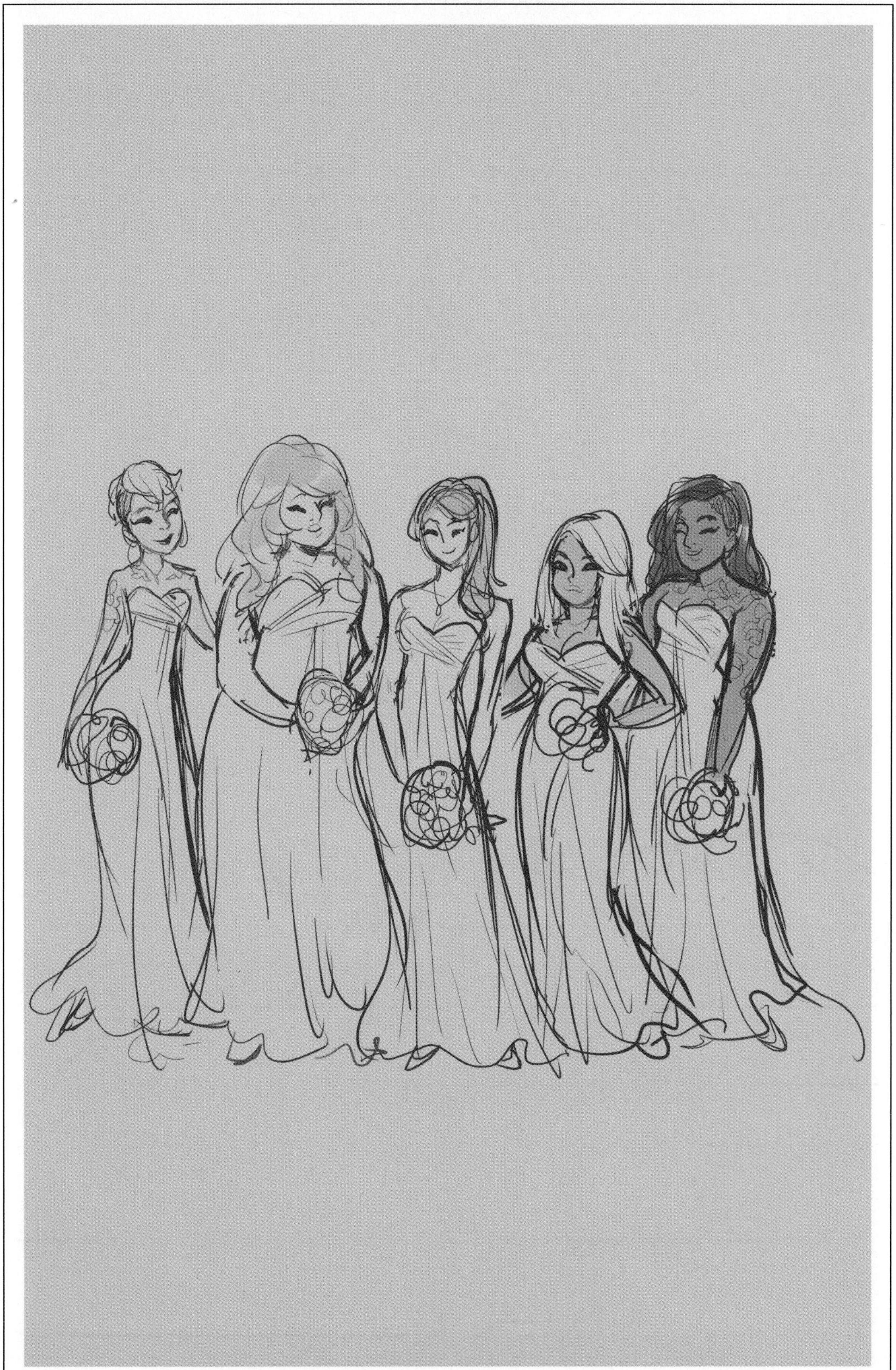

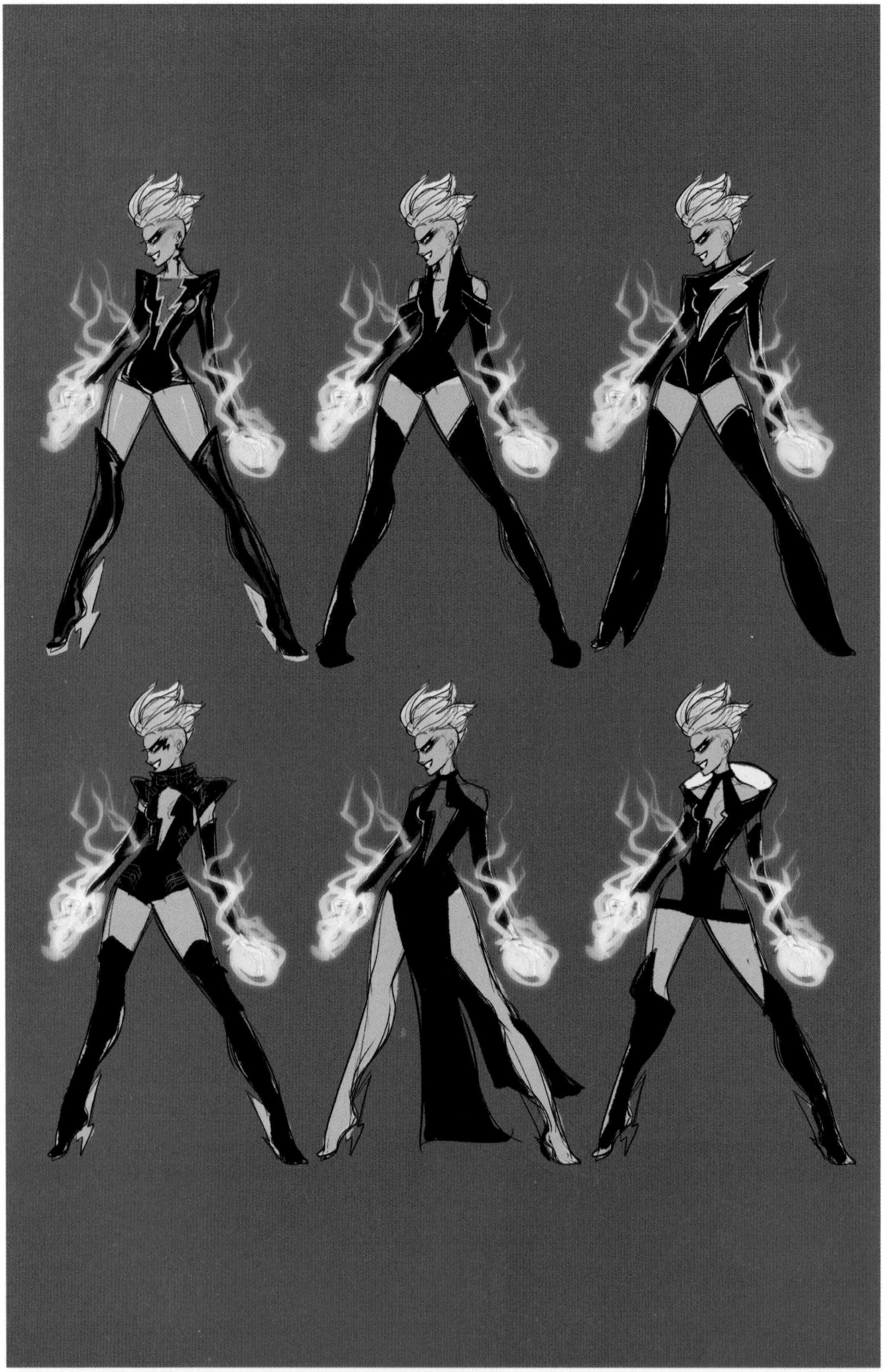

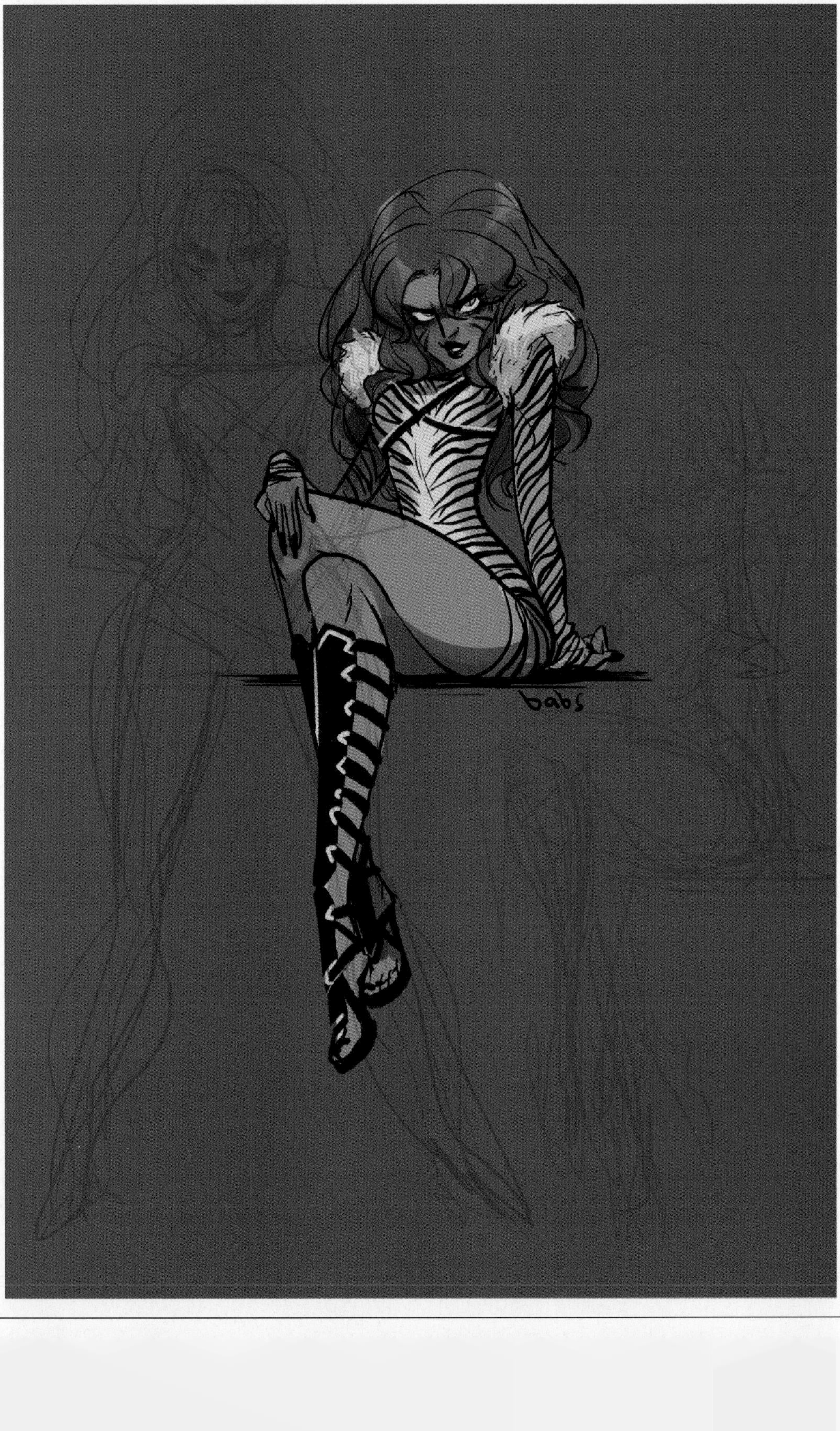
babs

BATGIRL POSTER FOR THE AMERICAN LIBRARY ASSOCIATION'S READ CAMPAIGN

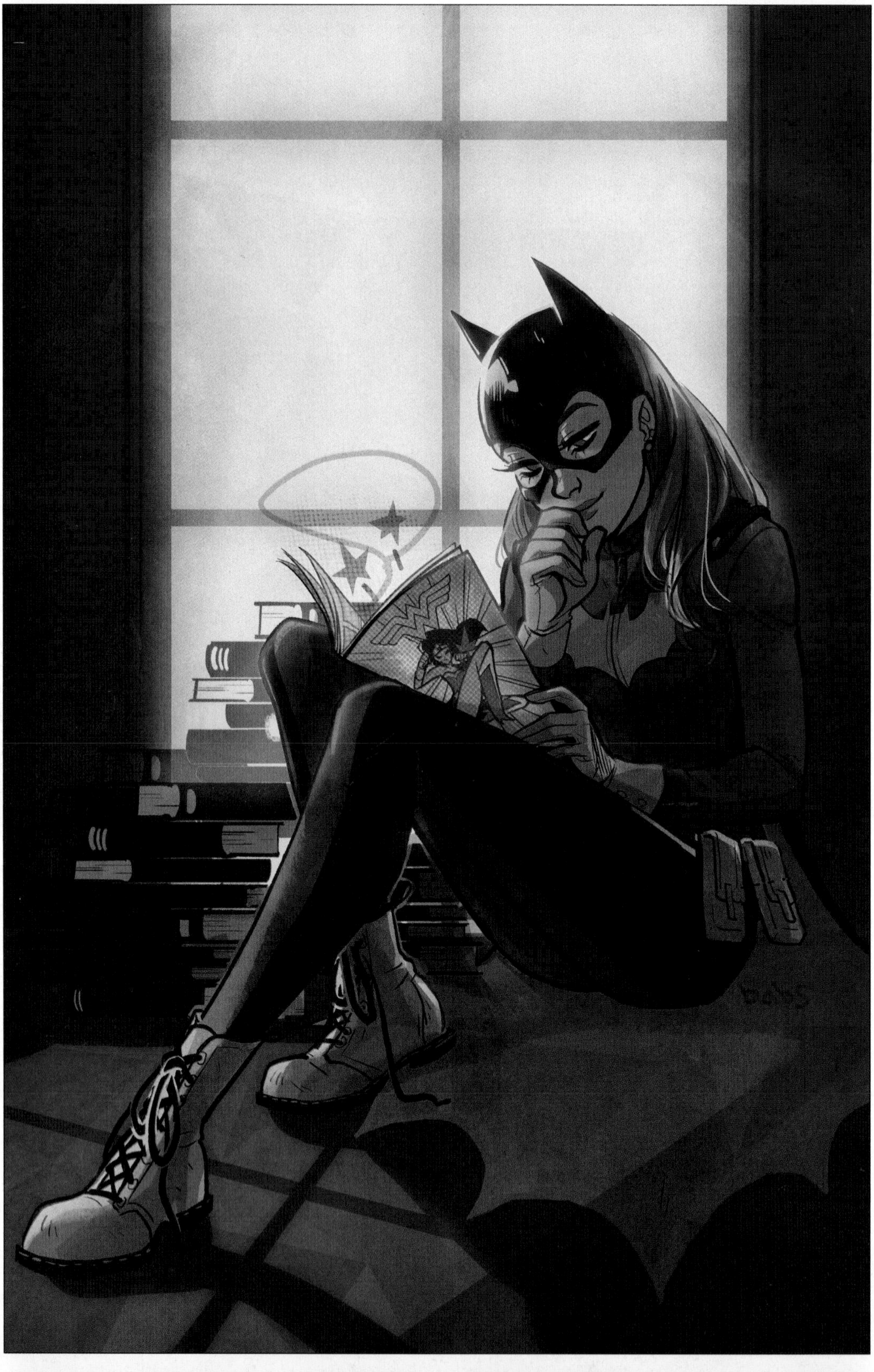

"Simone and artist Ardian Syaf not only do justice to Babs' legacy, but build in a new complexity that is the starting point for a future full of new storytelling possibilities. A hell of a ride."—IGN

START AT THE BEGINNING!

BATGIRL
VOLUME 1: THE DARKEST REFLECTION

BATGIRL VOL. 2: KNIGHTFALL DESCENDS

BATGIRL VOL. 3: DEATH OF THE FAMILY

BATWOMAN VOL. 1: HYDROLOGY

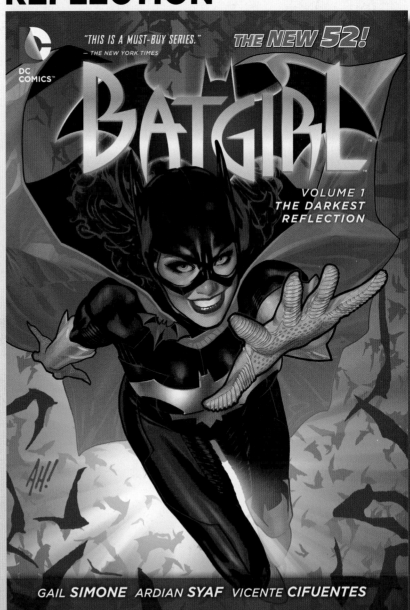

"Chaotic and unabashedly fun."—IGN

*"I'm enjoying HARLEY QUINN a great deal;
it's silly, it's funny, it's irreverent."*
—COMIC BOOK RESOURCES

HARLEY QUINN
VOLUME 1: HOT IN THE CITY

**SUICIDE SQUAD VOL. 1:
KICKED IN THE TEETH**

**with ADAM GLASS and
FEDERICO DALLOCCHIO**

**HARLEY QUINN:
PRELUDES AND
KNOCK-KNOCK JOKES**

**with KARL KESEL and
TERRY DODSON**

**BATMAN: MAD LOVE
AND OTHER STORIES**

**with PAUL DINI
and BRUCE TIMM**

THE NEW 52!

DC COMICS™

HARLEY QUINN

VOLUME 1
HOT IN THE CITY

*"CHAOTIC AND UNABASHEDLY
FUN AS ONE WOULD EXPECT."*
— IGN

AMANDA **CONNER** JIMMY **PALMIOTTI** CHAD **HARDIN**
STEPHANE **ROUX** ALEX **SINCLAIR** PAUL **MOUNTS**